Analyzing Grammar

Analyzing Grammar is a clear introductory textbook on grammatical analysis, designed for students beginning to study the discipline. Covering both syntax (the structure of phrases and sentences) and morphology (the structure of words), it equips them with the tools and methods needed to analyze grammatical patterns in any language. Students are shown how to use standard notational devices such as Phrase Structure trees and word-formation rules, as well as prose descriptions, and are encouraged to practice using these tools through a diverse range of problem sets and exercises. Emphasis is placed on comparing the different grammatical systems of the world's languages. Topics covered include word order, constituency, case, agreement, tense, gender, pronoun systems, inflection, derivation, argument structure, and Grammatical Relations, and a useful glossary provides a clear explanation of each term.

PAUL R. KROEGER is Associate Professor and Head of the Department of Applied Linguistics at the Graduate Institute of Applied Linguistics, Dallas. He has previously published *Phrase Structure and Grammatical Relations in Tagalog* (1993) and *Analyzing Syntax* (Cambridge University Press, 2004). He has carried out linguistic fieldwork in East Malaysia, and has written for many journals including *Pacific Linguistics, Oceanic Linguistics,* and the *Philippine Journal of Linguistics.*

Analyzing Grammar
An Introduction

PAUL R. KROEGER

CAMBRIDGE
UNIVERSITY PRESS

CAMBRIDGE UNIVERSITY PRESS
Cambridge, New York, Melbourne, Madrid, Cape Town, Singapore, São Paulo

Cambridge University Press
The Edinburgh Building, Cambridge, CB2 8RU, UK

Published in the United Sates of America by Cambridge University Press, New York

www.cambridge.org
Information on this title: www.cambridge.org/9780521816229

First published 2005
Third printing 2007

Printed in the United Kingdom at the University Press, Cambridge

A catalogue record for this publication is available from the British Library

Library of Congress Cataloging in Publication data
Kroeger, Paul, 1952–
Analyzing grammar : an introduction / Paul R. Kroeger.
    p.   cm.
Includes bibliographical references and index.
ISBN 0-521-81622-9 – ISBN 0-521-01653-3 (pbk.)
1. Linguistic analysis (Linguistics)   2. Grammar, Comparative and general.   I. Title.
P126.K76   2005
415–dc22   2004057104

ISBN 978-0-521-81622-9 hardback
ISBN 978-0-521-01653-7 paperback

For Sarah, Ruth, and Katie

Contents

Preface and acknowledgments

This book provides a general introduction to morphology (the structure of words) and syntax (the structure of phrases and sentences). By "general" I mean that it is not specifically a book about the grammar of English, or of any other particular language. Rather, it provides a foundation for analyzing and describing the grammatical structure of any human language. Of course, because the book is written in English it uses English examples to illustrate a number of points, especially in the area of syntax; but examples from many other languages are discussed as well.

The book is written for beginners, assuming only some prior knowledge of the most basic vocabulary for talking about language. It is intended to be usable as a first step in preparing students to carry out fieldwork on under-described languages. For this reason some topics are included which are not normally addressed in an introductory course, including the typology of case and agreement systems, gender systems, pronoun systems, and a brief introduction to the semantics of tense, aspect, and modality. This is not a book about linguistic field methods, but issues of methodology are addressed in various places. The overall goal is to help students write good descriptive grammars. Some basic formal notations are introduced, but equal emphasis is given to prose description of linguistic structures.

In this book I am chiefly concerned with structural issues, but I do not attempt to teach a specific theory of grammatical structure. My basic assumptions about how human grammars work are those of Lexical Functional Grammar (LFG; see Bresnan 2001 and references cited there), but I have adopted a fairly generic approach which will hopefully be usable by teachers from a wide variety of theoretical backgrounds. For the sake of simplicity, I have adopted some analyses which are different from the standard LFG approach, e.g. the treatment of "pro-drop" in chapter 5. The main features of the book which are distinctive to LFG are the well-formedness conditions outlined in chapter 5 and the inventory of Grammatical Relations (including OBL_θ and XCOMP).

It is somewhat unusual for a single textbook to deal with both morphology and syntax. In adopting this broad approach, the present work follows and builds on a tradition of grammar teaching at various training schools of the Summer Institute of Linguistics (SIL). Earlier work in this tradition includes Pike and Pike (1982); Elson and Pickett (1988); Thomas et al. (1988);

Healey (1990a); Bickford (1998); and Payne (2002, MS). Bickford's book, in particular, has had a major influence on this one in terms of scope and organization, and in a number of specific details cited in the text.

Teaching morphology is much easier if the students have some basic background in phonology. For this reason, most of the chapters dealing with morphology are clustered at the end of the book (chapters 13–17), for the benefit of students who are concurrently taking a first course in phonology. In situations where this is not a factor, those chapters could be taught earlier, though some of the exercises assume material taught in previous chapters. Chapters 3–5 are a tightly knit unit and should be taught in that order; with the other chapters, the ordering is probably less crucial. Chapters 9 (Tense, Aspect, and Modality systems) and 17 (clitics) are relatively independent of the rest of the book, and could probably be taught wherever the instructor wants to fit them in.

The contents of this book can be presented in a standard semester-length course. However, this material is intended to be reinforced by having students work through large numbers of data analysis exercises. Many teachers have found the exercises to be the most important part of the course. In addition, it is very helpful to assign a longer exercise as a final project, to give students some practice at writing up and integrating their analyses of various aspects of the grammar of a single language. (A sample of such an exercise, using Swahili data, is included as an appendix at the end of the book.) For most beginning students, extra tutorial hours or "lab sessions" will be needed to complete all of these components in one semester.

Some data exercises are included at the end of each chapter, except chapter 1. Those labelled "Practice exercises" are suitable for classroom discussion; the others can be used for either homework or tutorial sessions. Model answers for some of these exercises are available from the author. For most chapters, additional exercises are suggested from two source books: Merrifield et al. (1987) and Healey (1990b). Of course, similar exercises are available from many other sources as well, and instructors should feel free to mix and match as desired. The discussion in the text does not generally depend on the students having worked any specific exercise, except for exercise 3A(ii) at the end of chapter 3, which is referred to several times.

(A new edition of the Merrifield volume was published in 2003; it contains the same exercises as the 1987 edition with some orthographic changes. A few of the data sets have been re-numbered, but there is a table at the beginning of the 2003 edition listing the changes in numbering. Numbers cited in the present book refer to the 1987 edition.)

So many people have helped me with this project that I cannot list all of their names. Special thanks must go to Joan Bresnan, René van den Berg, Dick Watson, Bill Merrifield, John Roberts, and Marlin Leaders for their contributions. To all of the others, I offer my thanks with apologies for not naming them individually. Thanks also to my students in Singapore,

Darwin, and Dallas who have pushed me to clarify many issues with their insightful questions and suggestions, and to my long-suffering family for their encouragement and support.

The copyright for data exercises that I have cited from Merrifield et al. (1987); Roberts (1999); Healey (1990b); and Bendor-Samuel and Levinsohn (1986) is held by SIL International; these exercises are used here by permission, with thanks.

Abbreviations

–	affix boundary
=	clitic boundary
[ ]	constituent boundaries
*	ungrammatical
#	semantically ill-formed or inappropriate in context
?	marginal or questionable
%	acceptable to some speakers
(X)	optional constituent
*(X)	obligatory constituent
Ø	null (silent) morpheme
1	1st person
2	2nd person
3	3rd person
A	transitive agent; Actor
A(DJ)	adjective
ABIL	abilitative mood
ABL	ablative case
ABS	absolutive
ACC	accusative
ACT	active voice
ADV	adverb
ADVBL	adverbializer
ADVRS	adversative
AGR	agreement
agt	agent
AP	Adjective Phrase
APPL(IC)	applicative
ASP	aspect
ASSOC	associative
AUX	auxiliary
BEN	benefactive
C	consonant
CAT	syntactic category
CAUS	causative
CLASS	classifier

COMIT	comitative (accompaniment)
COMP	complementizer
CONCESS	concessive
CONJ	conjunction
CONT	continuous
COP	copula
DAT	dative
DEB	debitive (must/ought)
DESID	desiderative
DET	determiner
DIR	directional
DIRECT	direct knowledge (eye-witness)
DU(AL)	dual
DUB	dubitative
DV	dative voice (Tagalog)
ERG	ergative
EVID	evidential
EX(CL)	exclusive
EXIST	existential
F(EM)	feminine
FOC	focus
FUT	future tense
GEN	genitive
GR	Grammatical Relation
HIST.PAST	historic past
HORT	hortative
IMPER	imperative
IMPERF	imperfective
IN(CL)	inclusive
INAN	inanimate
INDIRECT	indirect knowledge (hearsay)
INF	infinitive
INSTR	instrumental
INTERROG	interrogative
IO	indirect object
IRR	irrealis
IV	instrumental voice (Tagalog)
LNK	linker
LOC	locative
M(ASC)	masculine
N	Noun
N' / N̄	N-bar (see Glossary)
NEG	negative
N(EUT)	neuter

NMLZ	nominalizer
NOM	nominative
NONPAST	nonpast tense
NP	Noun Phrase
OBJ	primary object
O(BJ).AGR	object agreement
OBJ$_2$	secondary object
OBL	oblique argument
OPT	optative
OV	objective voice (Tagalog)
P	(1) preposition; (2) transitive patient
PASS	passive
PAST	past tense
pat	patient
PERF	perfect
PERM	permissive
PERS	personal name
PFV	perfective
pl / PL / p	plural
POSS	possessor
PP	Prepositional Phrase
PRE	prefix
PRED	predicate
PRES	present tense
pro/PRO	pronoun (possibly null)
PROG	progressive
PRT	particle
PS	Phrase Structure
Q(UES)	question
QUOT	quote marker
REC(IP)	recipient
REC.PAST	recent past tense
RECIP	reciprocal
REDUP	reduplication
REL	relativizer
REPORT	reportative
S	(1) sentence or clause; (2) intransitive subject
S′ / S̄	S-bar (see Glossary)
SBJNCT	subjunctive
sg /SG / s	singular
STAT	stative
S(UBJ)	subject
S(UBJ).AGR	subject agreement
SUBORD	subordinate

SUFF	suffix
TAM	Tense-Aspect-Modality
th	theme
TNS	tense
TODAY	today past
V	(1) verb; (2) vowel
VP	Verb Phrase
WFR	Word Formation Rule
WH	Wh- question marker
X*	a sequence of zero or more Xs (X is any unit)
XCOMP	predicate complement
XP	phrase of any category
YNQ	Yes–No question

1 Grammatical form

1.1 Form, meaning, and use

Why do people talk? What is language for? One common answer to this question is that language is a complex form of communication, and that people talk in order to share or request information. That is certainly a very important use of language, but clearly it is not the only use.

For example, what is the meaning of the word *hello*? What information does it convey? It is a very difficult word to define, but every speaker of English knows how to use it: for greeting an acquaintance, answering the telephone, etc. We might say that *hello* conveys the information that the speaker wishes to acknowledge the presence of, or initiate a conversation with, the hearer. But it would be very strange to answer the phone or greet your best friend by saying "I wish to acknowledge your presence" or "I wish to initiate a conversation with you." What is important about the word *hello* is not its information content (if any) but its use in social interaction.

In the Teochew language (a "dialect" of Chinese), there is no word for 'hello'. The normal way for one friend to greet another is to ask: "Have you already eaten or not?" The expected reply is: "I have eaten," even if this is not in fact true.

Now no one would want to say that *hello* means "Have you eaten yet?" But, in certain contexts, the English word and the Teochew question may be used for the same purpose or function, i.e. as a greeting. This example illustrates why it is helpful to distinguish between the meaning (or SEMANTIC content) of an utterance and its function (or PRAGMATIC content).

Of course, in many contexts there is a close relationship between meaning and function. For example, if a doctor wants to administer a certain medicine which cannot be taken on an empty stomach, he will probably ask the patient: "Have you eaten?" In this situation both the meaning and the function of the question will be essentially the same whether the doctor is speaking English or Teochew. The FORM, however, would be quite different. Compare the Teochew form in (1a) with its English translation in (1b):

(1)   a Lɨ chyaʔ pa boy?
         you eat full not.yet
    b *Have you already eaten?*

Obviously the words themselves are different, but there are grammatical differences as well. Both sentences have the form of a question. In Teochew this is indicated by the presence of a negative element ('not yet') at the end of the sentence, while in English it is indicated by the special position of the auxiliary verb *have* at the beginning of the sentence.

This book is primarily concerned with describing linguistic FORM, and in particular with describing grammatical structure. (What we mean by "grammatical structure" will be discussed below.) But in our study of these structural features, we will often want to talk about the meaning of a particular form and/or how it is used. The Teochew example illustrates how a particular form may be used for different functions, depending on the context. This means that the form of an utterance by itself (ignoring context) does not determine its function. But it is equally true that function by itself does not fully determine the form. In other words, we cannot fully explain the form of an utterance while ignoring meaning and function; at the same time, we cannot account for the form of an utterance by looking *only* at its meaning and function.

1.2   Aspects of linguistic form

In describing the grammar of a language, we are essentially trying to explain why speakers recognize certain forms as being "correct" but reject others as being "incorrect." Notice that we are speaking of the acceptability of the form itself, rather than the meaning or function which it expresses. We can often understand a sentence perfectly well even if it is not grammatically correct, as illustrated in (2).

(2)   a Me Tarzan, you Jane.
        b Those guys was trying to kill me.
        c When he came here?

Conversely, the form of a sentence may be accepted as correct even when the meaning is obscure or absurd. An extreme example of this is found in Lewis Carroll's famous poem *Jabberwocky*, from the book *Through the Looking Glass*. The poem begins as follows:

Jabberwocky
'Twas brillig, and the slithy toves
    Did gyre and gimble in the wabe;
All mimsy were the borogoves,
    And the mome raths outgrabe.

"Beware the Jabberwock, my son!
    The jaws that bite, the claws that catch!
Beware the Jubjub bird, and shun
    The frumious Bandersnatch!"

(Another five verses follow in a similar style.) After reading this poem, a native speaker of English will very likely feel as Alice did (pp. 134–136):

> "It seems very pretty," she said when she had finished it, "but it's *rather* hard to understand!" (You see she didn't like to confess even to herself, that she couldn't make it out at all.) "Somehow it seems to fill my head with ideas – only I don't exactly know what they are!"

In the second verse, we can at least guess that the Jabberwock is some kind of beast, the Jubjub is a kind of bird, and the Bandersnatch is something dangerous and probably animate. But the first verse is almost total nonsense; the "function" words (i.e. conjunctions, articles, prepositions, etc.) are real English words, but almost all the content words (nouns, verbs, etc.) are meaningless.

As noted in section 1.1, language is normally used to communicate some MEANING from the speaker to the hearer. In these verses very little meaning is communicated, yet any speaker of English will recognize the poem as being English. How is this possible? Because the FORM of the poem is perfectly correct, and in fact (as Alice points out) quite pretty. Thus in one sense the poem is successful, even though it fails to communicate.

Let us look at some of the formal properties of the poem which make it recognizable, although not comprehensible, as English. First, of course, the whole poem "sounds" like English. All of the nonsense words are pronounced using sounds which are phonemes in English. These sounds are represented in written form using English spelling conventions. And these phonemes are arranged in permissible sequences, so that each nonsense word has the phonological shape of a possible word in English. For example, *brillig* and *gimble* could be English words; in a sense it is just an accident that they do not actually mean anything. In contrast, *bgillir* and *gmible* are not possible English words, because they violate the rules for combining sounds in English.

In addition, Carroll has skillfully made many of the nonsense words resemble real words which could occur in the same position: *brillig* reminds us of *brilliant* and *bright*; *slithy* reminds us of *slippery*, *slimy*, *slithering*, etc.

Second, the sentence patterns are recognizably those of English, specifically of a poetic and slightly old-fashioned style of English. We have noted that most of the function words (*the*, *and*, *in*, *were*, etc.) are real English words, and they occur in their proper place in the sentence. Similarly real content words like *son*, *shun*, *jaws*, *claws*, etc. are used in appropriate positions. We can generally identify the PART OF SPEECH (or CATEGORY) of each of the nonsense words by the position in which we find it. For example, *slithy*, *frumious*, and (probably) *mome* must be adjectives, while *gyre* and *gimble* (and probably *outgrabe*) are verbs. (In chapter 3, section 3.4 we will discuss some of the specific clues which allow us to reach these conclusions.)

Besides the word order, there are other clues about word categories. For example, we can see that *toves, borogoves,* and *raths* are nouns, not only because they all follow the definite article *the* (and perhaps an adjective) but also because they all contain a final *-s* which is used in English to indicate PLURALITY (more than one). This marker can only be attached to nouns. Similarly, the final *-ous* in *frumious* is typically found only in adjectives, which reinforces our earlier conclusion that *frumious* must be an adjective. And in the following couplet (from a later verse):

> "And hast thou slain the Jabberwock?
> Come to my arms, my beamish boy!"

the word *beamish* contains an ending *-ish* which is found in many adjectives; this confirms what we could already guess based on position.

Finally, the form of the poem as a whole conforms to a number of important conventions. The poem is divided into stanzas containing exactly four lines each. The first stanza, which seems to provide a kind of setting, is repeated verbatim at the end of the poem to create a frame around the story. The last word in each line, whether it means anything or not, fits into the A–B–A–B rhyme pattern typical of much English poetry. Each line has exactly four stressed syllables, with stressed and unstressed syllables alternating in a fixed rhythmic pattern. These features serve to identify this extended utterance as a coherent text, or DISCOURSE, of a certain type.

So there are at least four kinds of formal properties that Carroll manipulates to make his poem effective: sound patterns, word shapes, sentence patterns, and discourse structure. In this book we will be very much concerned with sentence patterns (SYNTAX) and word shapes (MORPHOLOGY), but only indirectly concerned with sound patterns (PHONOLOGY). And, due to limitations of space, we will not be able to deal with discourse structure here.

1.3   Grammar as a system of rules

One way to evaluate a person's progress in learning a new language is to measure their vocabulary: how many words do they know? But it does not make sense to ask, "How many sentences does this person know?" Vocabulary items (words, idioms, etc.) are typically learned one at a time, but we do not "learn" sentences that way. Rather than memorizing a large inventory of sentences, speakers create sentences as needed. They are able to do this because they "know" the rules of the language. By using these rules, even a person who knew only a limited number of words could potentially produce an extremely large number of sentences.

Now when we say that a speaker of English (or Tamil, or Chinese) "knows" the rules for forming sentences in that language, we do not mean that the person is aware of this knowledge. We need to distinguish between two different kinds of rules. There are some rules about using language that must be consciously learned, the kind of rules we often learn in school. Rules of this kind are called PRESCRIPTIVE rules: rules which define a standard form of the language, and which some authority must explicitly state for the benefit of other speakers.

The rules we are interested in here are those which the native speaker is usually not aware of – the kind of knowledge about the language that children learn naturally and unconsciously from their parents and other members of their speech community, whether they attend school or not. All languages, whether standardized or not, have rules of this kind, and these rules constitute the grammar of the language. Our approach to the study of grammar will be DESCRIPTIVE rather than prescriptive: our primary goal will be to observe, describe, and analyze what speakers of a language actually say, rather than trying to tell them what they should or should not say.

We have seen that there are rules in English concerning the sequence of sounds within a word. Similarly there are rules for the arrangement of words within a sentence, the arrangement of "meaningful elements" within a word, etc. The term GRAMMAR is often used to refer to the complete set of rules needed to produce all the regular patterns in a given language. Another, perhaps older, way in which the term GRAMMAR is sometimes used means roughly "all the structural properties of the language except sound structure (phonology)," i.e. the structure of words, phrases, sentences, texts, etc. This book is concerned with grammar in both senses. It is intended to help prepare you to analyze and describe the word and sentence patterns of a language (sense 2) by formulating a set of rules (sense 1) which account for those patterns.

1.4 Conclusion

Even though there is a close relationship between linguistic form and meaning, there is also a certain amount of independence between them. Neither can be defined in terms of the other: speakers can produce both grammatical sentences which are meaningless, and meaningful sentences which are ungrammatical.

In our comparison of English with Teochew, we saw that both languages employ a special form of sentence for expressing Yes–No questions. In fact, most, if not all, languages have a special sentence pattern which is used for asking such questions. This shows that the linguistic form of an utterance is often closely related to its meaning and its function. On the other hand, we noted that the grammatical features of a Yes–No question in English are not the same as in Teochew. Different languages may use very different grammatical devices to express the same basic concept. So understanding the meaning and function of an utterance will not tell us everything we need to know about its form.

Many aspects of linguistic form are arbitrary conventions shared by the speakers of a given language. For example, in English (and in most other European languages) the subject of a sentence normally occurs before the verb; but in most Philippine languages the subject normally occurs after the verb. This difference might be called arbitrary, in that it does not reflect a contrast in meaning or function. But this does not mean that the difference is random. Word-order facts within any given language tend to show interesting patterns of correlation, and the patterns observed in different languages tend to vary in limited and systematic ways.

One of our primary goals as linguists is to discover the patterns of regularity that exist in the grammatical systems of individual languages, as well as the recurring patterns common to many languages. This book introduces some basic concepts and techniques that can help you in these tasks. Our study of grammatical structure will frequently involve a discussion of meaning (semantic content), and to a lesser extent of function as well. However, it has not been possible within the limitations of this volume to address either semantics or pragmatics in any systematic way. It is hoped that readers of this book will go on to study other books where those issues are discussed in greater detail.

2 Analyzing word structure

An important design feature of human language is the fact that larger units are composed of smaller units, and that the arrangement of these smaller units is significant. For example, a sentence is not just a long series of speech sounds; it is composed of words and phrases, which must be arranged in a certain way in order to achieve the speaker's goals. Similarly, words (in many languages) may be composed of smaller units, each of which has its own meaning, and which must be arranged in a particular way.

In order to analyze the structure of a word or sentence, we need to identify the smaller parts from which it is formed and the patterns that determine how these parts should be arranged. This chapter introduces some basic aspects of word structure (morphology), and some techniques for analyzing it. More complicated aspects of morphological structure will be discussed in chapters 13–17.

Section 2.1 deals with the problem of identifying the component parts of a word. The association between form and meaning, which we discussed in chapter 1, plays a critical role in this process. Some of the basic techniques we will need are also useful for analyzing sentences, and we will first introduce them in that context. Section 2.2 discusses the kinds of parts which can be combined to form words, sections 2.3–2.4 provide a method for displaying the arrangement of these parts, and section 2.5 gives a brief overview of the different types of word structure found in the world's languages.

2.1 Identifying meaningful elements

2.1.1 Identifying word meanings

Consider the following sentence in the Lotuko language of Sudan:

(1)   a idulak atulo ema   'The man is planting grain.'

Although we know the meaning of the sentence as a whole, we cannot be sure what any of the individual words mean. One sentence in isolation tells us almost nothing; we need to compare it with something:

(2)   a idulak atulo ema   'The man is planting grain.'
         b idulak atulo aful   'The man is planting peanuts.'

These two Lotuko sentences constitute a MINIMAL PAIR, because they are identical except for a single element (in this case the final words, *ema* vs. *aful*). The beginning of the sentence (*idulak atulo . . .*) provides a context in which the words *ema* and *aful* stand in CONTRAST to each other. Two linguistic elements are said to be in CONTRAST when (i) they can occur in the same environment(s), and (ii) replacing one with the other creates a difference in meaning.[1]

The examples in (2) allow us to form a HYPOTHESIS that the word *ema* means 'grain' and *aful* means 'peanuts.' It seems quite likely that this hypothesis will turn out to be correct, because it is based on a type of evidence (a minimal pair, or CONTRAST IN IDENTICAL ENVIRONMENTS) which is usually quite reliable. However, any hypothesis based on just two examples is only a first guess – it must be checked against more data. What information do the sentences in (3) provide?

(3)   c ohonya eito erizo   'The child is eating meat.'
         d amata eito aari   'The child is drinking water.'

Both of these sentences contain the word *eito*, and the English translation for both sentences contains the phrase *the child*. This observation suggests the hypothesis that the word *eito* means 'the child.' In this case our hypothesis is based on the assumption that there is a regular association between the recurring Lotuko word (*eito*) and the recurring element of meaning ('the child'). This process of identifying recurring elements of form which correlate with recurring elements of meaning is sometimes referred to as the method of RECURRING PARTIALS WITH CONSTANT MEANING (Elson and Pickett 1988:3).

Both of the hypotheses we have reached so far about Lotuko words are based on the assumption that the meaning of a sentence is composed in some regular way from the meanings of the individual words. That is, we have been assuming that sentence meanings are COMPOSITIONAL. Of course, every language includes numerous expressions where this is not the case. Idioms are one common example. The English phrase *kick the bucket* can mean 'die,' even though none of the individual words has this meaning. Nevertheless, the compositionality of meaning is an important aspect of the structure of all human languages.

Based on the four Lotuko sentences we have examined so far, which are repeated in (4), can we determine the meaning of any additional words?

(4)   a idulak atulo ema   'The man is planting grain.'
        b idulak atulo aful   'The man is planting peanuts.'
        c ohonya eito erizo   'The child is eating meat.'
        d amata eito aari   'The child is drinking water.'

We can at least make some guesses, if we assume that the word order is the same in each sentence. The minimal pair in (2) allowed us to identify the words expressing the direct object, and those words occurred at the end of the sentence. The repeated word in (3) expressed the subject, and it occurred in the middle. Assuming that all four sentences have the same word order, then the verb must come first and the order of elements must be Verb–Subject–Object (VSO). Based on this hypothesis, try to identify the unknown words in (4).

This kind of reasoning depends on another important feature of linguistic structure, namely that the arrangement of linguistic units often follows a systematic pattern of some kind. We arrived at a hypothesis about the structure of a simple sentence, and used that hypothesis to make some guesses about word meanings. But be careful – a hypothesis based on this kind of reasoning needs to be checked carefully. Many languages do not require consistent word order within a sentence, and most languages allow for some variation in word order. So we need to look for additional data to test our hypotheses. What evidence does the sentence in (5) provide as to the correctness of your guesses in (4)?

(5)   e ohonya odwoti aful   'The girl is eating peanuts.'

Now use the methods discussed above to find the meanings of any unknown words in (6), confirm or disprove the specific hypotheses stated above, and fill in the blanks for sentences h and i:

(6)   **Lotuko** (Sudan; adapted from Merrifield et al. 1987, prob. 131)
        a idulak atulo ema   'The man is planting grain.'
        b idulak atulo aful   'The man is planting peanuts.'
        c ohonya eito erizo   'The child is eating meat.'
        d amata eito aari   'The child is drinking water.'
        e ohonya odwoti aful   'The girl is eating peanuts.'
        f abak atulo ezok   'The man hit the dog.'
        g amata odwoti aari   'The girl is drinking water.'
        h _____   'The girl hit the child.'
        i ohonya ezok erizo   _____

Let us review what we have learned so far. We have identified three types of evidence that can be used to form hypotheses about the meanings of words: minimal contrast, recurring partials, and pattern-matching. These methods cannot be applied to a single example in isolation, but involve comparing two or more examples. The methods work best if the examples are reasonably similar to each other. In this data set, all the sentences contain the same three elements in the same order (verb, subject, object), and the same specific words are used over and over. So selecting the right data and organizing them in the right way are crucial steps in analyzing the grammatical patterns of a language.

The methods of recurring partials and minimal contrast simply allow us to identify new words. The recognition of structural patterns in the data (e.g. the VSO word order) not only helps us to identify new forms but also allows us to use the language creatively, that is, to produce or understand sentences we have never heard before (as in [6h, i]). In those examples, our hypothesis about the rule of sentence formation enabled us to make predictions that could be tested by consulting native speakers of Lotuko. It is important that our analysis of the grammar be stated in a way that allows us to make clear and testable predictions. Otherwise there is no way to be sure whether our claims about the language are correct or not.

2.1.2   Identifying meaningful elements within words

The kinds of reasoning discussed in the previous section can be used to identify parts of words as well. Consider, for example, the following data from the Isthmus Zapotec language of Mexico (Merrifield et al. 1987, prob. 9):

(7)   kañee   'feet'   kaʒigi   'chins'
        ñeebe   'his foot'   ʒigibe   'his chin'
        kañeebe   'his feet'
        ñeeluʔ   'your foot'   ʒigiluʔ   'your chin'
        kañeetu   'your (pl) feet'   kaʒigitu   'your (pl) chins'
        kañeedu   'our feet'   kaʒigidu   'our chins'

All of the words which contain the string /ñee/ have GLOSSES (translations) which involve the idea 'foot,' and all of the words which contain the string /ʒigi/ have glosses which contain the English word 'chin.' So the method of recurring partials allows us to identify the form *ñee* as meaning 'foot' and the form *ʒigi* as meaning 'chin.' Further data show that these forms, *ñee* and *ʒigi*, can occur as independent words in their own right.

We also notice that whenever the word begins with the sequence *ka–*, the English translation equivalent uses a plural form of the noun; so (again by the method of recurring partials) we might guess that *ka–* is a marker of plurality. This hypothesis can be confirmed by finding minimal pairs in (8). Why doesn't example (7) contain a form meaning 'his chins?' How would you say it if you needed to?

(8)   ñee   'foot'   ñeebe   'his foot'   ʒigi   'chin'
        kañee 'feet'   kañeebe   'his feet'   kaʒigi   'chins'

We can also use minimal contrasts to identify elements corresponding to the possessive pronouns in the English gloss. The forms *–be* 'his', *–tu* 'your (plural)', and *-du* 'our' occur in identical environments, as shown in (9), providing a minimally contrastive set.

(9)   kañeebe   'his feet'
        kañeetu   'your (pl) feet'
        kañeedu   'our feet'

There is a fourth ending, *–luʔ*, which seems to mean 'your (singular).' This ending is not shown in (9) because we do not have an example of it occurring in that precise context. That is, the data set (or CORPUS) does not contain the form *kañeeluʔ* 'your feet', although we would predict that this form could occur, based on the patterning of elements in other forms. As far as we can tell, this "gap" in the data is purely accidental, a result of how the examples were collected or arranged rather than a systematic fact about the language. The existence of forms like *kaʒikeluʔ* 'your shoulders' (compare *ʒike* 'shoulder', *ʒikebe* 'his shoulder') shows that *–luʔ* can co-occur with *ka–*.

Even though we have no example of *–luʔ* in the precise frame used in (9), the corpus contains other minimal contrasts which confirm its meaning:

(10)　　ñee　　'foot'　　　　ʒigi　　'chin'
　　　　ñeeluʔ　'your foot'　　ʒigiluʔ　'your chin'

2.1.3　Summary

We have discussed three types of reasoning that can be used to identify the meaningful elements of an utterance (whether parts of a word or words in a sentence): minimal contrast, recurring partials, and pattern-matching. In practice, when working on a new body of data, we often use all three at once, without stopping to think which method we use for which element. Sometimes, however, it is important to be able to state explicitly the pattern of reasoning which we use to arrive at certain conclusions. For example, suppose that one of our early hypotheses about the language is contradicted by further data. We need to be able to go back and determine what evidence that hypothesis was based on so that we can re-evaluate that evidence in the light of additional information. This will help us to decide whether the hypothesis can be modified to account for all the facts, or whether it needs to be abandoned entirely. Grammatical analysis involves an endless process of "guess and check" – forming hypotheses, testing them against further data, and modifying or abandoning those which do not work.

Using the methods of recurring partials and minimal contrast, we have identified the following meaningful elements in the Isthmus Zapotec examples:

(11)　　ñee　'foot'　　　　ka–　(plural marker)
　　　　ʒigi　'chin'　　　　–be　'his'
　　　　ʒike　'shoulder'　　–luʔ　'your (sg)'
　　　　　　　　　　　　　–tu　'your (pl)'
　　　　　　　　　　　　　–du　'our'

In predicting the existence of a word *kañeeluʔ*, which should mean 'your feet,' we also made use of a hypothesis about how these elements combine with each other; but we did not explicitly state this hypothesis. That is, we have not yet tried to define the order of elements in a Zapotec word. In sections 2.3–2.4 we will introduce a way of representing this kind of information.

2.2   Morphemes

2.2.1   Definition of "morpheme"

We have seen that a single word in Zapotec can be composed of several meaningful elements, or MORPHEMES. Of course, the same is true in English (13) and a large number of other languages.

(12)   kañeebe   ka-ñee-be   'his feet'
        kaʒigitu   ka-ʒigi-tu   'your (pl) chins'
        kaʒikelu?   ka-ʒike-lu?   'your shoulders'

(13)   chairman   chair-man
        distrust   dis-trust
        unbelievable   un-believ(e)-able
        unsparingly   un-spar(e)-ing-ly
        palatalization   palat(e)-al-iz(e)-ation

What do we mean when we say that a certain form, such as Zapotec *ka–*, is a "morpheme?" Charles Hockett (1958) gave a definition of this term which is often quoted:

> Morphemes are the smallest individually meaningful elements in the utterances of a language.

There are two crucial aspects of this definition. First, a morpheme is *meaningful*. A morpheme normally involves a consistent association of phonological form with some aspect of meaning, as seen in (7) where the form *ñee* was consistently associated with the concept 'foot.' However, this association of form with meaning can be somewhat flexible. We will see various ways in which the phonological shape of a morpheme may be altered to some extent in particular environments, and there are some morphemes whose meaning may depend partly on context.

Second, morphemes are the *smallest* meaningful elements. "Smallest" here does not refer to physical duration (time of articulation) or phonological weight. A morpheme may consist of a single phoneme (like the /a-/ in *a-moral, a-temporal, a-theism*) or long strings of phonemes (such as *elephant, spatula, Mississippi*, etc.) The real point is that a single morpheme may not contain any smaller element (or SUBSTRING) which is itself a meaningful element. For example, the word *unhappy* is not a single morpheme because it contains two substrings which are each "individually meaningful": *un–* means 'not' and *happy* means 'happy'. Thus, rather than saying that a morpheme is the smallest meaningful element, we might say that a morpheme is the MINIMAL meaningful element, in the sense that it can not be subdivided into smaller meaningful elements.

The words *catalogue*, *catastrophe*, and *caterpillar* are all single morphemes in modern English. Even though they all contain the sequence *cat–* (/kæt–/), they do not contain the English morpheme *cat*, because their meaning has nothing to do with cats. For the same reason, the word *caterpillar* does not contain the morpheme *pillar*. A recurrent element of form does not automatically indicate the presence of a common morpheme, unless the recurring phonological material correlates with some common element of meaning.

A final point should be made in relation to the definition stated above. Hockett identified the morpheme as the smallest "individually meaningful element" in the language. This phrase helps us to understand the difference between morphemes and phonemes. The contrast between two sounds (i.e. phonemes) is said to be SIGNIFICANT when substituting one for the other changes the meaning of a word, as in *bill* vs. *pill*, *lake* vs. *rake*, *mad* vs. *mat*, or the contrastive set *beat*, *bit*, *bait*, *bet*, *bat*. But even though such examples show that the contrast between /b/ and /p/ etc. is significant, the phoneme /b/ has no inherent meaning of its own. It is not "individually meaningful." So while the phoneme is "smaller" than the morpheme, in the sense that a single morpheme often consists of many phonemes, the morpheme is "meaningful" in a way that individual phonemes are not. In the following section, we will mention (in a very preliminary way) different types of meaning that a morpheme may carry.

2.2.2   Different kinds of morphemes

In the Zapotec data in section 2.1.2, we found some morphemes (including *ñee* 'foot,' *ʒike* 'shoulder,' and *ʒigi* 'chin') which can occur as independent words in their own right. Others (including *ka–* 'plural,' *–be* 'his,' *–tu* 'your (plural),' and *–du* 'our') only appear as part of a larger word, and never as a complete word on their own. Morphemes of the first type (those that may occur as complete words) are said to be FREE, while morphemes of the second type (those that may not) are said to be BOUND.

In the examples in (13), *trust*, *believe*, *spare*, and *palate* are all examples of free morphemes, because they can occur alone as complete English words. The morphemes *dis–*, *un–*, *-able*, *-ing*, *-ly*, etc. are all bound, because they only occur as part of a larger word. The word *chairman* is an interesting example, because it contains two free morphemes.

Consider the words *trusted*, *trusting*, *trusty*, *distrust*, *mistrust*, and *trust-worthy*. Intuitively it is obvious that all these words are "related" to each other in some way, and that this relationship is based on the fact that they all contain the morpheme *trust*. *Trust* is in some sense the "core" or "nucleus" of each of these words; it provides the basic element of meaning which all of the words have in common. The other morphemes in these words are in some sense "added on" to this core.

We refer to the morpheme that forms the core of a word as the ROOT. Other morphemes, which are added on to a root and modify its meaning in a consistent way, are referred to as AFFIXES. So the related words above all contain the same root (*trust*) but different affixes (*-ed*, *-ing*, etc.). It is not always easy to distinguish between roots and affixes, but there are three criteria (or "rules of thumb") that can help:

a   An affix is always bound, but a root is often free. If a particular morpheme occurs in isolation as a word, it must be a root.

b   A root normally carries LEXICAL MEANING, i.e. the kind of meaning you would look up in a dictionary or the "basic" meaning of the word (e.g. *trust*, *man*, *chin*). An affix, on the other hand, frequently carries only GRAMMATICAL MEANING, such as 'plural,' 'third person,' 'past tense,' etc.

c   An affix is always part of a CLOSED CLASS, meaning that there is only a limited (and typically small) number of other morphemes that could be found in the same position in the word. Roots, on the other hand, normally belong to an OPEN CLASS, meaning that there is a very large number of other morphemes of the same type. Moreover, new roots can be borrowed or invented quite freely, whereas new affixes enter the language only rarely.

An affix which occurs before the root is called a PREFIX, while an affix which occurs after the root is called a SUFFIX. We write affixes with a hyphen showing the relative position of the root. In the Zapotec data, we saw one prefix (*ka–* 'plural') and four suffixes: *-be* 'his,' *-lu?* 'your (singular),' *-tu* 'your (plural),' and *-du* 'our'.

Returning to the word *chairman*, we can now see that it contains two roots. Words of this type are called COMPOUND words.

2.3   Representing word structure

In discussing the Isthmus Zapotec data presented in section 2.1.2, we predicted that there might be a word of the form *kañeelu?* meaning 'your feet,' even though it was not found in the data. Of course, a hypothesis of this kind must be held very lightly until it can be confirmed with a native speaker – the phonological shape of a morpheme may change in certain environments, sometimes in unpredictable ways, and there may be other surprises as well. But the very fact that we could make such a prediction indicates that we have recognized a pattern that governs the way words are formed in Zapotec. In this section we will present a simple method for representing such patterns.

The Zapotec data set (including a few additional forms) is reproduced in (14). The meaningful elements that we can identify in this data are listed in (15).

(14)   **Isthmus Zapotec** (Mexico; Merrifield et al. 1987, prob. 9):

ñee	'foot'	ʒigiluʔ	'your chin'
kañee	'feet'	kaʒigidu	'our chins'
ñeebe	'his foot'	ʒike	'shoulder'
kañeebe	'his feet'	ʒikebe	'his shoulder'
ñeeluʔ	'your foot'	kaʒikeluʔ	'your shoulders'
kañeetu	'your (pl) feet'	diaga	'ear'
kañeedu	'our feet'	kadiagatu	'your (pl) ears'
ʒigi	'chin'	kadiagadu	'our ears'
kaʒigi	'chins'	biʃozedu	'our father'
ʒigibe	'his chin'	biʃozetu	'your (pl) father'
kaʒigitu	'your (pl) chins'	kabiʃozetu	'your (pl) fathers'

(15)   **ROOTS**   **AFFIXES**

ñee	'foot'	ka–	(pl. marker)
ʒigi	'chin'	–be	'his'
ʒike	'shoulder'	–luʔ	'your (sg)'
diaga	'ear'	–tu	'your (pl)'
biʃoze	'father'	–du	'our'

If we study the distribution of these affixes, we can make the following generalizations:

a   no word contains more than one prefix or more than one suffix;

b   morphemes which identify the possessor are always suffixes; the only prefix is the plural marker;

c   a word which contains no plural marker is interpreted as being singular;

d   no word contains more than one possessor marker (this follows as a logical consequence of (a) and (b));

e   the plural marker may occur with or without a possessor marker, and vice versa.

Most of this information is summarized in the simple chart shown in (16). This type of chart is called a POSITION CLASS CHART. Each column in the chart represents a position in which a certain class of morphemes can occur. The four possessive suffixes belong to the same POSITION CLASS, because they all occur in the same place in the word, and only one of them can occur at a time. In general, any two elements that belong to the same position class are MUTUALLY EXCLUSIVE, meaning that they cannot occur together in the same word.

(16)

−1	0	+1
NUMBER	ROOT	POSSESSOR
ka– 'plural'		–be '3sg' –lu? '2sg' –tu '2pl' –du '1pl'

The arrangement of the columns in the chart (from left to right) indicates the linear order of elements in a word. So whenever morphemes from different position classes co-occur, the one whose position is shown as being furthest to the left will occur first in the word. Rather than numbering the columns from left to right, linguists frequently assign numbers from the inside out, starting with 0 for the root position and using negative numbers for prefixes, positive numbers for suffixes. (These numbers have no special significance; they are only used for ease of reference.)

More significant than the position numbers are the labels at the top of each column. In the simplest case, all the elements belonging to a particular position class will have closely related meanings. In this example, all the elements in position +1 identify a possessor in terms of person (first, second, or third) and number (singular or plural). We normally try to assign each position in the chart a label which expresses the grammatical category or function that is shared by all the elements in that position class (in this case, "POSSESSOR").

Notice that we have not listed the root morphemes in their column. This is because roots belong to an open class (in this case, the class of common countable nouns). Even though only five roots are found in this corpus, in principle any number of other roots could occur in the same position, and it would be impossible to list them all. Affixes, however, belong to small closed classes, so it is normally both possible and helpful to list them all in their position in the chart.

There is still an important aspect of word structure in Zapotec which our chart does not reflect: every noun contains a root, but many nouns have no prefix, others no suffix, and some have neither prefix nor suffix. In other words, the root is OBLIGATORY (there must be an element in this position) whereas the prefixes and suffixes are OPTIONAL. A common way of indicating optionality is by using parentheses. So we might revise our chart slightly as follows:

(17)

−1 (NUMBER)	0 ROOT	+1 (POSSESSOR)
ka– 'plural'		–be '3sg' –lu? '2sg' –tu '2pl' –du '1pl'

In point (c) above we noted that a word which contains no plural marker is always singular. The chart in (17) shows that the plural prefix is optional, and that when it is present it indicates plurality; but it doesn't say anything about the significance of the *lack* of a prefix. One way to tidy up this loose end is to assume that the grammar of the language includes a DEFAULT RULE which says something like the following: "a countable noun which contains no plural prefix is interpreted as being singular."

Another possible way to account for the same fact is to assume that singular nouns carry an "invisible" (or NULL) prefix which indicates singular number. That would mean that the number prefix is actually obligatory for this class of noun. Under this approach, our chart would look something like (18):

(18)

−1 NUMBER	0 ROOT	+1 (POSSESSOR)
ka– 'plural' Ø– 'singular'		–be '3sg' –lu? '2sg' –tu '2pl' –du '1pl'

The use of null morphemes is a somewhat controversial issue. In general, this analysis is most plausible where the lack of an affix can be associated with a definite, specific meaning. For example, Turkish verbs carry an AGREEMENT suffix (see chapter 7) which indicates the person and number of the subject. The suffixes are: *-Im* '1sg,' *-sIn* '2sg,' *-Iz* '1pl,' *-sInIz* '2pl,' *-lAr* '3pl.'[2] When the subject is third person singular, there is no visible agreement suffix on the verb. In this case the lack of a suffix has a definite and specific meaning. By associating that meaning (third person singular) with a null morpheme, we can fill an otherwise puzzling gap in the PARADIGM (or set) of Turkish person–number agreement markers.

Contrast this pattern with the marking of English verbs, which take a suffix *-s* in the simple present tense when the subject is third person singular.

The absence of this suffix simply means that the verb is not a third person singular simple present form. The subject may be first or second person singular or a plural of any person, or the verb may be an infinitive, past or future tense, etc. Clearly no specific meaning can be associated with the lack of -*s* in this case, and it would not be appropriate to assume a zero suffix for these verbs.

English nouns can also take a suffix -*s* to indicate plural number. Here the lack of a suffix can be given a very specific interpretation, namely singular number, which might lead us to assume the presence of a zero suffix. On the other hand, there are many nouns (called MASS nouns) which do not normally take the plural suffix: *air, wheat, courage, static*, etc. For these nouns there is no contrast between singular and plural, and it seems odd to suggest that they always carry a null suffix. It seems preferable to assume that the singular is the "unmarked" or default number category for English nouns, as proposed for Zapotec under the analysis shown in (17).

2.4   Analyzing position classes

Let us work through the process involved in constructing a position class chart. The first step obviously is to identify each morpheme in the data, using the methods discussed in section 2.1. We will practice with the following (slightly regularized) data from the Gee language of West Africa. For simplicity, morpheme boundaries are already marked:

(19)   **Gee** (Togo; Bendor-Samuel and Levinsohn 1986; Roberts 1999, ex. M-4.8)

a	biʔ-ʃu-ni	'I came'
b	bai-ʃu-ni	'I went'
c	dos-ʃu-me	'you (sg) ran'
d	meʔ-ʃu-mi	'they spoke'
e	bai-te-mi-leʔ	'will they go?'
f	biʔ-paʔ-ni-do	'I am not coming'
g	dos-ʃu-ni-risa	'I ran first'
h	bai-paʔ-me-duʔa	'you (sg) only are going'
i	dos-te-mi-risa-leʔ	'will they run first?'
j	bai-ʃu-ni-tuʃi	'I went suddenly'
k	meʔ-te-mi-risa-do-leʔ	'will they not speak first?'
l	biʔ-te-me-duʔa-do	'you (sg) only will not come'
m	meʔ-paʔ-mi-tuʃi-leʔ	'are they suddenly speaking?'

Based on these data we can identify the following meanings for each morpheme:

(20)   **ROOTS**   **AFFIXES**
       bi? 'come'   *–ʃu*   'past tense'
       bai 'go'   *–pa?*   'present tense'
       dos 'run'   *–te*   'future tense'
       me? 'speak'   *–ni*   '1sg'
                           –me   '2sg'
                           –mi   '3pl'
                           –du?a 'only'
                           –risa 'first'
                           –tuʃi 'suddenly'
                           –do   'not'
                           –le?   'question'

We begin the position class analysis by re-writing each word in the data onto a chart, with the longest words (i.e. those which contain the greatest number of morphemes) at the top. We line up all the roots in one column and arrange the affixes in such a way that: (i) no column in the chart contains more than one morpheme in any given word; and (ii) each individual morpheme always appears in the same column in all the words where it occurs.

One obvious way to do this is to start out with a separate column for each morpheme; in this example, that would mean 12 columns (1 for the root plus 1 for each of the 11 affixes). But it is much more helpful to make some initial guesses about which affixes might belong to the same position class. When several affixes have closely related meanings, or belong to the same grammatical category (tense, person, number, etc.), and no two of them are found in the same word, there is a good chance they will belong to the same class. In that case, we can write them in the same column in our initial chart.

The charting procedure itself will help us to find out if an initial hypothesis of this sort was mistaken. There are at least two ways in which this could happen. First, we might discover that two of the affixes which we have tentatively grouped together really can occur in the same word after all. Second, we might discover that two affixes have different ORDERING RELATIONSHIPS with respect to some other morpheme. For example, if we find in a certain language that the masculine and neuter gender markers occur as prefixes to the adjective root, while the feminine marker occurs as a suffix, we must split these elements into two separate position classes, even though they all express the same grammatical category (namely gender). This is necessary because the columns in a position class chart represent fixed linear ordering constraints. Every element in a given position class must have the same order as its fellows with respect to all elements of every other position class.

In our present example, we can see that the three tense markers (*–ʃu*, *–pa?*, and *–te*) form a coherent group, as do the three subject-agreement markers (*–ni*, *–me*, and *–mi*); and there are no words which contain more than one element from either group. So our initial chart might look like (21).

(21)

k	meʔ	te	mi	risa			do	leʔ
i	dos	te	mi	risa				leʔ
m	meʔ	paʔ	mi		tuʃi			leʔ
l	biʔ	te	me			duʔa	do	
e	bai	te	mi					leʔ
f	biʔ	paʔ	ni				do	
g	dos	ʃu	ni	risa				
h	bai	paʔ	me			duʔa		
j	bai	ʃu	ni		tuʃi			
a	biʔ	ʃu	ni					
b	bai	ʃu	ni					
c	dos	ʃu	me					
d	meʔ	ʃu	mi					

The next step is to inspect each column to see whether elements in that column ever co-occur with elements in the neighboring column to the left or right. If we find two adjacent columns that are never both filled in the same row, it would be possible to merge the two into a single column. The two sets of elements are said to be in COMPLEMENTARY DISTRIBUTION, meaning that no single word ever contains elements from both sets.

We would definitely want to merge the two columns if the meanings of the elements are related or form a coherent class in some way. On the other hand, if two adjacent columns appear to be in complementary distribution but there is no plausible relationship between the meanings of their elements, it may be better to leave the columns separate for the time being. Rather than merging the two, add a note at the bottom of your chart stating that these two sets of elements have not been found to co-occur. When you have a chance to collect more data, try to find examples where elements from both sets can occur together. If there are no (or very few) such words in the language, you have discovered a CO-OCCURRENCE RESTRICTION, which needs to be stated as part of the grammar of the language. Attempting to find explanations for these restrictions often leads to interesting discoveries, either about the current structure of the language or about its historical development.

In our present example, we can see that the three forms –*risa*, –*tuʃi*, and –*duʔa* never co-occur with each other, so it would be possible to collapse all three columns into one. The corresponding meanings ('first,' 'suddenly,' 'only') do not appear to be closely related, but neither are they incompatible; they all provide some information about the manner in which the action was performed. Unless further data reveal that two or more of them may co-occur, it seems reasonable to combine them into a single position class, as in (22).

(22)

k	meʔ	te	mi	risa	do	leʔ
i	dos	te	mi	risa		leʔ
m	meʔ	paʔ	mi	tuʃi		leʔ
l	biʔ	te	me	duʔa	do	
e	bai	te	mi			leʔ
f	biʔ	paʔ	ni		do	
g	dos	ʃu	ni	risa		
h	bai	paʔ	me	duʔa		
j	bai	ʃu	ni	tuʃi		
a	biʔ	ʃu	ni			
b	bai	ʃu	ni			
c	dos	ʃu	me			
d	meʔ	ʃu	mi			

Since –*do* and –*leʔ* occur with each other and with elements of every other column in the chart, no further combination is possible. Tense and subject-agreement appear to be obligatory, while the other classes are optional, so our final position class chart would look like this:

(23)

0 ROOT	+1 TENSE	+2 SUBJ-AGR	+3 (MANNER)	+4 (NEGATIVE)	+5 (INTERROG)
	–ʃu 'past' –paʔ 'pres' –te 'fut'	–ni '1sg' –me '2sg' –mi '3pl'	–duʔa 'only' –risa 'first' –tuʃi 'suddenly'	–do 'not'	–leʔ 'ques.'

The identification of position classes is not a purely mechanical procedure. It involves judgments based on linguistic knowledge and intuition, which are developed with practice. Moreover, while position class charts are useful for a large number of languages, there are other languages for which they are less helpful. We will discuss some reasons for this in the following section.

2.5   A typology of word structure

Position class charts work best for languages which have the following properties:

a   each morpheme has a simple linear ordering relationship with all other morphemes in the same word;
b   each affix expresses only one grammatical feature or category;
c   all affixes which express the same grammatical category have the same ordering relationships with all other classes of morphemes.

In other words, these charts are most useful for languages in which affixes are strung together like beads on a string, and there is a one-to-one correspondence between grammatical categories and position classes. A traditional term used to refer to languages which have this type of word structure is AGGLUTINATING, suggesting that the word consists of a number of morphemes stuck together.

Obviously, this is not the situation in all languages. We will discuss several kinds of "non-linear" morphemes in chapter 16. In the remainder of this chapter, we will give a brief overview of the range of morphological structure found in the world's languages.

Some languages (especially in southeast Asia) have almost no affixes. Most words consist of a single morpheme (a bare root). Such languages have traditionally been called ANALYTIC (or ISOLATING) languages.

Another type of language is the SYNTHETIC type (also referred to as FUSIONAL or INFLECTIONAL languages). In languages of this type, a single affix frequently marks several grammatical categories at once. Such affixes are sometimes called PORTMANTEAU MORPHEMES.[3] A well-known example involves the Latin verbal suffixes, a small number of which are illustrated in (24).

(24)

amō	'I love'	amāvī	'I loved'	amor	'I am loved'
amās	'you love'	amāvistī	'you loved'	amāris	'you are loved'
amat	'(s)he loves'	amāvit	'(s)he loved'	amātur	'(s)he is loved'
amāmus	'we love'	amāvimus	'we loved'	amāmur	'we are loved'
amātis	'you (pl) love'	amāvistis	'you (pl) loved'	amāminī	'you (pl) are loved'
amant	'they love'	amāvērunt	'they loved'	amantur	'they are loved'

While the verbal endings contain some recurring elements, in many forms it is not possible to divide the ending into smaller morphemes which are consistently identifiable. For example, the suffix $-\bar{o}$ in 'I love' expresses all of the following categories at once: tense and aspect (simple present), subject agreement (first singular), voice (active), and mood (indicative). Similarly, the suffix $-(\bar{a})min\bar{\imath}$ expresses second person plural present passive indicative, all in one morpheme.

Another common pattern in synthetic (or fusional) languages is that a certain category may be expressed by SUPPLETION, i.e. a change in the form of the root, rather than by adding an affix.[4] This pattern is found in the past tense forms of some English verbs (25a), and in the comparative forms of some English adjectives (25b). In a sense, the suppletive form (e.g. *went*) is a portmanteau morpheme expressing both the basic meaning of the root ('go') and one or more additional grammatical categories ('past tense').

(25) a **PRES**   **PAST**
        go   went
        am   was
        buy   bought

    b **BASE**   **COMPARATIVE**
        good   better
        bad   worse
        much   more
        little   less

A fourth type of language is the POLYSYNTHETIC type. This term is generally used to designate languages which allow the INCORPORATION of one word into another (see chapter 14). In examples (26–27), the noun roots that express the direct object (*tobacco* and *sweat*, respectively) are morphologically part of the verb. As these examples illustrate, one word in a polysynthetic language often corresponds to a whole sentence in English.

(26) **Onandaga** (North America; Woodbury 1975, cited in Baker 1988:76)
      Wa?-ha-yv?kw-ahni:nu-?
      PAST-he/it-tobacco-buy-ASPECT
      'He bought tobacco.'

(27) **Rembarrnga** (Australia; Dixon 1980:223–224)
      yarran-məə?-ku?pi-popna-ni-yuwa
      1pl.IO/3sg.SUBJ-might-sweat-smell-INF-along.PRES
      'It (the kangaroo) might smell our sweat along (i.e. as we try to sneak up on it).'

To summarize, we have identified four broad types of languages based on their characteristic word structures:

1.   ANALYTIC (or ISOLATING): one morpheme per word;
2.   AGGLUTINATING: strings of affixes, each marking a single grammatical feature;

3.   SYNTHETIC (FUSIONAL or INFLECTIONAL): single affixes marking several grammatical categories at once (portmanteau morphemes); or suppletive forms;
4.   POLYSYNTHETIC: long strings of affixes or incorporated roots in a single word.

These terms are of only limited value as a system for classifying languages since many languages do not fit perfectly into any one category. However, the terms do help us to recognize and describe some of the differences in word structure found between languages, or even between different types of words in the same language.

Exercises

2A Finnish (Merrifield et al. 1987, prob. 13)
Identify the morphemes and prepare a position class chart to account for the following data.

1.	laulan	'I sing.'	7.	yuon	'I drink.'
2.	laulat	'You sing.'	8.	yuot	'You drink.'
3.	laulavi	'He sings.'	9.	yuovi	'He drinks.'
4.	laulamme	'We sing.'	10.	yuomme	'We drink.'
5.	laulatte	'You (pl) sing.'	11.	yuotte	'You (pl) drink.'
6.	laulavat	'They sing.'	12.	yuovat	'They drink.'

2B Swahili (East Africa; Healey 1990b, ex. A-5 and Roberts 1999, ex. M-3.5)
Identify the morphemes and prepare a position class chart to account for the following data.

1.	ninasema	'I speak.'
2.	unasema	'You speak.'
3.	anasema	'He speaks.'
4.	wanasema	'They speak.'
5.	ninaona	'I see.'
6.	niliona	'I saw.'
7.	ninawaona	'I see them.'
8.	nilikuona	'I saw you.'
9.	ananiona	'He sees me.'
10.	utaniona	'You will see me.'

Additional exercises

Merrifield et al. (1987) prob. 1, 4, 8, 11, 24, 28, 30, 34
Healey (1990b), ex. A.15, 24

Notes

1. When substituting one form for another does not produce a difference in meaning, we say that the two forms are in FREE VARIATION with each other, at least in that particular context.
2. The capital letters here indicate that the vowel quality in the suffix depends on the vowels in the root.
3. *Portemanteau* is a French word meaning 'coat rack,' while the English form *portmanteau* is used to refer to a kind of suitcase. In linguistics, this label is intended to indicate that a single morpheme expresses several concepts at once, just as a coat rack (or a suitcase) can hold several coats at the same time.
4. See ch. 15 for a fuller discussion.

3 Constituent structure

In chapter 1 we noted that MORPHOLOGY (the study of word structures) and SYNTAX (the study of phrase and sentence structures) are generally treated as separate sub-fields in linguistics. This is because words and sentences are different in certain fundamental ways. After studying chapter 2 you have some idea of how we might represent the arrangement of morphemes in a word, at least in the simplest cases. Describing the arrangement of words in a sentence will require some additional concepts.

In this chapter we discuss two fundamental aspects of sentence structure. First, the words of any language can be classified according to their grammatical properties. These classes are traditionally referred to as PARTS OF SPEECH (noun, verb, etc.); linguists refer to them as SYNTACTIC CATEGORIES. In describing the word-order patterns of the language, we need to refer to syntactic categories since it is obviously impossible to list every possible combination of specific words.

Second, the words in a sentence are not organized as a simple list. Rather, words cluster together to form groups of various sizes; these groups are referred to as CONSTITUENTS. The word-order patterns of human languages cannot be described adequately without reference to constituents.

In this chapter we will discuss the kinds of linguistic evidence we can use to identify constituents (groups of words) and categories (parts of speech). Then we will discuss "tree" diagrams, a commonly used method for representing both the grouping of words and the linear order of words in a sentence. But first, in order to see why these concepts are important, let us return to the issue addressed in chapter 1, namely the relation between form and meaning.

3.1 Ambiguity

Sometimes a sentence can have more than one meaning. Sentences of this type are said to be AMBIGUOUS, meaning that the same string of words can be interpreted in more than one way. Consider the following examples:

(1) a The hunter went home with five bucks in his pocket.
     b I drove my car into the bank.
     c Bill claimed that he saw her duck.
     d John hit a man with a telescope.

Each of the sentences in (1) contains a word which has more than one meaning. The word *buck* can mean either a male deer or (in American slang) a dollar. Similarly, the word *bank* can mean either a financial institution or a steep slope of land; the word *duck* can be used to refer to either a waterfowl or an action; and the preposition *with* can be used to express at least two different semantic relations (instrument vs. accompaniment; see chapter 4 section 4.2). These sentences provide examples of LEXICAL AMBIGU-ITY, sentences which are ambiguous because they contain ambiguous words.[1]

Now consider the examples in (2):

(2) a the tall bishop's hat
     b the woman on the committee that I met with yesterday

Neither of these phrases contains an ambiguous word, but each of them can be interpreted in more than one way. (Which one is tall, the bishop or his hat? Who did I meet with yesterday, the woman or the committee?) We can often find contexts which make one interpretation or the other more likely, as illustrated in (3). In isolation, however, both interpretations are possible.[2]

(3) a The short bishop hid the tall bishop's hat in his back pocket.
     b Archbishop Jones tried to compensate for his short stature by wearing his tall bishop's hat on formal occasions.

The ambiguity in (2) is not due to any ambiguous words. Rather, it arises because the words can be grouped together in two different ways, as shown in (4).

(4) a the [tall bishop]'s hat
        the tall [bishop's hat]
     b the woman on [the committee that I met with yesterday]
        the [woman on the committee] that I met with yesterday

These phrases provide examples of STRUCTURAL AMBIGUITY. This term means that the different interpretations of each phrase arise because we can assign different grammatical structures to the same string of words, even though none of the individual words is itself ambiguous in this context. Such examples demonstrate that words do form sub-groups (or CONSTITUENTS) within a phrase or sentence, and that these groupings are often crucial in determining what the sentence means.

Now consider sentence (5).[3] This sentence is ambiguous because each of the two words may belong to more than one syntactic category. One possible interpretation takes *mistrust* to be a noun and *wounds* to be a verb. This reading could be paraphrased: "Suspicion hurts (people)." The other possible interpretation takes *mistrust* to be a verb and *wounds* to be a noun. This reading could be paraphrased: "(We should) mistrust injuries." It requires a bit of work to imagine a situation where this would be a sensible thing to say, but it is nevertheless a possible interpretation of sentence (5).

(5)   Mistrust wounds.

This kind of ambiguity about the syntactic category of a word is frequently observed in newspaper headlines, where many function words are omitted and there is no discourse context to rely on. Sometimes this ambiguity produces amusing unintended readings. The examples in (6) are all reported to be actual newspaper headlines; try to identify the words whose category is ambiguous:

(6)   **Reagan Wins On Budget, But More Lies Ahead**
        Squad Helps Dog Bite Victim
        Eye Drops Off Shelf
        Teacher Strikes Idle Kids

These types of ambiguity illustrate the importance of constituency and category for making sense of what we hear. As we will see, these two concepts are fundamental to any description of sentence structure. In sections 3.2 and 3.4 we will consider the linguistic basis for identifying constituents and categories, respectively.

3.2   Constituency

Examples like (2) show that the words within a phrase or sentence are organized into sub-groups (or CONSTITUENTS), and that these groupings are often crucial in determining what the sentence means. Once we accept that fact a practical question arises, namely how are we to identify these significant sub-groups, since their boundaries are (in general) invisible? In some cases, the answer may seem obvious, even trivial. To see this, try (without looking below) to divide the Malay sentences in (7) into their major constituent parts:

(7)   a Ahmad makan nasi.
          Ahmad eat   rice
          'Ahmad is eating rice.'
        b Fauzi makan roti.
          Fauzi eat   bread
          'Fauzi is eating bread.'

    c   Orang ini   makan ikan.
        person this eat   fish
        'This person is eating fish.'

    d   Anjing itu   makan tulang besar.
        dog   that eat   bone big
        'That dog is eating a big bone.'

    e   Orang tua itu   makan pisang.
        person old that eat   banana
        'That old person is eating a banana.'

    f   Ahmad makan ikan besar itu.
        Ahmad eat   fish big   that
        'Ahmad is eating that big fish.'

Almost certainly, you would make the divisions in the places marked in (8). Why? First, these examples show that a single word (e.g. *Ahmad*) can be replaced by phrases containing two or three words (*anjing itu*, *orang tua itu*, etc.). Since a single word is obviously a "unit" of some kind, the phrases which can be substituted in the same position should also be units of the same kind. Moreover, each of these phrases forms a semantic unit: *orang tua itu* refers to a single, specific, individual. And, although it contains three words, the phrase bears only one GRAMMATICAL RELATION in sentence (7e), namely subject (see chapter 4).

(8)   a Ahmad | makan | nasi.   'Ahmad is eating rice.'
         b Fauzi | makan | roti.   'Fauzi is eating bread.'
         c Orang ini | makan | ikan.   'This person is eating fish.'
         d Anjing itu | makan | tulang besar. 'That dog is eating a big bone.'
         e Orang tua itu | makan | pisang.   'That old person is eating a banana.'
         f Ahmad | makan | ikan besar itu.   'Ahmad is eating that big fish.'

But we must be careful here. In some languages, a group of words which forms a semantic and functional (or relational) unit does not always form a unit for purposes of word order (i.e. a constituent). For example, the subject of the Warlpiri sentence in (9) ('small child') consists of two words, a noun and an adjective, which are widely separated from each other and so could not form a constituent in the normal sense.

(9)   **Warlpiri** (Australia; Hale 1981:10)
       Kurdu-ngku ka   maliki-Ø wajilipi-nyi   *wita-ngku.*
       child-ERG   ASPECT   dog-ABS chase-NONPAST small-ERG
       'The small child is chasing the dog.'

Such languages are the exception rather than the rule; but in all languages there are many contexts where semantics and Grammatical Relations alone will not enable us to determine the constituent boundaries. We need other kinds of evidence, in particular evidence that is more directly related to the linear arrangement of words in the sentence.

At this point, we can only offer a preliminary introduction to the kinds of tests used to determine the boundaries of syntactic constituents. Identifying constituents can be a complex issue and sometimes requires a fairly deep knowledge of the language. Moreover, tests that work for one language may not apply to another. But let us see how we might proceed with our Malay examples.

One reason for believing that the words *orang tua itu* in (7e) form a syntactic constituent is that the same string of words can occur in a variety of positions within the sentence: subject (10a), object (10b), object of a preposition (10c), etc. Each of these positions could equally well be filled by a single word, e.g. a proper name like *Ahmad*.

(10)   a [Orang tua itu] makan nasi goreng.
           person old that eat   rice fry
           'That old person eats fried rice.'

        b Saya belum kenal [orang tua itu].
           I   not.yet know person old that
           'I am not yet acquainted with that old person.'

        c Ibu   memberi wang kepada [orang tua itu].
           mother give   money to   person old that
           'Mother gives money to that old person.'

        d Ibu   belanja [orang tua itu] minum teh.
           mother treat   person old that drink tea
           'Mother bought a cup of tea for that old person.'

We noted above that strings of words which can replace a single word in a particular position must be "units" (i.e. constituents) of the appropriate type. This conclusion is supported by the discovery that only one such unit can occur as the subject or direct object of a single verb, as demonstrated in (11). (The asterisk "*" before the sentences in [11] indicates that they are ungrammatical.) Therefore, where several words occur together in these positions, as in (10a,b), those words must form a single constituent.

(11)   a *[Perempuan ini] [orang tua itu] makan nasi.
           woman   this person old that eat   rice
           *'This woman that old person is eating rice.'

        b *Fauzi makan [ikan itu] [nasi goreng].
           Fauzi eat   fish that rice fry
           *'Fauzi is eating fried rice that fish.'[4]

Malay, like most other languages, has various ways of changing the word order of a sentence. When a group of words can be "moved" as a unit, we can normally assume that the group forms a syntactic constituent. So examples like (12b–d) support the claim that the direct object phrase in (12a) is a constituent.

(12)   a   Saya makan [ikan besar itu].
            I   eat   fish big   that
            'I ate/am eating that big fish.'

        b   [Ikan besar itu] saya makan.
            fish big   that I   eat
            'That big fish I ate/am eating.'

        c   [Ikan besar itu]=lah   yang saya makan.
            fish big   that=FOC REL I   eat
            'It was that big fish that I ate.'

        d   [Ikan besar itu] di-makan oleh anjing saya.
            fish big   that PASS-eat by   dog   my
            'That big fish was eaten by my dog.'

Another reason for identifying the phrases we have been discussing here as constituents is that they can be replaced by question words to form a content question (sometimes called a CONSTITUENT QUESTION). This is illustrated in (13).

(13)   a   [Orang tua itu] makan [ikan besar itu].
            person old that eat   fish big   that
            'That old person ate the big fish.'

        b   *Siapa* makan [ikan besar itu]?
            who   eat   fish big   that
            'Who ate that big fish?'

        c   [Orang tua itu] makan *apa*?
            person old that eat   what
            'What did that old person eat?'

Similarly, constituents can form the answer to a content question, whereas a string of words which is not a syntactic constituent is not a possible answer, as illustrated in (14c).

(14)   a   Q: Siapa makan ikan besar itu?   A: Orang tua itu.
               who   eat   fish big   that   person old that
            Q: 'Who ate that big fish?'   A: 'That old person.'

        b   Q: Orang tua itu makan apa?   A: Ikan besar itu.
               person old that eat   what   fish big   that
            Q: 'What did that old person eat?' A: 'That big fish.'

        c   Q: Orang tua itu makan apa?   A: *Besar itu.[5]
               person old that eat   what   big   that
            Q: 'What did that old person eat?' A: * 'That big.'

Let us briefly summarize the kinds of evidence we have mentioned. We have claimed that certain strings of Malay words form a syntactic constituent because these strings:

a   can replace, or be replaced by, a single word;
b   occur in positions within the sentence which must be unique;
c   may occur in a number of different sentence positions, as illustrated in (10), and can be "moved" (or re-ordered) as a unit, as illustrated in (12);
d   can be replaced by a question word;
e   can function as the answer to a content question.

As mentioned above, gathering this kind of evidence often requires a significant amount of knowledge about the grammar of the language. When beginning to study a new language "from scratch," it is reasonable to make some initial hypotheses about constituent structure based on factors such as meaning and potential for substitution, as we did in our initial discussion of the Malay data. But keep alert for other kinds of evidence which can help you confirm or disprove these hypotheses.

3.3   Hierarchy

In the previous section we showed that a sentence is not just a string of words. Rather, the words in a sentence may be grouped into grammatical units of various sizes. One very important unit is the CLAUSE, which is sometimes defined as a "simple sentence." Perhaps a more useful definition would be to say that a clause is the smallest grammatical unit which can express a complete proposition (see chapter 4, section 4.1 for a discussion of what this means). A sentence may consist of just one clause or, as illustrated in (15), a single sentence may contain several clauses.

(15)   a   "[Foxes have holes] and [birds of the air have nests],
                but [the Son of Man has no place to lay his head]."
        b   [My wife told me that [I should introduce her little sister to the
                captain of the football team]], but [I assumed that [her sister
                was too shy]].

Another important unit is the PHRASE. (We will propose a definition of "phrase" in section 3.4.2 below.) A single clause may contain several phrases, as illustrated in (16a). A single phrase may contain several words, as seen in (16a) and in our Malay examples above. A single word may contain several morphemes, as illustrated in (16b).

(16)   a   [The coach's wife] introduced [her little sister]
                [to [the captain [of [the football team]]]].

b dis-taste-ful
   read-abil-ity
   dis-en-tangle

Each well-formed grammatical unit (e.g. a sentence) is made up of constituents which are themselves well-formed grammatical units (e.g. clauses, phrases, etc.). And there are only a small number of basic types of units. The set of types mentioned above is adequate for a large number of languages: sentence, clause, phrase, word, morpheme. This kind of structural organization is called a PART–WHOLE HIERARCHY: each unit is entirely composed of smaller units belonging to a limited set of types. This is an extremely important aspect of linguistic structure, not only in morphology and syntax but in phonology as well.[6]

3.4   Syntactic categories

Examples (5) and (6) illustrated how the part of speech (or CATE-GORY) of a word can help to determine its interpretation, and the meaning of the phrase or sentence in which it occurs. It turns out that phrases, as well as words, must be assigned to syntactic categories in order to understand their distribution in sentences. But, as with constituent boundaries, syntactic categories are not immediately visible; they must be identified on the basis of linguistic evidence. We will begin with the categories of words, i.e. LEXICAL CATEGORIES, and then consider categories of phrases.

3.4.1   Word-level (lexical) categories

Traditional definitions for parts of speech are based on "notional" (i.e. semantic) properties such as the following:

(17)   A NOUN is a word that names a person, place, or thing.
        A VERB is a word that names an action or event.
        An ADJECTIVE is a word that describes a state.

However, these characterizations fail to identify nouns like *destruction, theft, beauty, heaviness*. They cannot distinguish between the verb *love* and the adjective *fond (of)*, or between the noun *fool* and the adjective *foolish*. Note that there is very little semantic difference between the two sentences in (18).

(18)   They are fools.
        They are foolish.

In discussing the poem "Jabberwocky" in chapter 1, we found that we could identify the part of speech of most, if not all, of the nonsense words.

Obviously this identification could not be based on semantic factors, since those "words" actually have no meaning. Rather, we used the grammatical features of each word, specifically (i) its position in the sentence and (ii) its morphology, to guess its part of speech.

The task of assigning words to syntactic categories involves two problems, which need to be addressed separately. First we must ask the question, "Which words belong together in the same class?" This question must be answered in terms of specific grammatical properties which may be different for each particular language. Only then can we ask the second question: "What name (or label) should we assign to a given word class?" This second question is generally answered on the basis of semantic properties which are relevant in a very large number of languages.[7]

Let us work through the process in more detail. First, words that share a number of grammatical characteristics are assumed to belong to the same class, while words that have distinct grammatical characteristics are assigned to different classes. For example, the noun *fool* and the adjective *foolish* can be distinguished by properties like the following:

(19)   a **Modification by degree adverb vs. adjective**:
           They are utter fools.   *They are very fools.
           *They are utter foolish.   They are very foolish.

        b **Inflection for number**
           fool   fools
           foolish   *foolishes

        c **Comparative forms**
           fool   *fooler/*more fool
           foolish   more foolish

        d **Occurrence as subject of a clause**
           Fools rush in where angels fear to tread.
           *Foolish rush in where angels fear to tread.

Thus *fool* belongs to the class of words which can be modified by adjectives and inflected for number, have no comparative form, and can occur as subjects.[8] Other words which share these properties, and so belong to the same class, include *man*, *house*, and *tree*. But *foolish* belongs to the class of words which can be modified by adverbs of degree (or INTENSIFIERS), do have a comparative form, cannot be inflected for number, and cannot occur as subjects. Other words which share these properties include *big*, *green*, and *angry*.

Once the word classes in a particular language have been defined in this way, they can be assigned a label (Noun, Verb, etc.) based on universal notional patterns. Words that exhibit all of the defining grammatical properties associated with a particular class are said to be PROTOTYPICAL members of that class. If there is a class whose prototypical members include most of the basic terms for concrete objects, e.g. *dog, man, house, tree*, etc., we would give that class the label NOUN. If there is a class whose proto-typical members include most of the basic terms for volitional actions, e.g. *run, dance, eat, cut*, etc., we would give that class the label VERB.

The grammatical criteria used to identify word classes should be thought of as diagnostic features or "symptoms," rather than definitions. A proto-typical member of a given category will normally exhibit most if not all of the properties listed for that category, but we also find examples of words which exhibit only some of these features. For example, adjectives can be identified by the ability to take comparative and superlative suffixes (*big, bigger, biggest; fat, fatter, fattest*). But some adjectives (including those more than two syllables long) cannot be inflected in this way (*beautiful, *beautifuller, *beautifullest*; cf. *more beautiful, most beautiful*).

To summarize, the number of categories and the identifying properties of each category must be determined separately for each individual language. The labels for each category are assigned based on universal seman-tic criteria. Almost all languages[9] have the lexical categories Noun and Verb, but beyond that there is a significant range of difference among lan-guages. A list of the most commonly used category labels will be given in section 3.4.2.

3.4.2 Phrases and phrasal categories

In everyday speech, people may refer to any group of words as a "phrase." In linguistics, however, this term has a more precise meaning. First, a phrase must be a group of words which form a constituent (i.e. a unit according to the criteria described in section 3.2). Second, a phrase is lower on the grammatical hierarchy than clauses. Intuitively this means that phrases are in some sense "smaller" than clauses. More precisely, simple clauses may (and usually do) contain phrases, but simple phrases do not (in general) contain clauses. As a preliminary definition, then, let us assume that a PHRASE is a group of words which can function as a constituent within a simple clause.

Just as words may be classified into different categories, so too there are different sorts (categories) of phrases. Phrases of a particular type will be appropriate in some contexts but not in others. Once again, we are faced with two basic questions: (i) how do we know whether two phrases belong to the same or different categories?; and (ii) how do we know what category label to assign to a particular class of phrases? These questions lead us into some fairly complex issues. We will attempt to provide some preliminary answers here, returning in section 3.6 to a further discussion of these questions.

Concerning the first question (identifying phrasal categories), the answer is much the same as the corresponding answer for word-level categories – two phrases belong to the same category if they have the same grammatical properties. Two basic types of evidence are useful for determining whether two phrases belong to the same category. These are: (i) mutual substitutability (i.e. sameness of distribution); and (ii) sameness of internal structure.[10]

In identifying word classes, "internal structure" means morphological structure, for example the capacity to be inflected for number (in the case of nouns) or tense (in the case of verbs). When we are dealing with phrases, "internal structure" means the category and order of the phrase's constituents. For example, an English noun phrase frequently begins with a DETERMINER (*a, the, this, that*).

The criterion of mutual substitutability (sameness of distribution) involves the general principle that two phrases of the same category could potentially occur in the same positions, unless one of them is inappropriate for semantic reasons. For example, phrases which can occur in subject or object position are generally noun phrases.

We turn now to the second question, how to assign labels to phrasal categories. In most phrases, we can identify one word as being the most important element.[11] (We will clarify what we mean by "most important" below.) This word is called the HEAD of the phrase. The normal practice in linguistics is to name a phrase by the category of its head. For example, the phrase *that big fish* is a noun phrase, because its head word (*fish*) is a noun. The phrase *very beautiful* is an adjective phrase, because its head word (*beautiful*) is an adjective.

If we accept the principle that the category of a phrase is normally the same as the category of its HEAD, an important practical question remains to be answered, namely: how do we know which word in the phrase is the head? How can we distinguish the head from its DEPENDENTS (all the other elements in the phrase)? Or, to put the question another way, what makes the head special? We will mention here three specific ways in which the head is more "important" than the other elements. These general properties can help us to identify the head of a phrase when we are in doubt.

First, the head of a phrase determines many of the grammatical features of the phrase as a whole. The contrast between the two sentences in example (20) shows that the head noun determines grammatical number for the subject noun phrase as a whole. Since *rice* is a mass noun, the whole noun phrase is grammatically singular in (20a) and so requires the singular form of the verb, *is*. Since *kittens* is a plural form, the subject noun phrase is grammatically plural in (20b) and so requires the plural form of the verb, *are*.

(20)   a [The new rice] *is* in the barn.
        b [The new kittens] *are* in the barn.

Second, the head may determine the number and type of other elements in the phrase. For example, we take the verb to be the head of a clause, and (as we will see in chapter 5) different verbs require different numbers and categories of phrases to occur with them in their clause. Dependents which are selected by the head word in this way are referred to as COMPLEMENTS. Thus subjects, objects, etc. are often referred to as complements of the verb. To take another example, many adjective phrases contain a prepositional phrase complement, as illustrated in (21). We know that these prepositional phrases are complements because the choice of preposition is determined by the identity of the head adjective:

(21)   a I am [very grateful *to* you].
        b John felt [sorry *for* his actions].
        c Mary looks [very proud *of* herself].
        d Bill is [angry *at* his lawyers].
        e Arthur seems [worried *about* the next election].

Third, the head is more likely to be obligatory than the modifiers or other non-head elements. For example, all of the elements of the subject noun phrase in (22a) can be omitted except the head word *pigs*. If this word is deleted, as in (22e), the result is ungrammatical.

(22)   a [The three little pigs] eat truffles.
        b [The three pigs] eat truffles.
        c [The pigs] eat truffles.
        d [Pigs] eat truffles.
        e *[The three little] eat truffles.

Of course, English noun phrases do not always contain a head noun. In certain contexts a previously mentioned head may be omitted because it is "understood," as in (23a). This process is called ELLIPSIS. Moreover, in English, and in many other languages, adjectives can sometimes be used without any head noun to name classes of people, as in (23b,c). But, aside from a few fairly restricted patterns like these, heads of phrases in English tend to be obligatory.

(23)   a [The third little pig] was smarter than [the second __].
        b [the good], [the bad] and [the ugly]
        c [The rich] get richer and [the poor] get children.

As noted above, the head of a phrase will generally be a lexical item of the same category – a noun phrase will be headed by a noun, an adjective phrase by an adjective, etc. However, not all lexical (word-level) categories can be heads of phrases. Those that can (including at least Noun, Verb, Adjective, and Preposition in English) are called MAJOR CATEGORIES; those that cannot (e.g. conjunctions) are called MINOR CATEGORIES. A listing of the most important lexical categories for English is given in (24):

(24)   a **MAJOR CATEGORIES** (can function as heads of phrases)
Noun (*dog, tree, water, kindness*, etc.)
Verb (*run, melt, hit, love*, etc.)
Adjective (*big, red, friendly, impossible*, etc.)
Adverb (*quickly, unexpectedly, fortunately*, etc.)[12]
Preposition (*on, under, from*, etc.)

b **MINOR CATEGORIES** (do not normally function as heads of phrases)
Conjunction (*and, or, but*, etc.)
Interjection (*oh, ah, well, ouch*, etc.)
Determiners: includes articles (*a, the*), demonstratives (*this, that*), and
quantifiers (*all, some, many*, etc.)

Major categories are typically OPEN CLASSES; these categories contain an indefinite but large number of words, and new words tend to be added frequently through borrowing or innovation. Minor categories are typically CLOSED CLASSES; such classes contain only a small, fixed number of words, and new words are added very slowly. But this correlation is not perfect. For example, Preposition is a major category but probably a closed class (although English has a larger inventory of prepositions than many other languages).

3.5   Tree diagrams: representing the constituents of a clause

3.5.1   Phrase Structure diagrams

An important part of our task in analyzing the grammatical structure of a sentence is to identify: (a) the constituent parts from which the sentence is formed; and (b) the order in which these constituents occur. For example, the sentence in (25) consists of three constituent parts: a noun phrase followed by a verb followed by another noun phrase.

(25)   Anjing itu | makan | tulang besar.
dog   that   eat   bone   big
'That dog is eating a big bone.'

Even for very simple sentences like this one, a purely verbal description is a bit tiresome to interpret. The vertical lines inserted between the constituents in (25) are helpful, but for more complex structures this approach rapidly proves to be inadequate. Moreover, as discussed in section 3.3, constituent structure is HIERARCHICAL – each constituent of a larger unit may itself be composed of smaller constituents. In sentence (25), for example, each noun phrase is composed of two words. So it is not enough to list the immediate constituents of the sentence in the correct order. Each of these constituents must in turn be analyzed as to its sub-constituents and their linear order, and so on down to the word level.

The most commonly used method of representing information about constituency and linear order is the TREE DIAGRAM. A simple tree diagram is shown in (26). This tree contains three NODES. The top-most node, *A*, is the MOTHER of the two lower nodes, *B* and *C*. *B* and *C* are DAUGHTERS of the same mother, and so we refer to them as SISTER nodes. Straight lines are used to connect mothers to their daughters.

(26)　　　A

　　　　B　　C

When a tree of this kind is used to represent the structure of a grammatical unit (e.g. a phrase or sentence), the mother node represents the larger unit, while the daughter nodes represent its constituents (or sub-parts). The linear order of the constituents is shown by the left-to-right order of the corresponding nodes. The lines from mother to daughter represent the part–whole relationship. So a partial interpretation of the diagram in (26) could be stated as in (26′):

(26′)　　Unit *A* is composed of two constituent parts, *B* and *C*, which occur in that order.

This interpretation of (26) treats the labels at each node of the tree diagram (*A*, *B*, and *C*) simply as names, or a handy way of referring to the individual units. In fact, the labels in a diagram of this kind are not names for specific units, but are used to indicate the class (or CATEGORY) of each unit. So a more adequate interpretation of the diagram in (26) would be something like the following:

(26″)　　A unit of category *A* is composed of two constituent parts, one of category *B* and the other of category *C*, occurring in that order.

When tree diagrams are used to represent linguistic structure, the node labels provide two kinds of information about each unit: (i) its SYNTACTIC CATEGORY (e.g. Noun, Verb, etc.); and (ii) its "size," or level in the grammatical hierarchy (word, phrase, clause, etc.). The list in (27) shows the category symbols that are generally used (we will introduce a few others later). A simple tree structure using these labels is given in (28). This tree represents a prepositional phrase which consists of two parts, a preposition followed by a noun phrase. The noun phrase, in turn, is composed of a determiner followed by a noun.

(27)   **Word level**   **Phrasal**
        N   = Noun   NP = Noun Phrase
        A   = Adjective   AP = Adjective Phrase
        V   = Verb   VP = Verb Phrase
        P   = Preposition   PP = Prepositional Phrase
        Adv = Adverb   S   = Sentence or Clause
        Det = Determiner
        Conj = Conjunction

(28)

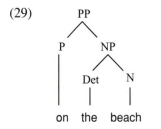

But, as far as we can tell from the tree in (28), this prepositional phrase contains no words. Obviously we need a way to represent the actual words that make up the phrase, in addition specifying their part of speech. We will represent words as daughters of nodes which bear lexical (word-level) category labels, as shown in (29).

(29)

```
        PP
       /  \
      P    NP
      |   /  \
      | Det   N
      |  |    |
     on the beach
```

Nodes which contain specific lexical items such as *on*, *the*, and *beach* will never themselves have daughters; they mark the bottom end of the tree structure. Nodes of this type, which do not dominate any other node, are called TERMINAL NODES. Lexical items such as *on*, *the*, and *beach* are TERMINAL ELEMENTS, and the sequence of terminal elements at the bottom of a tree (e.g. *on the beach*) is called the TERMINAL STRING.

We say that a non-terminal node DOMINATES all of its daughter nodes, the daughters of its daughters, daughters of its "grand-daughters," etc. A mother IMMEDIATELY DOMINATES its own daughters. This terminology gives us a way to define constituents in terms of tree structure:

(30)   A CONSTITUENT is a string of words which is
        EXHAUSTIVELY DOMINATED by some node.

The phrase "exhaustively dominated" means that the node in question dominates all the terminal elements which are part of the string but no terminal elements which are outside of the string. This definition tells us how constituents are represented in a Phrase Structure diagram, but it is important to remember that the linguistic facts are the primary reality. In analyzing the structure of a sentence, the constituents of the sentence must first be identified on the basis of linguistic criteria like those outlined in section 3.2. After we have identified the constituents in this way we can draw a tree of the appropriate shape to represent them.

Following standard usage, we will use the symbol "S" to represent both "sentence" and "clause," as indicated in (27). The highest node in the tree diagram of a sentence will normally be labeled S. This is because the sentence is itself a grammatical constituent, and so all the words in the sentence must be exhaustively dominated by a node of the appropriate category. Of course, a single sentence can contain several clauses, in which case the highest S in the tree will dominate several other S nodes (see chapter 12).

The top-most node in any tree diagram is called its ROOT NODE, while the terminal nodes at the bottom of the tree are sometimes called LEAVES. In the case of a sentence, S is the root node and the individual words are the leaves. So we might say that a Phrase Structure tree is upside down, with its root at the top, its leaves at the bottom, and its branches in between.

3.5.2   Constraints on tree structures

Phrase Structure diagrams for human languages are normally required to conform to two constraints:

a   the **No Crossing constraint**: lines from mother to daughter must not cross; i.e. no word belonging to one constituent can be embedded within another constituent; and

b   the **Single Mother constraint**: each node after the root (top-most) node must be the daughter of exactly one other node.

The motivation for imposing these constraints is that by allowing crossing lines or multiple parenthood, we would introduce the potential to construct extremely complex structures which are never found in real human languages. We will encounter data in certain languages which might tempt us to violate one or the other of these constraints. But it is possible to develop other methods for handling these "problem cases" without introducing unrealistic degrees of complexity into the system.

Practice exercise

Try to draw tree diagrams to represent the structure of the following two Malay sentences. Use the category labels shown in (27) for non-terminal nodes. (Answers given in (38) below.)

(31)   a Anjing itu   makan tulang besar.
        dog   that eat   bone big
        'That dog is eating a big bone.'

      b Orang tua itu   makan ikan besar.
        person old that eat   fish big
        'That old person is eating a big fish.'

3.5.3   Phrase Structure rules

In chapter 1 we pointed out that speakers of a language do not memorize sentences. Rather, they construct them using a set of rules (their "internal grammar"). The task of the linguist is to discover these rules. Analyzing the structure of specific sentences is an important step, but we cannot stop there. We need to identify a set of rules that could produce these structures and, ultimately, all other possible sentence patterns in the language.

An important feature of the Phrase Structure diagrams introduced above, and a major reason why they are so useful to the linguist, is that there is a direct and regular relationship between the arrangement of the tree structure and a particular set of rules. Moreover, the rules needed to produce Phrase Structure trees are of an especially simple type. They are known as PHRASE STRUCTURE RULES (PS rules), and have the following form:

(32)   A → B   C

Each Phrase Structure rule defines a possible combination of mother and daughter nodes. The mother is shown to the left of the arrow, the daughters to the right. The rule in (32) says that a node labeled "A" may immediately dominate two daughters labeled "B" and "C", in that order. Notice that there is no conditioning environment stated in this rule. In order to limit the complexity of the terminal strings which the rules can generate, we require them to be CONTEXT FREE. For the same reason, each rule has only one symbol on the left side of the arrow.

The specific relationship between tree structures and rules is this: each node of a Phrase Structure tree must be permitted (or LICENSED) by a Phrase Structure rule in order to be legal. The rule in (32) will license a subtree of the form shown in (26). To license (or "generate") the prepositional phrase structure in (28), we would need the rules shown in (33).

(33)   PP → P   NP
        NP → Det   N

Now, in order to generate the complete prepositional phrase shown in (29), we need rules to insert the terminal elements (lexical items), i.e. to "hang leaves on the tree." One way of doing this might be to write Phrase Structure rules like the following:[13]

(34)   P → {on, in, at, over, under, . . .}
         N → {beach, house, boy, girl, cat . . .}
         Det → {the, a, an, this, that, . . .}

But the LEXICON of a language, i.e. the speaker's "mental dictionary," is much more than just a list of words. As we will see in chapter 5, the lexical entry for each word must include various kinds of phonological, semantic, morphological, and syntactic information. So, if we used the kinds of rules shown in (34), we would actually have to list each word of the language twice – once in the word's lexical entry, and once more in a special rule that "hangs the leaves" of a particular category.

Rather than adopting the approach shown in (34), we will assume that there is a general rule of LEXICAL INSERTION which will license a word of any given category to appear as the only daughter of a node which bears the corresponding lexical category label. (The word's category will be specified in its lexical entry.) The rule of lexical insertion is similar to an ordinary Phrase Structure rule in that it defines a possible combination of mother and daughter nodes. The crucial difference is that the daughter node in this case is a real word, rather than an abstract category symbol. The rule could be stated roughly as in (35):

(35)   **Lexical Insertion**
         Any lexical category (N, V, etc.) may have a single daughter node
         which is a specific lexical item of the same category.

In most languages there are at least some phrasal categories that can be expanded in more than one way (i.e. that allow some variation in the string of daughters which they dominate). For this reason, it is normal for grammars to contain more than one Phrase Structure rule with the same element on the left side of the arrow. In this situation, certain notational devices (abbreviations) can be used to combine two or more Phrase Structure rules. Parentheses () are used to mark optional elements, and curly braces {} are used to mean "either–or." Thus the single rule in (36a) is equivalent to the pair of rules in (36b); and the single rule in (37a) is equivalent to the pair of rules in (37b):

(36)   a   A → B (C)
         b   A → B
             A → B C

(37)   a   X → $\begin{Bmatrix} Y \\ Z \end{Bmatrix}$
         b   X → Y
             X → Z

To summarize, a tree diagram is used to represent the structure of a particular sentence. The general word order patterns of the language are captured in the Phrase Structure (PS) rules. In order for a particular tree structure to be considered grammatical, each combination of mother and daughters in that tree must be licensed by one of the PS rules in the grammar. As we will see, a small number of PS rules can generate a very large number of different trees.

Practice exercise

Look back at the diagrams which you drew for the sentences in (31). (They should probably look something like the trees shown in (38).)

(38)   a

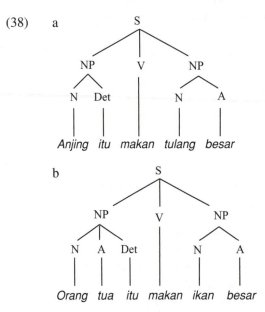

b

a   Now write a set of Phrase Structure rules which will generate your diagrams, or the tree diagrams in (38).
b   Check to see that your rules will also generate all the other Malay sentences in example (7); modify your rules if necessary.

3.6   Pronouns and proper names as phrasal categories

In section 3.4.2 we cited the criterion of mutual substitutability, or sameness of distribution, as an important kind of evidence for establishing that two phrases belong to the same category. But this principle leads us into an apparent contradiction, or paradox, in that certain lexical items seem to have the distribution of phrases. Specifically we noted at the beginning of section 3.2 that a proper name like *Ahmad* can be replaced by an entire phrase, and the same is true for pronouns. This fact presents a challenge to our proposed distinction between word-level and phrase-level categories, because in traditional grammar the term "phrase" refers to a unit consisting of more than one word. Pronouns and proper names are not thought of as "phrases" in this traditional sense.

Let us consider this problem in more detail. What Phrase Structure rules might we write to generate the following intransitive clauses?

(39)   I collapsed.
         John collapsed.
         The old school house collapsed.

These three clauses are identical in structure. Many other similar examples could be found to show that the subject of a clause may be expressed as a pronoun, a proper name, or a common noun phrase, without affecting the basic structure of the clause. We could express this fact using the Phrase Structure rule in (40). (For simplicity we will only consider intransitive clauses here.)

(40)
$$S \rightarrow \left\{ \begin{array}{l} \text{pronoun} \\ \text{proper name} \\ \text{noun phrase} \end{array} \right\} V$$

In the same way, the object of a preposition can be a pronoun, a proper name, or a common noun phrase, as illustrated in (41). Again, we could build this set of alternatives into the Phrase Structure rule which generates our prepositional phrase as in (42).

(41)   behind me
         behind John
         behind the old school house

(42)
$$PP \rightarrow P \left\{ \begin{array}{l} \text{pronoun} \\ \text{proper name} \\ \text{noun phrase} \end{array} \right\}$$

But notice that the material inside the braces in (42) is exactly the same as in (40). Moreover, the same set of alternatives will show up in many other Phrase Structure rules as well. In almost every position where a name can occur, we can substitute a pronoun or a common noun phrase. If we had to list all of these alternatives in every rule that mentions one of these positions, there would be a large amount of redundancy in the rules. We would obviously be missing an important generalization.

In order to avoid this massive redundancy, we will use the symbol "NP" in all the rules which would otherwise have to refer to a choice between pronoun, proper name, or common noun phrase, as in (43). That is, we will use the term "Noun Phrase" (NP) to refer to any unit which can appear in a "name-like" position in the Phrase Structure, whether it consists of one word or many.[14]

(43)   S → NP   V

PP → P   NP

One way of accounting for the kinds of words that can function as noun phrases in the grammar (as illustrated in (39) and (41)) might be to treat pronouns and proper names as special sub-categories of Noun. The Phrase Structure rules that expand NP could specify different expansions for each of these sub-categories. However, this approach seems to ignore the true function of pronouns.

Traditional grammars state that a pronoun "takes the place of a noun," but in fact pronouns replace whole NPs, as seen in (44).[15] As these examples illustrate, pronouns have a very different distribution from common nouns. Pronouns are never modified by determiners or (in normal usage) adjectives; they function on their own as complete NPs. Semantically, too, they are more similar to NPs than to simple nouns. For these reasons, it makes better sense to assume that they actually belong to the category NP, rather than N.

(44)   a The quick red fox jumped over the lazy brown dog.
        b *The quick red she jumped over the lazy brown him.
        c She jumped over him.

Proper names, when they refer to a specific individual, are similar to pronouns in that they have the distribution of NPs and are not modified by determiners or adjectives. In the unusual cases where they do take such modifiers, as in (45), one could argue that they are in fact being used as common nouns rather than names.

(45)   a It is very confusing to have three *Pauls* in the same office.
        b You are the first *Emily* I have ever met.
        c The Skinners have always wanted a *Joy*.

Again, we could treat proper names as a sub-class of nouns, using some lexical feature such as [– common] to distinguish them from other nouns. However, to be consistent it seems preferable to treat them in the same way we treat pronouns, i.e. as lexical items belonging to category NP.

We will assume, then, that pronouns and proper names are lexical items whose lexical entry specifies that they belong to category NP, rather than N. This means that they may appear in tree diagrams as immediate daughters of an NP node. Some examples are seen in the next few chapters.

3.7   Conclusion

This chapter has introduced two concepts which are crucial for understanding the structure of sentences: constituents and categories.

Syntactic constituents are groups of words that function as a unit in terms of word order: they may replace or be replaced by a single word, occur together in various positions in a variety of sentence types, be the "focus" of a content question, or function as the answer to such a question. A constituent is represented in a tree diagram as a string of words that is exhaustively dominated by a single node.

Syntactic categories are classes of words (or phrases) that share certain properties. Category names appear in a tree diagram as the labels for each non-terminal node. We have said that lexical category names (the traditional names for parts of speech) are assigned on the basis of semantic factors, and that phrases share the same category as their head. However, category membership for both words and phrases must be determined on the basis of shared grammatical properties. Two of the crucial types of evidence are (i) sameness of distribution, and (ii) sameness of internal structure. For lexical categories (words), we ask: (i) what kinds of phrases does this word occur in, and what is its function within the phrase (e.g. head, modifier, complement)?; and (ii) what kinds of affixes occur on this type of word? For phrasal categories we ask: (i) where may this type of phrase occur in a sentence, and what is its function in the sentence?; and (ii) what kinds of words occur, and what is their function, within this type of phrase?

Phrase Structure trees are a popular and efficient way to represent these aspects of sentence structure. However, there are other aspects of syntactic structure that are not directly represented in simple tree diagrams of the sort we have seen thus far. We will begin to explore some of these in the next chapter.

Practice exercises

A Give examples of tree structures that could be generated by the following two rules:

> PP → P   NP
> NP → Det   N   (PP)

B Based on these rules, parse (that is, determine the tree structures) for the following two phrases:

a   [a durian on the tree in the garden of that house in Penang]
b   [in the closet at the top of the stairs in that castle beside the river]

Exercises

3A Give five examples of possible tree structures that could be generated by each of the following simple grammars:

(i)   A → B C   (take A to be the root node)
        B → D (A)

        $C \rightarrow \left\{ \begin{array}{l} D \\ E \end{array} \right\}$

(ii)   S   → NP V (NP) (PP)   (take S to be the root node)
        NP → Det (A) N (PP)
        PP → P NP
        V   → {*runs, sings, yawns, likes, gives, pinches*}
        A   → {*small, big, young, white*}
        P   → {*to, in, behind, from*}
        Det → {*the, a, an*}
        NP → {*John, Mary*}
        N   → {*boy, girl, house, tree, cake, sausage, dog, cat*}

3B (from Baker 1978:41) Find the smallest set of Phrase Structure rules which will generate the following tree:

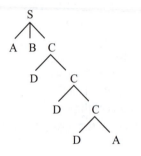

3C Ngbaka (Congo; Roberts 1999, ex. 5.7)
Write a set of PS rules which will generate all of the grammatical noun phrases (#1–9) but none of the ungrammatical ones (#10–18).

1.	toa kpo	'one house'
2.	toa ke	'this house'
3.	toa ge	'that house'
4.	gã folo kpo	'one big elephant'
5.	folo ge tũ	'that black elephant'
6.	bisĩ gbogbo kpo	'one small lion'
7.	gbogbo ge fẽ	'that white lion'
8.	bisĩ gbogbo ke fẽ	'this small white lion'
9.	gã folo kpo tũ	'one big black elephant'
10.	*ke	('this')
11.	*toa ke kpo	('this one house')
12.	*toa kpo ge	('that one house')
13.	*ge toa	('that house')
14.	*kpo toa	('one house')

15.   *folo kpo gã   ('one big elephant')
16.   *tũ folo ge   ('that black elephant')
17.   *gbogbo bisĩ kpo ('one small lion')
18.   *fẽ gbogbo ge   ('that white lion')

3D Mersthami (artificial language data; Bendor-Samuel and Levinsohn 1986, ex. D-4)

Based on the following examples, you are to: (i) identify the lexical and phrasal categories in Mersthami. State the grammatical criteria for identifying each category, and list the roots which belong to each lexical category; (ii) draw tree diagrams for #3, 5, and 7; (iii) write a set of PS rules which will generate all of these sentences.

1.   lopa   beli lale kuntu.
         walked man old slowly
         'The old man walked slowly.'

2.   lopa   fobeli lalepu kuntu.
         walked men   old   slowly
         'The old men walked slowly.'

3.   lopa   taha   onka   titam.
         walked woman young quickly
         'The young woman walked quickly.'

4.   lopa   fotaha onkapu titam.
         walked women young   quickly
         'The young women walked quickly.'

5.   tika sente titam   lale.
         ran dog   quickly very
         'The dog ran very quickly.'

6.   tika fobeli titam.
         ran men   quickly
         'The men ran quickly.'

7.   lopa   fotaha lalepu kuntu lale.
         walked women old   slowly very
         'The old women walked very slowly.'

8.   tika fosente titam   kindi.
         ran dogs   quickly unusually
         'The dogs ran unusually quickly.'

9.   lopa   taha   lale titam   onka.
         walked woman old quickly quite
         'The old woman walked quite quickly.'

10.   tika fobeli onkapu kuntu onka.
         ran men   young slowly quite
         'The young men ran quite slowly.'

11.   lopa   beli kindi   kuntu   lale.
       walked man   strange slowly very
       'The strange man walked very slowly.'

Additional exercises

Merrifield et al. (1987) prob. 139, 140, 146
Healey (1990b) ex. C.5

Notes

1. Example (1d) actually involves both structural and lexical ambiguity; can you identify the structural differences between the two readings?
2. In natural spoken English, the two different readings of (2a) would be distinguished
   by different intonation or stress patterns.
3. From Radford (1988:57).
4. The order of the duplicate object NPs is reversed in the English translation to clarify
   the nature of the ungrammaticality in Malay.
5. In order to be grammatical, this answer would have to be expressed as a headless
   relative clause preceded by *yang*.
6. Another important kind of hierarchy is a classification, or TAXONOMY, in which
   specific classes are grouped into more general classes. An example of this is the biol-
   ogist's classification of living things. Taxonomies are especially useful in analyzing
   certain aspects of word meaning.
7. This approach to defining lexical categories was proposed by Lyons (1966).
8. It is slightly inaccurate to say that a noun can function as the subject or direct object
   of a verb, or as the object of a preposition. These are functions (or positions) which
   must be filled by a noun phrase. The identifying property of nouns is the ability to
   appear as the head of a phrase in these positions.
9. The Salish and Wakashan languages are often cited as exceptions to this generalization.
10. See Bickford (1998:38–40).
11. The question of whether all phrases must have heads is a theoretical issue which
    will not be addressed in this book.
12. ADVERB is often considered a minor category, but I take the combination of inten-
    sifier + Adv to be an example of a "headed" (or ENDOCENTRIC) AdvP: *very
    quickly, rather unexpectedly, quite happily, most fortunately*, etc. However, it is true
    that many constituents which are called "adverbial phrases" do not have an adverb
    as head; they tend to be either subordinate clauses or prepositional phrases.
13. As explained below, the braces {} in this rule indicate that various alternatives are
    available: one element of the set within the braces is to be selected each time the
    rule is applied.
14. Similar arguments can be made for phrases of other categories. For example, in
    English (and many other languages) we recognize that adjective phrases can some-
    times consist of just a single adjective.
15. See also Radford (1988:78–79); and Bickford (1998:54–55).

4 Semantic roles and Grammatical Relations

The Phrase Structure model introduced in chapter 3 is a very useful tool for analyzing sentences. However, as we will see in this chapter, Phrase Structure rules by themselves cannot provide an adequate account of what speakers say. For example, the simple set of Phrase Structure rules listed in part A(ii) of the exercises in chapter 3 can produce odd sentences like those in (1) and (2).

(1)   a #The young sausage likes the white dog.
       b #Mary sings a white cake.
       c #A small dog gives Mary to the young tree.

(2)   a *John likes.
       b *Mary gives the young boy.
       c *The girl yawns Mary.

Even though the rules seem consistent with what we know about the grammar of English, we see that they can produce unacceptable sentences. These sentences are unacceptable for different reasons. The # sign before the sentences in (1) indicates that they are semantically ill-formed, i.e. they cannot be given an acceptable semantic interpretation. The * sign before the sentences in (2) indicates that they are ungrammatical. In (2a,b) we feel there is a phrase missing, while (2c) seems to contain an extra phrase.

We will discuss these problems in detail in chapter 5. For now the important point is that even though the Phrase Structure rules themselves may be correct, this will not necessarily ensure that the output of the rules is grammatical. Additional information is needed, information about the specific words which are used. This kind of information must be stored in the lexicon in some way.

Another type of complication that can arise is illustrated in (3). The PS rules in exercise 3A(ii) of chapter 3 could generate this sentence in two different ways. This means that the rules assign more than one possible Phrase Structure for this sentence, as shown by the two tree diagrams in (4). These two structures correspond to two different interpretations of the sentence. Can you identify the meanings which would be associated with these two structures?

(3)   John pinches the young girl behind the tree.

(4)   a

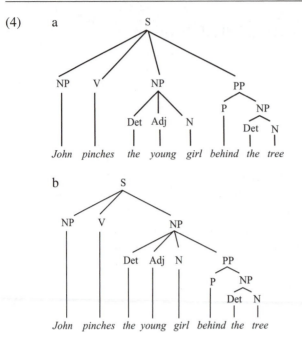

b

The sentence in (3) is an example of STRUCTURAL AMBIGUITY; the sentence as a whole is ambiguous because it has two possible Phrase Structures, even though none of the individual words is ambiguous in this context.[1] Is it some problem with our PS rules that allows the same sentence to be assigned two different structures in this way? Not at all. This is simply a fact about English grammar. Sentence (3) really is ambiguous, so it is actually a good thing that our PS rules generate both of the structures shown in (4).

In providing two analyses for (3), our miniature rule system is successful in the sense that it produces the same results as a native speaker's internal grammar. In contrast, when the rules produce sentences like those in (1) and (2) they are clearly failing to model what speakers actually say. In order to fix these problems we need to consider the unique properties of individual words, in particular of verbs; this will be the focus of chapter 5. We will also need to refer to two aspects of sentence structure we have not yet discussed, namely SEMANTIC ROLES and GRAMMATICAL RELATIONS. We will begin this discussion by considering certain aspects of word and sentence meanings.

4.1   Simple sentences and propositions

English teachers frequently remind their students that "each sentence must express a complete thought." In saying this, they are warning their students not to write "sentence fragments," i.e. sentences which are lacking some essential element.

In the following section, we will begin to consider the question of what the essential elements of a sentence are and how they fit together. But first we might ask ourselves what kind of "complete thought" a sentence may express. For the moment we will only consider the simplest, or most basic, kind of sentence, namely DECLARATIVE sentences (see chapter 11). Declarative sentences are typically used to make statements. A speaker uses a statement to assert or deny a PROPOSITION, i.e. a claim which can, at least in principle, be determined to be either true or false. Other kinds of sentences, which we will discuss further in later chapters, are typically used to perform other kinds of speech acts: giving commands, asking questions, offering wishes, blessings, curses, etc. Sentences of these kinds cannot be said to be either true or false.

A statement, then, is a sentence which asserts a proposition, i.e. a claim that a certain state of affairs does or does not exist. Normally statements are made *about* something or someone; they claim that a certain state of affairs is true of a given individual or set of individuals (where the individual may be a person, place, thing, etc.). They may indicate that a certain individual has a particular property, as in (5a,b), or that a certain relationship holds between two or more individuals, as in (5c,d):

(5)   a John is hungry.
        b Mary snores.
        c John loves Mary.
        d Mary is slapping John.

The element of meaning which identifies the property or relationship is called the PREDICATE: the words *hungry*, *snores*, *loves*, and *is slapping* express the predicates in the above examples. The individuals (or participants) of whom the property or relationship is claimed to be true (*John* and *Mary* in these examples) are called ARGUMENTS. The grammatical unit which expresses a single predicate and its arguments is called a simple sentence, or CLAUSE.

As we can already see from example (5), different predicates require different numbers of arguments: *hungry* and *snores* require just one, *loves* and *slapping* require two. Some predicates may not require any arguments at all. For example, in many languages comments about the weather (e.g. *It is raining*, or *It is dark*, or *It is hot*) could be expressed by a single word, a bare predicate with no arguments.

When a predicate is asserted to be true of the right number of arguments, the result is a well-formed proposition: a "complete thought."

4.2   Arguments and semantic roles

The properties or relationships described by different predicates may differ in any number of specific details, but many of these differences will have no effect on the grammatical structure of the sentence. For example, someone who *slaps* John (as Mary did in (5d)) is performing a different action from someone who *spanks*, *beats*, *whips*, *punches*, or *clubs* him. But, in most contexts, the semantic differences among these verbs are irrelevant to the grammar. Simple sentences which express the relationship between John and Mary will have exactly the same grammatical structure no matter which of these verbs is used. On the other hand, in some languages sentences like *Mary loves John* or *Mary sees John* would have different grammatical properties from *Mary slaps John*.

It is helpful to classify arguments into broad semantic categories according to the kind of role they play in the situations described by their predicates. For example in the sentence *Mary slaps John*, *Mary* plays the role of an AGENT, while *John* plays the role of a PATIENT. The same roles are involved if Mary *spanks*, *beats*, *whips*, *punches*, or *clubs* John. In the sentence *Mary sees John*, however, *Mary* plays the role of an EXPERIENCER; *John* is the perceived object, which we will call a STIMULUS. The use of a different role label implies a potential difference in grammatical properties.[2]

How many of these categories are there? How many role labels do we need to use? Different linguists have different opinions on this issue, and (unfortunately but not surprisingly) sometimes use the same labels in different ways. In this book we will make use of (at least) the following semantic roles:

(6)   INVENTORY OF SEMANTIC ROLES:[3]
    AGENT: causer or initiator of events
    EXPERIENCER: animate entity which perceives a stimulus or
        registers a particular mental or emotional process or state
    RECIPIENT: animate entity which receives or acquires something
    BENEFICIARY: entity (usually animate) for whose benefit an
        action is performed
    INSTRUMENT: inanimate entity used by an agent to perform
        some action
    THEME: entity which undergoes a change of location or
        possession, or whose location is being specified
    PATIENT: entity which is acted upon, affected, or created; or of
        which a state or change of state is predicated
    STIMULUS: object of perception, cognition, or emotion; entity
        which is seen, heard, known, remembered, loved, hated, etc.
    LOCATION: spatial reference point of the event (the SOURCE,
        GOAL, and PATH roles are often considered to be sub-types of
        LOCATION)
    SOURCE: the origin or beginning point of a motion
    GOAL: the destination or end-point of a motion

PATH: the trajectory or pathway of a motion

ACCOMPANIMENT (or COMITATIVE): entity which
    accompanies or is associated with the performance of an action

The examples in (7) illustrate how these terms are used:

(7)   a *John*   *gave*   *Mary*   *a bouquet of roses.*
            AGENT   RECIPIENT   THEME

       b *John*   *baked*   *Mary*   *a chocolate cake.*
            AGENT   BENEFICIARY   PATIENT

       c *John*   *opened*   *the lock*   *with a key.*
            AGENT   PATIENT   INSTRUMENT

       d *The key*   *opened*   *the lock.*
            INSTRUMENT   PATIENT

       e *Sherlock Holmes*   *heard*   *a piercing scream.*
            EXPERIENCER   STIMULUS

       f *Little Jack Horner*   *sat*   *in the corner.*
            AGENT/THEME   LOCATION

       g *Water*   *flows*   *through the aqueduct*
            THEME   PATH
           from mountain reservoirs   *to the city of San Francisco.*
           SOURCE   GOAL

4.3   Grammatical Relations

4.3.1   Subjects and objects

The terms "subject" and "object" are very familiar, but it may be helpful to clarify what they actually mean. English-speaking school children are often told that the subject of a sentence is the doer of the action, while the object is the person or thing acted upon by the doer. This definition seems to work for sentences like (8a,b), but is clearly wrong in examples like (8c,d):

(8)   a Mary slapped John.
       b A dog bit John.
       c John was bitten by a dog.
       d John underwent major heart surgery.

Phrases like "the doer of the action" or "the person or thing acted upon" identify particular semantic roles, namely agent and patient. But, as we can see in example (8), the subject is not always an agent, and the patient is not always an object. John is "acted upon" in all four of these sentences; but the word *John* appears as the object in (8a,b) and the subject in (8c,d).

Another traditional definition of the subject is "what the sentence is about." Again, this definition seems to work for many sentences (such as

9a), but fails in others (such as 9b,c). All three of these sentences seem to be "about" Bill; thus we could say that *Bill* is the TOPIC of all three sentences. But *Bill* is the subject in (9a), the object in (9b), and neither subject nor object in (9c). These sentences make it clear that the topic is not always the grammatical subject.

(9)   a Bill is a very crafty fellow.
       b (Jack is pretty reliable, but) Bill I don't trust.
       c As for Bill, I wouldn't take his promises very seriously.

It seems that we can not reliably identify the subject of a sentence with either the agent or the topic. Rather, we must use grammatical criteria to develop a workable definition. What grammatical properties do subjects have that other elements of the sentence do not share? Bickford (1998:43) notes the following properties of subjects in English:

a   **Word order**: In a basic English sentence, the subject normally comes before the verb, while the object and other parts of the sentence follow the verb.

b   **Pronoun forms**: The first and third person pronouns in English appear in a special form when the pronoun is a subject, as illustrated in (10). This form is not used when the pronoun occurs in other positions:[4]

     (10)   a She loves me.
             b I love her.
             c We threw stones at them.
             d They threw stones at us.

c   **Agreement with verb**: In the simple present tense, an *-s* is added to the verb when a third person subject is singular. However, the number and person of the object or any other element in the sentence have no effect at all on the form of the verb:

     (11)   a She angers him.
             b They anger him.
             c She angers them.

d   **Content questions**: If the subject is replaced by a question word (*who* or *what*), the rest of the sentence remains unchanged, as in (12b). But when any other element of the sentence is replaced by a question word, an auxiliary verb must appear before the subject. If the basic sentence does not contain an auxiliary verb, we must insert *did* or *do(es)* immediately after the question word, as in (12d,e):

     (12)   a John stole/would steal Mrs. Thatcher's picture from the British Council.
             b Who stole/would steal Mrs. Thatcher's picture from the British Council?
             c What *would* John steal, if he had the chance?

       d What *did* John steal from the British Council?

       e̅ Where *did* John steal Mrs. Thatcher's picture from?

e   **Tag questions**: A "tag question" (see chapter 11) is used to seek confirmation of a statement. It always contains a pronoun which refers back to the subject, and never to any other element in the sentence.

    (13)   a John loves Mary, doesn't he?

            b Mary loves John, doesn't she?

            c *John loves Mary, doesn't she?

A number of other properties could be added here, but many of them cannot be understood without a much deeper knowledge of English syntax than we can assume at this stage. The main point is that these are grammatical properties which uniquely identify the subject of an English sentence. Of course, for another language the list of specific properties would be different. We will not try to define SUBJECTHOOD as an abstract concept, but will assume that for each language there will be a set of grammatical criteria which allows us to identify subjects in that language.

The same considerations apply for objects: we cannot in general identify them on the basis of semantic roles or discourse functions. Rather, we need to find a set of grammatical properties which are characteristic of objects in a particular language. However, since subjects are in some sense more "prominent" than objects, there are (in many languages) fewer grammatical properties which are unique to objects; so it is sometimes more difficult to find objecthood tests than subjecthood tests.

4.3.2 Terms vs. oblique arguments

      Subjects and objects are often referred to as TERMS, or DIRECT ARGUMENTS. Arguments which are not subjects or objects are called INDIRECT or OBLIQUE ARGUMENTS. These labels reflect the idea that the grammatical relationship between a verb and its subject or object is closer, or more significant, than the grammatical relationship between the verb and other elements of the clause.

One indicator of the special status of subjects and objects in English is that all oblique arguments are marked with prepositions, whereas subjects and objects are expressed by bare noun phrases. Some examples of oblique argument phrases are given in the following examples:

(14)   a Michael Jackson donated his sunglasses

       [to the National Museum].   (RECIPIENT)

      b Samson killed the Philistines [with a jawbone].   (INSTRUMENT)

      c The Raja constructed a beautiful palace [for his wife]. (BENEFICIARY)

      d The Prime Minister deposited his money

       [in a Swiss bank].   (LOCATION)

We will use the abbreviations SUBJ, OBJ, and OBL to refer to subjects, objects, and oblique arguments, respectively. It is important to remember that these terms identify GRAMMATICAL RELATIONS, not semantic roles, and that these relations must be defined in terms of their syntactic and morphological properties. A few more Grammatical Relations will be introduced in subsequent chapters.

4.4   Adjuncts vs. arguments

Arguments are elements of a clause which have a close semantic relationship to their predicate. They are the participants which must be involved because of the very nature of the relation or activity named by the predicate, and without which the clause cannot express a "complete thought." For example, any event named by the predicate 'eat' must involve at least two participants, the eater and the eaten. (This is true even though one or the other of these participants may not be mentioned in a particular description of the event, e.g. *John is still eating*, or *The fish was eaten*.) For this reason we say that the predicate 'eat' takes two arguments. But speakers often need to convey other elements of meaning as well, elements which are not closely related to the meaning of the predicate but which are important to help the hearer understand the flow of the story, the time or place of an event, the way in which an action was done, etc. Elements of this type are not arguments; they are called ADJUNCTS.

Time and manner phrases are not, in most cases, related to the inherent meaning of the verb. They can be optionally added to almost any clause, as illustrated in (15):

(15)   George fell down the stairs *last night*.
         My daughter swallowed a penny *last night*.
         John gave Mary a bouquet of roses *last night*.

         George *intentionally* fell down the stairs.
         My daughter *intentionally* swallowed a penny.
         John *intentionally* gave Mary a bouquet of wilted roses.

It is not always easy to distinguish adjuncts from oblique arguments. One hint is that adjuncts are never obligatory, since they are not implied by (or directly related to) the meaning of the verb. To put it another way, adjuncts are always deletable (optional), whereas this may not be true of arguments. Example (16a) shows that the object of *use* is obligatory and therefore an argument. Similarly, (16b) shows that the verb *put* takes an obligatory PP argument. But adjuncts can always be omitted without creating any sense of incompleteness, as seen in (17).

(16) **ARGUMENTS**
    a Mary used *my shirt* for a hand towel.
       *Mary used for a hand towel.
    b Henry put the money *into his pocket*.
       *Henry put the money.

(17) **ADJUNCTS**
    a George fell down the stairs *last night*.
       George fell down the stairs.
    b My daughter *intentionally* swallowed a penny.
       My daughter swallowed a penny.

It is important to remember that arguments can also be optional. For example, many transitive verbs allow an optional beneficiary argument (18a), and most transitive verbs of the agent–patient type allow an optional instrument argument (18b). The crucial fact is that adjuncts are *always* optional. So the inference "if obligatory then argument" is valid; but the inference "if optional then adjunct" is not.

(18)   a John baked a cake (*for Mary*).
      b Bill cut the fish (*with a pocket knife*).

Second, adjuncts may be freely added to most clauses, whereas a particular kind of argument is permitted only with a verb of the appropriate type. As we will see in the next chapter, verbs can be "subclassified" according to the number and type of arguments they take. But adjuncts cannot be used to classify verbs, because adjuncts are semantically independent of the verb.

A third clue is that only arguments are normally eligible to bear the TERM relations (subject or object). The examples in (19) show that all three of the arguments in (19a) (agent, instrument, and patient) can be expressed as subject. The fact that the instrument can be expressed as a subject in (19b) shows that the instrument is an (optional) argument of the clause. Similarly, the fact that a beneficiary can be expressed as a direct object as in (20b) shows that the beneficiary is an (optional) argument of that clause. Adjuncts, in contrast, cannot normally be expressed as subjects or objects.

(19)   a John cuts his meat with a knife.
      b This knife cuts the meat easily.
      c This meat cuts easily.

(20)   a John baked a cake (*for Mary*).
      b John baked Mary a cake.

Finally, arguments must be unique within their clause; that is, each verb may have at most one of any particular type of argument. For example, the second sentence in (21a) is ungrammatical because it contains two recipient arguments. Adjuncts, on the other hand, may be freely multiplied, as shown in (21b,c). Sentence (21b) contains three time phrases, and sentence (21c) contains three manner phrases, yet these sentences are perfectly natural. This fact shows that time and manner phrases are adjuncts, rather than arguments.

(21)   a ARGUMENTS

John gave a bouquet of roses [to his mother].

*John gave a bouquet of roses [to his mother] [to Susan].

   b TIME ADJUNCTS

George fell down the stairs [last night] [at 3:00 AM] [during the typhoon].

   c MANNER ADJUNCTS

My daughter [suddenly], [impulsively], [without thinking], swallowed a penny.

We have listed four tests, or criteria, for distinguishing between adjuncts and arguments. These tests are summarized in (22). Often these criteria will provide a clear answer one way or another, but sometimes the evidence may be less than clear. This is not uncommon in linguistics. Linguists rely on tests of this kind for many different purposes. Even though such tests may not give an unambiguous answer in every case, they are extremely useful and, in fact, indispensable.

(22)

	ARGUMENT	ADJUNCT
Obligatory	maybe	never
"Subclassify" verb	yes	no
Subj/Obj	maybe	never
Unique within clause	yes	no

Arnold Zwicky (1985) points out that such tests should not be regarded as definitions, but as symptoms. We do not *define* adjuncts or arguments in terms of the properties listed in (22); but knowing which properties are characteristic of each class will help us to recognize them when we find them. Zwicky's point suggests a helpful analogy between linguists and medical doctors. The human body is a very complex system. Each part can affect the others in various ways, and a single symptom (e.g. a fever) can have several different underlying causes. Similarly, the grammar of a language is a very complex system. Just as the doctor looks for the diagnosis which will best account for the various symptoms, so the linguist tries to find the best "diagnosis" of the data, i.e. the hypothesis about the underlying patterns of the grammar that best accounts for the observable facts.

4.5 "Indirect objects" and secondary objects

There is a problem with the way the term "indirect object" is used in traditional grammar. This problem can be seen in relation to the pair of sentences in (23).

(23) a John gave Mary his old radio.
      b John gave his old radio to Mary.

In traditional grammar, *Mary* would be called the "indirect object" of both sentences (23a) and (23b). However, in (23b) *Mary* is preceded by the preposition *to* and occurs at the end of the sentence, while in (23a) *Mary* occurs immediately following the verb without any preposition. These facts suggest that the Grammatical Relation of *Mary* in (23a) is not the same as in (23b). (There are a number of other grammatical differences which support this conclusion as well, but we are not yet ready to discuss them.)

As this example illustrates, the term "indirect object" in traditional grammar is used to refer to the semantic role of recipient (or sometimes beneficiary), rather than to a specific Grammatical Relation. We have said that Grammatical Relations must be identified on the basis of grammatical properties, not semantic roles. The grammatical properties of *Mary* in (23a) are essentially the same as those of *Bill* in (24a); and the grammatical properties of *Mary* in (23b) are in many ways the same as those of *the attic* in (24b). Thus, based on grammatical properties, we would say that *Mary* bears the OBJ relation in (23a), but the OBL relation in (23b).

(24) a Susan slapped Bill.
      b John stored his coin collection in the attic.

If *Mary* bears the OBJ Relation in (23a), what is the Grammatical Relation of *his old radio* in that sentence? We will refer to it as the SECONDARY OBJECT, using the abbreviation OBJ$_2$. The sentences in (25) provide additional examples of this "double object" pattern. In these sentences the verb is followed by two NP objects. The first of these bears the OBJ relation; we call it the DIRECT or PRIMARY OBJECT. The second NP is the SECONDARY OBJECT (OBJ$_2$).

(25) a Mary gave [her son]$_{OBJ}$ [a new bicycle]$_{OBJ_2}$.
      b Reluctantly, Henry showed [Susan]$_{OBJ}$ [his manuscript]$_{OBJ_2}$.
      c Uncle George told [the children]$_{OBJ}$ [a story]$_{OBJ_2}$.

Many languages allow sentences like those in (25), in which the verb has two object NPs. In most languages, one of these NPs can be identified as the primary object (OBJ) and the other as the secondary object (OBJ$_2$). The specific grammatical criteria that distinguish OBJ from OBJ$_2$ will vary somewhat from one language to the next, but the following guidelines describe some of the more common differences:

a   **SPECIAL MARKING**: If one object is marked like the object of a simple (mono-) transitive clause while the other gets a special marker (e.g. dative case; see chapter 7), the one with the special marker is probably the OBJ$_2$.

b   **AGREEMENT**: If the verb agrees with only one of the two objects, it will normally agree with the primary object.

c   **PASSIVIZATION**: If only one of the two objects can be expressed as the subject of a passive clause (see chapter 14), it will normally be the primary object.

d   **POSITION**: If there is no difference in the marking of the two objects, e.g. if both are bare NPs, and if their relative ordering is fixed (or if one ordering can be shown to be more basic than the other), the object that occurs closest to the verb is more likely to be the primary object.

4.6   Conclusion

The elements of a simple clause (aside from the predicate itself) can be classified as either arguments or adjuncts. Arguments are those elements which are "selected" by the verb; they are required or permitted by certain predicates, but not by others. In order to be expressed grammatically, arguments must be assigned a Grammatical Relation within the clause. The Grammatical Relation of an argument, which is determined on the basis of morphological and syntactic properties, is not the same as its semantic role, which is determined by the meaning of the verb.

We have identified two basic classes of Grammatical Relations, obliques vs. terms (or direct arguments). These two classes are distinguished on the basis of grammatical properties. Terms (i.e. SUBJ, OBJ, OBJ$_2$) play an active role in a wide variety of syntactic constructions, while obliques are relatively inert. This classification of clausal elements is summarized in the following diagram:

(26)

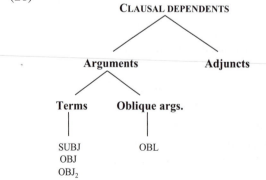

We will explore these ideas further in the next chapter. Before we move on, however, a word of warning is in order concerning the use of the term "predicate." In traditional grammars, the term "predicate" is frequently used to refer to everything in a clause that is not part of the subject. In this book we use the term in a quite different way: a predicate is a semantic element which names a property or relation involving some fixed number of arguments.

Strictly speaking, we should distinguish between predicates, which are abstract semantic entities, and the words (linguistic entities) which express them in a particular language. However, we will allow some slippage here. For example, in the preceding sections we have followed common usage among linguists by talking about the arguments of the *verbs*, rather than of the *predicates* which they represent. Where there is any danger of confusion, we will try to be more precise.

Exercises

4A English
Identify the semantic roles and Grammatical Relations of the arguments in the following examples.

1. Mary hit the crocodile with her umbrella.
2. John dropped a coin into the wishing well.
3. Susan donated her portrait of Winston Churchill to the National Museum.
4. Everyone in town heard the explosion.
5. The Queen of England keeps her jewels in the Tower of London.
6. Harry hit the ball with his tennis racquet.
7. Superman broke the window with the gangster.
8. The racquet hit the ball out of the stadium.
9. The ball fell to earth.
10. A large sack of rice sat in the corner of the room.
11. Three Afghan refugees swam the English Channel.
12. The police chased the smugglers from Jakarta to Bangkok.
13. My son was bitten by a snake.
14. Mary was given a silver ring by her mother.
15. These scissors cut well.
16. This paper cuts easily.
17. I am afraid.
18. That firecracker frightened me.

4B Indonesian (adapted from Sneddon 1996 and other sources)
Identify the semantic roles and Grammatical Relations of the arguments in the following examples. Assume that all PPs are arguments.

1. Mereka berenang ke seberang sungai.
   they　　swim　　to across　　river
   'They swam to the other side of the river.'

2. Siti memberikan surat itu　kepada ayah=nya.
   Siti give　　　　letter that to　　father=3sg
   'Siti gave the letter to her father.'

3. Pak Ali memotong kayu itu　dengan parang.
   Mr. Ali cut　　　　wood that with　　machete
   'Mr. Ali cut the wood with a machete.'

4. Saya berlibur di Bali berserta.dengan keluarga.
   1sg　vacation in Bali together.with　　family
   'I vacationed in Bali with my family.'

5. Ayah membeli sepeda baru untuk adik.
   father buy　　　bicycle new for　　yg.sibling
   'Father bought a new bicycle for my little brother.'

6. Pak Ali muncul dari　belakang rumah.
   Mr. Ali emerge from back　　　house
   'Mr. Ali appeared from behind the house.'

7. Hang Tuah tinggal di Kota Melaka.
   Hang Tuah dwell　in city　Malacca
   'Hang Tuah lived in Malacca.'

8. Pesakit itu　tidak kenal isteri=nya sendiri.
   patient that not　know wife=3sg self
   'The sick man does not know his own wife.'

9. Siti rindu kepada adik=nya.
   Siti miss　to　　　yg.sib=3sg
   'Siti misses her little sister.'

10. Budak itu　membuang buku saya ke dalam sumur.
    child　that throw　　book 1sg to in　　well
    'That boy threw my book into the well.'

Notes

1. In (4a) the PP is an adjunct describing the location of the event, while in (4b) the PP is a modifier indicating which girl was involved.
2. Of course, semantic-role categories do not reflect *all* the semantic differences which could be relevant to grammar. However, semantic roles generally play a crucial part in the assignment of Grammatical Relations, which, in turn, determine a number of important grammatical features. As we will see, these features often include case, agreement, word order, and participation in various syntactic processes.

3. Notice that this list is restricted to ARGUMENT roles. Some other commonly expressed types of semantic information, e.g. time, manner, purpose, etc., are not included here, because the elements which express these concepts are almost always ADJUNCTS rather than arguments. This distinction is discussed in section 4.4.

4. We are ignoring for now the use of nominative pronouns as predicate complements (see chapter 10), especially in relatively formal speech, e.g. *It is she*.

5 Lexical entries and well-formed clauses

Examples (1) and (2) of chapter 4 showed that good Phrase Structure rules can produce bad sentences. We hinted that the solution to this problem was to be found in the LEXICON, the speaker's mental dictionary, where information about the unique properties of individual words is stored. This topic is the focus of the present chapter. In particular, we will be interested in the lexical properties of the verb and the ways in which these properties determine the structure of the clause as a whole.

5.1 Lexical entries

Linguists use the term LEXICON to refer to the collection of all the words (or meaningful elements) in the language; we often think of it as the speaker's "mental dictionary." Each individual word is referred to as a LEXICAL ITEM. For each lexical item, the lexicon must specify how it is pronounced, what it means, and how it patterns in the grammar.

All of the phonological, semantic, and grammatical information which is specific to a particular word is included in its LEXICAL ENTRY. This lexical entry is somewhat analogous to an entry in a normal printed dictionary, which provides information about pronunciation, meaning, and part of speech. However, the grammatical information contained in a lexical entry may go far beyond the word's part of speech (syntactic category). For example, we noted in chapter 4 that one of the diagnostic features for nouns in English is that they can be inflected for number. There is, however, a large sub-class of nouns that cannot (in their most basic meanings) be pluralized. Nouns of this type are often called MASS NOUNS, while nouns which can be pluralized are called COUNT NOUNS. The contrast is illustrated in (1).

(1)   a MASS NOUNS: this rice/salt/mud/money
         COUNT NOUNS: this dog/house/tree/car
       b MASS NOUNS: *these rices/salts/muds/moneys
         COUNT NOUNS: these dogs/houses/trees/cars

Mass and count nouns exhibit other grammatical differences as well. Mass nouns cannot be modified by determiners such as *a, many, few, three, eight*, etc. (2a). Count nouns, on the other hand, cannot be used in their singular form with the determiner *some* (2b), or without any determiner (2c).

(2)   a *a rice/salt/mud/money
         a dog/house/tree/car
      b Please give me some rice/salt/mud/money
         Please give me some?dog/*house/*tree/*car
      c I like rice/mud/?dog/*tree/*car.[1]

These differences in grammatical patterning can be used to separate the words that belong to the category Noun into two sub-classes (or SUBCATE-GORIES), count vs. mass nouns. Which sub-class a particular noun belongs to must be indicated in its lexical entry. In cases like this, where there is a simple two-way distinction to be made, linguists often think in terms of binary FEATURES.[2] Features are used to represent a property that a given linguistic unit may or may not have. To distinguish between count vs. mass nouns, we could require the lexical entry of every noun to contain either the feature [+ count] (for count nouns) or [− count] (for mass nouns). Similarly the subclass of AUXILIARY verbs, which have a number of special grammatical properties, could be distinguished from regular verbs by a feature [+ aux].

To summarize, then, the lexical entry for each word must specify at least the following information:

a   phonological shape
b   meaning (semantic properties)
c   syntactic category (part of speech)
d   other grammatical information
e   irregular forms or patterns associated with that specific word

A lexical entry for the English noun *child* might look something like (3).

(3)
$$\begin{bmatrix} child \text{ /t\textipa{S}a}^{\text{j}}\text{1d/} \\ \text{'young human'} \\ \text{CAT: N} \\ [+ \text{ count}] \\ \text{PLURAL: } children \end{bmatrix}$$

5.2   Argument structure and subcategorization

In chapter 4 we noted two fundamental ways in which predicates may differ from each other: (i) different predicates may require different numbers of arguments; and (ii) predicates which require the same number of arguments may assign different semantic roles to those arguments. As we will see, these differences are crucial in determining the structure of the clauses in which each predicate occurs.

The ARGUMENT STRUCTURE of a predicate is a representation of the number and type of arguments it requires. The following examples show simple argument structure representations for the verbs *sing*, *slap*, *love*, and *give*:

(4)   *sing* <agent>
       slap <agent, patient>
       love <experiencer, stimulus>
       give <agent, theme, recipient>

In any particular sentence in which these verbs are used, each of the arguments will be associated with a specific Grammatical Relation. This is illustrated in (5), where both the semantic role and the Grammatical Relation are marked for each argument.

(5)   a SUBJ .... (Grammatical Relations)
         John   sings.
         AGENT .... (Semantic Roles)

       b SUBJ .... OBJ .... (Grammatical Relations)
         Mary   slapped   John.
         AGENT .... PATIENT .... (Semantic Roles)

       c SUBJ .... OBJ .... (Grammatical Relations)
         John   loves   Mary.
         EXPERIENCER .... STIMULUS .... (Semantic Roles)

       d SUBJ .... OBJ .... OBL .... (Grammatical Relations)
         John   gave   the roses   to his wife.
         AGENT .... THEME .... RECIPIENT .. (Semantic Roles)

We can use an enriched argument structure representation to show the alignment of semantic roles with Grammatical Relations for each verb, as illustrated in (6).

(6)   a *sing*   < agent >
                        |
                     SUBJ

       b *slap*   < agent,   patient >
                       | |
                     SUBJ   OBJ

       c *love* < experiencer, stimulus >
                        | |
                     SUBJ   OBJ

       d *give*   < agent,   theme,   recipient >
                       | | |
                     SUBJ   OBJ   OBL

Information about the set of Grammatical Relations which a particular verb assigns to its arguments is often referred to as SUBCATEGORIZA-TION, because it provides a way of dividing a single syntactic category (namely Verb) into several sub-categories (those that do not take an object, those that require an object plus an oblique argument, etc.). For example, the diagram in (6d) indicates that the verb *give* "subcategorizes" for a subject, a direct object, and an oblique argument. A verb's subcategorization is an important part of the information which must be found in its lexical entry. We will assume that this information is represented in roughly the form shown in (6).

We should point out that the representations in (6) are somewhat redundant, in that they contain information that is (usually) predictable. For example, a normal active transitive verb will almost always assign the SUBJ relation to its agent and the OBJ relation to its patient. Many linguists assume that a lexical entry should contain as little redundant or predictable information as possible. Now if the Grammatical Relation of each argument were fully predictable, so that it could be determined by applying a set of rules (often called LINKING rules), then we would not need to list the Grammatical Relations in the verb's lexical entry. However, getting this approach to work properly turns out to be a fairly difficult task, and introduces more complexity than we can deal with here. For this reason we will simply assume that all of the information contained in the representations in (6) is specified in the lexical entry for each verb.

5.2.1 Transitivity and valence

The concept of subcategorization is somewhat similar to the traditional classification of verbs as being either intransitive or transitive. The basic meaning of the term TRANSITIVE is "taking an object." Thus, an intransitive verb (e.g. *yawn*) does not take any object, a transitive verb (e.g. *like*) requires one object, and a ditransitive verb requires two objects. We considered some ditransitive examples in chapter 4; these are repeated in (7):

(7)   a Mary gave [her son]$_{OBJ}$ [a new bicycle]$_{OBJ_2}$.
      b Reluctantly, Henry showed [Susan]$_{OBJ}$ [his manuscript]$_{OBJ_2}$.
      c Uncle George told [the children]$_{OBJ}$ [a story]$_{OBJ_2}$.

Another way of specifying the transitivity of a verb is to ask, how many TERM (subject or object) arguments does it take? The number of terms, or direct arguments, is sometimes referred to as the VALENCE of the verb. Since most verbs can be said to have a subject, the valence of a verb is normally one greater than the number of objects it takes: an intransitive verb has a valence of one, a transitive verb has a valence of two, and a ditransitive verb has a valence of three.

It is important to notice that the valence of the verb (in this sense) is not the same as the number of arguments it takes. For example, the verb *donate* takes three semantic arguments, as illustrated in (8). However, *donate* has

a valence of two because it takes only two term arguments, SUBJ and
OBJ. With this predicate, the recipient is always expressed as an oblique
argument.

(8)   a Michael Jackson donated his sunglasses to the National Museum.
       b *donate*   < agent,   theme,   recipient >
                        | | |
                      SUBJ   OBJ   OBL

Some linguists use the term "semantic valence" to refer to the number of
semantic arguments which a predicate takes, and "syntactic valence" to
specify the number of terms which a verb requires. In this book we will use
the term "valence" primarily in the latter (syntactic) sense.

    To summarize, both valence and subcategorization tell us something
about the number of arguments that must be expressed in a clause which contains a particular verb. However, there is an important difference between
them. The valence of a verb tells us only the number of terms, or direct
arguments; it says nothing about the presence or absence of oblique arguments. The subcategorization of a verb tells us all the Grammatical Relations
which the verb assigns to its arguments, whether direct or oblique. So, for
example, the verbs *hit* and *put* have the same valence (two), but different
subcategorization sets, since *put* requires an oblique argument while *hit*
does not, as shown in (9). (As a practice exercise, the reader should make
up some example sentences to illustrate these argument structures.)

(9)   a *hit*   < agent,   patient >
                     | |
                   SUBJ   OBJ

       b *put*   < agent,   theme,   goal >
                     | | |
                   SUBJ   OBJ   OBL

5.2.2   Valence alternations

    We have already seen that some verbs can be used in more than
one way. In chapter 4, for example, we saw that the verb *give* occurs in
two different clause patterns, as illustrated in (10). We can now see that
these two uses of the verb involve the same semantic roles but a different
assignment of Grammatical Relations, i.e. different subcategorization. This
difference is represented in (11). The lexical entry for *give* must allow for
both of these configurations.[3]

(10)   a John gave Mary his old radio.
        b John gave his old radio to Mary.

(11)   a *give* < agent,   theme,   recipient >
                      | | |
                   SUBJ   OBJ$_2$ OBJ

        b *give* < agent,   theme,   recipient >
                      | | |
                   SUBJ   OBJ   OBL

It is not difficult to find examples of other verbs with more than one possible valence. For example, in the following pairs of sentences we see the same verb used either with or without an object:

(12)   a John has eaten his sandwich.
        b John has eaten.

(13)   a Bill is writing an autobiography.
        b Bill is writing.

These sentences seem to show that *eat* and *write* can be either transitive or intransitive. However, the same kind of event is described in both patterns. Whenever you eat, something must get eaten; whenever you write, something must get written. So even in the (b) sentences, it seems reasonable to assume that the argument structure contains a patient, although we don't know exactly what the patient is because it is not specified. It is even possible to refer to this unspecified patient, as illustrated in (14). The pronoun *it* in (14c) refers to the unspecified patient of (14b).

(14)   a John: I feel hungry.
        b Mary: Didn't you eat before we left?
        c John: Yes, but *it* wasn't very substantial.

We might say that such verbs are semantically transitive, but differ from other transitive verbs in that they allow the patient argument to remain unexpressed. (For historical reasons, the pattern illustrated in (12b) and (13b) is sometimes called "unspecified object deletion." A more precise term might be "unspecified patient suppression.") We could represent the argument structure of these verbs as in (15), indicating that the patient may either be an OBJ, or be syntactically unexpressed:

(15)   *eat* < agent,   patient >
                    | |
                 SUBJ   (OBJ)

But not all cases of variable transitivity can be treated in this way. Consider the following examples:

(16)   a John is walking the dog.
        b John is walking.

(17)   a The sunshine is melting the snow.
        b #The sunshine is melting.
        c The snow is melting.

In example (16), it is not so clear that the same kind of event is described by both sentences. In (16b) John is definitely walking; but in (16a), while the dog is clearly walking, John could be riding a bicycle or roller-skating. Similarly, even though the string of words in sentence (17b) is a proper sub-set of sentence (17a), its meaning is quite different. Compare this example with (12) and (13) above. The sentence *Bill is writing an autobiography* clearly implies that *Bill is writing*; and *John has eaten his sandwich* clearly implies that *John has eaten*. However, sentence (17a) implies not (17b) but (17c).

Thus the variable transitivity in examples (16) and (17) seems to be of a different type from that in (12) and (13). For cases like (16) and (17), we might want to say that the verb simply has two different senses, each with its own argument structure (as illustrated in (18)), and both senses must be listed in the lexicon.

(18)   a *walk₁* < agent >
                       |
                     SUBJ

         b *walk₂* < agent,   patient >
                       | |
                     SUBJ   OBJ

A number of languages have grammatical processes which, in effect, "change" an oblique argument into an object. The result is a change in the valence of the verb. This can be illustrated by the sentences in (19). In (19a), the beneficiary argument is expressed as an OBL, but in (19b) the beneficiary is expressed as an OBJ. So (19b) contains one more term than (19a), and the valence of the verb has increased from two to three; but there is no change in the number of semantic arguments. Grammatical operations which increase or decrease the valence of a verb are a topic of great interest to syntacticians. We will discuss a few of these operations in chapter 14.

(19)   a John baked a cake for Mary.
         b John baked Mary a cake.

5.3   Properties of a well-formed clause

Examples (1) and (2) in chapter 4, repeated below as (20) and (21), illustrate how good Phrase Structure rules can produce "bad" sentences. In both cases, the set of arguments available is not the right set for the particular verb involved: we have the wrong type of arguments in (20); the wrong number of arguments in (21). Let us consider each of these problems in turn.

(20)   a #The young sausage likes the white dog.

          b #Mary sings a white cake.

          c #A small dog gives Mary to the young tree.

(21)   a *John likes.

          b *Mary gives the young boy.

          c *The girl yawns Mary.

5.3.1   Selectional restrictions

The examples in (20) are grammatical but semantically ill-formed – they don't make sense.[4] The examples in (22) are similar. The problem stems from the combination of words used: the subjects of *know* and *sleep* must normally be animate beings; the object of *drink* must be a liquid, while the object of *bite* must be a solid.

(22)   a #My pencil doesn't know how to spell that word.

          b #John drank his sandwich and took a big bite out of his coffee.

          c #The idea is sleeping.

Constraints on what lexical items may occur in combination with each other are referred to as SELECTIONAL RESTRICTIONS. The violation of a selectional restriction, as in the examples in (20) and (22), is sometimes referred to as a COLLOCATIONAL CLASH. Sentence (20a) illustrates two different kinds of collocational clash. First, sausages cannot be said to 'like' anything because they are not the kind of thing that can feel emotions. This selectional restriction is based at least partly on our shared knowledge about the world. Second, the adjective *young* is normally used only for living things. Thus we may speak of *a new sausage, a fresh sausage*, or *an old sausage*, but not #*a young sausage*. This restriction seems to be an essentially arbitrary fact about the word *young*.

The famous example in (23) was used by Chomsky (1957) to show how a sentence can be grammatical without being meaningful. What makes this sentence so interesting is that it contains so many collocational clashes: something which is *green* cannot be *colorless*; *ideas* cannot be *green*, or any other color, but we cannot call them *colorless* either; *ideas* cannot sleep; *sleeping* is not the kind of thing one can do *furiously*; etc.

(23)   #Colorless green ideas sleep furiously.

In the first paragraph of this section, we noted some selectional restrictions on the subjects of *know* and *sleep*, and on the objects of *drink* and *bite*. However, this way of expressing the restrictions was slightly inaccurate. Selectional restrictions must be stated in terms of semantic roles (agent, patient, etc.) rather than Grammatical Relations (subject, object, etc.). This is illustrated by examples like the following:

(24)   a #John drank his sandwich.
        b #The sandwich was drunk by John.

(25)   a That book is loved by children around the world.
        b #Children around the world are loved by that book.

(26)   a #Mary taught her motorcycle classical Chinese.
        b #Mary taught classical Chinese to her motorcycle.

The examples in (24) show that the patient of *drink* must be a liquid, whether it appears as object or subject. The examples in (25) show that the verb *love* requires an animate experiencer, not an animate subject: (25b) which has an animate subject is extremely odd, whereas (25a) which has an inanimate subject is perfectly sensible. And (26) shows that the experiencer of *teach* must be animate, whether it appears as an object or an oblique argument.

Semantic constraints of various kinds are needed to prevent the grammar from producing sentences like those in (20) and (22). Some constraints would be included in the lexical entries of particular words, e.g. the fact that *young* is used only for living things. Others could perhaps be stated as general rules, e.g. the expectation that experiencers and recipients must normally be animate. Those problems which relate to our non-linguistic knowledge about the world, e.g. the fact that girls may own dogs but not vice versa, may not need to be stated as part of the grammar at all. The main point here is that the Phrase Structure rules themselves do not need to be modified to deal with these sorts of issues.

5.3.2   Subcategorization

As pointed out above, the sentences in (21) are bad because the number of participants in the clause does not match the number of arguments which the verb requires. More precisely, the SUBCATEGORIZATION requirements of the verbs, which are shown in (27), are not satisfied; the set of Grammatical Relations which the verb must assign does not match the number of phrases available to bear those relations. *Like* is a transitive verb which requires an object; *yawn* is an intransitive verb which does not take an object; and *give* requires three arguments, while only two NPs are present in (21b).

(27)   a *like*   < experiencer,   stimulus >
                         | |
                       SUBJ   OBJ

        b *give*   < agent,   theme,   recipient >
                        | | |
                      SUBJ   OBJ   OBL

        c *yawn*   < agent >
                       |
                     SUBJ

Our set of Phrase Structure (PS) rules allowed this kind of mismatch to occur because the rule which expands "S" (repeated in (28)) simply lists the post-verbal NP and PP as optional elements which can be freely included or omitted.

(28)   S → NP   V   (NP)   (PP)

Clearly we need some way to ensure that the number of NPs and PPs generated in the tree structure is appropriate for the specific verb which is chosen. One approach might be to break up the category of "verbs" (V) into three subsets: intransitive verbs (V_{INTR}), transitive verbs (V_{TRANS}), and ditransitive verbs ($V_{DITRANS}$). We could then write separate rules expanding "S" in the correct way for each of these subcategories.[5]

(29)   S   →   NP V_{INTR}
         S   →   NP V_{TRANS} NP
         S   →   NP $V_{DITRANS}$ NP   NP

However, as we expand our inventory of verbs we quickly discover that three rules are not enough. Some verbs require not only an object NP but also a PP as oblique argument. Other verbs take a PP but no NP. As we will see in future chapters, other verbs require or allow a following AP or S. If we tried to write additional rules to allow for every possible combination of these elements, the grammar would become hopelessly messy and redundant; we would also end up with a very large number of sub-classes for the category V.

A more efficient way of preventing sentences like those in (21) from being generated is to refer to the subcategorization information contained in the lexical entry of the verb. A fundamental assumption of most current approaches to syntactic analysis is that the structure of a clause is largely determined by the argument structure and subcategorization of its verb. We will express this principle through a set of constraints on possible clause structures, which we refer to as WELL-FORMEDNESS CONDITIONS.

5.3.3   Well-formedness conditions

Elements that are listed in the subcategorization of the verb (e.g. subjects, objects, etc.) are often referred to as the COMPLEMENTS of the verb. The constraints that we need to formulate will basically ensure that each clause contains the right number and type of complements.

The "right number" means neither too few nor too many. A clause will have too few complements if it lacks one which is required by the verb's subcategorization set. In that case, we would say that the clause is not COMPLETE. A clause will have too many complements if it contains one which is not listed in the verb's subcategorization set. In that case, we would say that the clause is not COHERENT. To these two conditions we will add a third, namely that the Grammatical Relation of each complement must be UNIQUE in its clause. In other words, there cannot be two subjects, two primary objects, etc. in a single clause.

As we will see in later chapters, many languages allow one clause to be embedded within another (i.e. one S may dominate another). For this reason, in order to determine whether a given clause contains the "right number" of complements, we need to be more precise about what it means for two elements to belong to the same clause. We will say that two elements are CLAUSE-MATES if the smallest clause that contains either one of them contains the other as well. To restate this definition in terms of tree structure, we say that *X* and *Y* are clause-mates if the smallest S which dominates *X* also dominates *Y*, and vice versa. For example, *A* and *B* are clause-mates in (30), as are *C* and *D*. But *A* and *C* are not clause-mates, and neither are *A* and *D*, *B* and *C*, or *B* and *D*.

(30)

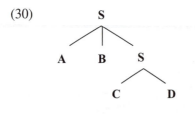

Our three well-formedness conditions can now be expressed as in (31).[6] These conditions do not apply to adjuncts, of course, because adjuncts by definition are not part of the subcategorization of the verb.

(31)   **WELL-FORMEDNESS CONDITIONS**
   a COMPLETENESS: every Grammatical Relation which is obligatory in the subcategorization of a verb V must be assigned to a clause-mate of V.

   b COHERENCE: every (non-adjunct) Grammatical Relation which is assigned to a clause-mate of V must be allowed in the subcategorization of V.

   c UNIQUENESS: no Grammatical Relation may be assigned more than once by a single verb.

In order to be considered grammatical, each sentence must conform not only to the PS rules of the language but also to these three well-formedness conditions. In other words, we define a grammatical (or WELL-FORMED) clause structure as being one in which: (a) every combination of mother and daughters is licensed by a PS rule; and (b) the well-formedness conditions are satisfied.

5.3.4 Annotated Phrase Structure trees

The well-formedness conditions above speak of assigning Grammatical Relations to phrases which occur in particular Phrase Structure positions, specifically to clause-mates of V. But there is no indication in our Phrase Structure diagrams of which Grammatical Relation is assigned to which constituent, thus no way to be sure whether or not a particular tree structure satisfies the well-formedness conditions. It would be helpful to add this information to our PS trees in some way. The simplest approach is to add an ANNOTATION to the appropriate nodes in the tree structure, as in (32).

(32)

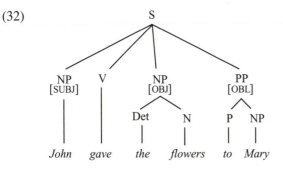

To see whether the well-formedness conditions are satisfied, we need to compare the subcategorization properties of the verb with the Grammatical Relations (GRs) assigned to its clause-mates. Although we normally write only a single word for each terminal element in our tree diagrams, this is just a short-hand notation which actually represents the full lexical entry. The rest of the information contained in the lexical entry, including (at least for verbs) the argument structure, is also assumed to be available. By making some of this information explicit in the tree diagram, as in (33), we can immediately check for completeness and coherence.

(33)

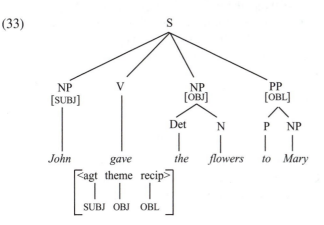

This kind of annotated tree diagram allows us to see at once what is wrong with the ungrammatical examples in (21) above: (21b) is incomplete, as demonstrated in (34a), while (21c) is incoherent, as demonstrated in (34b).

(34)   a (= 21b)

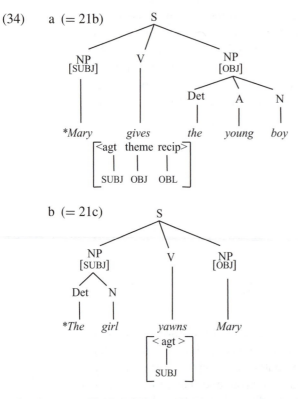

b (= 21c)

In a language like English, word order (or position in the Phrase Structure) is the most important signal for identifying the GR of a constituent: subjects normally come before the verb, direct objects immediately after the verb, etc. One way in which the grammar can specify the regular association of position with GR is by adding annotations to the PS rules themselves, as in (35). This rule will license tree structures like that shown in (33). The annotations can be thought of as extra units of information which must be true of the constituent that occupies a given position in the tree. The node labels for these constituents now specify not only syntactic category but also the GR which must be assigned.

(35)   S   →   NP   V   (NP)   (PP)
             [SUBJ]   [OBJ]   [OBL]

In some other languages, word order is quite free and GRs are distinguished primarily by morphological features (specifically case marking and/or agreement; see chapter 7). In these languages, the rules which assign GRs to phrases must be stated in terms of the relevant morphological features.

GRs form a crucial link in the association between individual phrases and semantic roles. They are associated with semantic roles in the argument structure of the verb, and with NPs or PPs in the Phrase Structure representation. (Both of these associations are illustrated in (33).) This linkage between a specific phrase and the semantic role which it bears is what allows the grammar to specify who did what in a particular situation. But the linkage is indirect, mediated by the GR.

5.4   Uniqueness of oblique arguments

The third of the well-formedness conditions in (31) (i.e. Uniqueness) states that "no Grammatical Relation may be assigned more than once by a single verb." This statement seems to be contradicted by examples like those in (36), which have more than one oblique argument:

(36)   a John carved a whistle [for his daughter] [with his pocket knife].
         b Mary threw breadcrumbs [into the water] [for the fish].
         c The farmer drew water [from the well] [with a wooden bucket].

There is a crucial difference between these examples, which are grammatical, and the ungrammatical example in chapter 4 (21a): *John gave a bouquet of roses to his mother to Susan.* That example is ungrammatical because it contains two oblique arguments of the same kind, namely two recipients. The grammatical sentences in (36), however, each contain two oblique arguments bearing distinct semantic roles.

These observations suggest that we can maintain the Uniqueness constraint, which seems to be needed in any case for the other GRs, by recognizing more than one oblique grammatical relation. The GRs of the various oblique arguments in (36) can be differentiated by reference to their semantic roles: OBL_{INSTR} for instrument phrases; OBL_{BEN} for beneficiary phrases; OBL_{GOAL} for goal phrases, etc. These various OBL relations are said to be SEMANTICALLY RESTRICTED, since each relation can only be associated with a particular semantic role.[7]

In English, the difference between the various Oblique GRs is signaled in the syntax by the choice of preposition: *with* for OBL_{INST}; *for* for OBL_{BEN}; *from* for OBL_{SOURCE}; *(in)to* for OBL_{GOAL}; *by* for OBL_{AGT}, etc. In some other languages, these GRs may be indicated by the use of specific case markers (see chapter 7).

5.5   Zero-anaphora ("pro-drop")

Another apparent problem for the well-formedness conditions in (31) is illustrated by the examples in (37a,b). Both of these examples contain two verbs, and all four of the verbs subcategorize for a SUBJ, but there is no subject NP to be seen in either example. Furthermore, the transitive verb *provei* 'I tried' in (37a) lacks an OBJ NP. The missing subjects and objects seem to violate the Completeness condition, yet the sentences are fully grammatical.

(37)   **Portuguese** (Parkinson 1992)

    a Provou   o   bolo?   Provei!
      try-PAST.2sg the(MASC.SG) cake   try-PAST.1sg
      'Did you try the cake? (Yes,) I tried (it).'

    b Digo   que vem.
      say-PRES.1sg that come-PRES.3sg
      'I say he is coming.'

    c (Eu) não sei.
      I   not know-PRES.1sg
      'I don't know.'

Subject pronouns are generally optional in Portuguese, as indicated in (37c); such pronouns could be added to examples (37a,b) as well. But subject pronouns are, in a sense, redundant, because the person and number of the subject are already indicated by the form of the verb. Since the pronoun adds no new information, it is not surprising that it can be easily omitted. (Third person pronouns, which add information about masculine vs. feminine gender, are less likely to be omitted than first and second person pronouns.) However, pronouns can sometimes be omitted even when there is no verbal morphology to preserve the information. Portuguese verbs do not agree with their objects, but object pronouns can be dropped when the referent can be identified from the immediate context, as in (37a).

This is an area where languages differ from each other in somewhat unpredictable ways. Some languages in which verbs agree with their subjects, including Portuguese and Italian, allow subject pronouns to be freely omitted. In other languages with similar agreement patterns, such as French and German, subject pronouns are not freely omitted. Certain other languages, including Chinese and Japanese, lack agreement morphology entirely, but nevertheless allow pronominal arguments to be omitted. Languages which allow pronouns to be omitted are sometimes referred to as "pro-drop languages." Some authors, however, prefer to restrict the term PRO-DROP to cases where information is preserved by verb agreement, using the term ZERO-ANAPHORA for cases where there is no verb agreement. (The term ANAPHORA will be discussed in chapter 8.)

In section 5.2.2 we noted that certain verbs in English allow their objects to be omitted, as illustrated in (38). We suggested that these verbs subcategorize for an optional OBJ relation.

(38)   a John has already *eaten*.
       b Mary *drinks* like a fish.
       c Arthur loves to *read*.

But these examples are different from the Portuguese sentences (37a,b) in several important respects. First, the omitted objects in (38) have no definite referent: we have no idea what John ate, what Arthur likes to read, etc. In (37), however, each of the verbs (including the 3rd person *vem* 'he is coming' in (37b)) is understood to have a definite, specific subject. Similarly, the omitted object NP in the answer of (37a) is understood to refer to a specific cake. A second difference is that only certain transitive verbs in English allow their objects to be omitted; this is a feature that must be listed in the verb's lexical entry. In languages like Portuguese, however, all verbs seem to allow the same patterns of pro-drop.

    In both of these respects, pro-drop and zero-anaphora are very much like using a normal, visible pronoun. A common way of analyzing examples like (37a,b) is to assume that they contain invisible (or NULL) pronouns, which are often represented as *pro*. Under this analysis, pro-drop languages are those which contain *pro* as an element of their lexicon, while non-pro-drop languages do not.

5.6   Further notes on English Phrase Structure

    The simple PS rules we have assumed up to now generate only "flat" clause structures, with the verb and all of its complements being immediate daughters of S as shown in (39a). This kind of analysis seems to be correct for many languages, e.g. Malayalam (Mohanan 1982). In English, however, and in a number of other languages, there is good reason to believe that the subject NP is not a sister of V. Rather, the verb, its object, and oblique arguments form a constituent labeled VP, and it is this VP which is a sister to the subject NP. The VP analysis for English is shown in (39b).

(39)   a S $\rightarrow$ NP   V   (NP)   (PP)
                    [SUBJ]   [OBJ] [OBL]

       b S $\rightarrow$ NP   VP
                    [SUBJ]
         VP $\rightarrow$ V   (NP)   (PP)
                         [OBJ] [OBL]

The evidence which supports a VP constituent for English is fairly complex, and we will not consider it in detail here.[8] A few of the relevant patterns are illustrated in (40–41). These examples show that the combination of V + OBJ(+ OBL) can function as a sentence fragment in answer to a question (40), and can be re-ordered or deleted as a unit (41). These are

some of the classic tests for constituency, similar to those we discussed in
chapter 3.

(40)   Q: What are you going to do now?
        A: [*Buy a birthday card for my mother.*]

(41)   a John promised that he will finish the assignment, and [*finish the
          assignment*] he will.[9]
        b What you need to do now is [*surrender these documents to the
          police*].
        c If Mary [*gives buns to the elephant*], then John will _ too.

Because the VP analysis for English is so widely assumed, we will adopt
it in the remainder of this book. However, we will continue to assume a
flat clause structure for other languages, because we will not have time
to examine the evidence for constituency in each individual language. In
general, we prefer to assume the simplest possible structure consistent with
the language-specific evidence. With respect to Phrase Structure, this means
assuming a flat clause structure unless we find specific evidence supporting
a VP constituent in a particular language.

Another question that arises in the analysis of English is the position of
the auxiliary verb (AUX). Here the evidence is slightly more ambiguous,
and several different analyses have been proposed over the years. Without
going into the details of the debate, we will assume that the AUX in English
is a daughter of S, a sister to both the VP and the subject NP, as shown in
(42).

(42)   S   →   NP   AUX   VP
                 [SUBJ]
        VP   →   V   (NP)   (PP)
                      [OBJ]   [OBL]

Based on these assumptions, we would assign the structure shown in (43)
to a basic clause like *Mary could sell air-conditioners to an Eskimo*.

(43)

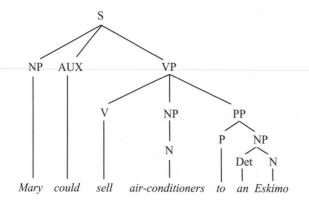

5.7   Conclusion

We began chapter 4 by asking what the essential elements of a clause are. We can now give a reasonably concise answer to this question: the essential elements of a clause are: (i) a word (frequently a verb) expressing the predicate; and (ii) phrases expressing the appropriate number and type of arguments for that predicate. Thus the structure of a clause is largely determined by the argument structure of its predicate. However, in addition to the predicate and its arguments, many clauses also contain extra elements referred to as ADJUNCTS.

The lexical entry of a verb must provide at least three pieces of information about that verb: (i) the number of arguments it takes; (ii) the semantic roles it assigns to its arguments; and (iii) the Grammatical Relation assigned to each argument. The set of Grammatical Relations assigned by the verb is referred to as its SUBCATEGORIZATION. The number of term (i.e. non-oblique) relations that a verb assigns is called its (syntactic) VALENCE. Valence is closely related to transitivity, which (in its basic meaning) is an expression of the number of objects the verb takes: an intransitive verb has no object; a transitive verb has one object; and a ditransitive verb has two objects.

As we have seen, simple PS rules alone will "over-generate"; that is, they will generate sentences which are not, in fact, grammatical. The subcategorization properties of the verb play an important role in avoiding this problem. In order for a PS tree to be "well-formed" (i.e. grammatical), the constituents which appear as complements of V must be precisely those which are required or allowed by the verb's subcategorization. Each clause must be complete (i.e. must contain all the complements required by the verb) and coherent (it may not contain any complements which the verb does not allow); and each GR must be uniquely assigned within its clause.

Exercises

5A Ngbaka (Congo; Roberts 1999, ex. S-9.2)
Write lexical entries for the verbs in the following examples. (Assume that all PPs are arguments, and not adjuncts.)

1.   a nea ko toa   geogeo.
       he went to house slowly
       'He went to the house slowly.'

2.   a yu.
       he runs
       'He runs.'

3.   *a ne.
       he goes
       ('He goes.')

4.   a yu   ko toa.
       he runs to house
       'He runs to the house.'

5.   a   ne   ko toa   do wili   a.
       she goes to house with husband her
       'She goes to the house with her husband.'

6.   a   gi   loso we wili   a.
       she cooks rice for husband her
       'She cooks rice for her husband.'

7.   a nyongo loso do   papa.
       he eats   rice with spoon
       'He eats rice with a spoon.'

8.   a a   mbeti ko sanduku.
       he puts book in box
       'He puts the book in the box.'

9.   *a a   mbeti.
       he puts book
       ('He puts the book.')

10.   a da   mbeti.
       he throws book
       'He throws the book.'

11.   a daa   mbeti ko sanduku ze.
       he threw book in box   yesterday
       'He threw the book in the box yesterday.'

5B Japanese (data from Hisatsugu Kitahara and Tom Pinson, North Dakota
Summer Institute of Linguistics, used by permission)

   Write lexical entries for the verbs in the following examples. Assume
that all arguments are NPs. For the purposes of this exercise, treat the
markers =*ga*, =*o*, and =*ni* as simple suffixes. What is the function of
these markers?

1.   a Taro=ga ookina inu=o mitsuke-ta.
         Taro   big   dog   find-PAST
         'Taro found the big dog.'

       b *Kare=ga mitsuke-ta.
         3sg.m   find-PAST
         ('He found.')

2.   a Kare=ga hashit-ta.
        3sg.m   run-PAST
        'He ran.'

     b *Kare=ga inu=o hashit-ta.
        3sg.m   dog   run-PAST
        ('He ran the dog.')

3.   a Kanojo=ga ne-ta.
        3sg.f   sleep-PAST
        'She slept.'

     b *Hanako=ga akanbou=o ne-ta.
        Hanako   baby   sleep-PAST
        ('Hanako slept the baby.')

4.   a Kare=ga boru=o nage-ta.
        3sg.m   ball   throw-PAST
        'He threw the ball.'

     b *Kare=ga nage-ta.
        3sg.m   throw-PAST
        ('He threw.')

5.   Taro=ga kare=ni boru=o nage-ta.
        Taro   3sg.m   ball   throw-PAST
        'Taro threw the ball to him.'

6.   a Hanako=ga inu=ni gohan=o age-ta.
        Hanako   dog   rice   give-PAST
        'Hanako gave the dog rice.'

     b *Hanako=ga inu=ni age-ta.
        Hanako   dog   give-PAST
        ('Hanako gave to the dog.')

7.   Kare=ga Hanako=ni inu=o age-ta.
        3sg.m   Hanako   dog   give-PAST
        'He gave the dog to Hanako.'

Additional exercises

Merrifield et al. (1987) prob. 190, 249

Notes

1. The word *dog* is possible in (2b,c) only when interpreted as a mass noun, i.e. a kind of meat.
2. This device is used more extensively in phonology.
3. The relationship between these two configurations can be expressed as a grammatical rule, since a number of other verbs allow the same kind of alternation. See Kroeger (2004, ch. 3) for a detailed discussion of this alternation.

4. One reason for saying that examples like (20) and (22) are grammatical, even though they sound so odd, is that it would often be possible to invent a context (e.g. in a fairy tale or a piece of science fiction) in which these sentences would be quite acceptable. This is not possible for ungrammatical sentences like those in (21).

5. Another way of adjusting the PS rules might be to make lexical insertion a context-sensitive rule, but we will not explore this option here.

6. See Kaplan and Bresnan (1982) for a more rigorous formulation.

7. In some languages, a single clause can contain more than one secondary object. In such languages several different secondary object relations can be identified, which are again semantically restricted.

8. See Radford (1988, ch. 2); and Kroeger (2004, ch. 2) for a discussion of the kinds of evidence which support this claim

9. From Radford (1988:101).

6 Noun Phrases

A Noun Phrase, as its name suggests, is a phrasal constituent whose head is a noun. NPs in English, and most other languages, can function as subjects, primary or secondary objects, and objects of prepositions. In this chapter we will discuss various kinds of dependents (non-head constituents) which may appear in NPs in a large number of languages. The three most important classes of these are DETERMINERS, COMPLEMENTS, and ADJUNCTS (or MODIFIERS). We will also look at POSSESSORS, which function as a kind of determiner in English, but as complements or adjuncts in some other languages. Finally we will discuss some structural features of NPs in English.

6.1   Complements and adjuncts of N

In studying the structure of a clause we have distinguished complements, which are selected by the verb, from adjuncts, which are not. Nouns, too, can take complements and adjuncts of various categories. In this section we will discuss some of the criteria for distinguishing complements from adjuncts within an NP.

As mentioned above, adjuncts to an NP are often referred to as MODIFIERS. The most common type of modifier in English is the adjective, which will be discussed in section 6.3. Besides adjectives, NPs can also contain PP modifiers, as illustrated in (1). The prepositional phrase *with long hair* in these examples functions as an adjunct; it is not selected by the head noun, but may be freely added to any number of NPs, subject to semantic and pragmatic plausibility.[1]

(1)   a a student [with long hair]
        b a boy [with long hair]
        c a girl [with long hair]
        d a teenager [with long hair]
        e a punk [with long hair]

On the other hand, a PP may also function as a complement within NP. In chapter 3, section 3.4.2, we defined a COMPLEMENT of a phrase as a dependent (non-head) constituent which is "selected by" the head word of that phrase. Complement PPs are LEXICALLY SPECIFIED; they only occur with certain specific head nouns and not with others. For example, all of the NPs in (2) contain the PP *of Physics*, but only (2a) is grammatical. This is because the noun *student* can take a complement of this type, while the other head nouns (*boy*, *teenager*, etc.) cannot.

(2)   a a student [of Physics]
        b *a boy [of Physics]
        c *a girl [of Physics]
        d *a teenager [of Physics]
        e *a punk [of Physics]

The contrast between complement PPs and adjunct PPs is also reflected in other ways. As (3) illustrates, when a given NP contains both a complement PP and an adjunct PP, the complement must always precede the adjunct, as in (3a). An adjunct may not separate the complement PP from its head N, as shown in (3b).

(3)   a a student [of physics] [with long hair]
        b *a student [with long hair] [of physics]

The phrases in (4) illustrate that a complement PP must be unique; no single NP can contain more than one complement PP of the same type (4a). Adjunct PPs, however, can be more freely multiplied as illustrated in (4b,c).

(4)   a *a student [of Physics] [of Chemistry]
        b a student [from Philadelphia] [with long hair]
        c a student [with long hair] [with an interest in Thomas Aquinas]

As the examples in (5) illustrate, a question phrase can be formed from a complement PP but not from an adjunct PP.

(5)   a What branch of Physics are you a student of?
        b *What kind of hair are you a student with?

The pro-form *one* can be used to refer to the head noun when it is followed by an adjunct PP, as in (6a), but not when it is followed by a complement PP as in (6b).

(6)   a The [student] with short hair is dating the *one* with long hair.
        b *The [student] of Chemistry was older than the *one* of Physics.

Finally, notice that PP complements of a noun can often be paraphrased as NP arguments of the corresponding verb; this is illustrated in (7).

(7)   a a student [of Physics]
        a′ John studies Physics

b the loss [of his passport]
b′ John lost his passport

c the attack [on Pearl Harbor]
c′ the Japanese attacked Pearl Harbor

Like PPs, clauses too may occur within NPs as either complements or modifiers. A clause that functions as a modifier within the NP is called a RELATIVE CLAUSE. This construction will be discussed in greater detail in chapter 12, but some examples are given in (8).

(8)   **Clausal modifiers (Relative clauses)**
       a the woman [that I love]
       b the food [that I love]
       c the color [that I love]
       d the idea [that I love]
       e the theory [that I love]

Because the modifying clause is a kind of adjunct, nearly any head noun can occur in this pattern. In contrast, clausal complements are allowed only with certain specific head nouns, most commonly with nouns describing verbal or mental activities. Example (9) shows that some nouns accept such complement clauses while others do not.

(9)   **Clausal complements**
       a the report [that I love Margaret Thatcher]
       b the idea [that I love Margaret Thatcher]
       c the theory [that I love Margaret Thatcher]
       d *the woman [that I love Margaret Thatcher]
       e *the food [that I love Margaret Thatcher]
       f *the color [that I love Margaret Thatcher]

6.2   Determiners

In English, many noun phrases begin with an ARTICLE (*a* or *the*) or a DEMONSTRATIVE (*this* or *that*). Articles and demonstratives are the most common types of determiner. English QUANTIFIERS (*some*, *all*, *no, many, few*, etc.) also function as determiners, though in some other languages determiners and quantifiers belong to distinct categories.

Determiners typically provide information about definiteness, number (singular vs. plural), and (in the case of demonstratives) distance from the speaker. In some languages they also indicate other grammatical information such as case (chapter 7) and gender (chapter 8).

Determiners do not behave like typical adjuncts, because the choice of determiner is often limited by the grammatical and semantic properties of the head noun. For example, in chapter 5, section 5.1, we noted the important distinction between MASS NOUNS, which cannot be pluralized (e.g. *these rices*), vs. COUNT NOUNS, which can be pluralized (e.g. *these dogs*). Mass and count nouns require different determiners. Count nouns cannot be used in the singular with the determiner *some*, nor can they appear in the singular form without a determiner. Mass nouns, on the other hand, cannot occur with determiners such as *a*, *many*, *few*, or numerals (*three*, *eight*, etc.).

On the other hand, determiners do not behave like typical complements either. Some linguists analyze determiners as being heads of a phrasal category DetP, which takes the rest of the NP as its complement. In this book, we will simply treat determiners as a new type of dependent, which is neither a complement nor an adjunct.

6.3   Adjectives and Adjective Phrases (AP)

In many languages there is one lexical category whose primary function is to modify nouns. This category is generally labeled ADJECTIVE. Adjective modifiers in English normally occur before the head noun. Thus the basic order of constituents in the English NP (ignoring modifying and complement clauses for now) is: Det-A-N-PP, as seen in the examples in (10).

(10)   a that little dog under the table
         b a secret admirer in the Ministry of Education

But it is not unusual for more than one word to occur between the determiner and head noun. For example, sentences like those in (11) show that adjective modifiers can themselves be modified by adverbs of degree (sometimes called INTENSIFIERS).

(11)   a You have [a *very* beautiful daughter].
         b [A *surprisingly* large majority] voted in favor of the amendment.
         c Mary coaxed her son to swallow [the *extremely* bitter medicine].
         d John has just discovered [a *rather* interesting species of flatworm].

What is the internal structure of these NPs? Does the combination of intensifier plus adjective form a constituent (an AP), as indicated in (12b), or are both of these elements individually daughters of the NP, as in (12a)?[2]

(12)   a NP → Det (Adv) (A) N (PP)
         b NP → Det (AP) N (PP)
            AP → (Adv) A

The examples in (13) show that both the intensifier and the adjective
are optional within the NP. This is, of course, what we would expect since
neither of them is the head of the NP. But these examples also show that,
while the adjective can occur without the intensifier, the intensifier cannot
occur without the adjective.

(13)   a You have [a very beautiful daughter].
         b You have [a beautiful daughter].
         c *You have [a very daughter].
         d You have [a daughter].

This fact could not be explained using the PS rule in (12a). However, the
rule in (12b) offers an immediate explanation: the AP as a whole is optional,
so we can get an NP with neither adjective nor intensifier as in (13d). But
if there is an AP, it must include an adjective, since that is the head.

Another piece of evidence supporting the analysis in (12b) is the fact that
there may be several adjectives modifying the head N of the same NP, as in
(14a); and each of these adjectives can be modified by an intensifier, as in
(14b).

(14)   a You have a [beautiful, intelligent, considerate] daughter.
         b You have a [very beautiful, extremely intelligent, unusually
            considerate] daughter.

There is no fixed limit on how many modifiers can appear in such a sequence.
But in order to represent an arbitrarily long string of alternating adjectives
and intensifiers, it is necessary to treat each such pair as a single unit.

The "star" notation used in (15) is one way of representing arbitrarily
long sequences of the same category. For any category X, the symbol "X*"
stands for "a sequence of any number (zero or more) of Xs." So the symbol
"AP*" stands for "a sequence of zero or more APs." It is easy to modify the rule in (12b) to account for examples like (14b); this analysis is
shown in (15b). Under the analysis in (12a), we would need to write a more
complex rule something like (15a).[3] Because simplicity tends to be favored
in grammatical systems, (12b) and (15b) provide a better analysis for this
construction.

(15)   a NP → Det ((Adv) A)* N (PP)
         b NP → Det AP* N (PP)

Further evidence for the existence of the AP constituent is seen in the
fact that the combination of intensifier plus adjective can be conjoined in
coordinate structures like (16). This is significant because only constituents
can normally be conjoined in this way.

(16)   You have a [[very beautiful]$_{AP}$ but [slightly crazy] $_{AP}$]$_{AP}$ daughter.

Finally, the combination of intensifier plus adjective appears in other contexts as well, and not just as a modifier inside NP. The sentence in (17) contains an AP functioning as a "predicate complement."[4] If we did not recognize the AP as being a constituent, we would be forced to repeat the same sequence found in (12a) in the PS rules for these other constructions as well, leading to a highly redundant description of the facts.

(17)   Your daughter is [very beautiful].

For all of these reasons, we will adopt the analysis in (12b). Of course, an AP in English may be more complicated than those we have been considering. Some examples are shown in (18), but we will not try to develop a rule to account for all of these possibilities here. Our purpose is not to present a detailed analysis of English, but to give an example of the kinds of evidence that can be used to identify sub-constituents, i.e. phrases embedded within other phrases.

(18)   a The [smaller than normal] crowd disappointed the organizers.
        b The minister's [too numerous to mention] mistakes have
           seriously embarrassed the government.

6.4   Possession and recursion

Most languages allow a Noun Phrase to contain another NP which names the POSSESSOR of the head noun. This phrase is called a "possessor" because it can always be used to express the concept of possession or ownership; but in many languages it can be used to express a wide variety of other relationships as well. For example, the phrase *my picture* can be used to indicate that I am the owner of the picture (I bought it), I am the creator of the picture (I painted it), or I am the subject of the picture (it shows my likeness). Similarly, phrases like *John's leg*, *John's son*, or *John's reputation* indicate various kinds of association between the possessor (John) and the head noun, none of which involves ownership in the normal sense of the word.

In English, a possessor phrase functions as a kind of determiner. We can see this because possessor phrases do not normally occur together with other determiners in the same NP:

(19)   a the new motorcycle
        b Mary's new motorcycle
        c *Mary's the new motorcycle
        d *the Mary's new motorcycle

In some other languages, however, this is not the case. Example (20) shows that possessor phrases may co-occur with definite articles in Portuguese, and with demonstratives in Malay.

(20)   a **Portuguese**

o   meu   filho 'my son'
the(masc.sg) my(masc.sg) son

b **Malay**

anak Ramli itu   'Ramli's child'; 'that child of Ramli's'
child Ramli that

In section 6.4.1 we will discuss a grammatical distinction that is made in some languages between two different kinds of possession. Section 6.4.2 discusses the structure of "nested" possessor phrases, e.g. *John's sister's husband*.

6.4.1   Alienable vs. inalienable possession

In a number of languages, including many in New Guinea, Australia, and the Americas, possessor phrases can be marked in two different ways depending on the kind of relationship being expressed between the possessor and the head noun. The term INALIENABLE possession is used to indicate that there is a necessary and permanent relationship between the possessor and the possessed item. Nouns that require this kind of marking typically include body parts and kinship terms. The term ALIENABLE possession is used for things which are possessed only conditionally or temporarily, that is, for items that can be bought, sold, given away, lost, found, etc.

In Hatam (Irian Jaya; Reesink 1999), for example, inalienably possessed nouns (including body parts, kin terms, and a few other words) carry an obligatory prefix that indicates the person and number of the possessor. This pattern is illustrated in (21). Alienable possession is indicated using the possessive particle *de*, as illustrated in (22).

(21)   **Hatam** (adapted from Reesink 1999:48–49, 80–84)
di-cig 'my father'   di-bou 'my head'
a-cig 'your (sg) father'   a-bou 'your (sg) head'
ni-cig 'his/her father'   ni-bou 'his/her head'
i-cig 'our (incl) father'   i-bou 'our (incl) head'
*cig (for: 'father')   *bou (for: 'head')

(22)   a a-de   singau
2sg-POSS knife
'your knife'

b andigpoi Miller de   ig
old.man Miller POSS house
'Mr. Miller's house'

c a-cig ni-de nab
 2sg-father 3sg-POSS pig
 'your father's pig'

The Australian languages Warrgamay and Malak-Malak both have genitive case markers which are used to mark the possessor phrase only for
alienable possession. To express inalienable possession, on the other hand,
the possessor phrase appears as a bare NP. Note also the change of word
order in Malak-Malak.

(23) **Warrgamay** (Dixon 1980:293)
  a ŋulmburu-ŋu mindi
   woman-GEN grass.dilly.bag
   'the woman's grass dilly-bag'

  b ŋulmburu bingany
   woman foot
   'the woman's foot'

(24) **Malak-Malak** (Blake 1987:98)
  a muyiny yinya-noe
   dog man-GEN
   'the man's dog'

  b alawarr tyet
   woman leg
   'the woman's leg'

6.4.2 Recursive rules

In the practice exercises at the end of chapter 3 we proposed two
simple PS rules for NP and PP, repeated in (25) below. These rules account
for the fact that one PP can be embedded within another. In fact, English
grammar allows PPs to be nested one inside another for as long as the
speaker's breath holds out; some examples from chapter 3 are repeated in
(26).

(25) PP → P NP
  NP → Det N (PP)

(26) a a durian on the tree in the garden of that house in Penang
  b in the closet at the top of the stairs in that castle beside the river

The tree structure for a portion of example (26a) is presented in (27). This
is an example of a RECURSIVE structure: that is, one in which a constituent of a particular category (namely PP) can be embedded inside another

constituent of the same category, which, in turn, can be embedded inside
another such constituent, etc.

(27)

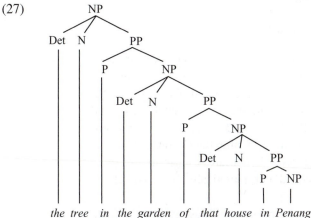

the tree   in   the   garden   of   that   house   in   Penang

The recursion in (26) is due to the fact that the rule for PP contains an
embedded NP, and the rule for NP contains an embedded PP. Now let us
consider another kind of recursive structure. Before proceeding further, try
to formulate a set of Phrase Structure rules which will generate noun phrases
like those in (28).

(28)   a [John]'s sister
        b [John's sister]'s husband
        c [John's sister's husband]'s uncle
        d [John's sister's husband's uncle]'s daughter (etc.)

In the simplest case (28a), the NP consists of a possessor phrase (marked
with –'s) followed by the head N. But, as the other examples illustrate, the
NP may contain any number of possessor phrases.

There are two facts that must be noted about this possessive construction
in English before we can arrive at an adequate analysis of its grammatical
structure. First, each possessor phrase is a full NP which can contain its
own modifiers etc.; it is not just a bare noun as the examples in (28) might
suggest.

(29)   a [my favorite uncle]'s youngest daughter
        b [my favorite uncle's youngest daughter]'s oldest son
        c [my favorite uncle's youngest daughter's oldest son]'s best friend
        d [my favorite uncle's youngest daughter's oldest son's best friend]'s
           new bicycle

Second, as noted above, a possessor phrase marked with –'s never co-
occurs with a determiner; in fact, the possessor phrase seems to take the
place of a determiner.

(30)   the old cabin
        my old cabin
        Abraham Lincoln's old cabin
        *the my old cabin
        *the Abraham Lincoln's old cabin

In addition to generating an appropriate Phrase Structure tree for these NPs, we will obviously need to account for the possessive marker –'*s* itself in some way. Several analyses have been proposed. We will treat the possessive –'*s* as a kind of genitive case marker (see chapter 7), i.e. an element which marks possessive NPs. We will recognize a new Grammatical Relation, POSSESSOR, which is assigned within the NP rather than the clause. Under this approach, our PS rules do not have to mention the possessive marker –'*s* at all; it will be added morphologically to any NP which bears the POSSESSOR function.[5]

To summarize, we have said that the possessor phrase is an NP which takes the place of a determiner within another NP, and bears the POSSESSOR function within that NP. These facts are represented in the revised PS rule in (31).

(31) $NP \rightarrow \left(\left\{ \begin{array}{c} Det \\ NP_{[POSS]} \end{array} \right\} \right) AP^* \; N \; (PP)$

This rule has an interesting property, namely, that the category on the left side of the arrow (NP) also appears on the right side. Any rule that has this property is called a RECURSIVE rule. The rule says that one NP can have another NP (a possessor phrase) embedded inside it; but it also implies that the possessor NP itself can contain a possessor NP, and so on. In this way, the rule in (31) captures another important fact about the genitive construction: there is no set limit to the number of possessor NPs which can be nested one inside the other, as indicated in (28d) and (29d). This rule would assign the structure shown in (32) to the NP in (28d).

(32)

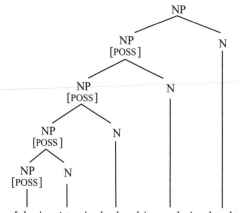

John-'s sister-'s husband-'s uncle-'s daughter

English has a second type of possessive construction using the preposition *of*, as in *the father of the bride*. The phrase *of the bride* is a normal PP, and this example could be generated by the rules we have stated in (25). We have already seen that these rules can recursively embed a PP within a PP; the same pattern can occur with possessive PPs, as illustrated in (33):

(33)   a friend of a friend of a friend

6.5   English NP structure (continued)

The structure of the English NP is unusually complex, and we will not try to analyze it in any detail in this book. However, we will use some further examples from English to illustrate a few more general principles about Phrase Structure. Let us begin by considering the distribution of the "pronominal" element *one* in the following sentences:

(34)   a The [dancing fountain] in Kuching is smaller than the *one* in
          Singapore.
        b The [pretty girl] in the window is my sister, the *one* on the
          swing is my cousin.
        c The [old car] your brother tried to sell me was a total wreck,
          but the *one* my neighbor showed me actually runs.

If we assume that only constituents can be replaced by a pronominal element, the examples in (34) suggest that adjective modifiers form a constituent with the noun that they modify. This constituent is commonly labeled N′ (pronounced "N-bar"). A similar pattern seems to emerge with PP complements:

(35)   a The present [King of Bhutan] is more popular than the previous
          one.
        b The president's public [reaction to the news] was much calmer
          than his private *one*.
        c This [request for help] is the last *one* we will consider.

Without trying to account for every detail at this point, these facts suggest that the Phrase Structure rules should look something like (36). A tree diagram showing an NP that could be generated by these rules is given in (37).

(36)   NP → Det   N′
        N′ → (AP)   N   (PP)

(37)

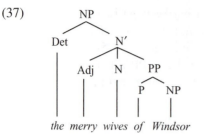

the merry wives of Windsor

The N′ constituent in these rules may seem like an odd sort of unit. Its head is the same N which is the head of NP; thus we might say that N′ and NP are CONCENTRIC. It is smaller than a complete phrase, but bigger than a single word. Such intermediate-level categories (N′, V′, etc.) have been identified in a number of languages, and some linguists assume they are used in all languages. However, in this book we will use these categories only where there is clear positive evidence for a distinct layer of constituent structure.

6.6   Conclusion

In addition to the head noun, most languages allow an NP to contain determiners and/or possessor phrases. Possessors are typically expressed as either NPs or PPs, either of which creates a structure which is potentially recursive.

Languages vary considerably in the number and type of complements and modifiers that may occur within a single NP. English is probably more liberal than most, allowing very complex NP structures. In languages which impose greater restrictions, it is fairly common for speakers to use a relative clause construction when they want to express more (or more complex) modifiers than would otherwise be allowed. For this reason, our discussion of relative clauses in chapter 12 will bring us back to the structure of the NP.

Practice exercise

Review ex. 3C (Ngbaka)

Exercises

6A Agatu (Nigeria; Roberts 1999, ex. 7.4; tone not marked)
Write a set of PS rules which will generate all of the following examples, and draw PS trees for # 5, 8, and 12. Use annotations to show all Grammatical

Relations. (Note: assume that the prefix labeled "GEN" is inserted by a rule
of morphology.)

1. ɔi   wa.
    child came
    'The child came.'

2. ewo wa   ɔlɛ.
    dog came compound
    'The dog came to the compound (i.e. to the houses round one courtyard).'

3. ada   wa.
    father came
    'Father came.'

4. ɔi   ma ewo.
    child saw dog
    'The child saw the dog.'

5. ada   g-ɔi   ɛpa wa.
    father GEN-child two came
    'The father of the two children came.'

6. ɔi   ma ewo g-ada.
    child saw dog GEN-father
    'The child saw the father's dog.'

7. ɔi   ma ewo ɛpa.
    child saw dog two
    'The child saw two dogs.'

8. ada   ma ewo ɛpa g-ɔi.
    father saw dog two GEN-child
    'Father saw the child's two dogs.'

9. ɔi   ma ɔlɛ.
    child saw compound
    'The child saw the compound.'

10. ada   g-ɔlɛ   ma ɛhi g-ɔi.
    father GEN-compound saw pot GEN-child
    'The compound-head (lit. father-of-compound) saw the child's pot.'

11. ewo ma ɔi g-ada   g-ɔlɛ.
    dog saw child GEN-father GEN-compound
    'The dog saw the compound-head's child.'

12. ewo ɛpa g-ada   g-ɔlɛ   wa.
    dog two GEN-father GEN-compound came
    'The compound-head's two dogs came.'

6B Bariba (Benin, W. Africa; Roberts 1999, ex. 7.5)
Write a set of PS rules which will generate the following examples, and draw
PS trees for # 9 and 10. (Note: assume that =*n* is a CLITIC post-position;

that is, your rules should treat it as a separate word belonging to category P. See chapter 17 for a discussion of clitics.)

1. sabii   'Sabi'
    Sabii

2. sabii=n   kurɔ   'Sabi's wife'
    Sabii=POSS wife

3. durɔ   'man'
    man

4. durɔ wi   'that man'
    man that

5. durɔ boko   'big man'
    man big

6. durɔ wi=n   kurɔ   'that man's wife'
    man that=POSS wife

7. durɔ boko=n   kurɔ   'the big man's wife'
    man big=POSS wife

8. durɔ geo   wi   'that good man'
    man good that

9. durɔ geo   wi=n   kurɔ   'that good man's wife'
    man good that=POSS wife

10. sabii=n   kurɔ geo   wi   'that good wife of Sabi'
    Sabii=POSS wife good that

11. sabii=n   wɔnɔ   geo 'Sabi's good younger brother'
    Sabii=POSS younger.brother good

6C Amele (PNG; Roberts 1999, ex. 7.7)
Based on the following examples, describe the structure of NPs in Amele. In addition to a prose description, you should include PS rules which will generate all of the examples and tree diagrams for # 3, 4, 7, 8, and 12. Use annotations to show all Grammatical Relations.

1. jo   nag   eu   'that small house'
    house small that

2. ho caub oso   'a white pig'
    pig white a

3. uqa na ho   'his pig'
    3sg of pig

4. Dege na jo   'Dege's house'
    Dege of house

5. *uqa ho   ('his pig')
    3sg pig

6.	*Dege jo				('Dege's house')
	Dege house				
7.	ija cot-i				'my brother'
	1sg brother-1sg.POSS				
8.	Dege cot-ig				'Dege's brother'
	Dege brother-3sg.POSS				
9.	*ija na cot-i				('my brother')
	1sg of brother-1sg.POSS				
10.	*Dege na cot-ig				('Dege's brother')
	Dege of brother-3sg.POSS				
11.	Dege cot-ig	na ho			'Dege's brother's pig'
	Dege brother-3sg.POSS of pig				
12.	ija cot-i	na jo	ben		'my brother's big house'
	1sg brother-1sg.POSS of house big				

Additional exercises

Merrifield et al. (1987) prob. 151, 172, 173
Healey (1990b) ex. F.4, 5, 6, 15

Notes

1. The examples in (1–6) are taken from Radford (1988:176ff.); (4b,c) have been modified.
2. This discussion is patterned after Bickford (1998, ch. 7).
3. Note that even in (15a) the outer parentheses mark the intensifier plus adjective as forming a single unit.
4. See ch. 10 for a discussion of this construction.
5. Of course, –'s is not a normal affix but rather a CLITIC, as discussed in ch. 17.

7 Case and agreement

As we pointed out in chapter 5, word order (or position in the Phrase Structure) is the most important clue for identifying Grammatical Relations in English: subjects normally come before the verb, direct objects immediately after the verb, etc. This kind of clue would not be very helpful for a language like Malayalam, in which (as the examples in (1) show) word order is relatively free. Yet speakers of Malayalam must have some way of distinguishing subjects from objects, or they would never be able to understand each other.

Every language must have some way of indicating the Grammatical Relations of clausal elements, and of distinguishing one relation from another. As we have seen, prepositions are often used to mark oblique arguments and adjuncts. For identifying the term relations (subjects and objects), three basic devices are available: word order, CASE marking, and AGREEMENT. Any particular language will make use of one or more of these options. Since we have already introduced some basic ideas about word order in earlier chapters, this chapter will focus on the other two options, beginning with case.

7.1   Case

How are subjects, direct objects, and secondary objects identified in the following Malayalam sentences?

(1)   **Malayalam** (Dravidian, southern India; adapted from Mohanan 1982, 1983)
    a kuṭṭi kaṟaññu.
       child cried
       'The child cried.'

    b puucca uraṇṇi.
       cat   slept
       'The cat slept.'

    c kuṭṭi aana-ye ṇuḷḷi.
       child elephant pinched
       'The child pinched the elephant.'

d kuṭṭi-ye aana   ikkiḷiyaakki.
 child elephant tickled
 'The elephant tickled the child.'

e eli-ye puucca ṭiṇṇu.
 rat   cat   ate
 'The cat ate the rat.'

f kuṭṭi amma-kkə aana-ye wittu.
 child mother   elephant sold
 'The child sold the elephant to Mother.'

g kuṭṭi-kkə puucca-ye aana   koṭuttu.
 child   cat   elephant gave
 'The elephant gave the cat to the child.'

h amma pakṣi-ye puucca-kkə koṭuttu.
 mother bird   cat   gave
 'Mother gave the bird to the cat.'

As these examples illustrate, Malayalam relies on noun morphology for identifying Grammatical Relations: direct objects take the suffix *–ye*,[1] recipient secondary objects take the suffix *-kkə*, and subjects are "unmarked" (no suffix is added).

Affixes of this kind, which are added to a noun or NP to indicate the Grammatical Relation of that NP, are referred to as CASE markers. More generally, any system in which the Grammatical Relation of an NP is indicated by some kind of morphological marking on the NP itself is referred to as a CASE SYSTEM. For example, the first and third person pronouns in English appear in variant forms which reflect case distinctions (*I, me, my*; *he, him, his*; *we, us, our*; etc.).[2] This is virtually all that remains of the case system which affected nouns as well as pronouns in Old English.

7.1.1   Grammatical case vs. semantic case

The case marking of the nouns in (1) is determined by the Grammatical Relations which the NPs bear in the clause. Case affixes of this type are sometimes referred to as GRAMMATICAL CASE markers, to distinguish them from SEMANTIC CASE markers, which are determined on the basis of semantic roles.

Grammatical cases are normally used only for TERM relations (SUBJ, OBJ, OBJ₂). A case form that is used to mark direct objects (like Malayalam *–ye* in examples (1c), (1g), and (1h)) is traditionally referred to as the ACCUSATIVE case. A case form like Malayalam *-kkə* (examples (1f), (1g), (1h)) that is used for "indirect objects," i.e. recipient secondary objects, is traditionally referred to as the DATIVE case. A case form that is used for subjects is normally called the NOMINATIVE case; thus we could say that the nominative case is unmarked in Malayalam, because no suffix is added to the subject.

Malayalam also has semantic case markers; some examples are given in the following sentences:

(2) a joon̯-*inte* kuṭṭi aana-ye ṇuḷḷi.
     John's   child elephant pinched
     'John's child pinched the elephant.'

    b kuṭṭi skuuḷ-*il* pooyi.
     child school went
     'The child went to school.'

    c amma kuṭṭi-ye waṭi-*yaal* aṭiccu.
     mother child   stick   beat
     'Mother beat the child with a stick.'

Semantic cases are normally used for oblique arguments (and perhaps some adjuncts). If a special case marker is used for possessors (like Malayalam –*inte* in (2a)), it is normally called the GENITIVE. If a special case marker is used for locations (like Malayalam -*il* in (2b)), it is often called the LOCATIVE. If a special case marker is used for instruments (like Malayalam -*(y)aal* in (2c)), it is normally called the INSTRUMENTAL. The Malayalam case suffixes are summarized in (3):[3]

(3)   **Malayalam case suffixes**

	Case name	Suffix	Primary usage
GRAMMATICAL	nominative	-∅	SUBJ
CASES	accusative	-*(y)e*	OBJ
	dative	-*(kk)ə*	OBJ$_2$
SEMANTIC CASES	genitive	-*inte* ~ -*(u)ṭe*	possessor
	instrumental	-*(y)aal*	instrument
	locative	-*il*	location

In addition to the use of semantic case, another common way of marking oblique arguments and adjuncts is through the use of prepositions or (as in Malayalam) POST-POSITIONS. Sometimes there are two different ways to indicate the same semantic role. For example, the instrument role is marked by semantic case in (4a), but by a post-position in (4b). The two sentences have the same meaning, but (4a) would be used primarily in formal speech, while (4b) would be preferred in informal speech (K. P. Mohanan, p. c.).

(4)   a amma kuṭṭi-ye   waṭi-*yaal*   aṭiccu.
        mother child-ACC stick-INSTR beat
        'Mother beat the child with a stick.'

b amma kuṭṭi-ye   waṭi *konṭə* aṭiccu.
mother child-ACC stick with   beat
'Mother beat the child with a stick.'

7.1.2   Ergativity

Most languages that have grammatical case markers follow one of two basic patterns. The more common of these patterns can be observed in English. As mentioned above, case marking in modern English is found only in pronouns, so our interest will be focused on the distribution of the pronominal forms in examples like the following:

(5)   a I dance.
       b He dances.
       c I like him.
       d He likes me.

As these examples illustrate, subject pronouns have the same form (*I* and *he*) whether the clause is intransitive, as in (5a,b), or transitive, as in (5c,d). Following standard terminology, we would call this the nominative form. Direct objects occur in a different form (*me* and *him*). We could call this the accusative form. This pattern of case marking is referred to as a Nominative–Accusative system, or ACCUSATIVE for short. Example (6), showing the distribution of English pronoun forms in transitive vs. intransitive clauses, illustrates the Nominative–Accusative pattern.

(6)   **Standard English**
       INTRANSITIVE SUBJECT: *I, he*
       TRANSITIVE   AGENT: *I, he*   PATIENT: *me, him*
                     [nominative]   **[accusative]**

Now imagine that you are shipwrecked on a South Pacific island where you find people speaking a previously undescribed variety of Pidgin English, which we will call "Pseudo-English." You record the following utterances:

(7)   a mi dans.   'I dance.'
       b him dans.   'He dances.'
       c ai laik him. 'I like him.'
       d hi laik mi.   'He likes me.'

In these examples, we see that direct objects of transitive clauses take the same form as subjects of intransitive clauses, namely *mi* or *him*. Subjects of transitive clauses take a special form, *ai* or *hi*. This kind of case-marking pattern, summarized in (8), is referred to as an ERGATIVE system. The form used for transitive subjects is called ERGATIVE case, while the form used for transitive objects and intransitive subjects is called ABSOLUTIVE case.

(8)   **"Pseudo-English"**

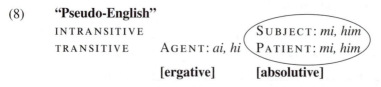

INTRANSITIVE   SUBJECT: *mi, him*
TRANSITIVE   AGENT: *ai, hi*   PATIENT: *mi, him*
              [ergative]   **[absolutive]**

The accusative and ergative patterns are compared in (9), using "S" for the subject of an intransitive clause, "A" (Agent) for the subject of a transitive clause, and "P" (Patient) for the object of a transitive clause. As this diagram illustrates, the defining characteristic of the ergative pattern is a unique case marker for transitive subjects, while the defining characteristic of the accusative pattern is a unique case marker for transitive objects.

(9)   (based on Comrie 1978:332)

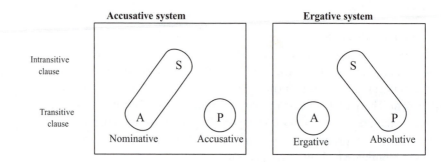

Based on the examples in (1), how should we classify the case-marking pattern of Malayalam? We can see that subjects get the same marking (namely -Ø) whether the clause is intransitive, as in (1a,b), transitive, as in (1c-e), or ditransitive, as in (1f-h). Direct objects get a special case marker (-*ye*) which is distinct from the marking for subjects. This distribution, which is summarized in (10), clearly fits the Nominative–Accusative pattern.

(10)   **Malayalam**

INTRANSITIVE   SUBJECT: -*Ø*
TRANSITIVE   AGENT: -*Ø*   PATIENT: -*ye*
              [nominative]   **[accusative]**

Based on the examples in (11), how would you classify the case-marking pattern of Walmatjari?

(11)   **Walmatjari** (Australia; adapted from Healey 1990b, ex. E-17; data
        from Hudson 1978)
        a parri pa   laparni.
          boy AUX   run
          'The boy ran.'

b manga pa   laparni.
  girl   AUX run
  'The girl ran.'

c wirlka pa   laparni.
  lizard AUX   run
  'The lizard ran.'

d parri pa   pinya manga-ngu.
  boy AUX hit   girl
  'The girl hit the boy.'

e wirlka pa   nyanya parri-ngu.
  lizard AUX   see   boy
  'The boy saw the lizard.'

These examples show that in Walmatjari, direct objects of transitive clauses get the same case marking as subjects of intransitive clauses, namely -Ø. Subjects of transitive clauses get a special case marker (-*ngu*). This distribution, which is summarized in (12), follows the ergative pattern.

(12)   **Walmatjari**

INTRANSITIVE   SUBJECT: -Ø
TRANSITIVE   AGENT: -*ngu*   PATIENT: -Ø
               [ergative]   **[absolutive]**

The Malayalam and Walmatjari data illustrate an interesting fact about case systems. If a language has an "unmarked" case, or zero case marker, it is most likely to be the case that is used for intransitive subjects: the nominative in an accusative language like Malayalam, and the absolutive in an ergative language like Walmatjari.[4]

7.1.3   Split ergativity

In some languages we find both the ergative and accusative case marking patterns. For example, pronouns may take Nominative–Accusative marking while common nouns take Ergative–Absolutive marking; or animate nouns may take Nominative–Accusative marking while inanimate nouns take Ergative–Absolutive marking.

The term "SPLIT ERGATIVITY" refers to a situation in which both ergative and non-ergative patterns are found in the grammar of a single language. In other words, one sub-system of the grammar follows an ergative pattern while a different sub-system does not. A typical example is found in Pitjantjatjara, another Australian language:

(13)   **Pitjantjatjara** (Australia; Merrifield et al. 1987, prob. 208)

a kuḻpir-pa ŋalyapityaṉu.
kangaroo came
'The kangaroo came.'

b yuṉṯal-pa pakanu.
daughter   got.up
'(My) daughter got up.'

c ŋali   ŋalyapityaṉu.
we(DUAL) came
'We (2) came.'

d ɲura pakanu.
you   got.up
'You got up.'

e ampin-tu kuḻpir-pa ɲaṉu.
Ampin   kangaroo saw
'Ampin saw the kangaroo.'

f ɲura yuṉṯal-pa kulinu.
you   daughter   heard
'You heard my daughter.'

g kuḻpir-tu ɲura-ɲa ɲaṉu.
kangaroo you   saw
'The kangaroo saw you.'

h yuṉṯal-tu ŋali-ɲa   kulinu.
daughter   we(DUAL) heard
'My daughter heard us (2).'

i ŋali   kuḻpir-pa ɲaṉu.
we(DUAL) kangaroo saw
'We (2) saw the kangaroo.'

The case endings for nouns and pronouns are listed in (14). This chart shows that pronouns follow a Nominative–Accusative pattern, with the same (zero) case marker being used for intransitive subjects and transitive subjects and a different marker (-ɲa) being used for transitive objects. Common nouns and proper names, on the other hand, follow an ergative pattern, with the same case marker (-pa) being used for intransitive subjects and transitive objects and a different marker (-tu) being used for transitive subjects.

(14)

Pitjantjatjara case markers	**pronouns**	**common nouns/proper names**
intransitive subjects (S)	–∅	–pa
transitive subjects (A)	–∅	–tu
transitive objects (P)	–ɲa	–pa

Some further examples of split-ergative case-marking systems, taken from Dixon (1979:87), are listed in (15). The Cashinahua third person pronouns illustrate a TRIPARTITE pattern, in which three distinct forms occur (15b).

(15)   a **Dyirbal** (Australia)

	1st and 2nd person pronouns	**3rd person pronouns**	**common nouns/ proper names**
intransitive subjects (S)	–∅	–∅	–∅
transitive subjects (A)	–∅	–ŋgu	–ŋgu
transitive objects (P)	–ɲa	–∅	–∅

b **Cashinahua** (Peru)

	1st and 2nd person pronouns	**3rd person pronouns**	**common nouns/ proper names**
intransitive subjects (S)	–∅	– *habu*	–∅
transitive subjects (A)	–∅	– *habũ*	–nasalization
transitive objects (P)	–*a*	– *haa*	–∅

These examples illustrate split systems based on the PERSON–ANIMACY HIERARCHY, which is shown in (16). In almost every instance of split ergativity in which case marking is based on the inherent properties of the noun phrases themselves, categories near the left (= higher) end of the scale will follow the accusative pattern, while categories near the right (= lower) end of the scale will follow the ergative pattern. The dividing point between the two patterns, however, varies from language to language, as we have already seen.

(16)   PERSON–ANIMACY HIERARCHY[5]

1st person pronoun	2nd person pronoun	3rd person pronoun	Proper nouns	Common nouns		
				human	animate	inanimate

(high)   (low)

It is tempting to ask why languages should be so consistent in this respect. One might suppose that it would be just as easy for pronouns to follow the ergative pattern while common nouns follow the accusative pattern, or for proper names to follow one pattern while all other NPs follow the other; but this does not seem to happen. A number of authors have suggested that the motivating factor is the relative likelihood of a participant's functioning as agent vs. patient. Since inanimate objects rarely function as transitive agents, this is the situation that requires a distinctive marker (ergative case). Human participants (e.g. those generally named by first and second person pronouns) frequently serve as agents, so what is uniquely marked is the situation where they serve as patients (accusative case).[6]

This explanation seems quite plausible in the case of inanimate common nouns, but it is not so persuasive as a basis for distinguishing pronouns

from proper names, or first and second person pronouns from third person
animate pronouns, all of which seem equally likely to function as agents.
Moreover, as pointed out by Wierzbicka (1981), frequency alone cannot
be the relevant factor.[7] There is no reason to think that first and second
person pronouns occur more often as agents than patients in natural speech;
Wierzbicka suggests that the opposite may, in fact, be true, at least for the
first person. Perhaps a more general concept of "newsworthiness" would
prove more useful than raw frequency. A speaker will take a special interest
in events that affect himself (first person) or other people with whom he can
identify (including the addressee, second person). This inherent interest
may help to explain the tendency to mark these participants in a special way
when they are affected by an action, i.e. when they occur as patients.

Split ergativity can also be conditioned by tense or aspect. Hindi is a
well-known case. As the examples in (17–18) show, the case marking of
the transitive agent depends on aspect: it takes ergative case when the verb
is marked for perfective aspect, nominative in other aspects. Note that the
ergative case marker -*ne* is distinct from both the genitive (-*ka*) and instrumental (-*se*). This is interesting because in many languages ergative case
marking is identical to either the genitive or the instrumental.

(17) a Mai-ne bite saal ek ghar   banawaayaa.
         I-ERG last year one house(NOM) make-CAUSE-PFV-3sg.MASC[8]
         'I had someone build a house last year.'

      b Mai   agale saal ek ghar   banawaungaa.
         I(NOM) next year one house(NOM) make-CAUSE-FUT-1sg.MASC
         'I will have someone build a house next year.'

(18) a Raam-ne kal   apane bete-ko (chhaḍi-se) maaraa.
         Ram-ERG adjacent.day self's son-ACC stick-INSTR beat-PFV-3sg
         'Ram beat his son yesterday (with a stick).'

      b Raam   kal   apane bete-ko (chhaḍi-se) maaregaa.
         Ram(NOM) adjacent.day self's son-ACC stick-INSTR beat-FUT-3sg
         'Ram will beat his son tomorrow (with a stick).'

Based on this very small sample of data, can we say anything about
the case marking of direct objects in Hindi? At first glance, the evidence
seems to be contradictory: the object takes accusative case in (18), but
nominative case in (17). It turns out that the case marking of objects is
sensitive to animacy: accusative case is used only for animate objects, a
pattern consistent with our discussion of the animacy hierarchy above. This
pattern is found in a number of widely scattered languages, but is especially
characteristic of south Asian languages, including Malayalam. Note the
following contrast (Mohanan 1982:539):

(19)   a puucca eli-ye   ṭinṇu.
              cat   rat-ACC   ate
              'The cat ate the rat.'

         b puucca roṭṭi   ṭinṇu.
              cat   bread(NOM)   ate
              'The cat ate the bread.'

This contrast is obligatory. Sentence (19a) would be ungrammatical if the nominative form of 'rat' were used, because 'rat' is animate. Sentence (19b) would be ungrammatical if the accusative form of 'bread' were used, because 'bread' is inanimate.

7.2   Agreement

AGREEMENT is a general term used to describe a situation in which the grammatical features of a noun or noun phrase determine the morphological shape of a word that is syntactically related to the N or NP in some way (Lehmann 1988; Haspelmath 2002:65ff). This syntactic relationship may be anaphoric, as when a pronoun agrees with its antecedent (see chapter 8), or it may involve a relation between a head and its dependent, as when a verb agrees with its subject or object.[9]

Other examples of heads that agree with dependent NPs include possessed nouns, which in some languages agree with their possessor NP, and prepositions, which in a few languages agree with their "object" NP. The features of the NP which may be reflected in the form of the agreeing head are gender, number, and person.

Within a noun phrase, the reverse pattern can occur: one or more dependents within the NP may agree with their head noun (N). These dependents typically include adjectives, determiners, and/or possessive pronouns. Some linguists use the term CONCORD to refer to this kind of agreement. The features of the head noun which may be reflected in the agreeing dependent forms are gender, number, and case.

7.2.1   Verb agreement

VERB AGREEMENT refers to a system in which the form of the verb reflects the person, number, and/or gender of one or more arguments. Verbs normally agree only with TERMS, i.e. arguments which bear the Grammatical Relations of subject, object, or secondary object. If a verb agrees with only one argument, it will be normally the subject; if two, they will be the subject and direct (or primary) object; if three, they will be the subject, primary object, and secondary object.

Modern English still retains some traces of the old subject–verb agreement pattern, which is more fully preserved in other Germanic languages. We used this fact as one of the tests for identifying the subject of a sentence in chapter 4. When the agreement features (specifically number and person) of the verb do not match those of the subject NP, the result is ungrammatical:

(20)   a *John are my cousin.
        b *John am my cousin.
        c *I is a native speaker.

Portuguese is another language in which the verb agrees with its subject. Unlike English, Portuguese verbs show agreement marking in all persons and most tenses. Only the present tense forms are listed in (21).

(21)   **Portuguese**

eu falo   'I speak'   nós falamos 'we speak'
tu falas[10] 'you (sg) speak'   vós falais   'you (pl) speak'
ele fala   'he speaks'   eles falam   'they speak'

Nahuatl (or Aztec), from Mexico, is a language in which a transitive verb agrees with both subject and direct object, as illustrated in (22b). An intransitive verb, of course, agrees only with the subject (22a). Notice that, in addition to the agreement prefixes which register the person and number of the subject and object, the verb also bears a plural agreement suffix -(e)h when the subject is plural. The agreement affixes are summarized in the chart in (22c).

(22)   **Huasteca Nahuatl** (Eastern dialect; Beller and Beller 1979; allomorphic alternations omitted)

a Intransitive verbs

ni-kotʃi   'I sleep'   ti-kotʃi-h   'we sleep'
ti-kotʃi   'you (sg) sleep'   in-kotʃi-h   'you (pl) sleep'
Ø-kotʃi   'he sleeps'   Ø-kotʃi-h   'they sleep'

b Transitive verbs

ni-mic-ita   'I see you (sg)'   ti-netʃ-ita 'you (sg) see me'
Ø-mic-ita   'he sees you (sg)'   ti-k-ita   'you (sg) see him'
ti-mic-ita-h   'we see you (sg)'   ti-tetʃ-ita 'you (sg) see us'
Ø-mic-ita-h   'they see you (sg)' ti-kin-ita   'you (sg) see them'

c Position class chart:

Subj-Agr	Obj-Agr	root	Subj-number
ni- '1sg'	*netʃ-* '1sg'		*-Ø* 'singular'
ti- '2sg'	*mic-* '2sg'		*-(e)h* 'plural'
Ø- '3sg'	*k-* '3sg'		
ti- '1pl'	*tetʃ-* '1pl'		
in- '2pl'	*metʃ-* '2pl'		
Ø- '3pl'	*kin-* '3pl'		

An example of a language which agrees with subject, primary object, and secondary object is Southern Tiwa.[11] Agreement with these three arguments is shown in a single portmanteau prefix, as illustrated in (23–24).

(23)   **Southern Tiwa** (North American; Allen and Frantz 1983)

    a *bey*-mu-ban
       2sg:1sg-see-PAST
       'You (sg) saw me.'

    b *a*-mu-ban
       2sg:3sg-see-PAST
       'You (sg) saw him.'

    c *i*-mu-ban
       1sg:2sg-see-PAST
       'I saw you (sg).'

    d *ti*-mu-ban
       1sg:3sg-see-PAST
       'I saw him.'

(24)   a *ka*-khwien-wia-ban
       1sg:2sg:3sg-dog-give-PAST
       'I gave you (sg) the dog.'

    b *kam*-khwien-wia-ban[12]
       1sg:2sg:3pl-dog-give-PAST
       'I gave you (sg) the dogs.'

    c *ben*-khwien-wia-ban
       2sg:1sg:3sg-dog-give-PAST
       'You (sg) gave me the dog.'

    d *ta*-khwien-wia-ban   seuanide
       1sg:3sg:3sg-dog-give-PAST man
       'I gave the man the dog.'

As noted above, verb agreement normally reflects the grammatical features of person, number, and/or gender. An example of verb agreement which reflects gender is found in Russian, where the verb agrees with its subject for person and number in non-past tenses, and for gender and number in past tenses.

(25)   **Russian verb paradigm** 'to read' (Sussex 1992)

	PRESENT	FUTURE PFV	PAST PFV
1 sg (m/f/n)	ja čitáju	ja pročitáju	ja pročitál/-a/-o
2 sg (m/f/n)	ty čitáeš'	ty pročitáeš'	ty pročitál/-a/-o
3 sg masc	on čitáet	on pročitáet	on pročitál
3 sg fem	ona čitáet	ona pročitáet	ona pročitála
3 sg neut	ono čitáet	ono pročitáet	ono pročitálo
1 pl	my čitáem	my pročitáem	my pročitáli
2 pl	vy čitáete	vy pročitáete	vy pročitáli
3 pl	oni čitájut	oni pročitájut	oni pročitáli

7.2.2   Ergative agreement systems

In most of the languages we have looked at, including English, transitive and intransitive verbs show the same pattern of subject agreement, as illustrated in (26). Agreement in such languages can be said to follow the Nominative–Accusative pattern, because transitive and intransitive subjects trigger the same agreement marking while transitive objects are treated differently (either no agreement, as in English, or a different agreement marker). But the normal way to identify the agreement affixes in these languages is simply "subject agreement" or "object agreement," reserving the terms "nominative" and "accusative" for case markers.

(26)   a John *runs* every morning.
         b We *run* every morning.
         c John *eats* noodles every morning.
         d We *eat* noodles every morning.

However, there are other languages in which verb agreement follows the ergative pattern: intransitive subjects and transitive objects require one kind of agreement marking, while transitive subjects require another. One such language is Tabulahan, an Austronesian language of Sulawesi, Indonesia. The verb in Tabulahan carries two agreement markers in a basic transitive clause (28), but only one in an intransitive clause (27). One set of suffixes is used to agree with the subject of an intransitive clause or the object of a transitive clause, while a distinct set of prefixes is used to agree with the subject of a transitive clause. For example, the suffix *-ä'* is used for a first singular intransitive subject in (27a) and a first singular object in (28a); but the first singular subject of the transitive clause in (28b) requires the prefix *ku-*.

(27)   **Tabulahan** (Indonesia; Robin McKenzie, p.c.)

a Manaho-mi-ä'   naung di   tampo.
   fall-PFV-1sg.ABS down LOC ground
   'I fell to the ground.'

b La   le'ba'-koa'   dinoa?
   FUT leave-2pl.ABS now
   'Are you (pl.) leaving now?'

c Menge hahe-Ø   angkanna änä'.
   CONT sleep-3pl.ABS all   child
   'All the children are sleeping.'

d mao-ang.
   go-1pl.EX.ABS
   'We (excl.) are going.'

(28)   a Na-keki'-ä'   kampihsi'.
           3.ERG-bite-1sg.ABS mosquito
           'A mosquito bit me.'

b Haling ku-painsang[ng]i-koa'.
   already 1sg.ERG-cause.to.know-2pl.ABS
   'I have already told all of you.'

c La   malaraka uN-[ng]allingk-ä'   uhase?
   FUT possible 2pl.ERG-buy.for-1sg.ABS axe
   'Would you (pl) be able to buy me an axe?'

d uN-po-sabua'-ang.
   2sg.ERG-CAUS-servant-1pl.EX.ABS
   'You (sg) make us your servants.'

e dinoa la   ki-posolam-o.
   now FUT 1pl.EX.ERG-accompany-2sg.ABS
   'Now we will accompany you (sg).'

In order to see the patterns in a complex paradigm of this kind, it is often helpful to lay out the forms in some kind of work-chart. The chart in (29) lists the agreement affixes which occur in examples (27–28) according to their functions: S (intransitive subject), A (transitive subject), and P (transitive object). There are gaps in the chart, due to the limited amount of data in these examples, but we can see that wherever we have all three forms for a given person and number, the S and P forms are the same while the A form is different. For this reason we refer to the two sets of affixes as ergative vs. absolutive agreement, rather than subject vs. object agreement. The complete set of Tabulahan agreement affixes is displayed in the partial position class chart in (30).[13]

(29)

FUNCTION	1sg	2sg	3sg	1du.in	1pl.in	1pl.ex	2pl	3pl
S	*-ä'*					*-ang*	*-koa'*	*-Ø*
A	*ku-*	*uN-*	*na-*			*ki-*	*uN-*	
P	*-ä'*	*-o*				*-ang*	*-koa'*	

(30)

Ergative agreement	Root + other affixes	Absolutive agreement
ku- '1sg'		*-ä'* '1sg'
uN-/mu- '2sg'		*-o/-ko* '2sg'
na- '3sg'		*-Ø/-e'* '3sg'
ta- '1du.in'		*-ingke* '1du.in'
ta- '1pl.in'		*-ingkea'* '1pl.in'
ki- '1pl.ex'		*-ang* '1pl.ex'
uN-/mu- '2pl'		*-koa'* '2pl'
na- '3pl'		*-Ø/-ii* '3pl'

Of course, the terms "absolutive" and "ergative" are also used for case markers. However, in referring to absolutive agreement and ergative agreement, we are not saying that verbs in Tabulahan are marked for case. It is important to remember that case is, by definition, marked on NPs; verbs cannot take case marking unless they have been "nominalized" (see chapter 13). The use of similar labels for case and agreement systems reflects a similarity in function: both case and agreement can be used to distinguish subjects from objects. When either system marks S and P the same but marks A differently, we refer to these markers as "absolutive" and "ergative," respectively.

7.2.3   Possessor agreement

A number of languages have possessive affixes or clitics (see chapter 17) which attach to the possessed noun and indicate the person and number of the possessor. We refer to such patterns as POSSESSOR AGREEMENT only when the possessive markers can be used redundantly in the presence of a separate word or phrase referring to the same possessor. If the possessive marker *replaces* the possessor NP, i.e. if the two are in complementary distribution, it should probably not be analyzed as an agreement marker. This issue is discussed further in chapter 17.

In the Amele language of Papua New Guinea, possessor agreement indicates inalienable possession. Notice that the possessive suffix on the head noun co-occurs with an independent possessor NP.

(31)   **Amele** (PNG; Roberts 1999)
    a ija cot-i
      1sg brother-1sG
      'my brother'

b Dege cot-ig
Dege brother-3sG
'Dege's brother'

Another example is found in the Buru language of eastern Indonesia. The examples in (32) all contain a free pronoun (the possessor phrase) followed by the head noun, which bears a possessor agreement suffix.

(32)   **Buru** (Maluku, Indonesia; C. Grimes, unpublished lecture notes)
1 sg	yako faha-ng	'my hand'
2 sg	kae faha-m	'your (sg) hand'
3 sg	ringe faha-n	'his hand'
1 pl incl	kita faha-nan	'our (incl.) hands'
1 pl excl	kami faha-nam	'our (excl.) hands'
2 pl	kimi faha-nim	'your (pl) hands'
3 pl	sira faha-nin	'their hands'

7.2.4   Agreement with N

In many languages, certain dependents within a noun phrase are morphologically marked to agree with the number and gender of the head noun. In Portuguese, for example, the list of dependents which must agree with their head N for number and gender includes determiners, modifying adjectives, possessive pronouns, and the numerals 'one' and 'two.'

The examples in (33) involve the nouns *menino* 'boy' and *vestido* 'dress,' which are grammatically masculine, and *menina* 'girl' and *galinha* 'hen,' which are grammatically feminine. As we can see, the form of the demonstrative meaning 'this' depends on the gender of the head noun: *este* for masculine; *esta* for feminine. Similarly, the adjectives end in *–o* when the head noun is masculine, and in *–a* when the head noun is feminine. Moreover, whenever the head noun bears the plural suffix *–s*, the demonstratives and adjectives are also marked for plural number.

(33)   **Portuguese NPs** (adapted from Healey 1990b, ex. E.2)
a	este menino gordo	'this fat boy'
b	esta menina bonita	'this pretty girl'
c	estes meninos gordos	'these fat boys'
d	estas meninas bonitas	'these pretty girls'
e	este vestido bonito	'this pretty dress'
f	esta galinha gorda	'this fat hen'
g	estes vestidos bonitos	'these pretty dresses'
h	estas galinhas gordas	'these fat hens'

Case (as discussed in the first section of this chapter) is determined by the function of the noun phrase within a clause, and is assigned to the NP as a whole. In many languages, case is marked only once within each NP, e.g. on the head noun, or on a determiner, or with the addition of a separate particle or clitic. In other languages, however, more than one element of the NP may be inflected for case, and when that happens each element must get the same case marking.

Kalkatungu is an example of a language in which determiners and modifiers (including possessor phrases) within an NP must agree with their head N for case, as illustrated in (34). Notice that the elements of the possessor phrase in (34c) bear two case markers: genitive marking the function of the possessor NP itself; and ergative indicating the function of the larger NP to which the possessor phrase belongs. This kind of "case stacking" is relatively rare, but does occur in a number of languages.[14]

(34)   **Kalkatungu** (Australia; Blake 1987:87)

    a tyipa-yi   thuku-yu yaun-tu   yanyi   itya-mi
      this-ERG dog-ERG big-ERG white.man-ABS bite-FUT
      'This big dog will bite the white man.'

    b kalpin-ku yaun-ku thuku
      man-GEN   big-GEN dog-ABS
      'the big man's dog'

    c kalpin-ku[wa]-thu yaun-ku[wa]-thu thuku-yu ityayi=ngi
      man-GEN-ERG   big-GEN-ERG   dog-ERG   bite=me.ABS
      'The big man's dog bit me.'

7.3   Conclusion

Case and agreement are two of the most important devices that languages use to identify Grammatical Relations within a clause. Case may also be used to identify the semantic role of oblique arguments or adjuncts; we refer to this as SEMANTIC CASE. Grammatical case systems (those that mark Grammatical Relations) tend to follow one of two major patterns: the ACCUSATIVE pattern, in which S and A get the same marking while P gets a distinct marking; or the ERGATIVE pattern, in which S and P get the same marking while A gets a distinct marking. In some languages both patterns of case marking can be found; this situation is referred to as SPLIT ERGATIVITY.

Verbs normally agree only with term arguments. If the verb agrees with only one argument, it is normally the subject; if with two arguments, they will normally be the subject and primary object. However, verb agreement may also follow an ergative–absolutive pattern. Another very common type of agreement is between the head of a noun phrase and its modifiers and/or determiners. In this pattern the dependents are marked to agree with features of the head, whereas in verb agreement the head is marked to agree with features of its dependents (since the verb is the head of the clause).

Possessor agreement and preposition agreement (which we have not dis-cussed here) are less common; both patterns involve heads agreeing with NPs. The most common type of agreement pattern, found in every human language (as far as we know), is the agreement between a pronoun and its antecedent. This topic will be discussed in the next chapter.

Exercises

7A Quiché agreement (Guatemala; Larsen 1987; Trechsel 1993)[15]
Describe the verb agreement system of Quiché as revealed in the following examples, and provide a position class chart showing the structure of the verb. *Note*: the prefix *r-* is realized as *u:-* before consonants. You should ignore vowel length in affixes, which is morphophonemic, and the verbal suffixes which are glossed as SUFF. *Hint*: it may be helpful to make a work-chart of the agreement markers similar to that shown in (29) above.

1.　　a　x-at-b'iin-ik.
　　　　　PFV-2sg-walk-SUFF
　　　　　'you (sg) walked.'

　　　b　x-oj-b'iin-ik.
　　　　　PFV-1pl-walk-SUFF
　　　　　'we walked.'

　　　c　ka-Ø-b'iin-ik.
　　　　　IMPERF-3sg-walk-SUFF
　　　　　'he walks.'

　　　d　k(a)-e'-war-ik.
　　　　　IMPERF-3pl-sleep-SUFF
　　　　　'they sleep.'

　　　e　x-in-war-ik.
　　　　　PFV-1sg-sleep-SUFF
　　　　　'I slept.'

　　　f　laa ix　x-ix-tzaaq-ik?
　　　　　Q　2pl　PFV-2pl-fall-SUFF
　　　　　'Were you (pl) the ones who fell?'

2.　　a　x-at-qa-ch'ay-o.
　　　　　PFV-2sg-1pl-hit-SUFF
　　　　　'we hit you (sg).'

　　　b　x-oj-a-ch'ay-o.
　　　　　PFV-1pl-2sg-hit-SUFF
　　　　　'you (sg) hit us.'

     c jachin x-at-u-ch'ay-o?
      who   PFV-2sg-3sg-hit-SUFF
      'Who hit you (sg)?'

     d aree   ri at x-in-a-ch'ay-o.
      FOCUS the 2sg PFV-1sg-2sg-hit-SUFF
      'You (sg) were the one who hit me.'

     e x-Ø-ii-to'-o.
      PFV-3sg-2pl-help-SUFF
      'you (pl) helped him.'

     f k(a)-ix-r-il-o.
      IMPERF-2pl-3sg-see-SUFF
      'he/she sees you (pl).'

3.   a x-Ø-inw-il   ri aaq.
      PFV-3sg-1sg-see the pig
      'I saw the pig.'

     b ka-Ø-q'ab'ar   ri ixoq.
      IMPERF-3sg-get.drunk the woman
      'The woman gets drunk.'

     c k(a)-e'-q'ab'ar   ri ixoq-iib'.
      IMPERF-3pl-get.drunk the woman-PL
      'The women get drunk.'

     d x-Ø-u:-paq'   ri sii'   ri achii.
      PFV-3sg-3sg-split the firewood the man
      'The man split the firewood.'

     e jas x-Ø-u:-paq'   ri achii?
      what PFV-3sg-3sg-split the man
      'What did the man split?'

     f ee jachiin x-Ø-ki-tzaq   ki-jastaaq?
      pl who   PFV-3sg-3pl-lost 3pl-thing
      'Who are the ones who lost their thing(s)?'

7B Southern Azerbaijani case (Iran; Lee 1996)
Describe the case system of Iranian Azerbaijani as revealed in the following
examples. *Note*: vowel quality in suffixes is affected by "vowel harmony."
You should assume that /ə/ and /a/ are variant forms of the same vowel when
they occur in suffixes; and likewise for /ɨ/ and /i/. The consonants marked
with square brackets, [n] and [y], are inserted by a phonological rule and
can be ignored for the purposes of this problem.

1.   inək öldi.
      cow die
      'The cow died.'

2. Məməd inə[y]i öldürdi.
   Memed cow die-CAUS
   'Memed killed the cow (lit.: caused the cow to die).'

3. ev Ardabildə idi.
   house Ardabil was
   'The house was in Ardabil.'

4. saat altɨda evdən cixdɨ.
   hour six house came.out
   'He came out of the house at 6 o'clock.'

5. Fatma inəkinən evə qəyitdi.
   Fatma cow home returned
   'Fatma returned home with the cow.'

6. (siz) evdə kitabi oxursuz.
   2pl house book read-2pl
   'You are reading the book in the house.'

7. (siz) kitab oxursuz.
   2pl book read-2pl
   'You are reading a book.'

8. alma[n]i Məməddən aldɨm.
   apple Memed bought-1sg
   'I bought the apple(s) from Memed.'

9. kitablar Bakɨdan gəldilər.
   books Baku come
   'The books came from Baku.'

10. Bakɨ[y]a gedəcəksən?
    Baku go-FUT-2sg
    'Are you going to Baku?'

11. qɨz Məmədi gör-cək . . .
    girl Memed saw-when
    'As soon as the girl saw Memed . . .'

12. oğlan qɨza alma[n]i verdi.
    boy girl apple gave
    'The boy gave the apple to the girl.'

13. Məməd Fatma[y]a mektub verdi.
    Memed Fatma letter gave
    'Memed gave a letter to Fatma.'

14. Məməd Fatma[y]a mektubi verdi.
    Memed Fatma letter gave
    'Memed gave the letter to Fatma.'

15. Fatma inə[y]in ağzɨ[n]a yuni verirmiş.
    Fatma cow mouth-3sg wool was.giving
    'Fatma was giving wool to the cow's mouth.'

16.   indi dağda   qar   əriyir.
        now mountain snow melts
        'Snow is melting on the mountain now.'

17.   Həsən dağa   sarɨ   irəli   getdi.
        Hasan mountain toward forward went
        'Hasan went straight toward the mountain.'

18.   bir dağ   qələ[y]ə yaxɨn idi.
        one mountain castle   near   was
        'A mountain was near the castle.'

19.   Məmədin atɨ   təz   qaçdi.
        Memed   horse-3sg quickly ran
        'Memed's horse ran quickly.'

20.   arvad   bɨçağɨnan qarpɨzi   kəsdi.
        woman knife   watermelon cut
        'The woman cut the watermelon with a knife.'

21.   Fatma[n]ɨn anasɨ   dedi.
        Fatma   mother-3sg said
        'Fatma's mother said (it).'

22.   olar ipi   kəsdiler.
        3pl   rope cut
        'They cut the rope.'

23.   onun əl-ayağ-ɨ-[n]i ipinən bağladɨlar.
        3sg   hand-foot-3sg rope   bound
        'They bound his hands and feet with rope.'

24.   ağaclari təpə[y]ə daşɨdɨlar . . .
        trees   hill   carried
        'They carried the trees to the hill . . .'

25.   quşlar dağlara   sarɨ   uçüşürdi.
        birds   mountains toward were.flying
        'Birds were flying toward the mountains.'

7C Yidiny case (Australia; Dixon 1977, 1980)
Based on the following examples, describe the case system of Yidiny. Note: ignore changes in vowel length, which are phonologically predictable. Likewise, the endings *-du*, *-bu* and *-ŋgu* should be treated as phonological variants of the same morpheme.

1.   yiŋu wagu:ja galiŋ.
        this man   go
        'This man is going.'

2.   muja:mbu wagu:ja wawal.
        mother   man   look.at
        'Mother is looking at the man.'

3.   waga:ldu mujam wawal.
      wife   mother look.at
      '(My) wife is looking at mother.'

4.   wagujaŋgu wagal bunjaŋ baŋga:lda.
      man   wife hit   axe
      'This man hit (his) wife with (the back of) an axe.'

5.   galŋa:ŋ[gu] baŋgal budi:jiŋ.
      uncle   axe   keeps/owns
      'Uncle usually keeps (lit: 'puts down') an axe around.'
      (Note: in actual pronunciation of the first word, [gu] is
      deleted by a phonological rule.)

6.   ŋanyji mayi galŋa:nda wiwi:na.
      we   food uncle   give
      'We must give some food to uncle.'

7.   wagujaŋgu minya bujiŋ   waga:lnda.
      man   meat talk.about wife
      'This man is talking about meat to (his) wife.'

8.   yiŋu gurŋa   maŋgaŋ wagujanda.
      this kookaburra laugh   man
      'This kookaburra is laughing at the man.'

9.   gudagaŋgu mujam bajal.
      dog   mother bite
      'The dog is biting mother.'

10.   muja:mbu waga:lni guda:ga wawal.
      mother   wife   dog   look.at
      'Mother is looking at (my) wife's dog.'

11.   galŋa galiŋ digarrala.
      uncle go   beach
      'Uncle is going to the beach.'

12.   mujam galiŋ digarramu.
      mother go   beach
      'Mother is going away from the beach.'

13.   yiŋu wagu:ja galiŋ minya:gu.
      this man   go   meat
      'This man is going for meat (i.e. to spear animals).'

14.   ganyarraŋgu ŋuŋu burriburri baja:l.
      crocodile   that old.man   bit
      'The crocodile bit that old man.'

15.   ganyarrani wari bala:ny.
      crocodile mouth opened
      'The crocodile's mouth opened.'

7D Kalaw Lagaw Ya case (Torres Strait, Australia; Comrie 1981b; Kennedy 1985a,b)

Based on the following examples, analyze and describe the case system for singular NPs in Kalaw Lagaw Ya. No plurals are included in this data set. Hint: an /a/ in the final syllable of the stem often changes to /oe/ through a morphophonemic process; you do not need to account for this process. Do not try to identify morpheme boundaries within the first person pronoun(s).

1.   a moeginakoezin burum mathaman.
       boy   pig   hit
       'The boy hit the pig.'

     b garkoezin moeginakaz mathaman.
       man   boy   hit
       'The man hit the boy.'

     c moeginakaz uzariz.
       boy   go.away
       'The boy went away.'

     d burum uzariz.
       pig   go.away
       'The pig went away.'

     e garkaz uzariz.
       man   go.away
       'The man went away.'

     f umayn kazi iman.
       dog   child see
       'The dog saw the child.'

     g kazin umay iman.
       child dog   see
       'The child saw the dog.'

     h bupan bisi   mathaman.
       grass cassava hit
       'The grass choked the cassava.'

     i garkoezin bupa laban.
       man   grass cut
       'The man cut the grass.'

2.   a ngay uzariz.
       1sg   go.away
       'I went away.'

     b ngi uzariz.
       2sg go.away
       'You (sg) went away.'

c ngath ngin mathaman.
  1sg   2sg   hit
  'I hit you (sg).'

d ngidh ngoena mathaman.
  2sg   1sg   hit
  'you (sg) hit me.'

e nadh nuyn laban
  3sg.f 3sg.m cut.shallow
  'She cut him shallowly.'

f nuydh nan niay-pa   yoelpadhin.
  3sg.m 3sg.f dwelling-DAT lead-HIST.PAST
  'He took her as his wife (long ago).'

g na   patheoma.
  3sg.f embark-TODAY
  'She left by vehicle (earlier today).'

h nuy   koesa-pa   uzaraydhin.
  3sg.m river-DAT   went-HIST.PAST
  'He went to the river (long ago).'

3.   a Kala uzariz.
        Kala go.away
        'Kala went away.'

      b Gibuma uzariz.
        Gibuma go.away
        'Gibuma went away.'

      c Kala Gibuman mathaman.
        Kala Gibuma   hit
        'Kala hit Gibuma.'

      d Gibuma Kalan mathaman.
        Gibuma Kala   hit
        'Gibuma hit Kala.'

4.   a ngath burum mathaman.
        1sg   pig   hit
        'I hit the pig.'

      b ngath Kalan mathaman.
        1sg   Kala hit
        'I hit Kala.'

      c Kala ngin mathaman.
        Kala 2sg hit
        'Kala hit you.'

      d Kala garkaz mathaman.
        Kala man   hit
        'Kala hit the man.'

e garkoezin ngin mathaman.
man   2sg hit
'The man hit you.'

f nuydh wapi lumaypa.
3sg.m fish search-IMPERF
'He is searching for fish.'

g garkoezin Gibuman mathaman.
man   Gibuma hit
'The man hit Gibuma.'

h nadh kazi lumar.
3sg.f child search-CONT
'She keeps on searching for the child.'

i ngoena goeygin gasaman.
1sg   sun   catch
'The sun made me ill.'

Additional exercises

Merrifield et al. (1987) prob. 160, 205, 211
Healey (1990b) ex. E.7

Notes

1. This suffix is pronounced /-e/ following consonants, /-ye/ following vowels.
2. The 2nd person pronoun has only two distinct forms, *your* possessive vs. *you* nom/acc.
3. Some morphophonemic alternations are omitted from the table in (3). Mohanan (1982) refers to a second dative case category, "dative 2," which is also omitted here.
4. Greenberg (1963), universal #38.
5. The relative ordering of 1st vs. 2nd person pronouns cannot be justified on the basis of split ergativity alone. However, the person–animacy hierarchy is relevant to a number of other construction types as well, such as the INVERSE systems of many North American languages, in which this ordering is clearly motivated.
6. This proposal was first developed by Silverstein (1976); Comrie (1978); and Dixon (1979).
7. Wierzbicka (1981:67) suggests that the hierarchy effect in split case-marking systems can be explained in terms of "inherent topic-worthiness." She also makes the very helpful point that it is as experiencer, rather than agent, that the speaker enjoys a unique status.
8. Note that the verb in this example agrees with the nominative object, rather than the ergative subject. (I have been unable to locate the original source for examples 17–18.)
9. See Nichols (1986) for a discussion of "head-marked" vs. "dependent-marked" agreement.

10. These 2nd person pronouns are restricted to specific contexts in modern Portuguese: *tu* for indicating familiarity, and *vós* primarily for addressing the deity in prayer (Parkinson 1992). The polite second person pronouns, *você* (sg.) and *vocês* (pl.), trigger 3rd person agreement marking on the verb.

11. Following the analysis of Rosen (1990).

12. This example is based on the data in Allen and Frantz (1983), with very slight modification.

13. The 1st person inclusive refers to a group which includes both the speaker and the hearer, while the 1st person exclusive excludes the hearer; see ch. 8 for further discussion.

14. Lehmann (1988) cites case agreement like that illustrated in (34), along with other types of evidence, to argue that what we have referred to as "agreement with N" is actually agreement with the NP headed by N; in other words, the modifiers agree with the NP of which they are a part, rather than directly with the head noun that they modify. Case is assigned to the NP as a whole; what is required is that none of the dependents within the NP should have contradictory case features. The same kind of "unification" analysis can be given for number and gender as well.

15. Larsen refers to prefixes in the first two positions as "clitics"; I follow Trechsel and other authors in writing them simply as prefixes.

8 Noun classes and pronouns

In this chapter we discuss two topics relating to the syntax, morphology and semantics of nouns and noun phrases. In the first section we will look at ways in which the nouns in a particular language may be subclassified on the basis of grammatical markers. In the second section we will look at pronouns and pronoun systems.

8.1 Noun classes and gender

In the preceding chapter we made several references to the "gender" of a noun. The term GENDER has a very specific meaning in linguistics. Essentially, a gender system is a partitioning of the category N which has morphological consequences of a particular kind. In languages that have grammatical gender, each noun of the language is assigned to one of a small, fixed set of sub-classes, and the sub-class of each noun is reflected in some type of agreement morphology. In chapter 7 we saw examples of determiners and adjectives agreeing with the gender of their head noun in Portuguese (33), and of Russian past tense verbs agreeing with the gender of singular subjects (25).

Another common strategy for marking the sub-class of a noun is through the use of NOUN CLASSIFIERS. Classifiers are separate words that occur inside the NP in certain contexts (e.g. when the NP also contains a numeral or quantifier) and serve to indicate the sub-class of the head noun. We will discuss each of these strategies in turn. Then in section 8.1.3 we will summarize the crucial differences between gender and classifier systems.

8.1.1 Gender systems

A non-linguist is likely to assume that the gender of a noun is identical to the gender of the thing it refers to. However, it is easy to find counterexamples to this claim. The German word *Mädchen* 'girl,' for example, is grammatically neuter even though it refers to a female human. Such examples show how important it is to distinguish between grammatical gender and "natural" (or biological) gender. Biological gender (male vs. female) relates to reproductive functions and is relevant only to humans, the higher orders of the animal kingdom, and certain plant species. Grammatical gender is a sub-classification of nouns based on shared inflectional morphology, and must be specified for every noun in the language.[1]

Gender classes are determined on the basis of agreement patterns. For example, we know that *Mädchen* belongs to the neuter class because it requires the neuter form of various determiners and modifiers, e.g. *das Mädchen* 'the girl'; compare *die Frau* 'the woman' (feminine), *der Mann* 'the man' (masculine).

Labeling gender classes is a bit like labeling syntactic categories (chapter 3): the classes are set up on the basis of grammatical criteria, but labels are assigned on the basis of semantic features and prototypes. We might use the labels MASCULINE and FEMININE where there is a statistical correlation between noun class (grammatical gender) and biological gender, or where the prototypical members of two of the classes include male humans and female humans, respectively. But the correlation is never perfect. Since every noun must belong to some gender class, the assignment may seem quite arbitrary in many cases. In Latin, for example, *ignis* 'fire' is masculine, while *flamma* 'flame' is feminine.

The classification of particular nouns may reflect interesting facts about the world view or traditional beliefs of the language group. For example, in Latin 'sun' is masculine while 'moon' is feminine; but in the Australian language Dyirbal, these genders are reversed. This is because the two cultures have different myths associated with these two heavenly bodies. (In the Dyirbal myth, the sun is a woman and the moon is her husband.) But, partly because languages are always changing, in most gender systems there are some nouns whose classification seems arbitrary or does not follow the basic semantic patterns in the rest of the system.

In a number of languages, gender is partly determined on the basis of phonological or morphological patterns as well as semantic features. Returning to our German example, the word *Mädchen* 'girl' must be grammatically neuter because all nouns which contain the diminutive suffix *-chen* are grammatically neuter.[2] However, we should emphasize the fact that, while there is often a correlation between a noun's phonological shape and the gender class it belongs to, its class membership should always be identified on the basis of the agreement patterns which the noun triggers. In Portuguese there are some words which end in /-a/ but are grammatically masculine, e.g. *o problema* 'the problem'; and a few words which end in /-o/ but are grammatically feminine, e.g. *a tribo* 'the tribe.'[3] The grammatical gender of these words is indicated by agreement patterns observed in the definite article (*o* 'masculine' vs. *a* 'feminine') and in any modifying adjectives that may be present.

Often there is no correlation between noun class and biological gender. Rather, some other semantic property may form the basis for the grammatical gender system. Isthmus Zapotec has three gender classes based on degrees of animacy: human vs. animal vs. inanimate (see (15) below). In other languages gender classification may correlate with size and shape, edible vs. inedible objects, etc.

As we saw in chapter 7, Portuguese distinguishes only two grammatical genders, masculine and feminine. German, Russian, and a number of other European languages distinguish three grammatical genders (masculine, feminine, and neuter). Dyirbal has four genders. The gender of the head noun is indicated by a determiner that also indicates the case of the NP and its proximity to the speaker ('here,' 'there but visible,' or 'there and not visible'). The various case and gender forms of the marker that signals 'there but visible' are listed in (1).

(1)   **Dyirbal demonstratives meaning 'that (visible)'** (Australia; Dixon 1972:44–47)

	ABS	ERG/INSTR	DATIVE	GENITIVE
Class I	bayi	baŋgul	bagul	baŋul
Class II	balan	baŋgun	bagun	baŋun
Class III	balam	baŋgum	bagum	—
Class IV	bala	baŋgu	bagu	baŋu

Examples of the kinds of Dyirbal words which belong to each gender class are listed in (2). Dixon (1972) presents a very interesting analysis of the semantic basis for the gender categories, showing how they relate to the traditional Dyirbal world view; but, as (2) suggests, the patterns are quite complex.

(2)   **Semantic correlates of Dyirbal gender classes** (Dixon 1972:306–311)

Class I   human males; moon; rainbow; storms; kangaroos, possums, bats; most snakes, fishes, insects; some birds (e.g. hawks); boomerangs

Class II   human females; sun and stars; anything connected with fire and water; dogs, platypus, echidna; harmful fish; some snakes; most birds; most weapons

Class III   edible fruits and the trees that bear them; tubers

Class IV   body parts, meat, bees and honey, wind, most trees, grass, mud, stones, etc.

Bantu languages are famous for their noun class systems, which involve not only agreement between nouns and their modifiers but also verbal agreement with subjects and (optionally) direct objects. The pattern is illustrated with a Swahili sentence in (3a). The agreement prefixes signal both noun class and number: class 2 is the plural form of class 1; class 6 the plural form of class 5, etc. Semantic correlates for some of these classes are listed in (3b).

(3)   **Swahili** (Hinnebusch 1992)

    a Wa-le   wa-kulima wa-zuri wa-na-(ya-)lima   ma-hindi
      2-those 2-farmers 2-good 2SUBJ-TNS-(6OBJ-)cultivate 6-maize
              mashamba-ni kw-ao.
              (17)farms-LOC 17-their
      'The/those good farmers are cultivating maize at their farms.'

    b **Class 1/2**   human beings, some animals
      Class 3/4   plants, natural phenomena (fire, smoke), spirit beings, some body parts
      Class 5/6   fruits, paired body parts
      Class 6   liquid mass nouns (water, oil), groups or collections
      Class 7/8   artifacts, defective humans
      Class 9/10 kinship terms, most animals, insects
      Class 11   linear objects (tongue, wall, fence, sword)
      Class 14   abstract nouns (freedom, beauty, humanity)

8.1.2 Classifier systems

Classifiers are independent words, often nouns, which occupy a special position in the noun phrase, but do not seem to contribute to the meaning of the NP in any definite way. English has no true classifiers; the closest parallels are probably a few frozen expressions like those in (4a). The function of a classifier is in some respects similar to that of MEASURE WORDS like those in (4b), which allow us to quantify (or count) mass nouns. This pattern is quite productive in English, and indeed most languages. But notice that, in terms of grammatical structure, the measure word itself is the head of the NP that contains it. This is not the case with classifiers.

(4)   a a *pair* of scissors
      five *head* of cattle

    b two *pounds* of salt
      three *liters* of wine
      five *bushels* of wheat
      10,000 *barrels* of oil

The Chinese noun phrases in (5) show some examples of true classifiers. Li and Thompson (1981) report that classifiers are obligatory when the noun is preceded by a numeral (5a,b), demonstrative (5c,d), or by certain quantifiers including 'a few,' 'a certain,' 'every,' etc. Notice that these classifiers, unlike measure words, are used primarily when the head of the NP is a count noun. Classifiers are <u>not</u> used in Chinese if the NP contains a measure word.

(5)   **Chinese** (Li and Thompson 1981:104–105)

    a sān *ge*   rén   'three people'
      three CLASS people

b wǔ *jià*   fēijī   'five airplanes'
  five CLASS airplane

c zhèi *zhǎn*   dēng   'this lamp'
  this CLASS   lamp

d nèi *tiáo*   niú   'that cow'
  that CLASS   cow

e jǐ   *jiàn*   yīfu   'a few garments'
  a.few CLASS garment

f zhèi jǐ   *mén*   pào   'these few cannons'
  this a.few CLASS cannon

g nèi liù *běn*   shū   'those six books'
  that six CLASS book

The choice of classifier depends on the specific noun that heads the NP. In many cases the nouns which take a particular classifier tend to have some semantic features in common, often relating to size and shape, but there are numerous exceptions. For example, the classifier *tiáo* is used primarily for long, thin objects (e.g. 'snake,' 'road,' 'river,' 'tail') and four-legged mammals; but it is also used for various other nouns such as 'news' and 'law.' Moreover, some long thin objects (e.g. 'brush-pen' and 'arrow') take a different classifier. So, for most nouns, the choice of classifier cannot be predicted but must simply be memorized (and specified in the noun's lexical entry).

The classifier system of Malay is somewhat similar to that of Chinese. Classifiers must be used with most countable nouns whenever a numeral is present, and also with certain definite quantifiers (e.g. 'several'). The classifier word, italicized in the following examples, forms a constituent with the numeral or quantifier, and that constituent may occur either before or after the head noun:

(6)   **Malay** (Asmah and Rama 1985)
       a [dua *orang*] budak   'two children'
         two person child
       or: budak [dua *orang*]
           child two person

       b [tiga *batang*] rokok   'three cigarettes'
         three stick   smoke
       or: rokok [tiga *batang*]
           smoke three stick

As in Chinese, the choice of classifier is partly determined on the basis of size and shape, but a number of other semantic features are involved as well. Many of the classifiers can also be used as independent nouns, though the meaning of these nouns is sometimes quite different from the semantic features associated with the classifier. The most commonly used classifier words are summarized in (7):

(7)   **Classifiers in Malay/Indonesian** (based on Coope 1976; Sneddon 1996)

CLASSIFIER WORD	LITERAL MEANING	USED FOR:
orang	'person'	humans
buah	'fruit'	large solid objects (houses, cars, ships, books, etc.); generic classifier
ekor	'tail'	animals, birds, fish
biji	'seed'	small round objects (eggs, fruits, cups, etc.)
batang	'stick, stem'	long cylindrical objects (trees, pencils, cigarettes, umbrellas*); roads, rivers
keping	'piece'	flat objects with some thickness (planks, slices of bread, etc.)
helai	??	flat objects with no thickness (cloth, paper, leaves)
pucuk	'shoot (of plant)'	letters, guns
bilah	'thin strip'	sharp objects (knives, swords, needles)
bidang	'expanse'	flat, spread-out things (mats, sails, land)
bentuk	'shape, curve'	round or curved objects (rings, fish-hooks)
utas	'coil'	rope, thread, chain
kuntum	'bud, blossom'	flowers
butir	'particle'	gem stones, bullets
patah	'break'	words
lembar	'thread, strand'	flat things (paper, photos)

*In Indonesian, the classifier *kaki* 'foot' can be used for umbrellas.

8.1.3   Distinguishing gender from classifier systems

We have discussed two different ways in which languages may indicate grammatically determined noun classes. Since gender systems and classifier systems are similar in many ways, it is not always easy to decide which kind of system we are dealing with. Dixon (1986) lists a few basic criteria that can help us distinguish the two.

a   **Number of categories**: gender systems involve a small, fixed number of classes, usually between 2 and 20. In classifier systems, Dixon says that 20 is typically the lower limit, with over 100 distinct classifiers reported in some languages (e.g. Cambodian, Vietnamese, Tzeltal). Moreover, since gender is an inflectional category, the number of gender classes is relatively stable over time. However, classifiers are independent words and new ones can be adopted into the system fairly readily.

b   **Coverage**: in gender systems, every noun in the language must belong to some gender class. Certain nouns may appear in more than one class, e.g. Latin "common gender" words such as *exsul* 'exile,' *parēns* 'parent,' *dux* 'leader.' These words may be either masculine or feminine, depending on the sex of the individual referred to. But the number of such words is normally small. In classifier systems, however, there may be many nouns that do not occur with any classifier, and many others that can occur with several different classifiers.

c   **Morphology**: classifiers are normally free forms, occurring as independent words within the NP. Gender is an inflectional category and is expressed morphologically on the agreeing element(s), i.e. the noun's dependents and/or the verb which assigns its Grammatical Relation.

d   **Syntax**: the gender of a noun is always reflected in some kind of agreement marking, whether inside the NP (on modifiers or determiners) or outside (on the verb). Classifiers, on the other hand, do not trigger agreement.

Gender and classifier systems are the most common ways of indicating noun classes, but several other patterns have been reported; see Aikhenvald (2000) for a very thorough survey. Moreover, we occasionally find noun class systems that seem to have "mixed" properties. Japanese, for example, has a classifier system that includes a few hundred classifiers, but these classifiers are expressed as suffixes on the numerals rather than independent words (Downing 1986; Matsumoto 1993).[4] Aikhenvald (2000:108) states that the Paleosiberian language Nivkh has 26 different noun classes which are indicated by inflected forms of the numerals. This seems to fit Dixon's description of a gender system, but with an unusually large number of classes.

However, most noun class systems fit reasonably well into one of Dixon's two categories, gender vs. classifiers; and we will not discuss the less common patterns here.

Practice exercise

In chapter 7 we discussed the case system of an imaginary variety of Pidgin English which we called "Pseudo-English." Now imagine that several other varieties are discovered on neighboring islands, and you are sent to investigate. As part of this study, you collect the following NP examples. For each language, based on the data available, determine whether it has a gender system or a classifier system. Give reasons for your decisions, and state the criteria which you would use for determining the class of each noun. (Hyphens represent affix boundaries.)

Pseudo-English B:

(i) this-i horse   this-u bottle
     this-i hound   this-u box
     this-i hare   this-u boulder
     this-i husband   this-u budget
     this-i housewife this-u bicycle

As you collect Swadesh lists and other basic vocabulary samples, you find that 90 per cent of the nouns fit the patterns shown in (i). However, in collecting additional data you find a few forms like those in (ii). (Comparative evidence suggests that many of these forms are loan words.) In what way do these forms complicate your analysis? How many noun classes are there in this language? What labels would you suggest for naming the classes? Which class do each of the words in (ii) belong to, and why?

(ii) this-i behemoth this-u helix
      this-i boy   this-u hippopotamus

Pseudo English C:

(iii) one plark pig   this flusp leaf
       that plark rooster   one flusp mat
       those three plark puppies those four flusp blankets
       my four plark buffalo

       that siggle rifle   this chorp house
       those two siggle blossoms two chorp bicycles
                                  those three chorp tables
                                  four chorp nations
                                  that chorp problem

You manage to find some bilingual speakers of this dialect and ask them to translate these phrases into standard English. The translations are not surprising: 'one pig,' 'this leaf,' 'that rifle,' etc. You ask what *plark* means, and they tell you it means 'tail.' You learn that *chorp* means 'fruit.' You ask about *siggle* and *flusp* and are told: "Those words don't mean anything, but they make the phrases sound better." How many noun classes are there in this language? Is it a gender system or a classifier system? Why?

8.2   Pronouns

In chapter 3 we argued that pronouns are a special kind of noun phrase. Their syntactic distribution is (in many languages) similar to that of proper names. But semantically there is an important difference between pronouns and names.

A proper name refers to a specific individual. Of course, it is possible for two individuals to have the same name; I have a colleague named Winston Churchill, no relation to the late British Prime Minister. But names are generally used in contexts where there is no danger of confusion, i.e. where their reference is unique.

The reference (or semantic interpretation) of pronouns, however, is not fixed. It depends very much on the context of use, i.e. who is speaking to whom on what occasion, what has already been said, etc. A pronoun may refer either to someone or something in the immediate context (time and place) where the speaking is taking place; or it may refer to something which has been previously mentioned in the same discourse. We will discuss these semantic issues very briefly, then give an equally brief summary of the features which can determine the form of a pronoun.

8.2.1   Anaphora vs. deixis

The time and place where a conversation takes place is sometimes referred to as the SPEECH SITUATION. There are a number of words whose interpretation (or reference) is not fixed, but depends on the specific details of the speech situation. Words of this type are called DEICTIC elements. The term DEIXIS comes from a Greek word which means 'to show' or 'to point.' Deictic elements typically refer to things that the speaker could actually point to while he is speaking. As the table in (8) indicates, first and second person pronouns (e.g. *I* and *you*) are always deictic. Their interpretation depends on who is speaking to whom.

(8)   **Deictic element   Referent**

here	where the speaker is
there	indicated or specified place away from speaker
now	the time of the speech act
this	something near the speaker
that	something away from speaker
I	speaker
you	addressee

The other way in which the semantic interpretation of pronouns may depend on the context of use is called ANAPHORA (literally 'referring back'). ANAPHORIC elements are words whose interpretation depends on the interpretation of some other element (e.g. a noun phrase) in the same discourse. This other element is called the ANTECEDENT. An anaphoric element refers to the same person, place, or thing as its antecedent.

Third person pronouns (*he*, *she*, etc.), demonstratives (*this* or *that*), the locative pro-form *there*, as well as a few other words, may be used either as deictics or as anaphors. The sentences in the following examples illustrate the anaphoric usage: in each case, the interpretation of the word in italics depends on the interpretation of some other phrase in the same discourse. Identify the antecedent for each anaphoric element:

(9) a Mrs. Thatcher promised John Major that *she* would not interfere with *his* campaign.
 b John gave Mary a dozen roses, but asked *her* to share *them* with *his* sister.
 c I walked all the way to the stadium, but found no one *there*.
 d By the time *he* arrived at the river, John was too tired to swim.

(10) Smith: Mrs. Thatcher is supposed to visit the Pope tomorrow.
  Jones: I wonder what *she* wants to talk to *him* about?

The antecedent usually precedes the anaphoric element, but, as (9d) shows, this is not always the case. And (10) shows that it is not necessary for the antecedent to be part of the same sentence as the anaphoric element, or even spoken by the same speaker.

8.2.2 Reflexive vs. emphatic pronouns

REFLEXIVE PRONOUNS are anaphoric elements with special grammatical properties. They are subject to certain restrictions which do not apply to normal pronouns. For example, in a large number of languages a reflexive pronoun must find its antecedent within its immediate clause. Some English reflexive pronouns are illustrated in (11).

(11) a John has bought *himself* a new Mercedes.
 b I surprised *myself* by winning the dancing competition.
 c Mary tried to control *herself*, but could not resist tickling the Governor.

EMPHATIC PRONOUNS in English, and in many other languages, have the same form as reflexive pronouns, but their function and distribution are quite different. Each of the reflexive pronouns in (11) bears its own semantic role and Grammatical Relation, which are distinct from the semantic role and Grammatical Relation of its antecedent. But emphatic pronouns, like those in (12), do not have this kind of independent status within the clause. Rather, they are used simply to highlight the identity of some other phrase, namely the phrase which functions as their antecedent.

(12) a The Governor *himself* will appoint the new police chief.
 b I gave that money to the Governor *myself*.
 c I have a letter of authorization signed by the Governor *himself*.

Of course, there are also many languages in which emphatic pronouns are distinct from reflexives, e.g. German *sich* (reflexive) vs. *selbst* (emphatic). We can describe the status of emphatic pronouns more precisely by saying that they stand in APPOSITION to their antecedents. Two phrases are said to be in apposition when they: (i) bear the same Grammatical Relation; and (ii) refer to the same individual. The two phrases often occur next to each other as well, as in the examples in (13):

(13)   a President Reagan, *a former movie star*, was very effective on television.
   b My brother-in-law, *the new Mayor of Chicago*, has promised to get me a job.

The crucial difference between reflexive and emphatic pronouns, then, is that a reflexive pronoun has a different function in the sentence from its antecedent, while emphatic pronouns have the same function in the sentence as their antecedents. There are often other differences as well in particular languages. For example, in English (and many other languages) a reflexive pronoun may not occur as the subject of a sentence. Emphatic pronouns, on the other hand, frequently occur as subjects; in fact, this seems to be their most common usage.

8.2.3   Personal pronouns: agreement features

Agreement between a pronoun and its antecedent helps the listener to interpret the pronoun correctly. In English a pronoun must agree with its antecedent for person, number, and gender. This requirement prevents the pronoun *she* in sentence (14) from finding an antecedent within its sentence, since there is no feminine NP available. The antecedent must come from the discourse context, or from the speech situation.

(14)   John told Bill that *she* had won the election.

All languages appear to have some kind of pronoun agreement. We noted in the preceding chapter that person, number, and gender are the most commonly marked categories in pronoun systems, as in verb agreement systems. Of these, person and number appear to be marked in all languages. Joseph Greenberg (1963), in his pioneering study of language universals, stated:

"All languages have pronominal categories involving at least three persons and two numbers."   (Universal 42)

So all languages distinguish first, second, and third person pronouns, although in some languages third person pronouns have the same form as articles or demonstratives. Beyond these three basic categories, the most common further distinction is a contrast in the first person plural between INCLUSIVE and EXCLUSIVE forms. A first person inclusive pronoun (e.g. Malay *kita*) refers to a group which includes both the speaker and the hearer ('you, me, and [perhaps] those others'). A first person exclusive pronoun (e.g. Malay *kami*) refers to a group which includes the speaker but excludes the hearer ('me and those others but not you').

In the years since Greenberg published his study a few languages have been found in which pronouns are not specified for number.[5] Most languages, however, do make a distinction between singular and plural pronouns, at least in the first person (*I* vs. *we*). Modern English has lost its number distinction in the second person, and many languages have no number distinction in the third person. In addition to the basic contrast between singular and plural, many languages have a DUAL category for groups containing exactly two individuals. Dual number is found most commonly in first person forms. Any language that has a distinct dual form in the third person will almost certainly have distinct dual forms for the first and/or second persons as well.[6]

A few languages have a further distinct number category, TRIAL (for groups of three) or PAUCAL (for groups containing a few individuals).[7] Even in languages which have a trial number category, it is fairly common for the trial forms to be used at times in an extended, paucal sense to refer to more than three individuals.

The Susurunga language of Papua New Guinea is reported to have a complete set of quadral pronouns, which contrast with singular, dual, trial, and plural forms in all four persons (first inclusive, first exclusive, second, third).[8] The dual, trial, and quadral forms each contain incorporated numeral morphemes ('two,' 'three,' 'four,' respectively). However, the quadral forms actually have the meaning 'four or more,' rather than 'exactly four.' They are primarily used in two specific contexts: first, with relationship terms, as in 'we (four or more) who are in a mother–child relationship,' where plural forms are not allowed; and second, in hortatory discourse (speeches of exhortation), where speakers make frequent use of first person inclusive quadral forms to maintain a sense of identity with the listeners.

In addition to person and number, many languages have distinct pronoun forms to indicate the gender or noun class of the antecedent. Gender is most commonly marked in third person forms, and is never distinguished in the first person unless it is also distinguished in the second and/or third person.[9]

As mentioned in section 8.1, European languages tend to distinguish two genders (masculine and feminine, as in Portuguese) or three genders (masculine, feminine, and neuter, as in German). Another common gender classification is human vs. animal vs. inanimate, as found in

Isthmus Zapotec. Note that gender is distinguished only in the third person forms:

(15)   **Isthmus Zapotec pronouns** (Mexico; Elson and Pickett 1988:37–38)

	HUMAN	ANIMAL	INANIMATE
1 sg	naa	—	—
2 sg	lii	—	—
3 sg	laabe	laame	laani
1 pl incl	laanu	—	—
1 pl excl	laadu	—	—
2 pl	laatu	—	—
3 pl	laakabe	laakame	laakani

There is one important category which is not relevant to verb agreement systems but is often marked on pronouns because of the fact that pronouns function as noun phrases, and that is case. In languages where all NPs are marked for case, it is not uncommon for pronouns to have special inflected forms, rather than taking the normal set of case markers. Even where other NPs are not marked for case, pronouns may be inflected for case. This is the situation in English (*I, me, my; we, us, our; he, him, his*; etc.). And, as we saw in chapter 7, the case-marking pattern for pronouns may be accusative even when the case marking pattern for other NPs is ergative.

Some languages have distinct third person pronoun forms which indicate degree of PROXIMITY, i.e. how far the third person is from the speaker and hearer. Often this involves a distinction between someone who is visible to the speaker and hearer vs. someone who is invisible.

Finally, the choice of pronoun is often used to signal politeness. It is quite common for languages to have two different second person singular forms, one formal and the other informal or familiar (e.g. German *du* vs. *Sie*; French *tu* vs. *vous*; Biatah Land Dayak *ku'u* vs. *ka'am*). More complex systems are common in southeast Asia. Malay speakers must choose among half a dozen or more possible forms for both the first and second person singular category, depending on the relative social status and degree of intimacy between the speaker and hearer. Often speakers will use kinship terms or proper names for both first and second person reference, to avoid having to make this potentially embarrassing choice.

8.2.4   Examples of pronoun systems

Ingram (1978) states that the most commonly occurring pronoun system among the world's languages is one containing six different forms, representing all the possible combinations of three person categories with two number categories. This pattern can be illustrated with Mandarin Chinese:

(16)   **Mandarin pronouns**

	SINGULAR	PLURAL
1st person	wǒ	wǒmen
2nd person	nǐ	nǐmen
3rd person	tā	tāmen

The next most common system in Ingram's corpus is one which adds the dual number category and distinguishes inclusive from exclusive in the first person. This produces eleven distinct combinations of person and number features, as in Samoan:

(17)   **Samoan pronouns** (Mosel and So'o 1997:39)

	SINGULAR	DUAL	PLURAL
1st excl	a'u	mā'ua	mātou
1st incl	—	tā'ua	tātou
2nd person	'oe	'oulua	'outou
3rd person	ia	lā'ua	lātou

The third most common system in Ingram's study is one which has no dual number category but does distinguish inclusive from exclusive, for a total of seven distinct forms. This is the basic pattern found in Malay, if we ignore the politeness factors discussed above:

(18)   **Malay pronouns**

	SINGULAR	PLURAL
1st excl	saya	kami
1st incl	—	kita
2nd person	awak/kamu	kamu/kalian
3rd person	dia	mereka

These examples have referred only to the categories of person and number. If we take into account other features as well, such as case and/or gender, the systems can obviously become quite complex. And there can be significant variations even between relatively closely related languages. To illustrate this last point, consider the following systems from two western Malayo-Polynesian languages spoken within a few hundred miles of each other: Kayan, spoken in central Borneo; and Kimaragang Dusun, spoken in northeastern Borneo. Kimaragang has only one dual form, namely the first person inclusive; but Kayan has not only a complete dual set but also a complete paucal set. As is often the case, the Kayan dual and paucal forms contain reduced forms of the words meaning 'two' and 'three,' *dua'* and *təlo'*, respectively.

(19)   **Kimaragang Dusun pronouns** (northeastern Borneo)

	NOMINATIVE	GENITIVE	DATIVE
1 sg	oku	ku	dogon
2 sg	ikau/ko	nu	dikau
3 sg	yalo'	yo	dialo'
1 dual incl	kito	to	daton
1 pl incl	tokou	—	daton
1 pl excl	okoi	ya	dagai
2 pl	ikoo'/kou	duyu	dikoo'
3 pl	yaalo'	(yo)	daalo'

(20)   **Kayan pronouns** (central Borneo; Clayre and Cubit 1974)[10]

	SINGULAR	DUAL	PAUCAL (3–10)	PLURAL (more than 10)
1st excl	akui	kawa'	kalo'	kame'
1st incl	—	itu'	təlo'	itam
2nd	ika'	kua'	kəlo'	ikam
3rd	iha'	dawa'	dalo'	daha'

8.2.5   Summary

A speaker chooses the appropriate pronominal form in a given context based on an interesting variety of factors. Features of person, number, and gender are determined by the intended reference (whether anaphoric or deictic). The pronoun may be inflected for case on the basis of its syntactic position. And the speech situation may also be relevant, if the language uses pronouns to encode features such as politeness and proximity.

In describing the pronouns of a given language, the first step is to define the parameters of the system: how many categories of person, number, and (perhaps) gender are distinguished? These parameters define the number of possible forms. The second step is to determine the inventory, i.e. the forms which actually occur in the language. In the systems charted in (16–18), the number of actual forms is equal to the number of possible forms; the only gaps in these charts correspond to the logically impossible "1st singular inclusive" category. But this will not always be the case. For example, look at the nominative case set for Kimaragang in (19). We can see that Kimaragang uses the same parameters as the Samoan system in (17); but there are fewer distinct forms in the Kimaragang nominative set, because only one dual form is attested. In other words, there are systematic gaps in the Kimaragang paradigm. (Can you identify these gaps?)

Pronoun systems around the world tend to fall into familiar patterns, and to vary in familiar ways. For example, we have said that gaps in the pronoun inventory are more likely to occur in the third person than in the first or second person. However, any particular language may surprise us. Standard Arabic, for example, has distinct dual forms in the second and third persons, but not in the first person. Moreover, it is important to check whether apparent gaps in the inventory are systematic (i.e. truly a feature of the language) or just an accident due to insufficient data. Even in a fairly large corpus of data, it is quite easy for one or two pronoun forms to be unattested, and eliciting the missing forms from a native speaker can sometimes be surprisingly difficult.

Exercises

8A Walmatjari pronouns

The following sentences contain all the pronominal forms which occur in the examples of Hudson's (1978) excellent grammar sketch. Based on these examples, make a chart of the Walmatjari pronoun system. Does your chart predict the existence of any forms that are not attested in this corpus? If so, can you form a hypothesis as to what the missing forms might look like?

1. ngaju-Ø ma-rna-rla linya yawiyi-wu.
   I-ABS   AUX   cried sorrow-DAT
   'I cried because of my sorrow.' [ex. 85]

2. nyantu-Ø pa-Ø kirrarnana mayaru-rla kayili.
   s/he-ABS AUX sitting   house-LOC north
   'He is sitting in the house in the north.' [ex. 95]

3. mayaru-Ø pa-Ø-lu   ngartakanana nyurrajarra-kura-rla marnparni.
   house-ABS AUX-3p.SUBJ building   you(two)-POSS-LOC   nearby
   'They are building a house near yours.' [ex. 97]

4. nyuntu-ngu   ma-n-Ø ngarnung-karra kangku.
   you(sg)-ERG AUX   eat-MANNER   will.carry
   'Carry them and eat them.' [ex. 136]

5. ngalijarra-rla   pa-Ø-jarra-ngu-rla laparni rayin-Ø.
   we(two.incl)-COMIT AUX-3s.SUBJ   ran   fear-ABS
   'He ran away from us two in fear.' [ex. 61]

6. nyurrawarnti-Ø ma-rna-n-ta-lu nyanya nganampa-rlu.
   you(pl)-ABS   AUX   saw   we(excl)-ERG
   'We all (excl) saw you (pl).' [ex. 217]

7. yanku-lu   kanarlany-karti   nyantuwarnti-kura-rlawu.
   will.go-PL.SUBJ another-ALLATIVE   they-POSS-ALLATIVE
   'They should go another way to their home.' [ex. 115]

8B Yimas noun classes (Papua New Guinea; Foley 1991:119ff.)

How many distinct noun classes are found in the Yimas phrases below? Is this a gender system or a classifier system? Why? What criteria do you use to identify each class? List the nouns that belong to each class. Note: (*k*) is an epenthetic consonant, inserted by phonological rule, while (*u*) is an underlying vowel that gets deleted (i.e., is not pronounced).

	NP	**GLOSS**
1.	apwi ama-na-kn	'my father'
2.	apwi yua-n	'good father'
3.	kalakn m-n	'that child'
4.	panmal yua-n	'good man'
5.	narmang yua-nmang	'good woman'
6.	apak yua-nmang	'good sister'
7.	apak ama-na-(k)nmang	'my sister'
8.	murang ama-na-ng	'my paddle'
9.	murang m-ng	'that paddle'
10.	nangkpuk m-ung	'that meat'
11.	nangkpuk yua-wng	'good meat'
12.	impram yua-m	'good basket'
13.	matn ama-na-kn	'my brother'
14.	kalakn yua-n	'good child'
15.	tanm ama-na-m	'my bone'
16.	tanm m-m	'that bone'
17.	antuk ama-na-wng kpa-wng	'my big (i.e. loud) voice'
18.	trng ama-na-ng urkpwica(k)-ng	'my black tooth'
19.	impram ama-na-m kpa-m	'my big basket'
20.	tnum ama-na-(u)m kawngkra(k)-um	'my tall sago palm'
21.	irpm m-um	'that coconut palm'

8C Jacaltec noun classes (Guatemala; based on Craig 1977, 1986a; Day 1973)[11]

Describe the noun class system(s) that are revealed in the Jacaltec phrases below. What criteria do you use to identify each class? List the nouns that belong to each class. Note: the letter "x" represents a retroflex fricative [ʂ]; "ñ" represents a velar nasal [ŋ]; the symbol "š" is used here to represent the palato-alveolar fricative [ʃ], which is written in Jacaltec orthography as "ẍ."

ch'en botella	'the bottle'	noʔ chibe	'the meat'
ch'en ch'en	'the rock'	noʔ šic	'the rabbit'
ch'en óme	'the earrings'	noʔ oj	'the coyote'
ix ix	'the woman'	noʔ txitam	'the pig'
ix malin	'Mary'	teʔ hubal	'the beans'
ixim awal	'the cornfield'	teʔ ñah	'the house'
ixim bitx	'the tamale(s)'	teʔ oñ	'the avocado'
ixim ixim	'the corn'	teʔ teʔ	'the tree/stick/log'

ixim ulul	'the *atole* (corn drink)'	te? txat	'the bed'
ixim wah	'the tortilla(s)'	te? šila	'the chair'
k'ap camiše	'the shirt'	no? šila	'the saddle'
k'ap schañ	'the skirt'	tx'otx' tx'otx'	'the dirt'
metx' tx'i?	'the dog'	tx'otx' xih	'the pot'
naj elk'om	'the robber'	ya? comam	'the older man'
naj pel	'Peter'	ya? cumi?	'the older lady'
naj policia	'the policeman'	ya? malin	'Mary' (elder/respect)
naj winaj	'the man'	ya? manel	'Manuel' (elder/respect)
no? cheh	'the horse'	tx'umel	'the star'
tx'umel tu?	'that star'	te? ñah ac tu?	'that new house'
no? txitam tu?	'that pig'	hin no? txitam	'my pig'
metx' tx'i? tu?	'that dog'	hin no? wácax	'my cow'
k'ap camiše ti?	'this shirt'	hin metx' tx'i?	'my dog'
ch'en óme tu?	'those earrings'	hune? no? balam	'a/one tiger'
no? cheh c'ej'iñ	'the black horse'	hune? no? pay	'a/one fox'
heb ix ix	'the women'	heb naj winaj	'the men'
heb naj elk'om	'the robbers'	hej no? txitam	'the pigs'
heb naj policia	'the policemen'	hej te? ñah	'the houses'
hune? no? cheh saj'iñ	'a/one white horse'		
hune? no? hin txitam tu?	'that one pig of mine'		
hune? no? txitam bak'ich tu?	'that one fat pig'		
cab te? ñah	'two houses'	oxeb te? ñah	'three houses'
cab k'ap camiše	'two shirts'	oxeb no? caj-ch'elep	'three rainbows'
cab ch'en botella	'two bottles'	oxeb tx'umel	'three stars'
cac'oñ (hej) no? txitam	'two pigs'		
cac'oñ (hej) no? cheh	'two horses'		
cac'oñ (hej) metx' tx'i?	'two dogs'		
oxc'oñ (hej) no? cheh	'three horses'		
oxc'oñ (hej) metx' tx'i?	'three dogs'		
cawañ heb naj winaj	'two men'		
cawañ heb ix ix	'two women'		
cawañ heb ya? cumi?	'two older ladies'		
oxwañ heb naj winaj	'three men'		
oxwañ heb ix ix	'three women'		

Additional exercises

Merrifield et al. (1987) prob. 294, 295
Healey (1990b), ex. E.3, 12

Notes

1. See ch. 13 for the distinction between inflectional and derivational morphology.
2. See ch. 13.
3. Bill Merrifield (p.c.) points out that the masculine forms ending in /-a/ tend to be derived from Greek roots.
4. Downing (1986) states that the average Japanese speaker uses only 30–80 different classifiers in everyday speech.
5. Foley (1986:70–71) mentions several Papuan languages from the island of New Guinea which do not have distinct singular vs. plural pronoun forms. Asheninca Campa (Peru) may be another counter-example to Greenberg's generalization. Reed and Payne (1986) report that Asheninca pronouns can optionally be pluralized using the same plural suffix used for nouns, but in fact this is rarely done where the number can be inferred from the context.
6. Again, there are parallels between pronouns and agreement systems. An interesting fact about the very complex Southern Tiwa agreement pattern, discussed in ch. 7, is that dual number is marked in subject agreement but not in direct or indirect object agreement, which distinguish only singular vs. plural.
7. Greenberg's Universal 34 states: "No language has a trial number unless it has a dual. No language has a dual unless it has a plural."
8. Hutchisson (1986).
9. Greenberg's Universal 44. Moreover, there are many languages in which gender is distinguished only in singular forms, but there appears to be no language in which gender is distinguished only in plural forms (Universal 37).
10. There are minor variations in some Kayan forms relating to case functions. These variant forms are not shown here.
11. My thanks to Jean Stratmeyer for helpful comments on these examples.

9 Tense, Aspect, and Modality

The terms TENSE, ASPECT, and MODALITY refer to three kinds of information that are often encoded by verbal morphology. TENSE marking indicates, to varying degrees of precision, the time when an event occurred or a situation existed. In other words, it specifies the situation's "location" in time. ASPECT relates to the distribution of an event over time: is it instantaneous or a long, slow process?; completed or ongoing?; once only or a recurring event?

MODALITY covers a wide range of semantic distinctions, but generally relates to either the speaker's attitude toward the proposition being expressed (e.g. his degree of certainty about whether the proposition is true or not), or the actor's relationship to the described situation (e.g. whether he is under some kind of obligation to act in a certain way). We will distinguish modality from the related concept of MOOD, which indicates the speaker's purpose in speaking.

In many languages, we find that a single affix actually encodes information from more than one of these domains, e.g. tense and aspect; or tense and modality. For this reason, many linguists prefer to treat Tense–Aspect–Modality (TAM) as a single complex category. In this chapter we treat them as being logically distinct, while recognizing that there is often some overlap in their grammatical expression.

9.1 Tense

Every language has ways of talking about time. In most languages there is a variety of expressions that can be used to show when something happened or will happen. These may include temporal adverbs (*soon, later, then*), PPs (*in the morning, after the election*), NPs (*last year, that week, the next day*), auxiliary verbs (*will, has, did*), affixes on the verb, etc. The term TENSE is used only for time reference which is marked grammatically – that is, by purely grammatical elements such as affixes, auxiliaries, or particles. This distinction is reflected in standard definitions of tense such as the following:

Comrie (1985): "**TENSE** is grammaticalised expression of location in time."

Bybee (1985): "**TENSE** refers to the grammatical expression of the time of the situation described in the proposition, relative to some other time."

Some linguists use the term TENSE only when the time reference is indicated by verbal morphology. We will take a slightly more flexible approach, as indicated above; but where we are specifically interested in verbal morphology, we will speak of MORPHOLOGICAL TENSE. Following this usage, the familiar English paradigm *look, looked, will look* involves a three way semantic distinction, but only two morphological tenses: past (*looked*) vs. non-past (*look*).

As our two definitions indicate, tense systems provide a way of "locating" an event, i.e. specifying its position, in time. Notice that when we talk about time reference we often use the vocabulary of spatial location: *on the table* ~ *on Tuesday*; *in the house* ~ *in ten minutes*; *at school* ~ *at midnight*; *next door* ~ *next week*; *plan ahead, think back*, etc. This is not an accident, nor is it unique to English. In many languages, there are strong similarities between the way we think and speak about time and the way we think and speak about space.

Of course, there are important differences as well. Our experience of space is normally three-dimensional, with no one direction having a specially favored status. Time is one-dimensional and moves in only one direction. Picture yourself traveling down a one-way street with no turn-offs, and you will have a good spatial analogy for thinking about tense systems. Another possible analogy, reflected in the words used to refer to time in some languages, is to picture yourself sitting on the bank of a river facing downstream. Time flows past in one direction, like the water of the river. You can "see" what has flowed past, but not what is flowing toward you.

As noted in Bybee's definition, tense systems always define the time of a situation with reference to some other time. Normally this reference point is the time of the speech event, in which case we speak of an ABSOLUTE TENSE system. In some languages, another time can be selected as the reference point; this is called a RELATIVE TENSE system (see below).

In terms of spatial location, the place where the speaker is (i.e. the place of the speech situation) is called *here*. Other positions which lie in the direction toward which the speaker is facing or moving are said to be *ahead* or *in front*, while positions which lie in the opposite direction are said to be *behind* or *in back*. In terms of time reference, the time of the speech situation is called *now*. All times which lie in the direction of "travel" relative to this point are called FUTURE, while those in the opposite direction are called PAST.

9.1.1   How many tenses?

While our words for speaking about time make a three-way distinction between past, present, and future, it is actually somewhat unusual for a language to encode all three of these categories morphologically. One language which does have this property is Lithuanian; note the different verb forms in the following examples:

(1)   **Lithuanian** (Chung and Timberlake 1985:204)

    a dirb-au   'I worked/was working'
       work-1sg.PAST

    b dirb-u   'I work/am working'
       work-1sg.PRES

    c dirb-s-iu   'I will work/will be working'
       work-FUT-1sg

The most common morphological tense systems involve a two-way distinction: either past vs. non-past, or future vs. non-future. We noted above that English has just two morphological tenses, past and non-past. Kimaragang Dusun has a similar system: the infix –*in*– is used to express actions in the past (2a), but not for actions in the present (2b) or future (2c).[1]

(2)   **Kimaragang Dusun**

    a M[in]ongoi oku   sid=talob.
      go[PAST] 1sg.NOM DAT=market
      'I went to the market (some time in past).'

    b Mongoi oku   sid=talob   (ditih).
      go   1sg.NOM DAT=market this
      'I am going to the market (on the way right now).'

    c Mongoi oku   sid=talob   suwab.
      go   1sg.NOM DAT=market tomorrow
      'I will go to the market tomorrow.'

In languages which distinguish future vs. non-future, the future tense form is often used in an extended sense for unrealized, possible, or potential situations, while the non-future form is used for actual situations. In such systems the future tense form may be called IRREALIS, in contrast to the non-future form which is called REALIS.

The Muna language of Sulawesi, Indonesia, provides a good example. Realis (non-future) tense is unmarked, while irrealis (future) tense is marked by the infix-*um*-and/or a change in the form of the subject agreement prefix. Irrealis is used for future events (3a,b); it is obligatory in negated clauses (3c); and it occurs in many conditional clauses (3d).

(3)   **Muna** (Indonesia; van den Berg 1989:58–59, 259)

a naewine   a-k[um]ala   we   Raha.   (IRREALIS)
   tomorrow   1sg-go[IRR]   LOC   Raha
   'Tomorrow I will go to Raha.'

cf: indewi   a-kala   we   Raha.   (REALIS)
    yesterday   1sg-go   LOC   Raha
    'Yesterday I went to Raha.'

b naefie   na-gh[um]use?   (IRREALIS)
   when   3sg-rain[IRR]
   'When will it rain?'

cf: na-ghuse.   (REALIS)
    3sg-rain
    'It is/was raining.'

c miina-ho   na-r[um]ato-a.   (IRREALIS)
   not.yet   3sg-arrive[IRR]-CLITIC
   'She hasn't arrived yet.'

cf. no-rato-mo   (REALIS)
    3sg-arrive-PERF
    'She has arrived.'

d ane   na-r[um]ato   kapala,   a-k[um]ala   we   Jakarta.
   if   3sg-arrive[IRR]   ship   1sg-go[IRR]   LOC   Jakarta
   'If a ship came, I would go to Jakarta.'

While tense systems involving two morphological tenses are the most common, a number of languages distinguish more than three tense categories. Let us return briefly to our analogy between tense and spatial location. Spatial deictics in virtually all languages distinguish between things which are near the speaker and things which are far from the speaker (*this/that, here/there*, etc.). However, many languages allow more than two choices. For example, demonstratives in Portuguese and Dusun distinguish three degrees of distance from speaker (or PROXIMITY).

(4)   **Portuguese Dusun Gloss**

	Portuguese	Dusun	Gloss
PROXIMAL	este	iti	'this' (near speaker)
MEDIAL	esse	ino	'that' (near hearer)
DISTAL	aquele	ilo'	'that' (far from both speaker and hearer)

Similarly, the tense systems of some languages distinguish various degrees of distance in the past or future. The Wishram–Wacso dialect of Chinook has four distinct past tenses:

(5)   **Wishram–Wacso (Chinook)** (Chung and Timberlake 1985:208)

REMOTE PAST	*ga* -tʃ-i-u-χ	'he did it long, long ago'
FAR PAST	*ni* –tʃ-i-u-χ	'he did it long ago'
RECENT PAST	*na* -tʃ-i-u-χ	'he did it recently'
IMMEDIATE PAST	*i* –tʃ-u-χ	'he just did it'

In this language the boundaries between the various categories are rather vague, but recent past is the most likely choice for something which happened in the past week, while far past could be used for events which took place during the past several months at least. Some other languages have very specific cut-off points such as 'today' vs. 'yesterday,' 'yesterday' vs. 'before yesterday,' etc. A beautiful example is found in the Bantu language ChiBemba, which has (in addition to the present tense, illustrated in (37) below) a symmetric set of four past and four future tenses.

(6)   **ChiBemba (Bantu)** (Chung and Timberlake 1985:208)

REMOTE PAST	ba-*àlí* -bomb-*ele*	'they worked (before yesterday)'
REMOVED PAST	ba-*àlíí* -bomba	'they worked (yesterday)'
NEAR PAST	ba-*àcí* -bomba	'they worked (today)'
IMMEDIATE PAST	ba-*á* -bomba	'they worked (within the last 3 hours)'
IMMEDIATE FUTURE	ba-*áláá* -bomba	'they'll work (within the next 3 hours)'
NEAR FUTURE	ba-*léé* -bomba	'they'll work (later today)'
REMOVED FUTURE	ba-*kà* -bomba	'they'll work (tomorrow)'
REMOTE FUTURE	ba-*ká* -bomba	'they'll work (after tomorrow)'

9.1.2   Absolute vs. relative tense (reference point)

The time of the speech event normally functions as the reference point relative to which other events are located in time. This type of tense marking is called ABSOLUTE TENSE. In a RELATIVE TENSE system, a different reference point is used – tense marking is used to locate the time of one situation relative to another situation, rather than in relation to the speech event. This pattern is most common in subordinate clauses, especially with non-finite verb forms, but is also found in main clauses in some languages (e.g. classical Arabic).

We can illustrate this pattern using participial clauses in English, which allow (and often prefer) a relative tense interpretation. The most natural interpretation of the participle *flying* in the following examples is that the flying event takes place at (approximately) the same time as the giving event. Relative to the time of the speech event, we interpret the participle as referring to the past in (7a), but to the future in (7b).

(7)   a Last week Qantas gave free tickets to all passengers *flying* to Darwin.
        b Next week Qantas will give free tickets to all passengers *flying* to Darwin.

Comrie (1985) states that in Imbabura Quechua, main clause verbs have absolute tense reference while most subordinate verbs get relative tense interpretation.[2] In the following examples, the subordinate verb 'live' is marked for past, present, or future tense according to whether it refers to a situation which existed before, during, or after the situation named by the main verb. But, since the main verb is marked for past tense, the actual time referred to by the subordinate verb may have been before the time of the speech event even when it is marked for 'future' tense, as in (8c):

(8)   **Imbabura Quechua** (Peru; Cole 1982:143)

    a [Marya Agatu-pi kawsa-j]-ta   kri-rka-ni
      Mary   Agato-in live-PRES-ACC believe-PAST-1SUBJ
      'I believed that Mary was living (at that time) in Agato.'

    b [Marya Agatu-pi kawsa-shka]-ta kri-rka-ni
      Mary   Agato-in live-PAST-ACC believe-PAST-1SUBJ
      'I believed that Mary had lived (at some previous time) in Agato.'

    c [Marya Agatu-pi kawsa-na]-ta   kri-rka-ni
      Mary   Agato-in live-FUT-ACC believe-PAST-1SUBJ
      'I believed that Mary would (some day) live in Agato.'

9.2   Aspect

We have said that tense defines the location of an event in time. Aspect, on the other hand, defines the shape, distribution, or "internal organization" (Bybee 1985) of the event in time. Aspect relates to questions like the following:

Is the situation changing or static?
Is the event spread over a period of time, or is it thought of as being instantaneous?
Does the situation have a definite end point, or is it open-ended?
Does the situation involve a single unique event, or an event which is repeated over and over?

In this chapter we are primarily interested in morphological aspect, that is, the kinds of aspectual distinctions which are frequently signaled by verbal affixation. However, aspect is also an important part of the basic meaning of many predicates. We will refer to these aspectual components of meaning as LEXICAL ASPECT.

9.2.1   Lexical aspect

One of the most basic ways of classifying predicates relates to the first of the questions listed above: does this predicate describe a situation which is changing over time, or a situation which is relatively static (unchanging)? Predicates of the first type are called EVENTS, while those of the second type are called STATES.

Jackendoff (1983:170ff.) lists several simple tests for distinguishing states from events in English. First, events can be said to "happen," while states cannot. If a particular verb (or verb phrase) can be used naturally to answer the question *What happened?*, then it expresses an event (9a–d); if not, it expresses a state (9e–h).

(9)   What happened was that . . .
    a Mary kissed the bishop.
    b the sun set.
    c Peter sang Cantonese folk songs.
    d the grapes rotted on the vine.
    e *Sally was Irish.
    f *the grapes were rotten.
    g *William had three older brothers.
    h *George loved sauerkraut.

Second, only events can normally be expressed in the progressive aspect (10a–c). When states are expressed in this form, the result is normally ungrammatical as in (10d–g). Sometimes, however, speakers may use this construction to express temporary states (contrast 10g with 10h); or for states that are re-interpreted as events, e.g. behaving in a certain way as in (10i).

(10)   a Mary is kissing the bishop.
    b The sun is setting.
    c Peter is singing Cantonese folk songs.
    d *This room is being too warm.
    e *Sally is being Irish.
    f *William is having a headache.
    g *George is loving sauerkraut.
    h George is loving all the attention he is getting this week.
    i Arthur is being himself.

A third test involves the use of the simple present tense. In English, events which are expressed in the simple present tense take on a habitual interpretation, whereas states do not. Examples (11a–c), involving event predicates, imply that the subject is in the habit of performing the actions described by the predicate. Examples (11d–e), however, involving stative predicates, imply only that the state of affairs being described is true at that particular time. They do not imply that the room is always too warm, or that William always has a headache.

(11)   a Mary kisses the bishop (every Saturday).
    b The sun sets in the west.
    c Peter sings Cantonese folk songs.
    d This room is too warm.
    e William has a headache.

Events may be classified into two basic groups, bounded (or TELIC) vs. unbounded (or ATELIC). Telic events are those which have a natural end point. For example, consider the verbs *die* and *give birth*. When a person is dead, the act of dying is over. When the baby is fully delivered, the act of giving birth is over. These end points are an inherent part of the meaning of the predicates themselves. Contrast these telic examples with atelic verbs like *walk* or *shine*. Logically, we know that a person must eventually stop walking; we even know that the sun must eventually stop shining. But there is nothing in the meaning of the verbs themselves that implies the existence of an end point, or specifies when these events can be said to be complete.

Dowty (1979:56ff.) lists several tests for distinguishing telic vs. atelic events. To mention just one, atelic predicates occur quite naturally with phrases expressing duration such as *for ten minutes* (12a–c), whereas telic predicates are less natural with such phrases (12d–f). Conversely, telic predicates occur quite naturally with phrases expressing a time limit such as *in ten minutes* (13d–f), whereas such phrases are much less natural with atelic predicates (13a–c).[3] Similar contrasts occur with the phrases *spend an hour x-ing* vs. *take an hour to x*.

(12)   For ten minutes Peter . . .
    a sang in Cantonese.
    b chased his pet iguana.
    c stared at the man sitting next to him.
    d *broke three teeth.
    e *recognized the man sitting next to him.
    f *found his pet iguana.

(13)   In ten minutes Peter . . .
    a ??sang in Cantonese.
    b *chased his pet iguana.
    c *stared at the man sitting next to him.
    d broke three teeth.
    e recognized the man sitting next to him.
    f found his pet iguana.

These examples indicate that *break, recognize*, and *find* are telic, while *sing*, *chase*, and *stare at* are atelic. With this brief introduction to lexical aspect, let us turn our attention to aspectual features which tend to be marked morphologically.

9.2.2   Morphological aspect

Many linguists, following Comrie (1976a), make a fundamental distinction between PERFECTIVE vs. IMPERFECTIVE aspect. Perfective aspect presents the event as a single, unanalyzable whole, ignoring the stages which make up that event. Imperfective aspect focuses in some way on the "internal structure" of the event, the process involved. Comrie notes two primary types of imperfective aspect: the PROGRESSIVE, e.g. *John was working (when I entered)*; and the HABITUAL, e.g. *John used to work here*.

English does not have a specific marker for perfective aspect, but it does have a progressive form. The contrast between the simple past tense and the past progressive form can, in certain contexts, be used to illustrate the contrast between perfective vs. imperfective aspect. The simple past in (14a) has a perfective interpretation; the event is viewed as a whole, including beginning and end, so it seems contradictory to say that it was not completed. The past progressive in (14b) has an imperfective (specifically progressive) interpretation; it refers to the "middle" of the event, whether or not the intended outcome was in fact achieved.

(14)   a When I got home from the hospital, my wife *wrote* a letter to my doctor (?? but she never finished it).   (PERFECTIVE)
       b When I got home from the hospital, my wife *was writing* a letter to my doctor (but she never finished it).   (IMPERFECTIVE)

Comrie (1976a) notes that Spanish has a morphological contrast between two past tense forms: the perfective (15a), traditionally referred to as the PRETERIT, and imperfective (15b). Notice that the imperfective form is ambiguous between progressive and habitual senses, as reflected in the English translation.

(15)   a Juan leyó   el   libro.
         Juan read(PFV) the book
         'Juan read the book.'

       b Juan leía   el   libro.
         Juan read(IMPERF) the book
         'Juan was reading/used to read the book.'

Spanish also has a specific progressive form involving the auxiliary *estar*; this is illustrated in (16). Again, the imperfective form in (16c) is ambiguous in a way that the progressive form (16b) is not.

(16)   a Juan *estaba.cantando* cuando entré.
         Juan was.singing   when I.entered
         'Juan was singing when I entered.'

       b Juan sabía   que *estaba.hablando* demasiado de.prisa.
         Juan knew(IMPERF) that was.speaking   too.much   fast
         'Juan knew that he was speaking too fast.'

    c Juan sabía   que *hablaba*   demasiado de.prisa.
      Juan knew(IMPERF) that speak(IMPERF) too.much   fast
      'Juan knew that he was speaking too fast.'
      or: 'Juan knew that he always spoke too fast.' (Comrie 1976a:34)

When a telic predicate is expressed in the perfective aspect, it implies that the "end point" of the event was actually achieved; but with the imperfective aspect there is no such implication. In Russian, for example, where the contrast between perfective and imperfective aspect is very prominent, examples like (17) are perfectly normal (Comrie 1976a:48).

(17)   a Kolja umiral,   no ne umer.
          Kolja die(IMPERF) but not die(PFV)
          'Kolja was dying but didn't die.'

         b on ugovarival   menja, no ne ugovoril.
          he persuade(IMPERF) me   but not persuade(PFV)
          'He was persuading me, but he didn't persuade (me).'

However, perfective aspect is not the same as "boundedness" or "telicity" in the sense used in the previous section. Comrie points out that in a number of languages, phrases like *for ten minutes* can be used with both perfective and imperfective verbs. Both of the Spanish sentences in (18) are fully grammatical, yet there is a subtle difference between them. The perfective form (18a) is like a snapshot of the whole thirty-year period, and might be used in a summary statement. The imperfective form (18b) describes the reign as a process that went on for thirty years; at any point within that period, Don Carlos was ruling. This form might be used to introduce a more detailed, year-by-year account of the reign.

(18)   a Don.Carlos reinó   treinta años.
          Don.Carlos rule(PFV) thirty   years
          'Don Carlos ruled for thirty years.'

         b Don.Carlos reinaba   treinta años.
          Don.Carlos rule(IMPERF) thirty   years
          'Don Carlos ruled for thirty years.'

Inherently stative predicates may be more naturally expressed in the imperfective. The normal way to express the past tense of the Spanish verb meaning 'to know' is in the imperfective, as in (16b,c) and (19a). The perfective aspect (19b) would give the predicate an eventive meaning, in this case 'came to know.' As noted above, states cannot normally be expressed in the progressive (19c).

(19)   a sabía (IMPERF)   'I knew'
         b supe (PFV)   'I realized, came to know'
         c *Juan estaba sabiendo (PROG) 'Juan was knowing . . .'

English, unlike Spanish, has two distinct imperfective forms in the past tense, progressive vs. habitual; and the progressive form does not allow a habitual interpretation (20).

(20) When we were in high-school, John *used to swallow* / **was swallowing* goldfish.

Comrie (1976a:27–28) states that HABITUAL aspect describes a recurring event or ongoing state which is a characteristic property of a certain period of time. Clearly there is no hard and fast rule as to how often an event must occur in order for it to be considered "characteristic" of the time period being discussed. But some sense of what this means can be seen in the contrast between (21) and (22). If Mary uses the habitual form in (21), John seems justified in objecting on the grounds that the action being described only happened a few times. On the other hand, if Mary uses the simple past as in (22), the same objection seems illogical.

(21) Mary: "When we were in high-school, John *used to swallow* goldfish to frighten the teachers."
      John: "Don't exaggerate, I only did it a few times."

(22) Mary: "When we were in high-school, John *swallowed* goldfish to frighten the teachers."
      John: #?"Don't exaggerate, I only did it a few times."

Another type of imperfective aspect is the ITERATIVE (or REPETITIVE), which is used in some languages to refer to events which occur repeatedly (*keep on X-ing*). Such forms are often translated into English using phrases like *over and over, more and more, here and there,* etc.

Some languages have a special aspectual category, the INCEPTIVE, for referring to the beginning of a situation (e.g. *about to X, on the point of X-ing*). The term INCHOATIVE is sometimes used in the same way, but more often this term refers to a change of state or entering a state (*to become X*; e.g. *get fat, get old, get rich*). A number of languages have inchoative affixes which derive change of state verbs from stative verbs or adjectives (see chapter 13). Finally, the COMPLETIVE aspect is used to describe an event which has been completed. Such forms are often translated into English using phrases like *he finished X-ing.*

A number of other aspectual distinctions are marked in particular languages, but we will not list any more of them here. Instead, let us turn our attention to the PERFECT, which is often classified as an aspect but in some ways functions more like a tense.

9.3   Perfect vs. perfective

The terms PERFECT and PERFECTIVE are often confused, or used interchangeably, but there is an important difference between them. As stated in the preceding section, the PERFECTIVE is an aspectual category which refers to an entire event as a whole. The PERFECT (e.g. English *I have arrived*) is used to express a past event which is relevant to the present situation. That is, it signals that some event in the past has produced a state of affairs which continues to be true and significant at the present moment.

To illustrate what this means, compare the pairs of sentences in (23–24). The adverbial clause in (23) specifies a time so long ago that a broken bone should be completely healed by now, and hence no longer relevant. The simple past tense is fine in this context but the perfect is quite unnatural. In the same way, the second clause in sentence (24a) is perfectly natural, but the same clause in (24b) sounds quite odd. (24b) could only be used in the "experiential perfect" sense (see below), e.g. in answer to the question *Have you ever lost your glasses?*; and in that context it would probably require a slightly marked intonation pattern (*I háve lost my glasses, but . . .*).

(23)   a **Simple past**: When I was a small boy, I *broke* my leg.
         b **Perfect**: *When I was a small boy, I *have broken* my leg.

(24)   a **Simple past**:
             I *lost* my glasses, but fortunately my husband found them the next day.
         b **Perfect**:
             I *have lost* my glasses (??but fortunately my husband found them the next day).

The use of the perfect form in the Russian example (25a) implies that the state of affairs brought about by the described event continues to be true at the present moment: the house is still standing. The use of the simple past in the same context (25b) does not carry any such implication: the house may or may not be standing (Comrie 1976a:54).

(25)   a dom   postroen   v prošlom godu.
             house was.built(PERF) last year
             'The house has been built last year.' (implies still standing)
         b dom   byl postroen   v prošlom godu.
             house was.built(PAST) last year
             'The house was built last year.' (no implication about present state)

The perfect in English cannot be used with a phrase indicating the specific time of a past event (26a,b). It is possible to use phrases indicating the time of relevance (26c) or a span of time within which the past event occurred (26d,e). Note, however, that in some other languages (e.g. Spanish) sentences like (26a,b) would be acceptable.[4]

(26)   a *I have interviewed ten students *yesterday*.
         b *I have arrested 20 drug dealers *last Monday*.
         c I have *now* arrested 20 drug dealers.
         d I have interviewed ten students *today*.
         e I have arrested 20 drug dealers *in the past year*.

Linguists disagree over whether to classify the perfect as tense or aspect. It seems to have features of both, since it includes both the notions of completion (aspect) and location relative to some temporal reference point (tense). This is a good example of the overlap between tense and aspect which we referred to at the beginning of this chapter.

Comrie identifies four major uses of the perfect: (a) perfect of result; (b) experiential perfect; (c) perfect of persistent situation; (d) perfect of recent past. The term "perfect of result" means that a perfect verb is used to describe a result state. For example, if I say *The governor has arrived* my hearers can normally assume that the governor is here right now. Ashton (1947:37) points out that the Swahili perfect may be used to express either completion of the action or the state resulting from the action. In the latter case (the perfect of result), it is often best translated into English using the verb *to be* or some other stative predicate (e.g. *understand*).

(27)   **Swahili** (Ashton, 1947:37)
         ROOT   **PERFECT FORM**
         -fika   'arrive'   a-me-fika   'he has arrived'
         -iva   'ripen'   ki-me-iva   'it is ripe'
         -choka   'get tired'   a-me-choka   'he is tired'
         -simama   'stand up'   a-me-simama   'he is standing'
         -sikia   'hear, feel' a-me-sikia   'he understands'

The "experiential perfect" indicates that an event has occurred at least once in the past, without specifying any particular time. In English, a simple past tense often implies a specific time reference, whereas the corresponding perfect form does not. So, as illustrated in (28), a person might well give opposite answers depending on the form of the verb used in a question:

(28)   a   I spent my holidays in Sabah last month.
         b   Did you climb Mt. Kinabalu?   No(, not this time.)
         b' Have you climbed Mt. Kinabalu?   Yes(, many years ago.)

Comrie (1976a:59) uses the pair of sentences in (29) to illustrate the difference between the experiential perfect and the perfect of result. The perfect of result (29b) implies that Bill is still in America, or is still on his way there, whereas the experiential perfect (29a) only implies that he has been there at least once in his life and most likely is back home now.

(29)   a Bill has been to America. EXPERIENTIAL PERFECT
        b Bill has gone to America. PERFECT OF RESULT

Mandarin Chinese has a specific particle, *guo*, which is used to mark the experiential perfect. This is illustrated in (30b), in contrast to the perfective construction in (30a). Similarly, Malay has a specific auxiliary verb *pernah* which is only used to express the experiential perfect.

(30)   a nǐ   kànjian=le wǒ=de yǎnjìng ma?
           you see=PFV   my   glasses Q
           'Did you see my glasses?' (recently; I'm looking for them)
        b nǐ   kànjian=guo   wǒ=de yǎnjìng ma?
           you see=EXPER.PERF my   glasses Q
           'Have you ever seen my glasses?' (Li and Thompson 1981:227)

Comrie's "perfect of persistent situation" is used to describe a situation that began in the past and continues up to the present moment, e.g. *I have known him for 10 years* or *I have been waiting for hours*. (Note that this second example involves a combination of the perfect tense with imperfective aspect. This shows how important it is to distinguish between perfect and perfective.) Time expressions which cover an extended period up to the present moment occur more naturally in English with the perfect than with the simple past tense:

(31)   He has lived/?*lived in Canberra since 1975.
        In the past four days I have eaten/?*ate three dozen doughnuts.

This usage of the perfect is common in English, but Comrie points out that in some other languages a simple present tense would be used instead. German is one such language, as illustrated in (32).

(32)   Ich warte   schon   drei   Tage.
        I   wait(PRES) already three days
        'I have been waiting for three days.' (Comrie 1976a:60)

The "perfect of recent past" refers to the use of a perfect form to describe a past event which is relevant to the present situation because it is so very recent. This use of the perfect is often heard in news broadcasts on the radio or television (33), where events are reported within hours or even minutes of their occurrence.

(33)   A terrorist has just assassinated the Mayor.
        Brazil has won its fifth World Cup championship.
        The American president has announced new trade sanctions against the Vatican.

In all of the examples thus far, the reference point to which the situation expressed by the perfect verb has relevance is the present (i.e. the time of the speech event). This form of the verb is called the PRESENT PERFECT. But it is also possible to specify some other reference point to which the perfect form is relevant. The PAST PERFECT (or PLUPERFECT) indicates that a given situation was completed before and relevant to some reference point in the past, as in (34b). The FUTURE PERFECT indicates that a given situation will be completed before and relevant to some reference point in the future, as in (34c).

(34)   a **Present perfect**:
          My secretary *has destroyed* the evidence.

       b **Past perfect (pluperfect)**:
          When the police arrived, my secretary *had* (already) *destroyed* the evidence.

       c **Future perfect**:
          Before the police arrive, my secretary *will have destroyed* the evidence.

The past perfect and future perfect forms can be thought of as combinations of absolute and relative tense. The form of the auxiliary *have* indicates the absolute time of the reference point (past or future), while the time of the described situation is always past relative to that reference point.

9.4   Combinations of tense and aspect

Tense and aspect are in principle independent categories, so that a language with three tenses and four aspectual categories could potentially have twelve distinct tense–aspect combinations. In practice, however, there are often restrictions on which combinations are possible in a particular language.

ChiBemba has three morphological aspect categories: perfect, perfective, and imperfective. However, a complete three-way contrast is possible only in some (not all) of the past tenses. Chung and Timberlake (1985:227–228), based on data from Givón (1972), state that perfective is used for events which are completed, perfect for events which have enduring results, and imperfective for continuous or iterative events:

(35)   **ChiBemba (Bantu)** – REMOTE PAST
       a ba-*àlí* -bomb-*ele* 'they worked (before yesterday)' (PERFECTIVE)
       b ba-*àlí* -bomba   'they had worked (before yesterday)' (PERFECT)
       c ba-*àléé* -bomba   'they were working/kept on working/worked repeatedly (before yesterday)' (IMPERFECTIVE)

Future tense can combine with perfective (36a) or imperfective (36b) aspect, but not with the perfect. Present tense allows only the imperfective aspect; but a distinction is made between the PROGRESSIVE (37a), which uses the normal imperfective morphology, and ITERATIVE (37b), which uses a special habitual form.

(36)   **ChiBemba (Bantu)** – REMOTE FUTURE
    a ba-*ká* -bomba   'they will work (after tomorrow)' (PERFECTIVE)
    b ba-*káláá* -bomba 'they will be working/keep on working/work repeatedly
          (after tomorrow)' (IMPERFECTIVE)

(37)   **ChiBemba (Bantu)** – PRESENT
    a ba-*léé* -bomba 'they are working' (IMPERFECTIVE)
    b ba-*là* -bomba 'they repeatedly work' (HABITUAL)

To conclude our discussion of aspect, let us consider some tense–aspect combinations in Tagalog. Each Tagalog verb has three basic finite forms which are often referred to as past tense, present tense, and future tense. But this labeling is misleading. The "present tense" form could be used as a past progressive ("She was singing the Ave Maria when I arrived") as well as a present progressive ("She is singing the Ave Maria") or present habitual ("She sings the Ave Maria beautifully"). Similarly, the Tagalog "past tense" form can be used like the English simple past ("she sang") present perfect ("she has sung"), or past perfect ("she had sung").[5]

These three forms involve two different affixes: (1) a nasal infix *-in-* (realized as an initial /n-/ in active voice forms beginning with *mag-*); and (2) reduplication (see chapter 16). The infinitival form of the verb lacks both of these, though it is marked for voice. Some examples of these forms are shown in (38):[6]

(38)   **Infinitive   "Past"   "Present"   "Future"**
    bigy-an   b[in]igy-an b[in]i-bigy-an bi-bigy-an   'to be given'
    mag-luto   nag-luto   nag-lu-luto   mag-lu-luto 'to cook'
    gawa-in   g[in]awa   g[in]a-gawa   ga-gawa-in 'to be made, done'

A number of authors have pointed out that this four-way contrast can be analyzed in terms of two fundamental distinctions.[7] The infix *-in-* marks actions as having been begun, which corresponds nicely to the contrast between REALIS VS. IRREALIS tense. CV reduplication marks actions as being non-completed; verbs which lack this reduplication are in COMPLE-TIVE aspect, while the reduplicated forms are NON-COMPLETIVE.

The following table shows how these two categories combine to produce the forms in (38). The "past tense" forms are those which are both begun and completed, i.e. realis tense and completive aspect. The "present tense" forms are those which are begun but not yet completed, i.e. realis tense and non-completive aspect. The "future tense" forms are those which are nei-ther begun nor completed, i.e. irrealis tense and non-completive aspect. Of course, something which is not begun cannot be completed, so the combination of irrealis tense and completive aspect should be impossible. In fact, this combination, which corresponds to the morphologically unmarked form, is used for "tenseless" categories such as infinitives and imperatives.

(39)

	Realis (-in-)	**Irrealis (Ø)**
Non-completive (REDUP)	Present	Future
Completive (Ø)	Past	(Infinitive)

9.5   Mood

Bybee (1985:22) defines mood as an indication of "what the speaker wants to do with the proposition" in a particular discourse context. In other words, mood is a grammatical reflection of the speaker's purpose in speaking.

Linguists refer to the DECLARATIVE, IMPERATIVE, and INTERROGATIVE moods as MAJOR MOOD categories. Each of these categories corresponds to one of three basic speech acts: statements, commands, and questions, respectively. These are perhaps the most straightforward examples of how mood indicates "what the speaker is doing." Most of the examples we have considered in this book up to now have been statements expressed in the declarative mood. The use of the imperative and interrogative moods will be discussed in chapter 11. In this section we will introduce some other mood categories which are found in a number of languages. Then, in the next section, we will discuss MODALITY.

Some linguists do not distinguish between MOOD and MODALITY (or MODE), using one label or the other as a cover term for all the categories discussed below. We will attempt to maintain a distinction between these terms along the lines suggested at the beginning of this chapter: MOOD (as we have just said) is an expression of what the speaker is trying to do, so certain moods are closely associated with particular speech acts. MODALITY expresses (i) the speaker's attitude toward the proposition being expressed (e.g. his degree of certainty about whether it is true or not); or (ii) the actor's relationship to the described situation (e.g. whether he is under some kind of obligation to act in a certain way).

Some languages have a special mood for softened commands or exhortation, often called the HORTATIVE. Hortative mood is often used with first person inclusive reference, as in the English pattern *Let's go!* Another similar category is the OPTATIVE, which marks something the speaker hopes for, or wishes would be true. Note the following three-way contrast in Gurung:

(40)   **Gurung** (Nepal; Glover 1974:123–124)

    a **Imperative**

      tʰai-dú!   togó ax-cá-d!

      wait-IMPER now not-eat-IMPER

      'Wait, don't eat (me) now!'

    b **Hortative**

      kʰiba-d   bi-di,   "dxeró ró-le."

      old.man-ERG say-PAST now   sleep-HORT

      'The old man said, "Let's go to sleep now."'

    c **Optative**

      saẽ   ramailó ta-rgé.

      mind pleasant become-OPT

      'May (our) minds be happy.'

SUBJUNCTIVE is a category used to mark propositions which the speaker does not assert to be true. English still retains a few traces of subjunctive inflected forms, mostly in archaic or frozen expressions. These can be recognized by the failure of normal subject–verb agreement patterns:

(41)   English subjunctive examples:

    a If I *were* you, I wouldn't do that.

    b God *bless* you!

    c Long *live* the king!

The most common context where subjunctives may be required is in conditional (41a) or contrafactual constructions, e.g. *If you <u>had</u> been on time, we <u>could</u> have caught that bus.* The subjunctive may also have optative and/or hortative uses in main clauses (42b–c), and it may be required in certain kinds of dependent clauses. The following examples show some of the uses of the subjunctive in Latin:

(42)   **Latin subjunctives** (Allen and Greenough 1931:278–283, 327–328)

    a **potential event**

      aliquis   dīcat

      somebody say-3sg.PRES.SBJNCT

      'somebody may say . . .'

    b **Hortative**

      hōs   latrōnēs   interficiāmus

      those(ACC) thieves(ACC) kill-1pl.PRES.SBJNCT

      'Let us kill those robbers!'

    c **Optative**

      dī   tē   perduint

      gods(NOM) you(SG.ACC) ruin-3pl.PRES.SBJNCT

      'May the gods confound you!'

d **Conditional**

sī quis   deus   mihi   largiātur,
if some   god(NOM) me(DAT) grant-1sg.PRES.SBJNCT
     valdē   recūsem
     strongly reject-1sg.PRES.SBJNCT
'If some god were to grant me this, I would stoutly refuse it.'

e **Contrafactual**

sī vīveret,   verba   êius audīrētis
if live-3sg.IMPERF.SBJNCT words(ACC) his hear-2pl.IMPERF.SBJNCT
'If he were living, you would hear his words.'

The subjunctive, optative, and hortative moods are similar in certain important ways. All of them indicate that the speaker is not asserting the truth of the proposition expressed by the clause, and that the situation described by the clause is not an actual one. For this reason, the three are sometimes referred to as the "irrealis" moods.

We have seen that there is often an association between irrealis mood and future tense, in tense systems that distinguish future vs. non-future, because future tense expresses situations which are not yet actual. These categories may also span the boundary between mood and modality. The optative and hortative moods can be associated with specific speech acts (wishing and exhorting) or intentions, and so fit into our basic definition of mood. But certain uses of the subjunctive (e.g. that in 42a) seem to relate primarily to the speaker's degree of certainty about what he is saying. This is a type of modality, the category to which we now turn our attention.

9.6 Modality

The term MODALITY covers a fairly wide range of semantic contrasts. In order to get a feeling for some of the parameters involved, let us consider the behavior of some English modal auxiliary verbs. What type of ambiguity is illustrated in the following examples?

(43)   a The older students *may* leave school early (unless the teachers watch them carefully).

        b The older students *may* leave school early (if they inform the headmaster first).

(44)   a Your agent *must* be a close personal friend of the ambassador (otherwise he would never have gotten into the embassy).

        b Your agent *must* be a close personal friend of the ambassador (in order to carry out this mission successfully).

These two pairs of sentences show that *may* and *must* can be used in two different senses. In the (a) sentences, the modal carries a meaning which relates to the speaker's state of knowledge or belief about the proposition being expressed. *May* in this sense (43a) indicates that the speaker believes the proposition is possibly true; and *must* (44a) indicates that the speaker is fairly certain that the proposition is true, though this certainty is based on inference or supposition rather than direct knowledge. In the (b) sentences, the modal carries a meaning which relates to some kind of obligation or permission on the part of the agent. *May* in this sense (43b) indicates that the agent is permitted to do something, while *must* (44b) indicates that the agent is required or obligated to do something.

Semantic contrasts relating to the speaker's state of knowledge or belief (possibility, probability, certainty, etc.) are said to involve EPIS-TEMIC MODALITY. Semantic contrasts relating to obligation or permission on the part of the agent are said to involve DEONTIC MODALITY. But these categories can be seen as sub-sets of a more general distinction between SPEAKER-ORIENTED and AGENT-ORIENTED modalities. Speaker-oriented categories which have special grammatical marking in various languages include: possibility or potential, certainty, supposition, doubt (dubitative), and evidentiality (reflecting the speaker's basis for belief, e.g. hearsay vs. direct observation). Agent-oriented categories include ability, permission, obligation, desire (desiderative), intention, etc.

As we have noted, there are often connections between modality and tense or aspect. For example, only the deontic interpretation (obligation) is possible for *must* with future time reference, so (45a) can only be interpreted to refer to obligation. Only the epistemic interpretation (certain inference) is possible in the perfect, as in (45b). The ambiguity demonstrated above is only possible with present tense states or habitual actions; so the simple present tense as in (45c,d) allows both interpretations, but the present continuous form (45e) is unambiguous. (Which reading is the correct one for 45e?)

(45)   a You must leave tomorrow.
        b You must have offended the Prime Minister very seriously.
        c You must read the market reports every day.
        d You must be very patient.
        e You must be reading the market reports every day.

We cannot attempt a detailed survey of this topic here, but it will be helpful to give some examples of other modal categories found in various languages. One fairly common type of agent-oriented modality is the DESIDERATIVE, which expresses a desire rather than an actual event. The following examples are from Kimaragang Dusun, a language of East Malaysia.

(46)   **Kimaragang desideratives**
         BASE   DESIDERATIVE
         mang-akan 'eat'   ti-akan   'want to eat'
         m-odop   'sleep'   ti-odop   'feel sleepy, want to sleep'
         s[um]obu' 'urinate'   ti-sobu' 'feel urge to urinate'

Turning to speaker-oriented modality, some languages have a special
DUBITATIVE marker, which indicates that the speaker has some doubt
about the truth of the proposition expressed.

(47)   **Walmatjari dubitative** (Hudson 1978:82–83)
         a mimi-jarti   pa-lu
            sick-COMITATIVE AUX-3pl
            'They are sick.'

         b mimi-jarti   pa-rta-lu
            sick-COMITATIVE AUX-DUB-3pl
            'Maybe they are sick.'

Many languages have some means of indicating the speaker's basis for
asserting the proposition, i.e. how the knowledge was acquired. Common
distinctions in this area include direct knowledge (eye-witness report) vs.
hearsay vs. inference; some examples are presented in (48–49).

(48)   **Sherpa evidentials** (Givón 1984:308)
         a ti-gi   cenyi caaq-sung
            he-ERG cup   break-PFV/DIRECT
            'He broke the cup (eyewitness or direct evidence).'

         b ti-gi   cenyi caaq-no
            he-ERG cup   break-PFV/INDIRECT
            'He broke the cup (hearsay or indirect evidence).'

(49)   **Huallaga Quechua evidentials** (Weber 1989:421)
         a Qam-pis maqa-ma-shka-nki   =mi
            you-also hit-1OBJ-PERF-2SUBJ =DIRECT
            'You also hit me (I saw and/or felt it).'

         b Qam-pis maqa-ma-shka-nki   =shi
            you-also hit-1OBJ-PERF-2SUBJ =HEARSAY
            '(Someone told me that) you also hit me (I was drunk and can't remember).'

         c Qam-pis maqa-ma-shka-nki   =chi
            you-also hit-1OBJ-PERF-2SUBJ =INFERENCE
            '(I infer that) you also hit me.'
            (I was attacked by a group of people, and I believe you were one of them).

Some languages have a special marker to indicate that the speaker is
surprised at what he is reporting. This form is often called the MIRATIVE:

(50)   **Lhasa Tibetan** (Payne 1997:255)

    a ngar   dngul tog=tsam yod.

       1sg.DAT money some   EXIST

       'I have some money.' (expected)

    b ngar   dngul tog=tsam 'dug.

       1sg.DAT money some   EXIST.MIRATIVE

       'I have some money!' (unexpected)

Tamil (a Dravidian language of southern India) has a fairly complex system of moods and modalities, involving both inflectional suffixes and modal verbs. Some of the modalities are illustrated in (51). Note that the suffix *-laam*, which marks a kind of hortative mood, is also used for the modalities of permission and possibility. It is glossed as "PERM" (for 'permissive') in these examples.

(51)   **Tamil modalities** (Asher 1985:167–172)

    a **Obligation (DEBITIVE)**

       avan angke pooka-ṇum

       he   there go-DEB

       'He must go there.'

    b **Physical ability**

       ennaale   naalu mail duuram naṭakka   muṭiyum.

       1sg.INSTR four mile distance walk-INF able

       'I can walk 4 miles.'

    c **Permissive**

       avan kuuṭṭattile   peeca-laam

       he   meeting-LOC speak-PERM

       'He can speak at the meeting.'

    d **Possibility**

       Kantacaami   vantaalum   vara-laam

       Kandaswami come-CONCESS come-PERM

       'Kandaswami may perhaps come.'

    e **Hearsay/indirect knowledge**

       neettu   cengkattle   maẓe peñcut-aam

       yesterday Chengam-LOC rain   fall-PAST-3sg.N-HEARSAY

       'Apparently it rained in Chengam yesterday.'

9.7   Conclusion

This chapter has touched on a number of difficult and complex issues, about which many books have been written and much more is still to be learned. One of our primary goals has been to help you to understand and use correctly the terminology that linguists have developed for describing TAM systems.

A second goal, of course, is to lay a foundation for analyzing these systems. The semantic contrasts that we have discussed in this chapter are not always easy to identify, and languages often differ from each other in quite subtle ways in these areas. Even where two languages have superficially similar sets of TAM affixes, the specific semantic content of a particular affix in one language often has no exact equivalent in the other language. For this reason, we cannot base our analysis of these systems on simple translations into English or the local trade language. Instead, we must look for examples of minimal contrast between two related affixes or markers, and then try to identify specific contexts where one would be acceptable but the other would not. This is a time-consuming process, but it is the only way we can be sure which semantic features are relevant to an observed grammatical distinction.

Exercises

9A Ekpeye (Nigeria; Roberts 1999, ex. M-4.5)
Use a position class chart to represent the structure of the following verbs:

1.	edi	'he will eat'
2.	edikpo	'he will finish eating'
3.	edilɛ	'he has eaten'
4.	adikpolɛ	'we have finished eating'
5.	edikpohwɔ	'he will eventually finish eating'
6.	adigbalɛ	'we have eaten again'
7.	emekpohwɔlɛ	'he has eventually finished making'
8.	emegba	'he will make again'
9.	amekpogbalɛ	'we have finished making again'
10.	amegbahwɔ	'we will eventually make again'
11.	eme	'he will make'

9B Ngiyambaa (Australia; Donaldson 1980; Palmer 1986)
Based on the following examples, state the meaning/function of the morphemes glossed with '??' Some of these elements are clitic auxiliary particles, which must attach to the first word of their clause (see chapter 17). Describe the TAM system of Ngiyambaa as reflected in these examples.

1. yuruŋ-gu ŋidj-iyi.
    rain-ERG rain-PAST
    'It rained.'

2. yuruŋ-gu   ŋidja-ṛa.
    rain-ERG rain-PRES
    'It is raining.'

3. yuruŋ-gu   ŋidjal-aga.
    rain-ERG rain-??
    'It might/will rain.'

4. guya=ndu   dha-yi.
    fish=2NOM   eat-PAST
    'You ate a fish.'

5. guya=wa:=ndu   dha-yi.
    fish=??=2NOM   eat-PAST
    'So you ate a *fish*!!'

6. minja=wa:=ndu   dha-yi.
    what=??=2NOM   eat-PAST
    'You ate *what?!*'

7. guya=ga:=ndu   dha-yi.
    fish=??=2NOM   eat-PAST
    'Maybe you ate a fish, I don't know.'

8. minjaŋ=ga:=ndu   dha-yi.
    what=??=2NOM   eat-PAST
    'You ate something, I don't know what.'

9. ŋalu=ynja   walga-dha.
    that=up   climb-??
    'Climb up (that tree)!'

10. ŋindu bawuŋ-ga   yuwa-dha.
    you   middle-LOC lie-??
    '(You) lie in the middle!'

11. ŋadhu bawuŋ-ga   yuwa-giri.
    1sg   middle-LOC lie-??
    'I must lie in the middle.'

12. yana-buna-giri.
    go-back-??
    'We must go back.'

13. ŋadhu dhi:rba-nha guruŋa-giri.
    1sg   know-PRES swim-??
    'I know how to swim.'

14. ŋindu giramb-iyi.
    you   sick-PAST
    'You were sick.'

15. ŋindu=gara giramb-iyi.
    you=??   sick-PAST
    'One can see that you were sick.'

16. ŋindu=dhan giramb-iyi.
     you=??   sick-PAST
     'They say you were sick.'

17. wara:y=gara=dhu=na bungiyam-iyi dhiŋga:=dhi:.
     bad=??=1NOM=3ABS burn-PAST   meat=1POSS
     'I have burned my meat so it's no good, to judge by the smell.'
     (said outside the house where the meat was cooking)

18. gabuga:=gara=lu ŋamum-iyi.
     egg=??=3ERG   lay-PAST
     'It has laid an egg, by the sound of it.'
     (said of a chicken that was out of sight)

19. ŋadhu=dhan wiri-nji.
     1sg=??   cook-PAST
     'People say I have cooked.'

20. guni:m=baṟa=nu: baluy-aga.
     mother=??=2POSS die-??
     'Your mother will certainly die (if you point at a rainbow).'

21. wiriwal=baṟa=ni ga-ṟa.
     heavy=??=3ABS be-PRES
     'It certainly is heavy, that's for sure.'

22. guyan=baga:=dhu ga-ṟa.
     shy=??=1NOM   be-PRES
     'But I'm shy (contrary to what you seem to think)!'

23. gali:-ŋinda=gila ŋiyanu baluy-aga.
     water-desired=?? we   die-??
     'I guess maybe we will die for lack of water.'

24. guya=gila=ga:=lu dha-yi.
     fish=??=??=3ABS eat-PAST
     'I guess maybe he ate a fish, I don't know.'

25. minjaŋ=ga:=ma=ndu dha-yi.
     what=??=??=2NOM eat-PAST
     'You might have eaten I don't know what, but you didn't.'

26. waŋa:y=baga:=dhan=du ŋudha-nhi.
     NEG=??=??=2NOM   give-PAST
     'But people say you *didn't* give anything (contrary to what you claim).'

27. ŋindu=gila=ga:=dhan guṟuŋay-aga.
     you=??=??=??   swim-??
     'I don't know, but I hear that maybe you will swim.'

28. ŋinu:=ma=ni   bura:y giyi,   ŋindu=ma=ni yada guraw-iyi.
     your=??=3ABS child be-PAST you=??=3ABS well look.after-PAST
     'If this child had been yours, you would have looked after it well.'

Additional exercises

Merrifield et al. (1987) prob. 30, 32, 38, 150; and for a challenge, prob. 29
Healey (1990b), ex. A.17, 19, 25, 26, 27; D.9

Notes

1. See ch. 16, sec. 16.2.1 for a discussion of infixation.
2. A distinct set of tense markers is also used to distinguish between relative and absolute tense reference.
3. In some contexts examples like (13a–c) may be acceptable, but only when the time phrase is interpreted as specifying the beginning of the event, rather than the completion of the event as in (13d–f).
4. Comrie (1976a:61) notes that in several other Romance languages, including French, Italian, and Romanian, the construction that formerly marked the perfect has lost the perfect meaning and is now used simply as a past tense marker.
5. As this example suggests, certain constructions in Tagalog employ a "relative tense" system. Note the use of the "future" form *aalis* with past reference in the following example:

> Nang aalis   na   ako, tinawag   niya   ako.
> when leave(FUT) COMP 1sg called(PAST) by.him 1sg
> 'When I was <u>about to leave</u>, he called me.'   (Schachter and Otanes 1972:477)

6. Notice in the last example that the passive suffix *-in* does not appear in the presence of the aspect-marking infix *-in-*. As far as I know, this is true in every Philippine language.
7. Bloomfield (1917); Wolfenden (1961); de Guzman (1978).

10 Non-verbal predicates

In chapter 5 we saw that many predicates impose selectional restrictions on their arguments, as illustrated in (1). Each of the verbs in these examples requires one if its arguments to belong to a particular semantic class: animate beings in (1a,c); important public figures in (1b). When these restrictions are violated, the resulting sentences are semantically odd or unacceptable.

(1) a #My pencil doesn't know how to spell that word.
     b #John assassinated a big cockroach.
     c #Mary taught her motorcycle classical Chinese.

The examples in (2a,b) also involve selectional restrictions, but with an interesting difference: the same verb is used in all of these examples, namely *is*. This shows that, unlike previous examples we have considered, the contrast between *John is in love* vs. *#My guitar is in love*, or *#John is easy to play* vs. *My guitar is easy to play*, etc. cannot be determined by the lexical properties of the verb itself. Rather, the words or phrases that follow the verb seem to determine the selectional restrictions on the subject of the clause.

(2) a $\left\{ \begin{array}{c} \text{John} \\ \text{\#My guitar} \end{array} \right\}$ is happy/sick/in love/eager to play.

     b $\left\{ \begin{array}{c} \text{\#John} \\ \text{My guitar} \end{array} \right\}$ is broken/out of tune/easy to play.

The fact that the AP and PP constituents in (2a,b) can impose selectional restrictions suggests that they are functioning as semantic predicates. Up to now, most of the clauses we have considered have contained verbal predicates, but in this chapter we will examine various types of clauses whose semantic predicate is expressed by a word or phrase of some other category. (Recall that in chapter 4, section 4.1 we defined a predicate as "the element of meaning which identifies the property or relationship" described by a clause.)

The verb *to be*, realized as *is* in (2a,b), has almost no meaning of its own. It is grammatically a verb, being inflected for tense and agreement, but semantically it is essentially empty. For this reason it is often referred to as a LINKING VERB, or COPULA. The meaning of the clause is determined by the phrase which follows the linking verb, e.g. *in love* or *eager to play* in (2a). This phrase is called a PREDICATE COMPLEMENT, for reasons to be discussed in section 10.1.1.

The linking verb contributes very little to the meaning of a sentence, but it does satisfy a basic requirement of English grammar which states that every sentence must contain a verb. This requirement does not hold for all languages, however. In a number of languages, sentences like those in (2) would be expressed without any verb at all. Some Tagalog examples are presented in (3).[1] The semantic predicates of these three sentences are expressed by phrases belonging to the categories AP, NP, and PP, respectively. (In a Tagalog verbal clause, the verb usually comes first; in non-verbal clauses, the predicate phrase normally comes first.[2]) In each case the English translation contains the linking verb *is*, but there is no corresponding form in the Tagalog.

(3)   a [Matalino]$_{AP}$ ang=batà.
   intelligent NOM=child
   'The child is intelligent.'

  b [Anak ni=Belen]$_{NP}$ si=Romy.
   child GEN=Belen NOM=Romy
   'Romy is Belen's son.'

  c [Nasa Maynila]$_{PP}$ ang=gusali.
   at.DAT Manila NOM=building
   'The building is in Manila.'

In chapter 4 we defined a CLAUSE as the smallest grammatical unit which expresses a predicate and its arguments. The examples in (3) are unlike any we have discussed thus far in that they lack a verb; but they are still clauses under this definition, because they each contain a predicate and its argument. What is special about them is the fact that their predicates are not expressed by verbs.

English and Tagalog represent two basic patterns of clause structure involving non-verbal predicates. Many languages use a linking verb to express such predicates, as English does. In other languages, like Tagalog, no verb is needed. And there are a significant number of languages which use a linking verb in some contexts and not in others. In this chapter we will discuss examples of each type.

10.1 Basic clause patterns with and without the copula

There is a correlation between the syntactic category of a non-verbal predicate and its semantic function. Clauses like (3a), in which the semantic predicate is expressed by an adjective phrase, generally describe a quality or attribute which is said to be true of the subject. We will (following Payne 1997) refer to examples of this type as ATTRIBUTIVE CLAUSES.

An EQUATIVE CLAUSE is one in which the semantic predicate is expressed by a noun phrase, like (3b). The semantic function of the clause depends on whether the predicate NP is definite or indefinite. If the predicate NP is definite, as in (4a), the equative clause basically states that the two NPs refer to the same individual. If the predicate NP is indefinite, as in (4b,c), the equative clause states that the subject NP is a member of the class named by the predicate NP.

(4)   a George Washington was the first President of the United States.
        b George Washington was a surveyor.
        c George Washington was a tall man.
        d George Washington was tall.

In the latter case, the meaning of the equative clause is very much like that of an attributive clause; compare the equative clause in (4c) with the attributive clause in (4d). But the grammatical structure of an equative clause is normally the same whether the predicate NP is definite or indefinite. In Mandarin Chinese, for example, no copula is used for attributive clauses (those with AP predicates), as illustrated in (5a). However, a copula (linking verb) is used for equative clauses, whether the predicate NP is definite (5b) or indefinite (5c). (The predicate phrase is enclosed in brackets in these examples.)

(5)   **Mandarin Chinese**
        a **Attributive** (AP as predicate):
          Nèi ge   nǚrén   [hěn piàoliàng].
          that CLASS woman very pretty
          'That woman is very pretty.'

        b **Equative** (predicate NP is definite):
          Nèi ge   nǚrén   *shì*   [wǒ tài-tai].
          that CLASS woman COPULA my wife
          'That woman is my wife.'

        c **Equative** (predicate NP is indefinite):
          Nèi ge   nǚrén   *shì*   [Cháozhōu rén].
          that CLASS woman COPULA Teochew   person
          'That woman is a Teochew.'

A clause like (3c), in which the semantic predicate is expressed by a prepositional phrase, is often referred to as a LOCATIVE CLAUSE. As this name suggests, clauses of this type are often used to identify the location of the subject, as in (3c). However, this construction can also be used to express

a wide range of other semantic functions; some of these are illustrated in
the Tagalog examples in (6).

(6)   a Galing sa=Maynila si=Ben   dati.[3]
         from   DAT=Manila NOM=Ben previous
         'Ben is originally from Manila.'

       b Para sa=iyo   ang=mga=liham na   iyon.
         for   DAT=2sg NOM=PL=letter LNK that
         'Those letters are for you.'

       c Para sa=mga=Nasyonalista ang=kapatid niya.
         for   DAT=PL=Nationalist NOM=sibling 3sg.GEN
         'His brother is for (i.e. supports) the Nationalists.'

       d Nasa   babae   ang=libro.
         at.DAT woman NOM=book
         'The woman has the book.'

10.1.1 English: copula plus predicate complement

As noted above, attributive, equative, and locative clauses in
English must contain the copula, or linking verb, *be*. The AP, NP, or PP
which follows the copula, as in (7a, b, c, respectively), is called a PREDI-
CATE COMPLEMENT. A traditional definition of this term is "a constituent
which is needed to complete the meaning of the predicate."

(7)   a The Mayor is [extremely angry at the press]$_{AP}$.   ATTRIBUTIVE
       b Arthur is [a former Governor]$_{NP}$.   EQUATIVE
       c His money is [under the mattress]$_{PP}$.   LOCATIVE

In chapter 3 we defined a COMPLEMENT as a phrasal dependent which
is selected by the head word. The complements of a verb are those elements
which are specified in the verb's subcategorization set. Up to this point, we
have discussed complements which bear the Grammatical Relations SUBJ,
OBJ, OBJ$_2$, and OBL and generally identify participants. But (for reasons
we will discuss in section 10.5) the phrases that follow the copula in sentences like (7a–c) do not bear any of these relations; they are a different kind
of complement. In semantic terms, these complements express predicates,
rather than participants; hence the name PREDICATE COMPLEMENT.

The copula is by no means the only verb in English that takes a predicate
complement. Some examples of other verbs that require predicate complements are given in (8).

(8)   a Arthur *became* [the Governor of Texas].
       b The Mayor *seems* [extremely angry].
       c We *elected* John [chairman of the board].
       d They all *consider* me [crazy].

We will use the annotation XCOMP to designate the Grammatical Relation of a predicate complement. The "X" stands for any major category (N, A, V, or P), reflecting the fact that predicate complements may be NPs, APs, PPs, or even VPs (though we will not discuss VP complements here). We can represent the structure of an English sentence containing a predicate complement with a rule like (9), where XP stands for any phrasal category (NP, AP, PP, or VP). Notice that this single rule will account for the sentences in (7), which contain a copula, as well as those in (8), which contain other verbs.

(9)   S →   NP   V (NP)   (XP)
                [SUBJ]   [OBJ] [XCOMP]

The lexical entries for the verbs in (8), and for the copula, must include a predicate complement as part of the verb's subcategorization. The problem of specifying the category (NP, AP, or PP) of the predicate complements which can occur with a particular English verb is somewhat complex.[4] For simplicity, we will assume that the lexical entry for each verb specifies the possible categories of its XCOMPs. As predicted by the rule in (9), no verb takes more than one predicate complement in the same clause, regardless of category. Possible lexical entries for the verbs *consider* and *become* are proposed in (10–11).

(10)   a I consider John honest/my friend/?*out of the country.
        b *consider*   < exper,   patient,   state >
                          | | |
                        SUBJ   OBJ   XCOMP
                    [XCOMP CAT = AP, NP]

(11)   a Mary became very sick/a world-famous poet/?*in trouble.
        b *become*   < patient,   state >
                          | |
                        SUBJ   XCOMP
                    [XCOMP CAT = AP, NP]

Designing a lexical entry for the copula is somewhat more challenging, largely due to the lack of lexical semantic content.[5] However, ignoring this complication for the moment, we can adopt the entry in (12) as a first approximation (example sentences given in (7)).

(12)   *be*   < th/pat,   state >
                   | |
                 SUBJ   XCOMP
              [XCOMP CAT = AP, NP, PP]

10.1.2　Tagalog: verbless clauses

　　　As we saw in (3), attributive, equative, and locative clauses in Tagalog do not contain a copula. Some slightly more complex examples are given in (13). (13a) shows an equative clause with an indefinite predicate NP; (13b) shows an equative clause with a definite predicate NP; (13c) shows an attributive clause with a complex AP as predicate; and (13d) shows a locative clause.[6]

(13)　　a　Opisyal　sa=hukbo　　ang=panganay.
　　　　　　officer　　DAT=army　　NOM=eldest
　　　　　　'The eldest child is an officer in the army.'

　　　　b　Si=Rosa　　　ang=paborito　ko=ng　　　kaklase.
　　　　　　NOM=Rosa　NOM=favorite　my=LNK　classmate
　　　　　　'My favorite classmate is Rosa.'

　　　　c　Talaga=ng　　ma-ya-yaman　ang=mga=doktor.
　　　　　　really=LNK　STAT-PL-rich　NOM=PL=doctor
　　　　　　'The doctors are really rich.'

　　　　d　Nasa　　　gitnâ　　ng=silíd　　　ang=mesa.
　　　　　　at.DAT　middle　GEN=room　NOM=table
　　　　　　'The table is in the middle of the room.'

How shall we represent the structure of these verbless clauses? Some linguists assume that languages like Tagalog employ a "silent" (or invisible) copula, and that the structure of these clauses is essentially the same as the structure of their English translations. However, at least for Tagalog there seems to be no language-internal evidence for this assumption. In fact, there is good evidence that the structure of verbless clauses is very different from the structure of clauses which contain a verb.[7] Rather than assuming an invisible copula as the grammatical head of these clauses, it seems preferable (at least for Tagalog) simply to assume that the grammatical head is the NP, AP, or PP which expresses the semantic predicate. This analysis is indicated in the PS rules in (14).

(14)　　a　**Attributive clause:**
　　　　　　S → AP　　NP
　　　　　　　　　　　[SUBJ]

　　　　b　**Equative clause:**
　　　　　　S → NP　　NP
　　　　　　　　　　　[SUBJ]

　　　　c　**Locative clause:**
　　　　　　S → PP　　NP
　　　　　　　　　　　[SUBJ]

But these rules raise an interesting question. The Coherence condition stated in chapter 5 implies that the complement relations (SUBJ, OBJ, OBJ$_2$, OBL, and now XCOMP) can only occur in a clause when they are subcategorized, i.e. selected by the lexical entry of their predicate. If Tagalog verbless clauses have the structure shown in (14), how are the SUBJ phrases in (3) and (13) subcategorized? Can adjectives, nouns, and prepositions assign the SUBJ relation?

Bresnan (2001) has argued that the answer is "yes," not just for languages like Tagalog but even for English. She presents a variety of evidence, which we will not discuss here, showing that an XCOMP of any category must assign the SUBJ relation to the phrase of which it is predicated. For example, the XCOMPs in (8a,b) assign the SUBJ relation to the subjects of those sentences, and the XCOMPs in (8c,d) assign the SUBJ relation to the objects of those sentences.[8] Bresnan argues that adjectives have argument structures similar to verbs, which include a SUBJ argument; and that nouns and prepositions may optionally acquire argument structures by a regular process of predicate formation.

Without going into the formal details, we will adopt Bresnan's analysis. Clauses generated by the PS rules in (14) will be well-formed because their non-verbal predicates have argument structures and assign the SUBJ relation.

Even languages which have no copula may contain other verbs that require a predicate complement. One such verb in Tagalog is *maging* 'become,' which can take either AP (15a) or NP (15b) complements.[9] The verb *maging* forms a tight constituent with its predicate complement, and is sometimes written as a prefix.[10] However, its complement is a full phrasal category and not just a single word, as shown by examples like (15c); so it is (at least in its syntactic properties) a free form, and not an affix. Some other Tagalog verbs which take predicate complements are illustrated in (16–17).

(15)   a Nagiging   mahal   ang=bigas.
         become-IMPERF expensive NOM=rice
         'Rice is getting expensive.'

     b Naging   opisyal ang=anak   ko.
         become-PFV officer NOM=child my
         'My son became an officer.'

     c Magiging   [unang presidente ng=samahan]   si=Armand.
         become-FUT first   president GEN=organization NOM=Armand
         'Armand will become the first president of the organization.'

(16)   a Ipinapalagay   ko   si=Juan=ng   matalino.
         consider-IMPERF 1sg NOM=Juan=LNK intelligent
         'I consider Juan intelligent.'

b Inihalal   namin   si=Ben=ng   presidente.
  elect-PFV 1pl.EXCL NOM=Ben=LNK president
  'We elected Ben president.'

(17)   a Nagkunwari si=Juan=ng   duktor.
          pretend-PFV NOM=Juan=LNK doctor
          'Juan pretended to be a doctor.'

        b Nagkunwari si=Juan=ng   galit.
          pretend-PFV NOM=Juan=LNK angry
          'Juan pretended to be angry.'

10.2   Existential and possessive clauses

As the Tagalog example (6d) shows, possession is one of the relationships which can be expressed by the locative (i.e. prepositional) clause type. But the possessive relation involved in that example is of a particular kind: temporary physical possession, rather than ownership. The sentence tells us where the book is, rather than whom it belongs to; thus the use of the locative clause pattern seems quite appropriate.

Compare (6d), repeated here as (18a), with the possessive constructions in (18b,c).[11] While all three of these sentences express some kind of possessive relationship, each of them has a distinct function. Example (18a) describes temporary physical possession, as we have already mentioned, while (18b) describes ownership; but in both cases the possessed item is a definite, specific object (one particular book). Sentence (18c) may describe either temporary physical possession or actual ownership, but the possessed item is some indefinite or generic object; the hearer cannot tell which specific book is intended, and the speaker may not even know.

(18)   a Nasa   babae   ang=libro.   (= ex. 6d)
          at.DAT woman NOM=book
          'The woman has the book.' (or: 'The book is in the woman's possession.')

        b Sa=babae   ang=libro.
          DAT=woman NOM=book
          'The woman owns the book.' (or: 'The book belongs to the woman.')

        c May   libro ang=babae.
          EXIST book NOM=woman
          'The woman has/owns a book.'

Corresponding to these semantic differences, we find differences in grammatical structure as well. In (18a) the subject (the possessed item) is a definite NP and the predicate (expressing the possessor) is a PP. In (18b) the subject again expresses the possessed item as a definite NP, and the predicate again expresses the possessor, but this time as a bare dative NP rather than a PP. Aside from this one difference, the two clauses are structurally identical. Example (18c), however, has a very different structure: the subject NP expresses the possessor, while the possessed item appears as part of the predicate phrase, which contains the EXISTENTIAL predicate *may*.

Compare the indefinite possessive example (18c) with the EXISTEN- TIAL CLAUSE in (19a). As you can see, both sentences contain the same existential predicate (*may*) followed by a bare NP, i.e. an NP with no case marker.[12] (19b) is another example of an existential clause, but it contains a different existential predicate: in place of *may*, which expresses positive existence (something does exist), (19b) has *walâ*, which expresses negative existence (something does not exist). These same two existential predicates can also be used to express positive and negative possession, respectively, as illustrated in (20).

(19) a May tao   sa=bahay.[13]
         exist person DAT=house
         'There is someone in the house.'

      b Wala=ng   mais sa=palengke.
         not.exist=LNK corn DAT=market
         'There is no corn in the market.'

(20) a May pera   si=Juan.
         exist money NOM=Juan
         'Juan has (some) money.'

      b Wala=ng   pera   si=Juan.
         not.exist=LNK money NOM=Juan
         'Juan has no money.'

The existential predicates in (19–20) do not fit neatly into any syntac- tic category. Verbs in Tagalog take a rich assortment of inflectional and derivational affixes, but the existential *may* (or the longer form, *mayroon*) cannot take any of these affixes.[14] On the other hand, existential *may* does not share the properties of any other lexical category either. (Such forms are found in many languages; often they are called DEFECTIVE verbs, meaning that they lack the normal range of inflected forms which most verbs in the language exhibit.) So it is difficult to say whether the existential construc- tions above are strictly speaking "non-verbal" clauses; but they are clearly different from normal verbal clauses.

10.3   Cross-linguistic patterns

Up to now we have used the terms COPULA and LINKING VERB interchangeably. However, some languages have a copula which is not a verb. In Hausa, for example, verbs normally occur in the middle of a clause;

the basic word order is S–Aux–V–O, with the auxiliary element indicating person, number, gender, and tense/aspect. The copula that appears in equative clauses, however, appears in final position and is inflected only for gender, as illustrated in (21). It does not fit well within either the category V or the category Aux.

(21)   **Hausa** (Nigeria; Schachter 1985:55)
    a Ita   yarinya *ce.*   'She is a girl.'
      she girl   COP.FEM
    b Shi yaro *ne.*   'He is a boy.'
      he   boy COP.MASC

In other languages, the copula may be an invariant particle: one that is never inflected but always appears in the same form, and only serves as the marker of a non-verbal clause type. Payne (1997:117) cites the Sùpyìré language of Brazil as one such example.

A number of languages have verbal copulae which are only used in non-present tenses. In Modern Hebrew, for example, attributive, equative, and locative clauses in the present tense do not contain any copula, as illustrated in (22), although they may optionally contain a nominative pronoun that doubles the subject NP (not shown here). In past or future tenses, however, an inflected copular verb (root: *h.y.y*) is obligatory, as illustrated in (23).

(22)   **Modern Hebrew** (Doron 1986:314–315)
    a dani more   ba-universita.
      Dani teacher in-the.university
      'Dani is a teacher at the university.'
    b dani ha-more   le-matematika.
      Dani the-teacher to-mathematics
      'Dani is the mathematics teacher.'
    c dani nexmad ad.meod.
      Dani nice   very
      'Dani is very nice.'
    d dani al ha-gag.
      Dani on the-roof
      'Dani is on the roof.'

(23)   a dani *yihye*   more   ba-universita.
      Dani be.FUT teacher in-the.university
      'Dani will be a teacher at the university.'
    b dani *haya*   ha-more   le-matematika.
      Dani be.PAST the-teacher to-mathematics
      'Dani was the mathematics teacher.'

c dani *haya*   nexmad ad.meod.
  Dani be.PAST nice   very
  'Dani was very nice.'

d dani *yihye*   al ha-gag.
  Dani be.FUT on the-roof
  'Dani will be on the roof.'

Spanish has two distinct copular verbs, *ser* and *estar*. The choice of which copula to use depends partly on the category of the predicate complement and partly on semantic factors. Cárdenas (1961) states that *ser* is always used when the predicate complement is an NP, as in (24a), while *estar* is always used when the predicate complement is an adverbial element, as in (24b).

(24)   a La señora Alvarez *es*   una profesora conocida.
         the Mrs.   Alvarez SER one teacher   known
         'Mrs. Alvarez is a well-known teacher.' (Schmitt 1972:125)

       b La madre   *está*   aquí/cerca/lejos.
         the mother ESTAR here/close/far
         'The mother is here/near-by/far away.' (Cárdenas 1961:3)

When the predicate complement is a prepositional phrase, *ser* is used with the preposition *de* 'of, from' in all its various senses; while *estar* is used with the prepositions *en* 'in, on' and *a* 'at.' Some examples are provided in (25–26).

(25)   a El señor González *es*   de   México.
         the Mr. González SER from Mexico
         'Mr. González is from Mexico.' (Schmitt 1972:126)

       b El coche *es*   del   señor González.
         the car   SER of.the Mr. González
         'The car belongs to Mr. González.' (Schmitt 1972:126)

       c El anillo *es*   de plata.
         the ring   SER of silver
         'The ring is (made of) silver.' (Schmitt 1972:126)

(26)   a Carlos *está*   ahora en Nueva York.
         Carlos ESTAR now   in New York
         'Carlos is now in New York.' (Schmitt 1972:126)

       b Madrid *está*   en España.
         Madrid ESTAR in Spain
         'Madrid is in Spain.' (Schmitt 1972:126)

c La hermana *está*   a la   derecha.
  the sister   ESTAR at the right
  'The sister is at the right.' (Cárdenas 1961:1)

Notice that the choice of copula in locative clauses depends only on the specific preposition used; *estar* is used with the preposition *en* whether the location is understood as being temporary (26a) or permanent (26b). When the predicate complement is an adjective phrase, however, either copula may be used. The choice is made on semantic grounds: *ser* is used to express inherent properties or characteristics; while *estar* is used to express temporary states. This contrast is illustrated in (27–28). Some adjectives can take on two different meanings depending on which copula is used, as illustrated in (29–30).

(27)   a Maria *está*   bonita (hoy).
          Maria ESTAR pretty today
          'Maria looks pretty (today).'

        b Maria *es*   bonita.
          Maria SER pretty
          'Maria is pretty/a pretty girl.' (Schmitt 1972:128)

(28)   a Carlos *está*   borracho.
          Carlos ESTAR drunk
          'Carlos is drunk.'

        b Carlos *es*   borracho.
          Carlos SER drunk
          'Carlos is a drunkard.' (Schmitt 1972:128)

(29)   a Maria *está*   aburrida.
          Maria ESTAR bored
          'Maria is bored.'

        b Maria *es*   aburrida.
          Maria SER bored
          'Maria is boring.'

(30)   a Carlos *está*   malo.
          Carlos ESTAR bad
          'Carlos is sick.'

        b Carlos *es*   malo.
          Carlos SER bad
          'Carlos is an evil person.'

In the preceding section we saw that the structure of a possessive construction may depend on the definiteness of the possessed item. This is not a special feature of Tagalog grammar, but is, in fact, a common pattern across languages: definiteness is often a major factor in determining the structure of a possessive clause. A Tagalog clause expressing ownership of a specific, definite item, like example (18b), is structurally very similar to a locative clause. Many other languages also exhibit strong similarities between definite possessive constructions and locative clauses (Clark 1978).

Tagalog clauses expressing possession or ownership of an indefinite or unspecified item, such as (18c), are structurally more similar to existential clauses. An important aspect of the similarity between indefinite possessives and indefinite existentials in many languages is that the same existential predicate is used for both constructions. It turns out that the predicate which is used for these two clause types in Tagalog is not used in stative, equative, or locative clauses. The same situation is found in Dusun, Land Dayak, and a large number of other Austronesian languages: there is a unique predicate for existentials and indefinite possessives, not used in other clause types. Outside of the Austronesian family, Clark (1978) notes the following languages where this same pattern is found: Amharic, Irish, Mandarin, Eskimo, French, Modern Greek, Hebrew, Twi, and possibly Arabic.

Of course, other patterns are also common. In Malay, the existential predicate is used for both possessive and locative clauses, and Clark reports the same pattern in Turkish and Yurok. English uses the copula *be* for existential and locative clauses, but *have* for possessives. Some languages use the same copula for all of these clause types.[15]

As noted above, Tagalog has two existential predicates: the positive *may* (or *mayroon*) and the negative *walâ*. The negative existential is different from the various negatives used in other contexts. Again, a number of other languages also have special negative existential forms. Some examples from various languages are shown in the following table:

(31)

Language	Exist	Not exist
Tagalog	may(roon)	walâ
Kimaragang Dusun	waro	aso?
Biatah Land Dayak	əgi	mating
Hokkien	wu	bo
Eskimo[16]	qar	-it-
Hebrew	yeš	e^{y}n

10.4 A note on "impersonal constructions"

We have noted several times that sentences (19a) and (20a) are very similar in structure. However, there is an important difference between the two sentences as well. In both sentences, the existential predicate *may* is followed by a caseless NP complement. In the possessive clause (20a), the other NP (the possessor) is marked for nominative case, indicating that it is the subject. But there is no nominative NP in (19a); this sentence appears to lack a subject. Various syntactic tests confirm that sentences like (19a) and (19b) have no grammatical subject. This fact is not surprising: indefinite existentials in most languages are either subjectless or involve dummy subjects, like the *there* in the English translations of (19a) and (19b).[17]

Sentences that contain no subject are referred to as IMPERSONAL CON-STRUCTIONS. However, we must distinguish between true impersonal constructions and clauses in which the subject is simply not expressed by a distinct word or phrase. For example, in many languages which have a fully developed system of subject–verb agreement, subject pronouns may be optional or used only for special emphasis (recall our discussion of "pro-drop" in chapter 5). As another example, the subject is usually not expressed in imperative sentences in English (and in many other languages), although it is "understood" to be present. Neither of these examples counts as a true impersonal construction.

Impersonal constructions are frequently used for METEOROLOGICAL clauses like the Tagalog examples in (32–33). The predicates in such clauses are sometimes called "weather verbs," but they need not be verbs at all. The clauses in (32a) and (33a–c) all have verbal predicates, as indicated by their morphological structure, but the predicate in (32b) is an adjective.

(32)   a Umuulan. 'It is raining.'
            raining

         b Mainit. 'It is hot.'
            hot

(33)   a Lumindol   nang   malakas.
            earthquake-PAST ADVBL strong
            'There was a strong earthquake.'

         b Babagyo   raw   bukas.
            storm-FUT REPORT tomorrow
            'They say there will be a storm tomorrow.'

         c Bumabaha   sa=Maynila.
            flood-PRES DAT=Manila
            'There is flooding in Manila.'

Notice that the English translations of the examples in (19), (32), and (33) all contain a DUMMY subject, *it* or *there*. A dummy is an element which has no semantic content but simply occupies the subject position. Dummies often have the form of a pronoun, but they do not actually refer to anything. Some German examples of impersonal constructions containing the dummy subject *es* 'it' are given below. Example (34c) is a typical meteorological clause, while (34d) is an indefinite existential.

(34)   a Es wurde   getanzt.
            it PASSIVE danced
            'There was dancing.' (lit: 'It was danced.')

b Es tut   mir   leid.
  it   does to.me sad
  'I am sorry.'

c Es schneit.
  it   snows
  'It is snowing.'

d Es gibt   ein Buch auf dem Tisch.
  it   gives a   book on the   table
  'There is a book on the table.'

10.5   Further notes on the predicate complement (XCOMP) relation

In section 10.1.1 we stated that predicate complement phrases like those in the English examples (7) and (8) must bear a new kind of Grammatical Relation, which we labeled XCOMP. But what evidence do we have that this assumption is actually correct? For example, how do we know that these phrases are really complements and not just adjuncts?

One very important piece of evidence is the fact that predicate complements are often obligatory; compare the examples in (35) with those in (8). Adjuncts are never obligatory, as illustrated by the examples of DEPICTIVE predicate adjuncts in (36). Thus the fact that the predicate phrases in (7–8) are obligatory provides evidence that they are complements.

(35)   a *Arthur became.
       b *The Mayor seems.
       c *They all consider me.[18]

(36)   a Henry arrived at the courtroom (*drunk*).
       b Susan served the oysters (*raw*).

Bresnan (2001:267ff.) presents several other kinds of evidence demonstrating the difference between predicate complements and predicate adjuncts. We will mention two of these briefly. First, adjuncts can often occur in a variety of positions within the sentence, as illustrated in (37); but the position of predicate complements is relatively fixed, as illustrated in (38).

(37)   **PREDICATE ADJUNCTS**
       a Mary ran from the room, *ashamed of herself*.
       b Mary, *ashamed of herself*, ran from the room.
       c Woolsey, *as a loyal officer*, refused to join the rebellion.
       d *As a loyal officer*, Woolsey refused to join the rebellion.

(38)   **PREDICATE COMPLEMENTS**
  a Mary didn't sound *ashamed of herself.*
  b *Mary, *ashamed of herself*, didn't sound.
  c Woolsey strikes me *as a loyal officer.*
  d # Woolsey, *as a loyal officer*, strikes me. (different meaning!)

A second difference is that multiple adjuncts may occur within a single clause, as illustrated in (39). Predicate complements, however, like other arguments, must be unique within their clause as illustrated in (40).

(39)   **PREDICATE ADJUNCTS**
  a *Ashamed of herself*, Mary returned to her office *ready to apologize.*
  b *As an outspoken critic*, Woolsey had made a number of enemies *as a junior officer.*

(40)   **PREDICATE COMPLEMENTS**
  a *Mary didn't sound [*ashamed of herself*] [*ready to apologize*].
  b *Woolsey strikes me [*as a loyal officer*] [*as an outspoken critic*].

Well, then, how do we know that these complement phrases are not, in fact, grammatical objects? At least in the case of post-verbal NPs like those in (7b) and (8a), this might seem like a reasonable hypothesis. (Of course, the fact that APs can occur as predicate complements is itself an important piece of evidence, since an object cannot normally be an AP.) In some languages, e.g. Latin, there is evidence from case marking: direct objects take accusative case, while predicate complement NPs and APs agree with the case marking of the subject (normally nominative).[19] Even in English, where case is marked only on personal pronouns, there is a weak difference in case-marking potential between objects and predicate complements, as shown in (41).

(41)   a That's her/ That is she.[20]
         b John loves her/*she.

But this difference is rarely observed, since (aside from certain equative clauses like (41a)) personal pronouns are hardly ever used as predicate complements. This restriction on pronouns, which is illustrated in (42), is another piece of evidence for distinguishing predicate complements from objects.

(42)   a Arthur became a policeman.
         b *Arthur became him.
         c Arthur slugged a policeman.
         d Arthur slugged him.

Number agreement proves to be more useful than case marking in English: as (43) shows, predicate complements must agree with the subject NP for number, but there is no such restriction on objects.

(43)   a Arthur is/became a lawyer.
        b *Arthur is/became some lawyers.
        c Arthur hired a lawyer.
        d Arthur hired some lawyers.

Another kind of evidence comes from the fact that predicate complement NPs cannot appear in certain constructions where direct objects can. For example, an object NP can become the subject of a passive sentence (44b) or of certain adjectives (like *hard*, *easy*, etc.) which require a verbal or clausal complement (44c). However, predicate complement NPs never occur in these positions, as illustrated in (45).

(44)   a Mary tickled an elephant.
        b An elephant was tickled (by Mary).
        c An elephant is hard (for Mary) to tickle.

(45)   a Mary became an actress.
        b *An actress was become (by Mary).
        c *An actress is hard (for Mary) to become.

Finally, the definite article is often optional in predicate complement NPs, but not in object NPs; this is illustrated in (46). Thus, we have very strong evidence for distinguishing between NPs that function as objects and those that function as predicate complements.

(46)   a Mary became (the) Queen of England.
        b Mary tickled *(the) Queen of England.

10.6 Conclusion

We have discussed two different ways in which languages may allow a non-verbal phrase (NP, AP, or PP) to express the semantic predicate of a clause. Some languages, like English, make use of a semantically empty linking verb, or copula, which selects the predicate phase as a complement (XCOMP). Other languages, like Tagalog, allow a predicate NP, AP, or PP to function as the grammatical head of the clause, with no verb (visible or invisible) required. Some languages make use of both of these patterns in different contexts, e.g. present vs. non-present tense; or attributive vs. equative clauses. Both structures have the same essential function, namely to assert that the subject NP has a certain property, location, or identity.

Another type of clause that often has special properties is the EXISTEN-TIAL construction, which is used to assert either the existence or the non-existence of something. Existential clauses often involve a special predicate word, which has different properties from normal verbs. In many languages the same basic pattern is also used to express possession or location of indefinite or non-specific items.

Exercises

10A Tok Pisin (PNG; Woolford 1979; Verhaar 1995; Dutton 1973)
Describe the structure of the clauses found in the following examples, and write one or more PS rules showing the possible expansions of S. Write a lexical entry for any verb you find that requires a predicate complement. **Note**: you do not need to account for the internal structure of NP and AP, or for the distribution of the "predicate marker" *i*. The presence of this marker is partly conditioned by the person and number of the subject, as illustrated in (1), from Verhaar (1995:71); but other more complex factors are relevant as well.

1. mi amamas.   'I am happy.'
    yu amamas.   'You (sg) are happy.'
    em i amamas.   'He/she is happy.'
    yumi amamas.   'We (incl.) are happy.'
    mipela i amamas.   'We (excl.) are happy.'
    yupela i amamas.   'You (pl) are happy.'
    ol i amamas.   'They are happy.'

2. yu paitim pik bilong mi.   'You hit my pig.'
    ol meri i brumim ples.   'The women are sweeping the village.'

3. dispela meri i tisa.   'This woman is a teacher.'
    nem bilong en Ikolichimbu.   'His name is Ikolichimbu.'
    yu man bilong giaman.   'You are a liar (lit: a man of lies).'
    mi bos bilong dispela ples ia.   'I am the boss of this place here.'
    em masalai bilong papa bilong mipela.   'It is the spirit of our father.'
    mi kol tumas.   'I am very cold.'
    yu kros?   'Are you angry?'
    win i gutpela.   'The wind is good.'
    skin bilong pikinini i hat tumas.   'The child's skin is very warm.'
    dispela haus i [moa bik long arapela].   'This house is [bigger than the other one].'
    nus bilong en i [sotpela nogut tru].   'His nose is [extremely short].'
    em i stap bos.   'He is in charge.'
    ol i stap as nating.   'They were naked.'
    mi stap gut.   'I am well.'

em Praim Minista.	'That person over there (unknown to hearer) is the Prime Minister.'
em i stap Praim Minista.	'He (a person already known to hearer) is (currently) the Prime Minister.'

4. em i stap long haus. — 'He is in the house.'
    *em (i) long haus.
    ol pik i stap long ples. — 'The pigs are in the village.'
    olgeta abus i stap long bus. — 'All the animals are in the bush (i.e. forest).'

5. mi gat tripela pikinini meri. — 'I have three daughters.'
    Malolo i gat sampela buai. — 'Malolo has some betel nut.'
    yu gat hamas krismas nau? — 'How old are you now?'
    meri i gat bel. — 'The woman has a stomach (i.e. is pregnant).'

    i gat tupela tim. — 'There are two teams.'
    i gat kaikai bilong mi. — 'I have some food.'
    i gat wanpela draipela meri — 'There is a huge woman in the store.'
       i stap long stua.
    no gat supia long haus. — 'There is no spear in the house.'
    no gat papa bilong yu? — 'Don't you have a father?'
    bipo tru i no gat poteto long — 'A long time ago there were no potatoes
       Papua Niugini. —   in Papua New Guinea.'

6. Devit i kamap king. — 'David became king.'
    pikinini bilong mi i kamap dokta nau. — 'My child is becoming a doctor now.'
    meri bilong en i kamap sik. — 'His wife got sick.'
    tupela i kamap bikpela. — 'The two of them grew up (became big).'
    as bilong diwai i kamap waitpela. — 'The base of the tree becomes white.'

10B Amele (PNG; Roberts 1999, ex. 14.3)

Describe the structure of the Amele clauses found in the following examples. In addition to a prose description, you should: (a) write two lexical entries, one for each sense, for *lec* 'to go/to become,' *mec* 'to put/to become,' and *nijec* 'to lie (down)/to be'; and (b) write a set of PS rules that will generate all the clauses in the data. (Note: assume that PPs expressing a goal are arguments, not adjuncts.)

1. Dana leia.
    man   he.went [PAST]
    'The man went.'

2. Leia.
    he.went [PAST]
    'He went.'

3.   Dana eu jo   na leia.
       man that house to he.went [PAST]
       'That man went to the house.'

4.   *Dana eu jo   leia.
        man   that house he.went [PAST]
       '(That man went to the house.)'

5.   Caja   cabi   na leia.
       woman garden to she.went [PAST]
       'The woman went to the garden.'

6.   *Caja   cabi   leia.
        woman garden she.went [PAST]
       '(The woman went to the garden.)'

7.   Ho cus   leia.
       pig wild it.went [PAST]
       'The pig went wild.'

8.   *Ho cus   na leia.
        pig wild to it.went [PAST]
       '(The pig went wild.)'

9.   Cus leia.
       wild it.went [PAST]
       'It went wild.'

10.   Ma qao   leia.
       taro rotten it.went [PAST]
       'The taro went rotten.'

11.   *Ma qao   na leia.
        taro rotten to it.went [PAST]
       ('The taro went rotten.')

12.   Qao   leia.
       rotten it.went [PAST]
       'It went rotten.'

13.   Dana eu   bahu leia.
       man   that bush he.went [PAST]
       'That man went bush, i.e. he went to live in the forest.'

14.   Dana eu   bahu na leia.
       man   that bush to he.went [PAST]
       'That man went to the bush, i.e. he went to the toilet.'

15.   Tu   lena.
       dark it.is.going [PRESENT]
       'It is getting dark.'

16.   Dana eu sigin   cabal na meia.
       man   that bushknife bed   on he.put [PAST]
       'That man put the bushknife on the bed.'

17. Sigin   meia.
    bushknife he.put [PAST]
    'He put the bushknife.'

18. Meia.
    he.put [PAST]
    'He put.'

19. Mel eu   ben.
    boy that big
    'That boy is big.'

20. Mel eu   dana.
    boy that man
    'That boy is a man.'

21. Mel eu   ben meia.
    boy that big he.became [PAST]
    'That boy has become big.'

22. Mel eu   dana meia.
    boy that man he.became [PAST]
    'That boy has become a man.'

23. Toia meia.
    old   he.became [PAST]
    'He has become old.'

24. Wa   camasac mena.
    water clear   it.is.becoming [PRESENT]
    'The water is becoming clear.'

25. Dana cabal na nijia.
    man   bed   on he.lay [PAST]
    'The man lay on the bed.'

26. Dana nijia.
    man   he.lay.down [PAST]
    'The man lay down.'

27. Mel aid   eu   gohic.
    boy female that short
    'That girl is short.'

28. Mel aid   eu   gohic nijoloi.
    boy female that short she.used.to.be [PAST HABITUAL]
    'That girl used to be short.'

29. Dana eu   utuqa-ni.
    man   that neighbor-1sg.POSS
    'That man is my neighbor.'

30. Dana eu   utuqa-ni   nijoloi.
    man   that neighbor-1sg.POSS he.used.to.be [PAST HABITUAL]
    'That man used to be my neighbor.'

31.   Jo   i   ija   na.
        house this 1sg   of
        'This house is mine.'

32.   Jo   i   ija   na   nijina.
        house this 1sg   of   it.is [PRESENT]
        'This house is mine.'

33.   Jo   i   ija   na   nijigian.
        house this 1sg   of   it.will.be [future]
        'This house will be mine.'

34.   Sab   me   i   hina   nu.
        food good this 2sg   for
        'This good food is for you.'

35.   Sab   me   i   hina   nu   nijigian.
        food good this 2sg   for   it.will.be [FUTURE]
        'This good food will be for you.'

36.   Hatin ben we   nijia.
        cave   big like it.was [PAST]
        'The cave seemed big.'

37.   Ben we   nijia.
        big like it.was [PAST]
        'It seemed big.'

38.   Nijina.
        it.is.lying [PRESENT]
        'It is/It is lying.'

Additional exercises

Merrifield et al. (1987) prob. 230, 231, 233, 234, 238
Healey (1990b), ex. D.6

Notes

1. Many of the Tagalog examples in this chapter are taken from Schachter and Otanes (1972), often with minor modifications.
2. It would be more accurate to say that the head of the predicate phrase is normally the first element of the clause, because predicate phrases can be expressed as discontinuous constituents in Tagalog.
3. (6a) is from Sityar (1989:21).
4. Maling (1983) argues that the restrictions on which type of predicate complement can occur with which verb are actually semantic, rather than categorial. Other writers, however, have argued that some information about categories must be included in the verb's subcategorization.

5. The subject NPs in (7) should probably not be considered semantic arguments of the copula. Thus, the lexical entry for the copula should probably be similar to that for a Raising predicate; see Kroeger (2004), ch. 5.

6. The predicate in Tagalog normally occurs as the initial element in its clause, and this is clearly the case in (13a), (13c), and (13d). In (13b), where both NPs are definite, there is some disagreement as to which should be identified as predicate and which as the SUBJ. This construction is sometimes identified as a cleft sentence, and on this analysis the "clefted" NP, i.e. the one in initial position, is regarded as the subject.

7. This evidence relates to the potential for discontinuous constituency and the distribution of second position clitics; see Kroeger (1993, 1998) for details.

8. Under this analysis the SUBJ of the XCOMP gets two Grammatical Relations, just as Mary bears two Grammatical Relations (OBJ of *persuade* and SUBJ of *dance*) in the sentence *John persuaded Mary to dance*. See Kroeger (2004), ch. 5 for further explanation.

9. The initial /n-/ in these examples indicates realis aspect.

10. No clitic pronoun or particle may intervene between *maging* and its complement. See ch. 17 for a fuller discussion of clitics and related issues.

11. Data from Schachter and Otanes (1972:257).

12. In fact, the possessed objects in (18c) and (19) are just bare nouns; but the NP complement of *may* can contain modifiers as well, as in: *May tatlong bagong bahay sa aming kalye.* 'There are three new houses in our street.' (English 1986).

13. (19a–b) are taken from Ramos (1971:160–161).

14. The negative existential root *walâ* occurs in a number of derived forms; but in its basic usage (i.e. in existential clauses) it is "defective" in the same sense as *may(roon)*; it does not take any of the normal inflectional morphology which characterizes true verbs in Tagalog (e.g. for aspect, voice, and modality).

15. Clark cites several examples from the Finno-Ugric (Finnish, Hungarian, and Estonian) and Indo-Iranian (Hindi, Kashmiri, and Bengali [past tense]) families.

16. The Eskimo and Hebrew examples are from Clark (1978:109).

17. See Clark (1970); Schachter (1977). Definite existential clauses (e.g. *God exists*) often contain a normal intransitive verb (e.g. *exist*) which takes a normal subject NP. In languages which lack this kind of verb, it can be quite difficult to translate such sentences.

18. Sentence (35c) is grammatical with a different sense of the verb *consider*, but not with the sense used in (8d).

19. Huddleston (1984:188); Bickford (1998:184).

20. The nominative form *she* would be used primarily in formal speech styles.

11   Special sentence types

Speakers can use their language to perform various kinds of actions: making statements, asking questions, giving commands, offering wishes, blessings, curses; performing rituals and ceremonies (e.g. weddings), pardoning or sentencing a criminal, opening or closing a meeting, etc. Actions of this sort are often referred to as SPEECH ACTS. The first three of these (statements, questions, and commands) are the most common. People of all cultures need to perform these actions, and in most (if not all) languages we find distinct sentence patterns corresponding to each of them.

In chapter 4 we suggested that the most basic kind of sentence structure is a simple statement, i.e. a DECLARATIVE clause. In this chapter we will discuss questions, commands, and various other "non-basic" sentence patterns, focusing primarily on their grammatical structure rather than their pragmatic functions. Different languages use different combinations of morphological, syntactic, and phonological devices for marking sentence type, but certain patterns of similarity can be observed across languages, as we will see. Since we take the declarative to be the most basic sentence type, we will focus on those features which distinguish the other types from a basic declarative clause. We will begin with some brief comments about speech acts.

11.1   Direct vs. indirect speech acts

As we noted above, the three most common things that speakers do by speaking are: (i) making STATEMENTS (asserting or denying the truth of a proposition); (ii) asking QUESTIONS (questioning the truth of a proposition, or asking for additional information about a proposition); and (iii) giving COMMANDS. Most languages have specific grammatical patterns that are used to indicate which of these actions the speaker intends to perform: DECLARATIVE for statements; INTERROGATIVE for questions; and IMPERATIVE for commands. These three sentence types correspond to the MAJOR MOOD categories mentioned in chapter 9. The primary function of each major mood category is shown in (1).

(1) **SPEECH ACT SENTENCE TYPE (MOOD)**
    Statement   Declarative
    Command   Imperative
    Question   Interrogative

The table in (1) shows the typical or expected sentence type (i.e. grammatical form) that would be used for expressing a given pragmatic function. DIRECT SPEECH ACTS are those in which this expected correlation is preserved: the form of the sentence matches the purpose, or intended force, of the utterance. Some examples are given in (2).

(2)   a I don't care whether you vote for me or not. (statement in declarative form)
    b Would you like to buy this watch?   (question in interrogative form)
    c Be quiet!   (command in imperative form)

However, speakers do not always choose the expected sentence type to express their intended function. Sometimes a speaker uses some other form to create a desired effect. INDIRECT SPEECH ACTS are those in which there is a mismatch between the sentence type and the intended force. Some examples are given in (3). A RHETORICAL QUESTION is a very common type of indirect speech act which involves the use of the interrogative form for some purpose other than asking questions, as in (3a) and (3c).

(3)   a Why don't you just be quiet?   (command in interrogative form)
    b Don't tell me you lost it!   (question in imperative form)
    c Who cares?   (statement in interrogative form)
    d I don't suppose you'd like to   (question in declarative form, with
       buy this from me?   modified intonation)

In sections 11.3 and 11.4 we will focus on the grammatical features of imperative and interrogative sentence patterns; in section 11.5 we will discuss patterns of sentence negation. But first, in section 11.2, we make some general observations about variation in word order, since word order is often significant in distinguishing one type of sentence from another.

11.2 Basic word order

Variations in word order are often used to make one part of the sentence more prominent than another. Even in a language like English, which has fairly rigid word order, the elements of a sentence can be rearranged in various ways to produce different shades of meaning. Compare the effect of the "basic" word order in sentence (4a) with the "marked" orders in sentences (4b–d):

(4)   a I gave my Klingon dictionary to Mr. Spock.
       b My Klingon dictionary I gave to Mr. Spock.
       c As for my Klingon dictionary, I gave it to Mr. Spock.
       d What I gave to Mr. Spock was my Klingon dictionary.

All four of these sentences contain the same propositional meaning; that is, they all describe the same basic event and would be true under the same circumstances. However, they would not normally be spoken in the same contexts or for the same purposes. Sentence (4d) seems to assume that we already know that SOMETHING was given to Mr. Spock; the question is WHAT? The crucial piece of new information provided by this sentence (i.e. the FOCUS of the sentence) is the Klingon dictionary. Sentences (4b,c) also assign special prominence to the Klingon dictionary, this time as TOPIC (what the sentence is about). The act of giving in these sentences is new information, and not presupposed as in (4d). Sentence (4a), which follows the basic, normal, rules of English word order, does not assign special prominence to any particular constituent; it simply describes the event in a relatively "neutral" way.

As these examples illustrate, special (or MARKED) word order is often used to indicate special pragmatic functions such as topic or focus.[1] But we cannot recognize marked word orders unless we know the "unmarked," or basic, word order. In a language like English it is not too difficult to determine the basic order, at least with regard to the major constituents of the clause (SVO, followed by oblique arguments and complement clauses). But many other languages allow much more freedom of word order than English. How, then, can we decide which of the possible orders for a particular sentence type is the most basic? Bickford (1998:214–216) suggests the following criteria:[2]

a   **frequency**: the basic order is usually the one that is used most frequently in discourse.

b   **neutral semantics and pragmatics**: basic sentences are normally indicative (statements, not questions or commands) and positive (not negated); and they do not assign special (marked) pragmatic prominence to any constituent. In most theories of grammar, active sentences are also assumed to be more basic than passive.

c   **avoid pronouns**: pronouns often have special word-order properties, so basic word order should be based on the order of full NP and PP arguments.

d   **subordinate clauses take priority**: in many languages, main clauses allow greater variation in word order than do subordinate clauses (see chapter 12); thus the order observed in subordinate clauses is more likely to be the basic order.

e   **distribution**: marked sentence types tend to be appropriate only in certain specific contexts. Neutral word order is generally the order that has the widest distribution, i.e. which can occur in the greatest number of different contexts.

In some languages, however, it may not be possible to determine a "basic" word order. Mohanan (1982) states that in Malayalam any permutation of the constituents in a clause is allowed, as illustrated in (5), provided that the verb occurs in final position. Further, these variations in word order make no significant difference in the semantics or intonation of the sentence. Mohanan argues that Malayalam clause structure is best described by the PS rule in (5e), which says that a clause consists of an arbitrary number of phrasal constituents followed by the verb. In this language, word order is so free that there seems to be little point in identifying one particular order as being more basic than the others.

(5)   **Malayalam** (Dravidian, southern India); adapted from Mohanan (1982:509)

    a kuṭṭi   aana-ye   amma-kkə   koṭuṭṭu.
       child(NOM)   elephant-ACC mother-DAT gave
       'The child gave the elephant to the mother.'

    b amma-kkə   kuṭṭi   aana-ye   koṭuṭṭu.
       mother-DAT child(NOM)   elephant-ACC gave
       'The child gave the elephant to the mother.'

    c aana-ye   kuṭṭi   amma-kkə   koṭuṭṭu.
       elephant-ACC child(NOM) mother-DAT gave
       'The child gave the elephant to the mother.'

    d amma-kkə   aana-ye   kuṭṭi   koṭuṭṭu.
       mother-DAT elephant-ACC child(NOM) gave
       'The child gave the elephant to the mother.' (etc.)

    e S → XP* V

11.3   Commands (imperative sentences)

Now let us examine how commands are formed in various languages. The defining property of a command is that the hearer (or addressee) is being told to do something. This means that an imperative verb will always have a second person actor, which (in most languages) will be the subject. For this reason any overt reference to the subject, whether as an NP or by verbal agreement, is likely to be redundant. Imperative verbs are frequently unmarked for person, even in languages which normally require the verb to agree with the person of the subject; and imperative clauses frequently lack a subject NP. Where there is an overt subject NP, it will always be a second person pronoun.

These features can be observed in the English examples in (6). With most English verbs the lack of agreement marking is not obvious, since the imperative form is the same as the second person present tense. But the lack of agreement morphology can be seen with the verb *to be*, as in (6b), since the normal second person form would be *are*.

(6)   a (You) give me that letter!
       b (You) be good!
       c Don't (you) forget to lock the door!

In languages that have morphological tense, imperative verbs are not normally inflected for tense. This seems natural, since an imperative always refers to a future event, and is most often intended to mean immediate future. In Latin, for example, the imperative is not inflected for tense, aspect, or person. It is thus distinct from the infinitive or any finite form of the verb, as shown in (7).[3] However, imperative verbs are marked for number, and this is true in many other languages as well.

(7)

INFINITIVE	amāre	'to love'	portāre	'to carry'
PRESENT	amō	'I love'	portō	'I carry'
	amās	'you love'	portās	'you carry'
	amat	'(s)he loves'	portat	'(s)he carries'
	amāmus	'we love'	portāmus	'we carry'
	amātis	'you (pl) love'	portātis	'you (pl) carry'
	amant	'they love'	portant	'they carry'
FUTURE	amābō	'I will love'	portābō	'I will carry'
	amābis	'you will love'	portābis	'you will carry'
	amābit	'(s)he will love'	portābit	'(s)he will carry'
	amābimus	'we will love'	portābimus	'we will carry'
	amābitis	'you (pl) will love'	portābitis	'you (pl) will carry'
	amābunt	'they will love'	portābunt	'they will carry'
IMPERATIVE	amā!	'Love! (sg)'	portā!	'Carry! (sg)'
	amāte!	'Love! (pl)'	portāte!	'Carry! (pl)'

As these examples illustrate, imperative verbs are often morphologically simpler than a corresponding indicative form. In many languages, the imperative form is just a bare root. Even in languages which have a specific affix that marks imperative mood, imperative verbs often lack the normal markers for agreement and/or tense. Swahili provides another striking example. In most contexts, Swahili verbs bear obligatory prefixes which mark subject agreement and tense, as illustrated in (8).[4] Imperative verbs, however, do not bear these suffixes. They are not marked for tense or person but only for number: *-Ø* for singular, *-eni* for plural. Some examples are given in (9–10).

(8)   **Swahili** (Ashton 1944; Hinnebusch 1992).

a ni-li-soma   kitabu.
  1sg-PAST-read   book
  'I (have) read the book.'

b u-li-soma   kitabu.
  2sg-PAST-read   book
  'You (sg) (have) read the book.'

c a-li-soma   kitabu.
  3sg-PAST-read   book
  'He (has) read the book.'

d m-li-soma   kitabu.
  2pl-PAST-read   book
  'You (pl) have read the book.'

e u-ta-soma   kitabu.
  2sg-FUT-read   book
  'You (sg) will read the book.'

f m-ta-soma   kitabu.
  2pl-FUT-read   book
  'You (pl) will read the book.'

(9)   a soma kitabu!
         read   book
         '(you sg) read the book!'

       b someni   kitabu!
         read-PL book
         '(you pl) read the book!'

(10)   a ondoa   viti!
         remove chairs
         '(you sg) take away the chairs!'

       b ondoeni   viti!
         remove-PL chairs
         '(you pl) take away the chairs!'

In some languages, the "imperative" form of the verb is marked for person and can even take first or third person agreement markers. However, these uses of the imperative form are not really commands. The first person forms often have a hortative sense (e.g. *Let's eat!*), while the third person forms often function as optatives (*May he win the battle!*).

Aside from verbal morphology, another possible way of marking imperative sentences is by using a special particle. This is illustrated in (11) with examples from Cambodian (i.e. Khmer).

(11)   **Cambodian** (Spatar 1997:121)[5]

    a ku:n mak n'a:<u>m</u>.
      child come eat
      'The child came/comes to eat.'

    b ku:n mak n'a:<u>m</u> cu<u>h</u>.
      child come eat   IMPER
      'Child, come and eat!'

When we give a direct command to someone, we imply that we feel entitled to give such commands, whether this right is based on social status, official position, or personal familiarity. Status and familiarity are always sensitive issues, so most languages have a variety of methods for softening a command or making it sound more polite. In Malay, for example, a simple imperative is expressed using the bare verb stem. For transitive verbs like 'read,' this involves dropping the active voice prefix *meN-*; compare the verb in (12a) with the form used in (12b–e). One way of softening the command is by attaching the focus particle *=lah* to the imperative verb (12c).[6] Other ways of forming a more polite command include inserting the verb *tolong*, literally 'help,' as in (12d); or using the passive form of the verb, as in (12e).

(12)   a Saya telah mem-baca surat itu.
      I   PFV ACT-read letter that
      'I have read that letter.'

    b Baca surat ini sekarang juga!
      read letter this now   also
      'Read this letter right now!'

    c Baca=lah surat ini!
      read=FOC letter this
      'Read this letter.'

    d Tolong baca surat ini.
      help   read letter this
      'Please read this letter.'

    e Surat itu di-baca   nanti.
      letter that PASS-read later
      'Read that letter later.'

In Malay, as in many other languages, negative commands are formed using a special negative auxiliary verb *jangan* 'do not!' The same softening devices are available as with positive commands (13a,b).

(13)   a Jangan(=lah) baca surat itu!
      do.not(=FOC) read letter that
      'Don't read that letter!'

b Surat itu   jangan di-baca   sekarang.
  letter that do.not PASS-read now
  'Don't read that letter now.'

11.4 Questions (interrogative sentences)

Two basic types of questions are found in virtually all languages:
(a) YES–NO QUESTIONS; and (b) CONTENT QUESTIONS.[7] The difference is illustrated in (14):

(14)   a YES–NO QUESTIONS
          Did Mary win the marathon?
          Did Barry buy a new Land Rover?

        b CONTENT QUESTIONS
          Who won the marathon?
          What did Barry buy?

Yes–No questions are sometimes referred to as "closed questions," because
the set of possible answers is closed, containing just two members (*yes*
and *no*). Content questions are sometimes referred to as "open questions,"
because the set of possible answers is open, with (theoretically) no limit to
the number of potential responses. But in terms of grammatical structure,
the most important difference between these two types of question is that
content questions contain a question word (*who, what, where, why, when,*
etc.) whereas Yes–No questions do not. Content questions are sometimes
called "Wh- questions," because most of the question words in English
begin with *wh-*.

11.4.1 Yes–No questions

Since Yes–No questions do not contain a question word, there
must be some other means of distinguishing them from simple declarative
sentences. The most commonly used devices for marking Yes–No questions
are listed, in descending order of frequency, in (15):

(15)   a Intonation
        b Clitics[8] or particles
        c Verbal affix (interrogative mood)
        d Change in word order

Most languages have a special intonation pattern for Yes–No questions.
The question mark "?" is an orthographic device that is used in written
language to represent this special intonation. Often the question intonation
pattern involves a sentence-final rising pitch, in contrast to a final falling

pitch in declarative sentences, but this is by no means universal. In many languages, it is possible to change a declarative sentence into a Yes–No question simply by changing the intonation pattern, and in some languages (e.g. Jacaltec) this is the only available strategy.

In a large number of languages, Yes–No questions must contain a special clitic or particle. Interrogative particles typically occur in one of three positions: sentence initial, sentence final, or as the second element in the sentence. Interrogative clitics may attach to a specific constituent, e.g. the first or last element in the sentence, or to whichever element is "in focus" in the question.

The marking of interrogative mood by an inflectional affix on the verb seems to be much less common than the use of a clitic or particle. An interesting example of a language which does have interrogative mood affixation is Greenlandic, which actually has two different interrogative forms, one for true questions and another for rhetorical questions:

(16)　**Greenlandic** (Sadock and Zwicky 1985:180)
　　　DECLARATIVE　　　　　naalanngilatit 'You do not obey.'
　　　TRUE QUESTION　　　　naalanngilit 'Do you not obey?'
　　　RHETORICAL QUESTION naalanngippit 'Do you not obey?'
　　　　　　　　　　　　　　　　　(i.e. 'You should obey.')

A change in word order to mark questions usually involves the movement of a verbal or auxiliary element toward the front of the sentence, as illustrated in the English examples in (17). This is also a relatively uncommon strategy, though it is found in a number of well-known European languages.

(17)　Ken will be working this afternoon.
　　　Will Ken be working this afternoon?

A construction which is closely related to the Yes–No question is the ALTERNATIVE QUESTION. The choice which is offered to the hearer in this kind of question may be between *yes* and *no*, as in (18a); or between two (or more) other alternatives, as in (18b):

(18)　a Do you want to see the movie or not?
　　　b Do you want coffee or tea?

Another related construction is the TAG QUESTION. Tag questions in English, as illustrated in (19), consist of a copy of the first auxiliary element of the main clause (or *do* if the clause contains no auxiliary), followed by a pronominal copy of the subject of the main clause. The tag question normally has the opposite POLARITY from the main clause: negative if the main clause is positive, and positive if the main clause is negative.

(19)　a You have been studying Russian, haven't you?
　　　b Bill isn't going to Paris next week, is he?

Two different uses of tag questions can be distinguished. The normal use is a request for CONFIRMATION. This construction is much the same as a simple declarative statement, with the tag question serving only as a request for feedback from the hearer. A second use of tag questions in English is to form BIASED QUESTIONS. This construction is a true request for information, in the sense that the speaker requires an answer from the hearer; but it signals an expectation or preference on the part of the speaker for one particular answer to be given.

Biased questions are distinguished from confirmation tags in English primarily by intonation. If the examples in (19) are read with final falling intonation, they have the force of normal confirmation tag questions. If the same sentences are read with final rising intonation, they have the force of biased questions. Also, marked focal stress on the first auxiliary element, as in (20), is more common in biased questions. With confirmation tag questions (20b), this kind of stress pattern may convey a sense of newly discovered and surprising information.

(20)   a You áre singing in the school concert, aren't you?
          (with rising intonation: BIASED QUESTION
          You'd better have a very good reason if you say no!)

       b You áre singing in the school concert, aren't you?
          (with falling intonation: CONFIRMATION TAG QUESTION
          I suspected as much all along!)

11.4.2 Content questions

In content (or information) questions, a question word replaces one of the constituents of the corresponding declarative sentence (see (21)). This question word is always the focused element of the question, representing the crucial piece of new information that is being requested. With regard to the structure of the content question, the first issue to be addressed is: where does the question word appear in the sentence? Most languages use one of two basic strategies: either the question word appears at the beginning of the sentence,[9] as in English, or the question word appears in the place where the constituent which it replaces would normally occur in a declarative sentence (see examples in section 11.4.3.1). The first strategy is often called "Wh- fronting."[10] For languages which employ the second strategy, we say that the question word remains *in situ* (the Latin phrase meaning 'in place').

(21)   a John gave his mother a jade necklace on her birthday.
       b *Who* gave John's mother the jade necklace on her birthday?
       c *What* did John give his mother on her birthday?
       d *Who* did John give the jade necklace to?
       e *When* did John give his mother the jade necklace?

In some languages, devices which are used to mark Yes–No questions – particles, interrogative mood affixation, special intonation, etc. – also occur (either optionally or obligatorily) in content questions. For example, the interrogative mood is obligatory in Greenlandic in both Yes–No questions and content questions (22). But these features are of secondary importance in content questions. The crucial defining feature of a content question is the presence of an interrogative (Wh-) word.

(22)　　**Greenlandic** (data from Sadock and Zwicky 1985:184)
　　　　DECLARATIVE　　　　Piniarpoq.　　　　'He is hunting.'
　　　　YES–NO QUESTION　Piniarpa?　　　　'Is he hunting?'
　　　　CONTENT QUESTION　Kina piniarpa?　　'Who is hunting?'
　　　　　　　　　　　　　　(*Kina piniarpoq?)

11.4.3　Case studies

11.4.3.1　Mandarin

Mandarin has two basic strategies for forming Yes–No questions. One involves the use of a sentence-final particle *ma* (23c), while the other involves a kind of alternative question which is sometimes referred to as the "A-not-A" pattern (23d). As (24) shows, the alternative can involve either a repetition of the verb alone (24b), of the verb plus object as a unit (26c), or of the copular verb *shì* 'is' (24d).

(23)　　**Mandarin** (adapted from Merrifield et al. 1987, prob. 255)
　　　　a tā lái.　　　　'He is coming.'
　　　　b tā bù lái.　　'He is not coming.'
　　　　c nǐ lái ma?　　'Are you coming?'
　　　　d nǐ lái bù lái?　'Are you coming or not?'

(24)　　a tā mǎi shū.　　　　　　　'He is buying books.'
　　　　b tā [mǎi bù mǎi] shū?　　　'Is he buying books or not?'
　　　　c tā [mǎi shū] bù [mǎi shū]?　'Is he buying books or not?'
　　　　d tā [shì bù shì] mǎi shū?　　'Is he buying books or not?'

These two strategies, final particle vs. A-not-A alternative question, seem to have the same function, and pairs of sentences like (23c) and (23d) are often interchangeable. However, Li and Thompson (1981) state that there is a difference in the way the two patterns can be used. The A-not-A question can be used only in "neutral" contexts, i.e. where the questioner has no prior assumptions or expectations about the answer to the question. Particle questions, on the other hand, can be used either in neutral contexts or in contexts where the questioner wishes to signal some prior expectation about what the answer should be. Consider the sentences in (25), from Li and Thompson (1981:551):

(25)   a Nǐ   hē   jiǔ   ma?
          2sg drink wine QUES
          'Do you drink wine?'

        b Nǐ   hē   bù   hē   jiǔ?
          2sg drink not drink wine
          'Do you drink wine?'

If the speaker is dining in a restaurant with a new acquaintance, and wants
to find out whether it is appropriate to order wine with the meal, then either
(25a) or (25b) would be acceptable. This is a neutral context, because the
speaker has no prior knowledge or expectation about the answer. But if
the speaker is dining with an old friend whom he knows to be a strict
tee-totaling Baptist, and is surprised to see this friend order wine with the
meal, only (25a) would be appropriate. The A-not-A pattern (25b) would
be very unnatural, because the speaker has definite prior expectations about
the answer.

Tag questions are formed by adding a simple A-not-A question at the end
of a statement. The examples in (26) are from Li and Thompson (1981:546).

(26)   a Nǐmen shì jiǔ-diǎnzhōng kāi   mén de, duì   bù   duì?
          2pl   be nine-o'clock open door PRT right not right
          'You opened at nine o'clock, right?'

        b Tā zài   gēng-tián, shì bù shì?
          3sg PROG plow-field be not be
          'He is plowing the field, right?'

A very frequently used Yes–No question consists of just the copula followed by the question particle: *shì ma?* 'Really? Is that so? Is that right?'

In Mandarin content questions, the question word remains *in situ*, as
illustrated in (27–28). There is another sentence-final particle *ne* which
optionally occurs in content questions (29a,b), but the Yes–No particle *ma*
does not occur in content questions. If *ma* is added to a content question, the
question word is re-interpreted as a quantifier (29c) and the whole sentence
becomes a Yes–No question.

(27)   a wǒ yào   mǎi shū.
          1sg want buy book
          'I want to buy books/a book.'

        b *shéi* yào   mǎi shū?
          who want buy book
          'Who wants to buy books/a book?'

        c nǐ   yào   mǎi *shénme*?
          2sg want buy what
          'What do you want to buy?'

(28) a nǐ   qù-le   *nǎli?*
         2sg go-PERF   where
         'Where did you go?'

      b wǒ   qù-le   měiguó.
         1sg go-PERF   America
         'I went to America.'

(29) a *shéi* lái-le   (ne)?
         who   come-PERF   PRT
         'Who came?'

      b nǐ   yào   mǎi *shénme* (ne)?
         2sg want buy what   PRT
         'What do you want to buy?'

      c nǐ   yào   mǎi *shénme* ma?
         2sg want buy what   QUES
         'Do you want to buy something?'

11.4.3.2 Huallaga Quechua

Yes–No questions in Quechua are marked by a clitic particle =*chu.* If this clitic attaches to the verb, as in (30b), the entire proposition is being questioned. But often the clitic attaches to another element in the sentence, as in (30c). In this case the constituent which hosts the clitic is the focal element of the question: the rest of the proposition is assumed to be true, and the questioner is asking only whether this particular piece of information is correct.

(30)   **Huallaga Quechua** (Peru; Weber 1989:19–20, 328–330)
      a Maria Hwan-ta   maqa-sha.
         Mary John-ACC hit-3SUBJ.PERF
         'Mary hit John.'

      b Maria Hwan-ta   maqa-sha=chu?
         Mary John-ACC hit-3SUBJ.PERF=QUES
         'Did Mary hit John?'

      c Maria Hwan-ta=chu   maqa-sha?
         Mary John-ACC=QUES   hit-3SUBJ.PERF
         'Was it John that Mary hit?'

In alternative questions (31a,b), both alternatives are marked with the Yes–No clitic; the conjunction *o* 'or' may optionally appear between them. Confirmation tag questions (31c) are formed merely by adding the word *aw* 'yes,' spoken with rapidly rising intonation, to the end of a declarative sentence.

(31)   a Kanan=chu   o   wara=chu?
           today=QUES or tomorrow=QUES
           'Today or tomorrow?'

         b Aywa-nki=chu   mana=chu?
           go-2SUBJ=QUES not=QUES
           'Are you going or not?'

         c Pillku-ta   aywa-yka-nki,   aw?
           Pillku-DIR go-IMPERF-2SUBJ yes
           'You are going to Pillku, right?'

In content questions, the question word normally occurs at the beginning
of the sentence, and is marked by another interrogative clitic. This Wh-
clitic has two variant forms: =*taq* and =*raq*. If the question word is part of
a larger constituent (e.g. 'how much bread' in (32d)), the Wh-clitic attaches
to the end of the entire constituent and never to the question word itself
(32e).

(32)   a Pi=raq   suwa-paa-maa-sha?
           who=WH steal-BEN-1OBJ-3SUBJ.PERF
           'Who might have stolen it on me?'

         b Pi-ta=taq   qoyku-shka-nki?
           who-ACC=WH give-PERF-2SUBJ
           'To whom did you give it?'

         c Imay=taq aywa-nki?
           when=WH go-2SUBJ
           'When will you go?'

         d [Ayka   tanta-ta]=taq   chara-nki?
           how.much bread-ACC=WH have-2SUBJ
           'How much bread do you have?'

         e *[Ayka=taq   tanta-ta]   chara-nki?
           how.much=WH bread-ACC have-2SUBJ

11.4.3.3 Russian

Yes–No questions in Russian may be formed either by the use of
question intonation alone, as in (33b), or by the use of a clitic particle =*li*,
as in (33c). The element which hosts the clitic appears in sentence-initial
position. As in Quechua, the clitic may attach either to the verb or to some
other element of the sentence. If the clitic attaches to the verb, as in (33c)
and (34b), the entire proposition is being questioned. If the clitic attaches
to another element, as in (34c), that element becomes the focus of the
question.

(33) **Russian** (King 1995:137–139)

a On živet zdes'.
he live here
'He lives here.'

b On živet zdes'?
he live here
'He lives here?'

c živet=li on zdes'?
live=QUES he here
'Does he live here?'

(34) a Anna pročitala knigu.
Anna read book
'Anna read a book.'

b Pročitala=li Anna knigu?
read=QUES Anna book
'Did Anna read a book?'

c Knigu=li Anna pročitala?
book=QUES Anna read
'Was it a book that Anna read?'

Question words in Russian content questions always occur in initial position. The interrogative clitic =*li* may not co-occur with a question word (35f).

(35) **Russian** (King 1995:59, 67, 89, 91, 140)

a *Kto* priexal k vam?
who came to you
'Who visited you?'

b *čto* ty kupila?
what you buy
'What did you buy?'

c *Kuda* ty ideš'?
where you go
'Where are you going?'

d *Komu* ženščina xotela napisat'?
who-DAT woman want write-INF
'Who did the woman want to write to?'

e *S kem* vy ezdili v London?
with whom you went to London
'Who did you go to London with?'

f *čto=li ona delaet?
what=QUES she do

11.5   Negation

In this section we will briefly discuss the most common ways in which negative sentences may be formed. To begin with, we need to be able to distinguish negative sentences from positive sentences.

In section 11.4.1 we noted that English tag questions normally have the opposite polarity from the main clause: negative if the main clause is positive; and positive if the main clause is negative. Klima (1964) points out that this pattern provides a test which we can use to distinguish positive from negative sentences in English: if the sentence takes a negative tag, it is probably positive, and vice versa. What does this test tell us about the main clause in each of the following examples?

(36)   a Arthur is not happy, is he?
         b Arthur is unhappy, isn't he?

(37)   a Bill doesn't like sushi, does he?
         b Bill dislikes sushi, doesn't he?

Sentences (36a) and (36b) are nearly synonymous – they mean almost the same thing – but the polarity of their tag questions is different. According to the test suggested above, the main clause in (36a) is a negative sentence, while main clause in (36b) is a positive sentence even though it contains a negative word (*unhappy*). Similarly, (37a) and (37b) are nearly synonymous but differ in polarity: the main clause in (37a) is a negative sentence, while the main clause in (37b) is a positive sentence which contains a negative word (*dislikes*). These examples illustrate the difference between sentence negation, as in (36a) and (37a), vs. lexical or morphological negation, as in (36b) and (37b). We will discuss the morphological function of affixes like *un-* and *dis-* in chapter 13. In this section we will focus on sentence negation.

Klima suggests two other tests that can be used to identify negative sentences in English: only negative sentences can be continued with *neither* or *not even*. These tests are illustrated in (38–39). Note that they lead to the same conclusions as the tag question test in (36–37):

(38)   a Arthur is not happy, and neither is Peggy.
         b Arthur is unhappy, and so/*neither is Peggy.

(39)   a Bill doesn't like coffee, not even with sugar.
         b Bill dislikes coffee, (*not) even with sugar.

Of course, these tests are specific to English, and will not work in the same way in many other languages. But it is important to find some grammatical criteria for identifying negative sentences in each language we study.

As the preceding examples illustrate, we cannot assume that every sentence which contains some semantic component of negation is syntactically negative.

The negative sentences in (36a–39a) illustrate the primary strategy for marking clausal negation in English: the free word *not* and its reduced or contracted form *–n't*. Payne (1985) notes that there are several other ways of forming negative sentences, including negated quantifiers (40a), inherently negative quantifiers (40b), and inherently negative adverbs (40c).

(40)   a *Not many* Americans like durian, do they?
        b *Nobody* wears bell-bottoms anymore, do they?
        c Bill *rarely* eats sushi, and neither does Arthur.

Payne (1985) suggests that the primary marker for clausal negation in any particular language can be identified by using weather predicates which take no arguments, e.g. *It is not raining*. Sentences of this type may be very useful because they are unlikely to contain quantifiers or negative adverbs, and are also unlikely to involve derivational negation (e.g. *un-* and *dis-*). However, we should remember that some languages use more than one strategy for marking clausal negation. For example, Malay uses the negative element *tidak* when the predicate is a verb (41a) or adjective (41b), and *bukan* when the predicate is an NP (41c) or PP (41d). In addition, there are special negative forms for existential clauses (*tiada*, 41e) and imperative clauses (*jangan*, 41f).[11]

(41)   a Adek   saya *tidak* makan durian.
        yg.sibling 1sg NEG eat   durian
        'My little brother does not eat durian.'

        b Jawaban itu   *tidak* betul.
        answer   that NEG correct
        'That answer is not correct.'

        c Adek   saya *bukan/*tidak* guru   besar.
        yg.sibling 1sg NEG   teacher big
        'My little brother is not a headmaster.'

        d Keretapi itu   *bukan/*tidak* dari Ipoh.[12]
        train   that NEG   from Ipoh
        'That train is not from Ipoh.'

        e *Tiada* pokok durian di New York.
        NEG tree   durian in New York
        'There are no durian trees in New York.'

        f *Jangan* makan durian itu!
        don't eat   durian that
        'Don't eat that durian!'

These negative markers in Malay are all independent word forms, as is the English *not*.[13] This use of a free word or particle to express clausal negation is a very common pattern. In many other languages, however, negation is indicated by an affix on the verb.[14] Some examples are given in (42–43).

(42)   **Hebrew** (Givón 1984:337)

    a Yoáv axál et   ha-léxem.
      Yoáv ate ACC the-bread
      'Yoáv ate the bread.'

    b Yoáv ló-axál   et   ha-léxem.
      Yoáv NEG-ate ACC the-bread
      'Yoáv did not eat the bread.'

(43)   **Turkish** (Underhill 1976:48, 57)

    a kitab-ï   oku-du-nuz.
      book-ACC read-PAST-2pl
      'You (pl) read the book.'

    b kitab-ï   okú-ma-dï-nïz.
      book-ACC read-NEG-PAST-2pl
      'You (pl) did not read the book.'

In a smaller number of languages, clausal negation is marked by a special negative auxiliary verb. In Finnish, for example, the negative auxiliary must agree with the person and number of the subject, as illustrated in (44).

(44)   **Finnish** (Aaltio 1964:66)

    a minä *en*   lue.
      I   NEG.1sg read
      'I do not read.'

    b sinä   *et*   lue.
      you(sg) NEG.2sg read
      'You (sg) do not read.'

    c hän   *ei*   lue.
      he/she NEG.3sg read
      'He/she does not read.'

    d me *emme*   lue.
      we NEG.1pl read
      'We do not read.'

Finally, it is not uncommon to find negation indicated by a pair of markers. In Quechua, for example, the most common pattern of clausal negation involves the free form *mana* 'not' plus a clitic particle =*chu* 'NEG.' The particle =*chu* may occur on the main verb, as in (45a,b), or may attach to the focused element as in (45c).

(45)   **Huallaga Quechua** (Weber 1989:335–337)

    a *mana* rura-shka-:=*chu*.
      not   do-PERF-1SUBJ=NEG
      'I didn't do it.'

    b. *mana* papa   ka-ra-n=*chu* . . .
      not   potato be-PAST-3SUBJ=NEG
      'There were no potatoes.'

    c. *mana* rura-ra-n   Hwan-paq=*chu* . . .
      not   do-PAST-3SUBJ John-BEN=NEG
      'He didn't do it for *John*, (he did it for Paul).'

What all of these strategies have in common is that, in order to form a negative sentence, something must be *added* to a basic positive clause. This is one of the reasons that we consider the positive clause to be more "basic" than the corresponding negative clause.

11.6   Conclusion

    Our strategy for describing the structure of the special sentence patterns discussed in this chapter has been to start with a more "basic" pattern, i.e. one which is not special in any of the ways we have been discussing. We take positive, declarative, pragmatically neutral clauses as the basic form, then describe the ways in which imperative, interrogative, or negative sentences differ from these. Some of the features that are frequently relevant include verb morphology, special clitics or particles, word order, and intonation. Content questions always involve the use of a special question word, and may or may not require any additional marking.

The formal properties of imperative and interrogative clauses are clearly related to the nature of the speech acts which they typically express. This is especially clear in the case of imperatives: when one person gives a direct command to another, the speech situation itself makes the specification of tense and actor/subject redundant. However, as we noted in chapter 1, function alone cannot provide a complete account of linguistic form. Our grammatical description of these constructions will include some features that seem arbitrary and others that seem to be functionally motivated, all working together as part of a single coherent system.

Practice exercise

Tok Pisin questions (PNG; Woolford 1979; Verhaar 1995; Dutton 1973)
Describe the question-forming strategies used in the following examples:

(1) Q: ol kago i kam?   'Did the goods (cargo) arrive?'
     A1: yes, ol kago i kam.   'Yes, the goods have arrived.'
     A2: nogat, ol kago i no kam.   'No, the goods have not arrived.'

(2) mi kaikai pinis.   'I have eaten.'
     yu kaikai pinis o nogat?   'Have you eaten (or not)?'
     em i orait o nogat?   'Is he all right?'
     yu no sem a?   'Aren't you ashamed of yourself?'
     tru, a?   'Is that so?'

(3) Q: ol i no save tok pisin a?   'Do they not know how to speak Tok Pisin?'
     A1: yes, ol i no save tok pisin.   'Yes, they don't know Tok Pisin.'
     A2: nogat, ol i save tok pisin.   'No, they do know Tok Pisin.'

(4) yu givim mani long husat?   'Who did you give money to?'
     husat i sanap long rot?   'Who is standing on the road?'
     yu kisim ka bilong husat?   'Whose car did you get?'
     dispela pikinini i kukim wanem?   'What is this child cooking?'
     mama bilong yu i stap we?   'Where is your mother?'
     yu kisim haumas muli?   'How many oranges did you get?'
     yu gat haumas krismas?   'How old are you?'

Exercises

11A Yessan-Mayo commands (PNG; Roberts 1999, ex. S-17.2)
Describe the imperative construction in Yessan-Mayo, based on the following data:

1.   an sini yim.   'I went back'
2.   an yibwa.   'I am going'
3.   pere Wuswar ki yibwa.   'The canoe is going down the Wuswar River.'
4.   nim bi lam.   'We did not see.'
5.   ni lati.   'You will see.'
6.   rim otop yiti.   'They will go together.'
7.   nim bul ki toknati.   'We will sleep in the bush.'
8.   hayi!   'Go!'
9.   bul ki hatokna!   'Sleep in the bush!'
10. hala!   'Look!'

11B Finnish questions (Roberts 1999, ex. S-16.3)
Describe the basic clause structure and strategies for question formation in Finnish, based on the following examples. (Note that the particles *ko* and *kö* are variant forms [i.e. ALLOMORPHS] of the same morpheme.)

1.   Kuka kirjoitti kirjeen?
     who   wrote   letter
     'Who wrote the letter?'

2.   Pekka kirjoitti kirjeen.
     wrote letter
   'Pekka wrote the letter.'

3.   Mitä Pekka kirjoitti?
  what   wrote
   'What did Pekka write?'

4.   Hän kirjoitti kirjeen.
  3sg wrote letter
   'He wrote a letter.'

5.   Missä Pekka kirjoitti kirjeen?
  what.in
   'Where did Pekka write the letter?'

6.   Hän kirjoitti kirjeen koulussa.
  3sg   school.in
   'He wrote the letter at school.'

7.   Milloin Pekka kirjoitti kirjeen?
  when
   'When did Pekka write the letter?'

8.   Hän kirjoitti kirjeen eilen.
  3sg   yesterday
   'He wrote the letter yesterday.'

9.   Kenelle Pekka kirjoitti kirjeen?
  who.to
   'To whom did Pekka write the letter?'

10.   Hän kirjoitti kirjeen äidilleen.
          mother.to.his
   'He wrote the letter to his mother.'

11.   Kirjoitti=ko Pekka kirjeen?
  wrote   letter
   'Did Pekka write the letter?

12.   Meni=kö Pekka kouluun?
  go   school.to
   'Did Pekka go to school?'

13.   Hän otti omenan.
  3sg took apple
   'She took the apple.'

14.   Mitä hän otti?
  what 3sg took
   'What did she take?'

15.   Otti=ko hän omenan?
  took 3sg apple
   'Did she take an apple?'

16.   Omenan=ko hän otti?
        apple   3sg took
        'Was it an apple that she took?'

17.   Hän=kö otti   omenan?
        3sg   took apple
        'Was it she who took the apple?'

Additional exercises

Merrifield et al. (1987) prob. 228, 229, 259, 260
Healey (1990b), ex. D.7, 8, 9, 10, 11

Notes

1. For a more detailed discussion of these pragmatic functions, see Kroeger (2004), ch. 6.
2. Criteria (a–d) are from Bickford; (e) is derived from other work on markedness.
3. Latin does, however, have a distinct "future imperative" form, used when there is an overt adverbial phrase designating a future time, or in "timeless" permanent instructions which are always in force (Allen and Greenough 1931). Only the present and future tenses are shown in (7); see ch. 2 (24) for examples of past tense forms.
4. The precise function of the "indicative" suffix –*a* is a puzzle in many Bantu languages, and this suffix is not glossed in the following examples.
5. The orthography used in (11) is a transliteration of the Khmer script, rather than a representation of actual modern pronunciation. The symbol "m̲" represents the *anusvara*, or *nikhahit*, while symbol "h̲" represents the *visarga*.
6. This is true for Malaysian. However, Sneddon (1996:328) states that in modern spoken Indonesian =*lah* no longer has this function in imperatives for most speakers.
7. Sadock and Zwicky (1985) mention Hopi as a possible example of a language which lacks content questions.
8. A CLITIC can be defined as an element which is phonologically bound to another word, even though it functions as an independent word in the syntax. See ch. 17 for details.
9. More precisely, in focus position. In many languages this means sentence-initial. But in languages like Hungarian, in which focused elements occupy a non-initial position, the question word will appear there as well.
10. This name is inherited from the Transformational Grammar analysis of these constructions. Under the approach adopted here, we assume that these structures are directly generated by special PS rules. However, we will not go into the details of the analysis in this book; see Kroeger (2004) and references cited there.
11. *Bukan* is also used to negate the truth of an entire proposition. Several other languages which have a special negative existential predicate were listed in ch. 10 (31).
12. Nik Safiah et al. (1986).
13. The word *not* is sometimes referred to as an "adverb," but does not really fit naturally into any lexical category.
14. (42–43) involve inflectional negation, as opposed to the derivational negation in words like *unhappy* and *dislike*. See ch. 13 for a discussion of the difference.

12 Subordinate clauses

Most human languages have certain constructions which are "expandable" to any degree the speaker wishes to take them. We have already seen several different ways in which English NPs can be "expanded" without limit; two of these are illustrated in (1).

(1)   a my favorite uncle's youngest daughter's oldest son's best friend's new bicycle
        b the portrait at the top of the stairs in that castle on a hill beside the river

In order to account for the possessive NP construction in (1a), we proposed a RECURSIVE Phrase Structure rule (chapter 6, section 6.4.2). A recursive rule is one which permits a mother node of some category (in this case, NP) to have a daughter of the same category. Recursive structures can also be generated when there are two phrasal categories such that each of them can dominate the other. For example, as illustrated in (1b) an NP may optionally contain a PP modifier, which will normally contain an NP object, which in turn may contain a PP, and so on.

The existence of recursive structures is a very important aspect of human grammatical systems. A particularly interesting type of recursion arises when one clause (category S) is embedded inside another. This is a major focus of study for syntacticians. Over the past forty years a huge amount of research has been devoted to understanding the grammatical properties of such structures, and it would obviously be impossible to review all of this research in a single chapter, or even in a whole book. In this chapter, our goal will be simply to introduce the most common types of embedded clauses, and to discuss some of the structural features that must be identified in any adequate description of these constructions.

12.1 Coordinate vs. subordinate clauses

There are two basic ways in which one clause can be embedded within another: COORDINATION vs. SUBORDINATION. In a COORDINATE structure, two constituents belonging to the same category are conjoined to form another constituent of that category. Such a structure is usually considered to be doubly headed, since both of the conjoined elements function as heads of the larger unit. Some simple examples of coordinate NPs are shown in (2):

(2)   a [[Snow White]_{NP} and [the seven dwarfs]_{NP}]_{NP}
       b [[two turtle doves]_{NP} and [a partridge in a pear tree]_{NP}]_{NP}
       c [[the lady]_{NP} or [the tiger]_{NP}]_{NP}
       d

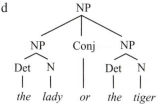

In a coordinate sentence, two (or more) S constituents occur as daughters and co-heads of a higher S. Each of the daughter clauses has the internal structure of an independent sentence, and neither is embedded in the other. Coordinate sentences in English are normally linked by conjunctions such as *and*, *but*, and *or*, as in the examples in (3). In other languages, coordinate sentences may be formed by simply juxtaposing two independent clauses, with only the second receiving final intonation.

(3)   a [[The Archduke was murdered by a Serb nationalist]_S and [the whole world was plunged into a terrible war]_S]_S
       b [[Give me liberty]_S or [give me death]_S]_S
       c [[The spirit is willing]_S but [the flesh is weak]_S]_S
       d

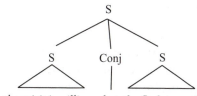

A SUBORDINATE clause is one which functions as a dependent, rather than a co-head. We will discuss three basic types of subordinate clause:

a   Complement clauses
b   Adjunct (or Adverbial) clauses
c   Relative clauses

COMPLEMENT CLAUSES are clauses that occur as complements of a verb; in other words, they are required or licensed by the subcategorization features of the verb. They typically function as the subject or object of another clause, which is referred to as the MATRIX clause. ADJUNCT CLAUSES, as their name suggests, are clauses which function as an adjunct or adverbial element of another clause. RELATIVE CLAUSES are clauses which function as modifiers within an NP.

For simplicity, we will use primarily English examples in our discussion of complement clauses and adjunct clauses (sections 12.2–12.4). In section 12.5, however, we will discuss examples of relative clauses from a wide variety of languages.

12.2   Complement clauses

In previous chapters we have dealt primarily with simple clauses whose complements are expressed as NPs or (in the case of oblique arguments) PPs. However, many verbs also allow or require a clausal complement. Examples (4–7) show that, for some verbs, either an NP or a complement clause may occur in the same position. The complement clause may be either FINITE (i.e. tense-bearing), as in (4b) and (5b), or NONFINITE as in (6b) and (7b).

(4)   a John believes [Mary's story].
       b John believes [that the airplane was invented by an Irishman].

(5)   a John told the girls [a story].
       b John told the girls [that their father had won the election].

(6)   a Mary planned [her trip] carefully.
       b Mary planned [for John to arrive in Dallas on New Year's Day].

(7)   a John promised his wife [a diamond ring].
       b John promised his wife [to stop smoking].

Notice that complement clauses are often introduced by a special word (or, in some languages, a particle) which is called a COMPLEMENTIZER. In English, the choice of verb form is related to the choice of complementizer. *That* is used to introduce a finite complement, as in (4b) and (5b). Infinitival complements take *for* if they have an overt (visible) subject, as in (6b); no complementizer is used when there is no overt subject, as in (7b).

As noted above, complement clauses frequently occupy the same position as NP objects. In languages where direct objects precede the verb, complement clauses often precede the verb as well. For example, the basic word order in Amele is SOV, as illustrated in (8a). Complement clauses in Amele normally precede the verb, as in (8b).

(8)   **Amele** (PNG; Roberts 1988:54–55)
       a Uqa sab   man-igi-an.
         3sg food roast-3sg-FUT
         'She will cook the food.'

       b Ija [dana age ija na   ho qo-ig-a]   d-ugi-na.
         1sg man PL 1sg POSS pig hit-3pl-REC.PAST know-1sg-PRES
         'I know that the men killed my pig.'

Some examples of complement clauses in subject position are given in
(9–10). In normal spoken style it is usually more natural to rephrase such
sentences using a dummy subject, as in (11–13); this construction is called
EXTRAPOSITION.

(9)   a [That John believes Mary's story] surprises me.
        b [That the airplane was invented by an Irishman] is not widely known.

(10)   a [For John to believe Mary's story] would surprise me.
        b [For the President to be re-elected] would cause panic on Wall Street.
        c ??[For you to read this book] is necessary.

(11)   a It surprises me [that John believes Mary's story].
        b It is not widely known [that the airplane was invented by an Irishman].

(12)   a It would surprise me [for John to believe Mary's story].
        b It is necessary [for you to read this book].

(13)   a It disappointed the General's supporters [that he refused to run].
        b It is obvious [that Mrs. Thatcher still controls the party].

The fact that the complementizer and the clause which it introduces always
stay together in the extraposition examples (11–13) suggests that these two
elements form a constituent in the Phrase Structure. Further evidence for
the existence of such a constituent is provided by examples like those in
(14):

(14)   a Simon believes [[that the Earth is flat] and
          [that the moon is made of green cheese]].
        b I sincerely hope, but unfortunately can't assume,
          [that Arthur will tell the truth from now on].

This constituent is normally labeled S′ or S̄ (pronounced "S-bar"). It contains two daughters: COMP (for "complementizer") and S (the complement
clause itself). This structure is illustrated in the tree diagram in (15), which
represents a sentence containing a finite clausal complement.

(15)

John   believes   that   my uncle   owns   Sentosa Island

As we noted in (4–7), complement clauses can often occur in the same position as NP complements. This observation suggests that a complement clause may bear the same Grammatical Relation as the NP which it replaces, as indicated in (16). This is a somewhat controversial issue; some linguists have argued that complement clauses must bear a distinct Grammatical Relation.[1] But, for the sake of simplicity, in this book we will assume the analysis suggested in (16). An annotated tree diagram based on example (16d) is shown in (17).

(16)   a John believes [Mary's story]$_{OBJ}$.
        b John believes [that the airplane was invented by an Irishman]$_{OBJ}$.
        c John told [the girls]$_{OBJ}$ [a story]$_{OBJ_2}$.
        d John told [the girls]$_{OBJ}$ [that their father had won the election]$_{OBJ_2}$.
        e [That John believes Mary's story]$_{SUBJ}$ surprises me.

(17)

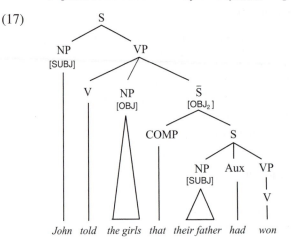

Subordinate clauses in general, and complement clauses in particular, often have structural features which are not found in main clauses or independent sentences. Some of the structural features that need to be considered in analyzing and comparing different types of subordinate clause include:

a   **VERB FORM**: Main clause statements and questions normally contain a finite verb. But the verb in some kinds of subordinate clause may be non-finite (e.g. an infinitive or participle), or appear in a different mood (e.g. subjunctive); or the subordinate verb may have to be nominalized.[2]

b   **SUBJECT**: Certain types of subordinate clause lack a subject NP, either obligatorily or optionally. In other cases, the only permissible subject of the subordinate clause is a pronoun which is co-referential with some element of the matrix clause. Other types of subordinate clause may contain an independent subject NP, just like a main clause.

c **WORD ORDER**: A subordinate clause may be subject to different word order constraints from a main clause. As we mentioned in chapter 11, there is often less freedom or variability in the word order of a subordinate clause than in a main clause.

d **MATRIX VERB**: Since complement clauses are selected (subcategorized for) by a specific matrix verb, it is important to identify which verbs select which type of clausal complement.

e **COMPLEMENTIZER**: Different types of complement clause may require different complementizers.

As mentioned in point (d), the form of a complement clause is often determined by the specific verb that occurs in the matrix clause. Verbs that belong to the same general semantic class often take the same type of complement. Some examples of various classes of English predicates follow. Example sentences for each class are given in (18) below.[3]

Semantic class	Examples	Complement V-form
a saying and knowing	*know, think, say, report, suspect, fear, hope, imply, tell*, etc.	finite
b influence verbs	*force, persuade, cause, request, urge, command, order*	infinitive
c modality predicates	*want, intend, plan, try, prefer, threaten, willing, afraid, eager, able, know how*	infinitive
d aspectual predicates	*begin, finish, keep on, go around*	progressive participle
e demands ("jussives")	*insist, demand, essential (that), important (that)*	present subjunctive (= bare infinitive)

(18) a John *believes* [that the airplane was invented by an Irishman].
b John *told* the girls [that their father had won the election].
c John *persuaded* his wife [to sell her old car].
d John *intends* [to buy his brother's rubber estate].
e Next week John will *begin* [studying for his A-levels].
f John *keeps on* [looking for a way to retire at age 35].
g I *insist* [(that) this man be arrested immediately].
h It is *essential* [that the President sign this document today].

In terms of the important structural features listed above, we might write brief descriptions of these constructions along the following lines:

(19) a English verbs of saying and knowing take a complement clause introduced by *that*. This complement clause has essentially the same structure as an independent sentence, including a finite verb, a full NP subject, normal word order, and the normal range of possible auxiliary verbs.

b English influence and modality predicates (verbs like *persuade* and *intend*) take a complement clause whose verb appears in the infinitive, preceded by *to*. These complement clauses have no complementizer and no subject. The subject of the complement clause is understood to be the same as the subject or object of the matrix clause.

Complement clauses which contain their own subject NP, like those in (18a,b,g,h) are sometimes referred to as SENTENTIAL COMPLEMENTS, because they contain all the essential parts of a sentence. In most languages, a complement clause will have its own subject whenever the complement verb is finite. Complement clauses which lack a subject NP, like those in (18c–f), can be analyzed as a special type of predicate complement.[4]

12.3 Direct vs. indirect speech

In many languages, including English, speakers have two different ways of reporting the words of another person. A DIRECT QUOTE contains (at least in theory) the exact words spoken by the other person, embedded in a simple clause (the QUOTE FORMULA) such as "John said . . ." An INDIRECT QUOTE expresses the content of what was said, but not the speaker's exact words. The following examples illustrate the difference between direct and indirect statements, questions, and commands.

(20) **Direct quotation**:
   a John said, "I do not want this kind of ice cream."
   b Mary asked, "Can you help me?"
   c Father asked Mother, "Who has been calling me?"
   d Mother told John, "Stop pinching that elephant!"

(21) a **Indirect statement**:
   John said (that) he did not want that kind of ice cream.
   b **Indirect Yes–No question**:
   Mary asked whether I could help her.
   c **Indirect content question**:
   Father asked Mother who had been calling him.
   d **Indirect command**:
   Mother told John to stop pinching the elephant.

In comparing the direct quotes in (20) with the corresponding indirect quotes in (21), we immediately notice changes in several kinds of words: pronouns (first person replaced by third person and second person replaced by first person); verbs (present tense becomes past tense); and other deictic elements (*this* changes to *that*, *here* to *there*, etc.). The seemingly complex "sequence of tenses" which is often memorized by students of English as a foreign language is just one part of this wider pattern of changes.

We can explain all of these changes in terms of the shift in pragmatic REFERENCE POINT which occurs in indirect speech. In a direct quote, the reference point is the time and place of the original (reported) speech event, and the point of view is that of the original speaker (*John* in (20a), *Mary* in (20b), etc.). In an indirect quote, the reference point is the time and place of the second speech event (the one which reports the first), and the point of view is that of the second speaker (the one doing the reporting). So all of the deictic elements (those which refer to something in the speech context) must be adjusted to fit the new reference point.

12.3.1 Indirect quotation

Indirect statements, questions, and commands are among the most common examples of complement clauses, and their grammatical features should be described in the same way as any other complement clause. Indirect questions often have special features, and in some languages there are structural differences between an indirect Yes–No question (21b) vs. an indirect content question (21c). Consider the following English examples:

(22)   a **Direct Yes–No question**:
          John asked Mary, "Will you marry me?"
        b **Indirect Yes–No question**:
          John asked Mary [whether she would marry him].
(23)   a **Direct content question**:
          Mary asked John, "What are you eating?"
        b **Indirect content question**:
          Mary asked John [what he was eating].

English main clause questions, including questions in direct quotes, exhibit a special word-order pattern: the first auxiliary verb must precede the subject, as in (22a) and (23a).[5] But, as the (b) examples illustrate, this "subject–Aux inversion" pattern is not found in indirect questions of either type. Both indirect Yes–No questions (22b) and indirect content questions (23b) exhibit the same basic word order found in statements, namely subject–Aux–verb–object.

Indirect content questions can be easily identified because they contain a question word, a feature they share with main clause content questions. Indirect Yes–No questions are identified in English by the use of a special complementizer, either *whether* or *if*.

12.3.2 **Direct quotation**

Direct quotes are actually not complements at all. As Weber (1989:20) points out (speaking of Huallaga Quechua), "Direct quotations are embedded in, but not subordinate to, the . . . clause that frames them." And: "they bear no grammatical relation (e.g. subject, object, etc.) to any verb." A direct quotation is, in fact, a separate discourse, and may contain any amount of linguistic material from a single word to an entire story.

Haiman (1992) states: "It has been widely noted that quoted material is grammatically independent" of the matrix clause. For example, even though the quote formula in English often contains the transitive verb *say*, the quote itself does not behave like a normal direct object. In (24a) the object of *say* has been fronted with subject–Aux inversion; but this construction is impossible with a direct quote (24b).

(24)   a Not a word did she say.
          b "Not a word," she said / *did she say.

Haiman uses the examples in (25) to illustrate the principle that quoted words are "mentioned" rather than "used."

(25)   a I don't like myself.
          b I don't like "I" in essays.

The first person pronoun which appears as the direct object in (25a) is used in the normal way, to refer to the speaker. Since it is co-referential with the subject of its clause, a reflexive form (*myself*) must be used. The quoted pronoun *"I"* in (25b) does not appear in the reflexive, or even the accusative (*me*), because it is not being used as a pronoun at all; it refers to a word (*I*) rather than a person (the speaker). When we use a direct quote we are reporting the linguistic expressions used by a speaker, rather than the content or message which the speaker expressed. As a result, there is generally no grammatical linkage between our words (the quote formula) and the speaker's words (the quotation).

While many languages (including English) use verbs of speaking in the quote formula, this is not always the case. In Kimaragang Dusun, a quote formula need not contain any verb at all, but almost always contains a quotative particle *kah*. This particle is neither a verb nor a noun: it is only one syllable long, whereas the minimum length for a content word in Kimaragang is two syllables; it cannot take any verbal affixes; and it ends in an *–h* (indicating lack of a final glottal stop), which is excedingly rare for content words but quite common among discourse particles and other functors.

The speaker may be indicated by a genitive NP or pronoun following the quote particle, as illustrated in (26). Only in clauses (b) and (d) does the quote formula contain a verb; in both cases the verb is *simbar* 'answer,' though, of course, many other verbs of speaking are possible. This passage is an excerpt from a story about the Roc, or Bird of Vishnu (Malay: *Garuda*), who abducts a woman to keep her from marrying her suitor.

(26) a "Ai, adi," *kah* di kurubau, "isai ot tulun sitih?" *kah*.
hey yg.sibling QUOT GEN Roc who NOM person here QUOT

b Simbar nopoh it tongondu, "Amuso," *kah*.
answer only NOM woman not.exist QUOT

c "Nokuroh.tu kiwaro ot tawau o-singud kuh?" *kah* di kurubau,
why exist NOM scent PASS-smell 1sg.GEN QUOT GEN Roc

d om simbar it tongondu, "Dogon dot tawau itih," *kah*.
and answer NOM woman 1sg.DAT LNK scent this QUOT

e "Amu, dikau dot tawau suwai, itih tawau ditih suwai,"
no 2sg.DAT LNK scent different this scent this different
kah di kurubau.
QUOT GEN Roc

f "M[in]an-sabun okuh," *kah* di tongondu.
use[PAST]-soap 1sg.NOM QUOT GEN woman

"Hey, little sister (i.e. wife)," said the Roc bird, "who is the person that is here?" The woman answered, "There is no one."
"Why is there a (human) scent which I smell?" said the Roc bird, and the woman answered, "That is my scent."
"No, your scent is different from this one," said the Roc bird. "I bathed with soap," said the woman.

12.4 Adjunct (or Adverbial) clauses

In chapter 4 we defined ADJUNCTS as elements which are not subcategorized by the verb, but which are added to the sentence to provide various kinds of information. Several different types of expression may function as adjuncts. The most common types are adverbs (27a), prepositional phrases (27b), and adjunct clauses (27c):

(27) a Mary *seldom* makes her bed.
b Mary makes her bed *on Tuesdays*.
c Mary makes her bed *when her mother comes to visit her.*

All three types of adjuncts can be used to express similar kinds of information: time, place, manner, reason, etc. Many of the prepositions used in English to introduce PP adjuncts can also be used to introduce adjunct clauses, both finite and non-finite (participial), as the examples in (28–29) illustrate.[6]

(28) a Mary opened her presents [before dinner].
b Mary opened her presents [before finishing her dinner].
c Mary opened her presents [before John finished his dinner].

(29) a The elephant's child was spanked [for his curiosity].
      b The elephant's child was spanked [for asking too many questions].

These prepositions are sometimes referred to as "subordinating conjunctions" when they are used to introduce adverbial clauses. Some linguists
prefer to analyze them as complementizers in this context, and to assign
the adverbial clauses which they introduce to the category S′. However, in
view of the parallelism illustrated in (28–29), we will treat them as prepositions and assign the adverbial clause to the category PP, as illustrated in
(30). This analysis requires us to modify our PS rules for English slightly, to
allow prepositions to take objects which belong to one of two categories, NP
or S.

(30)

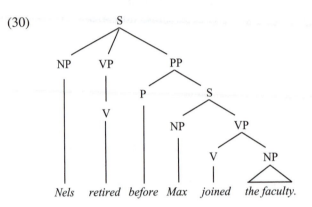

        Nels   retired   before   Max   joined   the faculty.

There are other "subordinating conjunctions" in English, including
because, while, if, unless, although, etc., which only introduce adjunct
clauses; they do not take NP objects like normal prepositions. In order to
have a single, consistent treatment for all adjunct clauses, we will assume
that these conjunctions also belong to the category P. It may seem odd
to call something a preposition that never appears in a "normal" prepositional phrase (i.e. never takes an NP object). But we face a somewhat similar
situation with verbs: some take NP objects (31a,b); others take clausal complements (31c,d); while still others can take either (31e,f) or both (31g). We
are analyzing *because, while, if*, etc., as prepositions which take only clausal
objects, similar to verbs like *realize* (in the sense illustrated in (31c,d)).[7] A
sample tree structure with an *if* clause is given in (32).

(31) a Sam kissed [my sister].
      b *Sam kissed [that Elvis was dead].
      c *Susan didn't realize [my sister].
      d Susan didn't realize [that Elvis was dead].
      e Arthur believed [my sister].
      f Arthur believed [that Elvis was dead].
      g Margaret told [my sister] [that Elvis was dead].

(32)

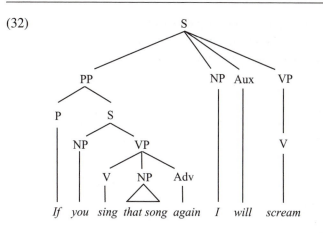

If you sing that song again I will scream

Treating adjunct clauses as PPs provides a more economical description for the sentence structure of English, but this is not true for all languages. In Southern Azerbaijani (Lee 1996), for example, the particle *ki* is used to mark a variety of complement clauses such as 'Hasan saw that X,' 'I hope that X,' 'He ordered the servants to X,' etc. However, the same particle can also be used to mark adjunct clauses of purpose as in 'He did X in order to Y.' In Warlpiri the clitic particle =*ku* is used to mark both complement clauses (for matrix verbs like the coercion and modality predicates listed in section 12.2) and adjunct clauses expressing purpose. Similarly, the Indonesian word *supaya* is used not only to introduce complement clauses corresponding to English *for . . . to* complements, as in (33), but also for certain adjunct purpose clauses as in (34) (examples adapted from Sneddon 1996). In such cases it makes sense to treat these markers as complementizers in both uses, analyzing both the complement and the adjunct clauses as S′ constituents, as indicated in diagrams (33b) and (34b).

(33)   a Bung Karno ingin *supaya* [kami   menolong dia].
         Bung Karno want COMP 1pl.EX help   3sg
         'Bung Karno wants us to help him.'

   b

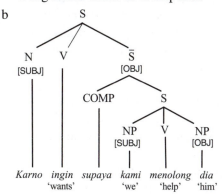

Karno ingin supaya kami menolong dia
      'wants'   'we' 'help'   'him'

(34)   a Dia jual sayur   *supaya* [anak=nya dapat bersekolah].
3sg sell vegetable COMP   child=3sg get   attend.school
'She sells vegetables so that her son can go to school.'

b

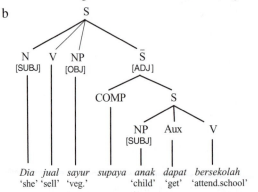

Dia jual sayur supaya anak dapat bersekolah
'she' 'sell' 'veg.'   'child' 'get' 'attend.school'

Remember that the term COMPLEMENTIZER is a label for a syntactic category, rather than a restriction on function. It is not meant to imply that elements belonging to this category can only appear in complement clauses. Indeed, it is quite common for them to mark not only adjunct clauses but also relative clauses, to which we now turn.

12.5   Relative clauses

In the beginning of this chapter we defined a RELATIVE CLAUSE as a clause which modifies the head noun within a noun phrase.[8] Consider the following example:

(35)   [The woman [that I love]$_{S'}$]$_{NP}$ is moving to Argentina.

This example illustrates the three basic parts of a relative clause construction: the head noun (*woman*), the modifying clause (*I love*), and the RELATIVIZER (*that*) which links the modifying clause to the head. Notice that the modifying clause is incomplete: it lacks a direct object, even though its verb (*love*) requires one. Of course, the reason this example is acceptable is that the head noun is "understood" to be the object of *love*. Thus the head noun actually has two different roles in this example: it functions as the subject of the main clause, but at the same time it is interpreted as being the object of the modifying clause.

In this section we will be primarily concerned with the internal structure of the relative clause. In addition to the structural features discussed in the preceding sections, which are potentially significant in all subordinate clause constructions, there are some additional issues which only arise in relative constructions. These include: the position of the modifying clause relative to the head noun; the nature of the relativizer, if any; the function which the head noun is understood to fill within the modifying clause, and the manner in which this function is indicated. But before we turn to these structural issues, let us briefly discuss the semantic function of relative clauses.

12.5.1   Restrictive vs. non-restrictive relative clauses

In (35) the head of the relative clause (*woman*) is a common noun which could refer to any one of a few billion individuals. The function of the modifying clause is to identify (uniquely, one would hope) which particular woman the speaker is referring to. This is a typical example of a RESTRICTIVE relative clause. In this construction, the reference of the NP as a whole is determined in two stages: the head noun designates a class which the referent must belong to; and the modifying clause restricts (or narrows) the identity of the referent to a specific member of that class.

Not all relative clauses work this way. A NON-RESTRICTIVE relative clause is one in which the referent of the head noun can be identified independently, and the clausal modifier simply presents additional information about that referent. The difference between restrictive and non-restrictive relative clauses is illustrated in (36). In (36a) the head is a common noun which identifies the class of men in general. The modifying clause serves to identify which particular man the speaker is talking about. In (36b), on the other hand, the head is a proper name; this indicates that the speaker assumes that the hearer already knows who Al Capone is. The clausal modifier serves only to provide additional background information about this individual.

(36)   a RESTRICTIVE:
             The police are looking for [the man who escaped from prison yesterday].
         b NON-RESTRICTIVE:
             The police are looking for [Al Capone, who escaped from prison yesterday].

Thus in restrictive relative clauses, like (36a), the modifying clause contains old or presupposed information while the identity of the referent is new information. But in non-restrictive relative clauses, like (36b), the identity of the referent is old information while the modifying clause contains new information.

In many languages there is little or no difference in grammatical structure between restrictive and non-restrictive relative clauses, but this is not always the case. In English the most obvious difference is intonational: non-restrictive relative clauses are always set off by pauses, usually indicated by commas as in (36b), whereas restrictive relative clauses are not. Another difference is illustrated in (37) and (38). In a restrictive relative clause like (37), the modifying clause may be introduced by *that*, a Wh- word, or Ø.

But in a non-restrictive relative clause like (38), the modifying clause must be introduced by a Wh- word; the use of *that* or Ø makes the construction ungrammatical.[9]

(37)　　a The woman whom I love is moving to Argentina.
　　　　b The woman that I love is moving to Argentina.
　　　　c The woman I love is moving to Argentina.

(38)　　a Mary Martin, whom I dearly love, is moving to Argentina.
　　　　b *Mary Martin, that I dearly love, is moving to Argentina.
　　　　c *Mary Martin, I dearly love, is moving to Argentina.

As we have seen, proper names occur quite naturally as heads of non-restrictive relative clauses, but they are quite unnatural in restrictive relative clauses. Conversely, phrases involving quantifier words such as *any*, *every*, or *some* are only acceptable as heads of restrictive relative clauses, and do not work in non-restrictive relative clauses:

(39)　　a Every student who failed the exam will be asked to repeat the course next year.
　　　　b *Every student, who failed the exam, will be asked to repeat the course next year.

(40)　　a Any student who brings cigarettes to school will be sent home.
　　　　b *Any student, who brings cigarettes to school, will be sent home.

(41)　　a No one who saw the new James Bond movie liked it.
　　　　b *No one, who saw the new James Bond movie, liked it.

12.5.2　Word order and morphology

12.5.2.1　Externally headed relative clauses

In English, as all of the preceding examples illustrate, the modifying clause always follows the head noun. This is probably the most common ordering of these elements across languages, but it is certainly not the only possibility. A large number of languages have the opposite order, with the modifying clause preceding the head noun. Both of these possibilities are examples of EXTERNALLY HEADED relative clauses, i.e. those in which the head noun occurs outside the modifying clause, whether before or after. The other possibility, namely an INTERNALLY HEADED relative clause, is quite rare; a brief example will be given in the next section.

If we examine externally headed relative constructions in many different languages, we will discover a partial correlation between the position of the modifying clause (before or after the head noun) and other word-order facts in the language. Verb-initial languages (those in which the verb occurs first in a basic declarative sentence, whether VSO or VOS) almost always have POSTNOMINAL (or POST-POSED) relative clauses, with the modifying clause following the head noun. A large number of verb-final (SOV) languages have PRENOMINAL (or PRE-POSED) relative clauses, with the modifying clause preceding the head noun. A Turkish example showing this structure is given in (42) (the abbreviation NMLZ stands for NOMINALIZER).[10] But other verb-final languages have postnominal relative clauses instead.

(42) [John='un Mary=ye ver-dig-i][11]   patates=i   yedim.
      John=GEN Mary=DAT give-NMLZ-his potato=ACC I.ate
      'I ate the potato that John gave to Mary.'
      (lit.: 'I ate the potato of John's giving to Mary.')

Most SVO languages (including English) use postnominal relative clauses. Some of these languages also have a prenominal relative construction, but these are typically more restricted in their distribution. We can summarize these observations by saying that, across languages, postnominal relatives are more common than prenominal, and that prenominal relatives are the preferred option only in SOV languages.

Aside from the prenominal order, there is another important difference between the Turkish example in (42) and the English examples in (35–41). In English relative clauses, the modifying clause contains a normal finite verb form, fully inflected for tense and agreement. In Turkish, however, the verb inside the modifying clause must be NOMINALIZED; that is, it is changed into a form which belongs to the category N.[12] Because of this change, the subject of the modifying clause is marked for genitive case, rather than the expected nominative. This kind of prenominal relative clause, with a nominalized verb form and a genitive subject, is found in a number of other SOV languages as well.

Another common pattern is for the verb inside the modifying clause to appear as a PARTICIPLE. German has two kinds of relative clauses: a prenominal relative containing a participial form of the verb (43a); and a postnominal relative containing a normal finite verb form (43b). Note that English also allows participial relatives, as illustrated in the translation of (43a).

(43) a der [in seinem Büro arbeitende] Mann
        the in his.DAT study working   man
        'the man working in his study'

      b der Mann, [der in seinem Büro arbeitet]
        the man   who in his.DAT study works
        'the man who is working in his study'

12.5.2.2 Internally headed relative clauses and related constructions

As mentioned above, a few languages have INTERNALLY HEADED relative clauses, in which the head noun appears inside the modifying clause. The examples in (44) are from Dogon, a language of West Africa. Notice that the head noun ('woman' in 44a, 'man' in 44b) lies inside the modifying clause in both examples. The two sentences are identical, except for the form of the verb in the modifying clause ('insult'), which indicates whether the head noun is the subject (as in 44b) or a non-subject element (as in 44a).

(44)   **Dogon** (Mali, W. Africa, Togo Kã dialect; Culy 1990:86)[13]
    a [yaa   nyɛ   ãrã   dɔɛ] iye.aga   Moti yei.
      yesterday woman man insult today.morning Mopti went
      'The man whom the woman insulted yesterday went to Mopti this morning.'
    b [yaa   nyɛ   ãrã   dɔsã] iye.aga   Moti yei.
      yesterday woman man insult today.morning Mopti went
      'The woman who insulted the man yesterday went to Mopti this morning.'

Another fairly rare type of relative construction is the CORELATIVE, in which the head noun occurs both inside and outside the modifying clause. The example in (45) is from Hindi.[14] Since these two constructions are relatively uncommon, we will not discuss them further in this book.

(45)   Jis   *aadmi*=ka kutta bemaar hai, us *aadmi*=ko mai=ne   dekha.
    which man=GEN dog sick   is   that man=OBJ 1sg=ERG saw
    'I saw the man whose dog is sick.'
    (lit.: 'Which man's dog is sick, that man I saw.')

12.5.3   Relative pronoun vs. relativizer

In discussing (35), we referred to the word *that* as a RELATIVIZER. A relativizer is basically a special type of complementizer which marks the modifying clause in a relative clause construction. In many languages (e.g. Chinese and Tagalog) the same particle which functions as a relativizer is also used to link other modifiers to the head noun.

In (37) we saw that English relative clauses do not always contain *that*. Another option, illustrated in (37a), is to use a Wh-word to introduce the modifying clause. An English Wh- word used in this way is called a RELATIVE PRONOUN. Relative pronouns in other languages may be derived from question words, definite articles, or demonstratives.

We can define a RELATIVE PRONOUN cross-linguistically by saying that it is an anaphoric element which introduces the modifying clause and takes the head noun as its antecedent. But if *that* and *whom* are often interchangeable, as illustrated in (37), what basis do we have for assigning them to different categories – for calling one a relative pronoun and the other a relativizer? More generally, why do we distinguish these two types of elements in any language, and how can we recognize them?

The crucial difference is that a relative pronoun is a special type of pronoun, i.e. an anaphoric NP, while a relativizer is not. The clearest evidence for the anaphoric nature of the relative pronoun is agreement, i.e. a change in the form of the relative pronoun depending on some features of the head noun (gender, number, animacy, etc.). Moreover, a relative pronoun is often inflected for case, which is a property of NPs. A relativizer, in contrast, is normally an invariant particle (one that doesn't change shape), much like a complementizer. If there are changes in the shape of the relativizer, they are usually morphophonemic in nature and do not reflect agreement or case features.

In English, as we have noted, neither case nor agreement is strongly reflected in the morphology. Vestigial case marking can be observed in the choice between *who* (nominative), *whom* (dative/accusative), and *whose* (genitive), as seen in (46).[15] A kind of animacy agreement determines the choice between *who* (for humans) and *which* (for non-humans), as illustrated in (47). The relativizer *that* could take the place of the relative pronoun in all of these examples except (46c,e), with no change in form; it is not marked for case or agreement.

(46)   a the spy who loves me
       b the spy who(m) I love
       c the spy from whom I bought these documents
       d the spy who I bought these documents from
       e the spy whose sister I love

(47)   a the professor who/*which my brother studied under
       b the monkey which/??who(m) my brother trained
       c the book which/*who(m) my brother edited

The case and agreement features of the relative pronoun are much more obvious in other languages. German provides a very clear example. The German demonstrative pronouns (*der, die, das* 'that one') also function as relative pronouns.[16] A relative pronoun agrees with the head noun for gender and number, while its case marking indicates the Grammatical Relation which the head noun is understood to bear within the modifying clause. The examples in (48) illustrate agreement with the grammatical gender of the head noun, while (49) illustrates the change in case marking.[17]

(48)   a der   Mann, [*den*   Marie liebt]
          the(MASC) man   who(SG.MASC.ACC) Marie loves
          'the man whom Marie loves'
       b die   Frau, [*die*   Hans liebt]
          the(FEM) woman who(SG.FEM.ACC) Hans loves
          'the woman whom Hans loves'
       c das   Mädchen, [*das*   Hans liebt]
          the(NEUT) girl   who(SG.NEUT.ACC) Hans loves
          'the girl whom Hans loves'

(49)   a der Reiseführer, [*der*   uns die Stadt zeigt]
           the guide   who(SG.MASC.NOM) us   the city   shows
           'the guide who shows us the city'

        b der Reiseführer, [*dessen*   Adresse wir haben wollen]
           the guide   who(SG.MASC.GEN) address   we have want
           'the guide whose address we want to have'

        c der Reiseführer, [*dem*   ich ein gutes Trinkgeld
           the guide   who(SG.MASC.DAT) I   a   good tip
              gegeben habe]
              given   have
           'the guide to whom I gave a good tip'

        d der Reiseführer, [*den*   ich Ihnen empfehlen kann]
           the guide   who(SG.MASC.ACC) I   you   recommend can
           'the guide whom I can recommend to you'

12.5.4 Relativization strategies

As noted above, the case marking of the relative pronoun in German indicates the Grammatical Relation that the head noun is understood to bear within the modifying clause.[18] This is clearly a very important function, since we cannot interpret the meaning of the NP correctly without understanding the semantic relationship between the head noun and the modifying clause. But not all languages have relative pronouns, and some languages that do have them (e.g. English) also allow relative clauses to be formed without using relative pronouns. How can the hearer identify the function of the head noun when the relative clause does not contain a relative pronoun?

Recall that in discussing (35), repeated below, we noted that the NP which contains the relative clause functions as the subject of the main clause. We might refer to this as the "external" Grammatical Relation of the NP. At the same time, the head noun (*woman*) is interpreted as being the object of the modifying clause. We will refer to this "internal" Grammatical Relation as the RELATIVIZED FUNCTION: the Grammatical Relation that is assigned to the head noun within the modifying clause.[19] Thus the relativized function in (35) is the direct object.

(35)   [The woman [that I love]$_{S'}$]$_{NP}$ is moving to Argentina.

But how can the hearer determine this, since the relativizer *that* provides no clues? The answer is related to our earlier observation that the modifying clause is incomplete: even though the verb *love* is transitive, the modifying clause lacks a direct object. This "missing" argument of the modifying clause must be the relativized function. Since the modifying clause needs an object in order to be grammatical, this relation must be assigned to the head noun.

This method of signaling the identity of the relativized function is often referred to as the GAP strategy, since the only clue is the "gap" or missing argument in the modifying clause. The head noun is interpreted as filling this gap. What is significant here is not merely the presence of a gap: an English relative clause contains a gap whether or not a relative pronoun is used, as illustrated in (50). The crucial point is that when the relative pronoun is present it provides at least some information about the relativized function. When there is no relative pronoun, the gap itself is the hearer's only clue. This is the situation we refer to as the gap strategy.

(50)

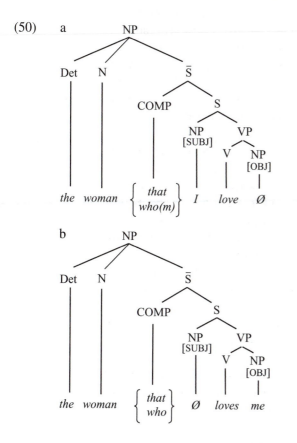

Gaps and relative pronouns are two different strategies which languages may use to accomplish the same goal, namely to identify the relativized function. The third commonly used strategy is PRONOUN RETENTION. In this pattern, the relativized function is represented by a pronominal "copy" of the head noun – a regular personal pronoun which occurs inside the modifying clause and agrees with the head noun in gender and number.

This pronominal copy is often called a RESUMPTIVE PRONOUN. The examples in (51) are from Keenan (1985:146).

(51)   a **Modern Hebrew**

> ha-sarim   she-ha-nasi   shalax *otam* la-mitsraim
> the-ministers REL-the-president sent   them to-Egypt
> 'the ministers that the President sent (them) to Egypt'

    b **Persian**

> Man [zan-i   râ   ke   John be *u*   sibe zamini dâd] mishenasam.
> 1sg woman-the ACC REL John to her   potato   gave know
> 'I know the woman that John gave the potato to (her).'

We have identified three basic strategies which languages commonly use to indicate the relativized function within a relative clause; (i) gaps; (ii) relative pronouns; and (iii) pronoun retention.[20] There are three interesting questions we might ask relating to the use of these strategies: (a) which languages use which strategy?; (b) which specific functions can be relativized in particular languages?; and (c) for languages which allow more than one strategy, is one of them preferred over the others for certain relativized functions?

The second and third questions lead to issues which are beyond the scope of the present book. Here we can only stress that it is the relativized function (the Grammatical Relation which the head noun bears inside the modifying clause) that is relevant to these questions, and not the external Grammatical Relation. This fact needs to be emphasized because it is a common source of confusion for beginning linguists. It is rare to find restrictions on the external Grammatical Relation of the NP which contains the relative clause; relative clauses can appear anywhere in the matrix sentence where a "normal" NP would be allowed. But languages do place interesting restrictions on the relativized function and how it is marked.

Investigations of the first question above have revealed some interesting correlations between relativization strategy and word order. The gap strategy is found in all types of languages, and is virtually the only strategy used in prenominal relative clauses. Relative pronouns have (so far) been found only in postnominal relative clauses. Pronoun retention is also found almost exclusively in postnominal relative clauses.[21]

12.5.5   Headless relatives and free relatives

At the beginning of section 12.5 we identified the basic parts of a relative clause construction as being a head noun, a modifying clause, and (optionally) a relativizer. Now consider the following Tagalog noun phrases. In each case the (a) example is a complete, normal, relative clause construction, but the corresponding (b) example seems incomplete. Specifically, the (b) examples contain no head noun; they are "headless."

(52)   a ang   mga baro=ng   binili   ko
           NOM PL   dress=REL bought by.me
           'the dresses that I bought'

       b ang   mga Ø binili   ko
           NOM PL   bought by.me
           'the ones that I bought'

(53)   a ang   babae=ng   nagbabasa ng=diyaryo
           NOM woman=REL read   GEN=newspaper
           'the woman reading a newspaper'

       b ang   Ø nagbabasa ng=diyaryo
           NOM   read   GEN=newspaper
           'the one reading a newspaper'

NPs like the (b) examples are referred to as HEADLESS RELATIVE
CLAUSES. They take the normal NP markers (case, determiners, etc.) and
contain a modifying clause, which may be preceded by a relative pronoun
or relativizer if these are present in normal relative clauses; but they lack a
head noun. Notice that the English translations of these examples include
a pronominal element *one* as head of the NP, since English does not allow
true headless relative clauses. The interpretation of a headless relative clause
will depend on context; *the ones that I bought* could refer to dresses, fish,
bicycles, shares of stock, etc., depending on the previous discourse. But
quite often headless relatives are used to refer to people; so (53b) could be
translated *the person reading a newspaper*.

There is no real headless relative construction in English. The closest
approximation is the "free relative" construction, as in *You can't always
get what you want*. However, headless NPs with adjectival modifiers (*the
rich*; *the poor*; etc.) are quite common, especially in movie and book
titles: *The good, the bad, and the ugly*; *The naked and the dead*; *Lonely
are the brave*; etc. These are quite similar to headless relative clauses
except that the modifier is just a single adjective, rather than an entire
clause.

The free relative construction mentioned in the previous paragraph is
basically an NP that looks like a content question; an example is given in
(54a). A free relative can easily be mistaken for an interrogative complement
clause (54b), i.e. an indirect question, because both of them begin with a
question word. The key difference is that the free relative is an NP and
typically refers to a thing, as in (54a); an interrogative complement clause
is an S̄ and typically refers to a proposition (the proposition that would
answer the embedded question), as in (54b).

(54)   a I don't eat [what he cooks on that old stove]$_{NP}$.   [FREE RELATIVE]
       b I don't know [what he cooks on that old stove]$_{S'}$. [INTERROG.COMPL.]

Recall that the verb *know* selects a clausal complement, whereas the verb *eat* does not. This means that the embedded clause in (54a) cannot be a complement clause; it must be the NP object of *eat*. Similarly, *ask* selects a clausal complement but *buy* does not; thus the embedded clause in (55a) can only be the NP object of *buy*.

(55)   (McCawley 1988:431–432)
          a I'll buy [what he is selling]$_{NP}$. [FREE RELATIVE]
          b I'll ask [what he is selling]$_{S'}$. [INTERROGATIVE COMPLEMENT]

Several grammatical differences between these two constructions are noted by Bresnan and Grimshaw (1978); and McCawley (1988).[22] Only in free relatives can the question word end with *–ever* (56). Only interrogative complements can be extraposed (57). Only in interrogative complements can the Wh- phrase contain a preposition (58) or a possessor (59). And only free relatives can trigger plural number agreement (60).

(56)   a I'll buy [whatever he is selling].   [FREE RELATIVE]
          b *I'll ask [whatever he is selling].   [INTERROGATIVE COMPLEMENT]

(57)   a *It isn't very popular [what he is selling]. [FREE RELATIVE]
          b It isn't important [how much he sold].   [INTERROGATIVE COMPLEMENT]

(58)   a *I'll buy [to what he was referring].   [FREE RELATIVE]
          b I'll ask [to what he was referring].   [INTERROGATIVE COMPLEMENT]

(59)   a *I'll buy [whose books he is selling].   [FREE RELATIVE]
          b I'll ask [whose books he is selling].   [INTERROGATIVE COMPLEMENT]

(60)   a [Whatever books he has written] haven't/*hasn't sold well.
                                                          [FREE RELATIVE]
          b [What books he has written] hasn't/*haven't been established.
                                                          [INTERROGATIVE COMPLEMENT]

12.6   Conclusion

All of the constructions we have discussed in this chapter have at least one thing in common: they all involve one clause embedded within another. These embedded clauses may have several different functions. A complement clause is one that functions as an argument of its matrix verb. An adverbial clause functions as an adjunct to the matrix clause. A relative clause functions as a modifier within an NP, and this NP in turn will (in most cases) function as a constituent of some larger clause.

As we noted at the beginning of this chapter, subordination is a very broad and complex area of syntactic research. This chapter has provided a basic introduction to the kinds of issues that are likely to be significant for any preliminary study of the subordinating constructions in a particular language. In describing these constructions, we need to address their internal structure (e.g. the form of the subordinate verb, choice of complementizer, word-order constraints, presence vs. absence of a subject NP). We also need to address their structural and functional relationship to the matrix clause (position within the larger sentence, complement vs. adjunct or modifier, semantic functions, etc.). Finally, we should look for any correlations between these external and internal features.

Some additional features are significant for describing relative clauses: the position of the head noun; the strategies available for marking the relativized function (most commonly the gap strategy, relative pronouns, or pronoun retention); and any restrictions on what Grammatical Relations may be relativized.

Practice exercise

English relative clauses
Find the relative clauses in the following examples. For each one, state whether it is restrictive or non-restrictive, what relativization strategy is used, and identify the relativized function.

1.   Mr. Darcy, whom everyone despises, wants to marry Lizzie, who is universally admired.

2.   Mrs. Bennet loves any man who wants to marry one of her daughters.

3.   The girl whom Mr. Darcy plans to marry has no hope of an inheritance.

4.   Lizzie tried to be polite to the cousin whose proposal she had refused.

5.   Mr. Bennet was astonished by the letter that his brother-in-law sent him.

6.   Mr. Collins was rejected by the first woman he proposed to.

7.   Mr. Collins was accepted by the second woman to whom he proposed.

8.   Lizzie is going to marry a man that her relatives can't imagine what she sees in him.

Exercises

12A Malay Noun phrases
(a) Formulate a set of Phrase Structure rules to account for the following examples; and (b) describe the relative clause patterns you observe. What relativization strategies are used? What relativized functions are possible

for each strategy? What generalization can you make about the distribution of AP? (Note: the clitic =*nya* functions grammatically as a normal third person pronoun. The notation "... *(X) ..." indicates that X is obligatory in that example. "AV" = 'active voice.')

1.   rumah itu   besar.   'That house is big.'
      house that big

2.   rumah ini   sangat besar.   'This house is very big.'
      house this very   big

3.   baju saya itu   terlalu kecil.   'That shirt of mine is too small.'
      shirt 1sg that too   small

4.   anak=nya rajin   dan pandai.   'His child is hardworking and clever.'
      child=3sg industrious and clever

5.   anjing besar itu   menggigit anak saya.
      dog   big   that AV-bite   child 1sg
      'That big dog bit my child.'

6.   anak saya digigit   (oleh) anjing.
      child 1sg PASS-bite (by)   dog
      'My child was bitten by a dog.'

7.   anjing yang menggigit anak saya itu
      dog   REL AV-bite   child 1sg that
      'the/that dog which bit my child'

8.   anak kecil yang digigit   (oleh) anjing
      child small REL PASS-bite (by)   dog
      'the small child who was bitten by a dog'

9.   *anak yang anjing itu   menggigit.
      child REL dog   that AV-bite
      (intended: 'the child whom that dog bit')

10.   *anjing yang anak saya digigit   (oleh)
      dog   REL child 1sg PASS-bite (by)
      (intended: 'the dog by which my child was bitten')

11.   rumah besar   'a big house'
      house big

12.   *rumah sangat besar   (intended: 'a very big house')
      house   very   big

13.   rumah yang sangat besar   'a house which is very big'
      house REL   very   big

14.   baju saya *(yang) terlalu kecil itu 'that shirt of mine which is too small'
      shirt 1sg (REL) too   small that

15. anak *(yang) rajin   dan pandai   'a child who is hardworking and clever'
    child (REL) industrious and clever

16. anjing besar *(yang) ganas   'a big dog that is fierce'
    dog   big   (REL) fierce

17. gadis yang abang=nya   memukul saya
    girl REL older.bro=3sg AV-hit 1sg
    'the girl whose elder brother hit me'

18. *gadis yang saya memukul abang=nya
    girl REL 1sg AV-hit   older.bro=3sg
    (intended: 'the girl whose elder brother I hit')

19. budak yang buku=nya dicuri   orang
    child REL book=3sg PASS-steal person
    'the child whose book was stolen by someone'

20. *budak yang orang mencuri buku=nya
    child REL person AV-steal book=3sg
    (intended: 'the child whose book someone stole')

12B Portuguese subordination (Sá Pereira 1948; Ellison et al. 1971)[23]
Describe the subordinate clause patterns in the following examples.

1. O médico acha que   o homem está doente.
    the doctor thinks COMP the man is sick
    'The doctor thinks that the man is sick.'

2. Sinto   que   ela esteja   doente.
    1sg.regret COMP she is(SBJNCT) sick
    'I regret that she is sick.'

3. Sei   que   êle me ama.
    1sg.know COMP he me loves
    'I know that he loves me.'

4. Nego   que   êle me ame.
    1sg.deny COMP he me loves(SBJNCT)
    'I deny that he loves me.'

5. É certo que   o Mário já   sabe   dançar.
    is certain COMP the Mario already knows to.dance
    'It is certain that Mario already knows how to dance.'

6. É provável que   o Mário já   saiba   dançar.
    is likely   COMP the Mario already knows(SBJNCT) to.dance
    'It is likely that Mario already knows how to dance.'

7. O João diz que   o pai dela é arquiteto.
    the John says COMP the father of.her is architect
    'John says that her father is an architect.'

8.   Espero   que   você goste   dêste restaurante.
      1sg.hope COMP you   like(SBJNCT) this   restaurant.
      'I hope that you like this restaurant.'

9.   O Dr. Campos proíbe que   êles subam   ao   Pão de Açúcar.
      the   forbids COMP they climb(SBJNCT) to.the bread of sugar
      'Dr. Campos forbids them to climb the Sugar Loaf.'

10.   Se eu fôr   amanhã ao   Rio, irei   de autómovel.
      if I go(FUT.SBJNCT) tomorrow to.the Rio 1sg.FUT.go by car
      'If I go to Rio tomorrow, I will go by car.'

11.   Quando eu vier,   falarei   com ela.
      when   I come(FUT.SBJNCT) 1sg.FUT.speak with her
      'When I come I will speak to her.'

12.   Depois que   os rapazes saírem,   nós faremos   o   trabalho.
      after COMP the boys   leave(FUT.SBJNCT) we 1pl.FUT.do the work
      'After the boys leave, we will do the work.'

13.   Elas   vão sair para que   os rapazes estudem.
      3pl.FEM FUT leave for COMP the boys   study(SBJNCT)
      'They (fem.) will leave so that the boys (can) study.'

14.   Vou   esperar aqui até que   ela volte.
      1sg.FUT wait   here until COMP she returns(SBJNCT)
      'I will wait here until she returns.'

15.   Êles estavam dormindo quando eu os   vi.
      they were   sleeping when   I them saw
      'They were sleeping when I saw them.'

16.   Ela veio aos   Estados Unidos para visitar a   filha.
      she came to.the States United for to.visit the daughter
      'She came to the United States to visit her daughter.'

Additional exercises

Merrifield et al. (1987) prob. 265, 267, 271, 273, 277, 281, 282, 283, 291
Healey (1990b), ex. F.8, 9, 10, 11, 14

Notes

1. For example, there are a few English verbs that take two NP objects (OBJ and OBJ_2)
   plus a clausal complement: *Henry bet* [*his cousin*] [*ten dollars*] [*that Brazil would
   win the World Cup*]. Since no English verb takes three NP objects, it is not clear
   what the GR of the complement clause would be in this example. Also, it has been
   argued that in some languages clausal complements which bear the OBJ relation
   have different grammatical properties from those which do not, even though they

may occur in the same phrase-structural positions. However, these issues are beyond the scope of the present book.

2. See ch. 13 for a discussion of nominalization.

3. Only the primary usage of each matrix verb is noted here. Of course, many verbs have more than one sense. Thus *say* can be used as a manipulation verb, as in *John says to meet him in the library*. Similarly, *persuade* can be used as a verb of speaking, as in *Arthur persuaded me that he was innocent*, etc.

4. See Kroeger (2004), ch. 5 for a detailed discussion of these constructions.

5. As noted in ch. 4, sec. 4.3.1, this does not apply when the subject of the sentence is itself a Wh- word, as in (20c).

6. See Kroeger (2004), ch. 5 for arguments that participial adjuncts like those in (28b) and (29b) are in fact clauses, even though they do not contain a subject NP.

7. Additional support for this analysis is provided by Emonds (1976:172ff.); and Radford (1988:134–137). The analysis is also adopted by McCawley (1988:191), citing Jespersen (1924:89).

8. Note: a number of authors use the term "Relative clause" to refer to the entire NP which contains a clausal modifier, including the head noun. In the present book, the term "Relative clause" refers only to the clausal modifier (or "modifying clause," as in the following paragraph); and the NP which contains a Relative clause is called a "Relative clause construction."

9. These differences are also discussed in Bickford (1998:332). For a more detailed discussion of these and several other grammatical differences between restrictive and non-restrictive relative clauses in English, see McCawley (1988:417–432).

10. (42–43) and (45) are from Keenan (1985), as are many of the typological generalizations in this section.

11. The possessor agreement marker *–i* on the nominalized verb agrees with the person and number of the genitive subject, in the same way that a possessed noun agrees with its genitive possessor in a Turkish noun phrase.

12. We will discuss morphological processes of this type in more detail in ch. 13.

13. My thanks to Chris Culy for discussion of these examples.

14. As Keenan (1985:164) points out, such examples are technically not relative clauses because the restrictive clause is not a modifier within a noun phrase. But they serve the same function as relative clauses in other languages.

15. The form *whom* is now rarely used in informal conversation. It is optional when the relativized function is the direct object (46b), and obligatory only when it follows a preposition as in (46c).

16. The German demonstrative pronouns are identical in form with the definite article except for the addition of *–en* in the dative plural and all genitive forms; a genitive example is seen in (49b).

17. (48) is adapted from Keenan (1985:149), while example (49) is taken from Stern and Bleiler (1961:46–47).

18. This is the normal case marking pattern for relative pronouns. There are, however, a few languages (e.g. Latin) in which the case marking of the relative pronoun may reflect instead the external Grammatical Relation, i.e. the Grammatical Relation which the NP containing the relative clause is assigned in the larger (matrix) sentence.

19. A number of other authors use the term RELATIVIZED POSITION for what we call here the relativized function. Our purpose in coining a different term is to emphasize the fact that we are concerned primarily with Grammatical Relations, rather than positions in Phrase Structure.

20. Relativizers may occur with either the gap or the pronoun retention strategies. The use of a relativizer is not a distinct strategy, since the relativizer itself provides no information about the relativized function.
21. Keenan (1985:149) cites Chinese as the only known counter-example to this generalization.
22. (55–57) are adapted from McCawley (1988:431–432).
23. Thanks to Rosalia Dutra for minor improvements to these examples. She points out that some of the diacritics shown here would not be used under the latest spelling reform, but I have chosen to retain the spelling of the published sources.

13 Derivational morphology

Consider the words in (1a,b), all of which contain the word *believe* plus at least one other morpheme. Intuitively, we might say that the examples in (1a) are really just different forms of the same word, while the forms in (1b) are actually different words, which are "derived from" *believe*.

(1)   base: *believe*
         a *believe-s, believe-d*
         b *believ-er, un-believ-able*

What is this intuition based on? One obvious factor is that the words in (1b) belong to different syntactic categories from *believe*: the first is a noun; the second an adjective. The words in (1a) on the other hand are both verbs, just as *believe* is. Another important factor is that the words in (1b) have meanings which are in some way different from the meaning of *believe*. In defining the (1b) forms we need to add some extra components of meaning: "a *believer* is a person who believes"; "something which is *unbelievable* is difficult or impossible for us to believe." But the forms in (1a) mean essentially the same thing as the base form (*believe*).[1] The suffixes in these forms simply add information about when it is appropriate to use that specific form, e.g. "*believes* describes the present time, but *believed* refers to some time in the past."

A more precise way to express this difference is to say that *believe*, *believes*, and *believed* are all forms of the same LEXEME, whereas *believer* and *unbelievable* are distinct lexemes. In section 13.2 we will present a more careful explanation of the term LEXEME, but intuitively it refers to all of the "variant forms" of a single lexical item.

The kind of affixation exhibited in (1a) is commonly referred to as INFLECTIONAL MORPHOLOGY; that in (1b) DERIVATIONAL MOR-PHOLOGY. The basic definition of these terms is that derivational morphology changes one word (or lexeme) into another, while inflectional morphology creates different forms of the same lexeme. We will have more to say about this definition in section 13.2, and in sections 13.3–13.4 we will discuss a wide variety of derivational affixes from a number of different languages. But first we need to introduce some additional terminology.

13.1   Stems, roots, and compounds

In chapter 2 we discussed the difference between two different kinds of morphemes, namely roots and affixes. All of the words in example (1) share the same root, namely the morpheme *believe*. But we have suggested that some forms which contain this root (those in (1a)) belong to the same lexeme, while others (1b) do not. It is often helpful to be able to refer to the portion of a word which all forms of a given lexeme have in common. This unit is generally called the STEM.

A stem is the part of a word that contains no inflectional morphology; it consists of the root plus any derivational morphology. So, while a root is always a single morpheme (by definition, a morpheme which is not an affix), a stem may consist of one or more morphemes. If a given word contains both derivational and inflectional morphology, then the root, stem, and word are all different (2a). If a word contains no inflectional morphology, then the stem and word are the same (2b). If a word contains no affixation at all, then the root, stem and word are all the same (2c).

(2)

	WORD	STEM	ROOT
a	civil-ize-d	civil-ize	civil
	organ-iz-ation-s	organ-iz-ation	organ
b	soft-en	soft-en	soft
	Marx-ist	Marx-ist	Marx
c	cat	cat	cat
	Mississippi	Mississippi	Mississippi

A root or stem is called BOUND if it cannot occur on its own without additional affixation; a FREE form is one that can occur as an independent word. In English, because there is relatively little inflectional morphology, most roots and stems are free, as illustrated in (2). Some examples which could be analyzed as bound roots are presented in (3).

(3)   a *culp + -able → culpable
       b *cran + berry → cranberry
       c re- + *cline → recline

A stem which contains more than one root is called a COMPOUND. Compounding can be considered a special type of derivational morphology.[2] At times, it can be difficult to distinguish a compound word (a word containing a compound stem) from a phrase (i.e. a group of two or more independent words). Some of the criteria which can help us to identify compounds include the following:

(i)   A compound word normally contains only one main stress. In a phrase, however, each word may contain its own stress. (Note that English spelling is not always a reliable guide.)

(4) | COMPOUND | PHRASE |
       |----------|--------|
       | hótdog | hòt dóg |
       | bláckboard | blàck bóard |
       | cóldcream | còld créam |
       | shórtstop | shòrt stóp |
       | búll's-eye | bùll's éye |
       | bútterfly | |
       | púnching bag | |
       | rúnning shoe | |
       | láughing gas | |

(ii)   The original meanings of the roots may be lost in a compound. For example, a *hotdog* is not a dog, and it can be cold (or even frozen); a *blackboard* might be green; etc. But in a phrase, each word retains its original meaning; so a *hot dog* must be both hot and a dog.

(iii) In a phrase, each individual word can take its normal range of affixes (5b). However, it is generally not possible to add extra suffixes to the first root of a compound in English, but only to the compound as a whole (5a).[3]

(5)   a | doghouse | *dogs-house | doghouses |
           |----------|-------------|-----------|
           | rat-trap | *rats-trap | rat-traps |
           | mousetrap | *mice-trap | mousetraps |
           | blackboard | *blackest-board | blackboards |
           | coldcream | *colder-cream | coldcreams |
           | babysit | *babies-sit | babysitter, babysitting |
           | runway | *running-way, | runways |
           | | *runner-way | |
           | jack-knife | *jack's-knife | jack-knife's, jack-knives |
           | (=pocket knife) | | |

       b   The *blackest board* is the one you should use.
           Colder cream would be easier to whip.
           I just found *Jack's knife* by the side of the road.

(iv)   Words in a phrase can often be separated by inserting one or more other words between them. This is never possible with compounds. When any other word separates the two elements in the compound, the compound sense is lost, as illustrated in (6).

(6)   a   I watched a *butterfly* out the window.
           I watched my *butter* suddenly *fly* out the window.
       b   I'll have a skinless *hotdog* with mustard and onion.
           I'll have a *hot*, skinless *dog* with mustard and onion.

13.2 Criteria for distinguishing inflection vs. derivation

At the beginning of this chapter we introduced the contrast between inflection vs. derivation by saying that derivational morphology changes one lexeme into another, while inflectional morphology creates different forms of the same lexeme. This statement captures the basic intuition behind these terms. However, it is not very useful as a definition unless we have a reliable way to determine whether two words which contain the same root are different lexemes or merely different forms of the same lexeme. If we do not have any independent criteria to guide us in making this judgment, the definition becomes circular.

In order to escape this circularity, let us adopt a different approach. We start with the notion of a STEM, which was introduced in the preceding section. The stem of a word consists of its root(s) together with all of the derivational affixes which it contains, but no inflectional affixes. As suggested above, we can say that two words are forms of the same lexeme just in case they share the same stem.

Under this approach, the terms STEM and LEXEME will be well-defined if we have some independent way to distinguish inflection from derivation. We must point out at once that this can be a very difficult task, because certain affixes do not fit neatly into either classification. Some scholars deny that it is possible to make such a distinction at all. We can, however, identify a number of properties which are typical of inflectional morphology and others which are typical of derivational morphology, as these terms have traditionally been used. These properties allow us to describe the distinction between inflection and derivation in terms of a contrast between two PROTOTYPES. Most affixes in most languages can be assigned to one class or the other according to which prototype they share the most properties with.

Here are some of the properties which define the two prototypes:[4]

a   Derivational morphology may change the syntactic category (part of speech) of a word, since it actually creates a new lexical item. Inflectional morphology, however, does not generally change syntactic categories.[5] As we noted above, the derivational suffix *-able* changes the verb *believe* into the adjective *believable*, whereas the inflected forms *believes* and *believed* are still verbs.

b   Derivational morphology tends to have "lexical" semantic content, i.e. meanings similar to the meanings of independent words (*X-er*: 'person who Xes'; *X-able*: 'able to be Xed'; etc.). Inflectional morphology, on the other hand, often has purely grammatical meaning (plural number, past tense, etc.).

c   Inflectional morphology is semantically regular; for example, the plural *-s* in English always means plural number. Derivational morphology may have variable semantic content which depends on the specific base form: a *sing-er* is a person who sings, a *cook-er* is an instrument which cooks things, a *speak-er* could be either the person who speaks or a device for amplifying his voice, and a *hang-er* is a hook or other device to hang things on.

d   Inflectional morphology may be, and often is, syntactically determined; but this is not true of derivational morphology.[6] Therefore, if a particular morphological marking is required or allowed only in specific syntactic environments, it is likely to be inflectional. For example, present tense verbs in English must agree with their subject for person and number. The suffix which marks this agreement (-*s*) is inflectional because it must occur in certain syntactic environments (e.g. 7b) and must not occur in others (e.g. 7a).

(7)   **3rd singular present** –*s:*
    a *We all likes Mary a lot.
    b *John like Mary too.

English is rich in derivational morphology, but has relatively few inflectional categories. Some additional examples include the plural (-*s*) on nouns and the two participial forms of verbs (-*ing* and -*en*). In both cases, there are certain syntactic contexts where the inflected form is required (8a, 9a), and others where it is not allowed (8b, 9b).

(8)   **Pural** –*s:*
    a *My three cat are sick.
    b *This cats is really sick.

(9)   **Past participle** –*en:*
    a *John has eat my sandwich.
    b *The tiger eaten John before we could save him.

On the other hand, there is no syntactic environment that requires an adjective ending in -*able*. Words containing this suffix may occur in the same positions as any other adjective, as illustrated in (10). This is exactly what we would expect, based on our earlier conclusion that -*able* is a derivational affix.

(10)   a Forsythe's latest novel is very good/long/*readable*.
    b Mary's silly/wild/*unbelievable* story failed to convince her mother.

e   Inflectional morphology is normally highly PRODUCTIVE, meaning that it applies to most or all of the words of the appropriate category. Derivational morphology, on the other hand, often applies only to certain specific words; and some derivational affixes are more productive than others.

When we speak of "productivity" in this sense, we are thinking of grammatical and semantic patterning rather than phonological regularity. For example, virtually every verb in English can be inflected for past tense. However, there are many different phonological processes that can be used to mark this inflectional category:

(11)   bake   baked
       stretch   stretched
       catch   caught
       buy   bought
       think   thought
       drink   drank
       sing   sang
       run   ran
       go   went
       is   was
       hit   hit

Thus, past tense is productive but not phonologically regular. Contrast this situation with the case of a derivational affix like *-ize*. This suffix is actually quite productive in English, being used in many new words (e.g. *digit-ize*, *Vietnam-iz-ation*). But, even so, there are numerous nouns and adjectives which cannot take this suffix. For example, we can *rubberize* something by coating it in rubber; but when we coat something in chocolate or sugar, we do not say *chocolatize or *sugarize. Similarly, we say *hospitalize* but not *prison-ize (cf. *im-prison*); *legalize, formalize, publicize, privatize*, etc., but not *good-ize (for 'improve') or *big-ize (for 'enlarge').

f   Inflectional morphology is often organized in paradigms, while derivational morphology is not. A PARADIGM can be defined as a set of forms which includes all of the possible values for a particular grammatical feature. For example, the table in (12) illustrates the subject-agreement paradigm in Finnish. The six verb forms in the table differ only in the categories of person and number; the categories of tense, voice, and mood remain constant. There is one suffix representing each possible combination of person and number, and no verb contains more than one of these suffixes. This illustrates the general principle that affixes which belong to the same paradigm are (normally) mutually exclusive (i.e. they cannot co-occur).

(12)   **Finnish** 'to pay' present active indicative (Aaltio 1964:34)

PERSON	SINGULAR	PLURAL
1st	maksa-n	maksa-mme
2nd	maksa-t	maksa-tte
3rd	maksa-:	maksa-vat

g   Portmanteau morphemes (i.e. single affixes which mark two or more grammatical categories at once, like the Finnish person–number suffixes in (12)) typically involve inflectional categories. Derivation is rarely marked by portmanteau forms.

h   Inflectional affixes are normally attached "outside" (i.e. further from the root than) derivational affixes, as in: *class-ify-er-s̲*; *nation-al-ize-d̲*.

i   Some derivational processes may apply twice in the same word, but each inflectional category will be marked only once.

These criteria are summarized in (13).

(13)

	DERIVATIONAL	INFLECTIONAL
category-changing	often	generally not
paradigmatic	no	yes
productivity	limited and variable (lexically specific)	highly productive
type of meaning	often lexical	often purely grammatical
semantic regularity	often unpredictable (conventionalized)	regular
restricted to specific syntactic environments	no	yes
position	central (near root)	peripheral (near edges of word)
portmanteau forms	rarely	often
repeatable?	sometimes	never

13.3   Examples of derivational processes

The range of meanings of derivational affixes around the world is very broad, and we will not attempt to present a comprehensive survey here. As noted above, derivational morphology may trigger a change in syntactic category, meaning, or (frequently) both. Let us illustrate each of these possibilities in turn.

13.3.1   Change in category with no change in meaning

As discussed in chapter 3, different parts of speech are typically associated with different semantic types: verbs tend to express events; adjectives tend to express states, etc. For this reason, a derivational process which changes the syntactic category of a word generally involves some semantic effect as well. But it is possible to find examples of category-changing processes that do not seem to involve any significant change of meaning.

Perhaps the most common such process is the formation of abstract nouns, which is illustrated in (14) using data from Malay. A process that derives nouns from roots or stems belonging to some other category, as in (14), is referred to as NOMINALIZATION. An affix which triggers such a change is called a NOMINALIZER. Notice that the nominalizing affix in (14) is actually a CIRCUMFIX (see chapter 16), *ke-* . . . *-an*. When this nominalizer combines with an adjective root, it forms a noun that refers to the state or quality named by the adjective. When it combines with a verb root, it forms a noun that refers to the event or process named by the verb.

(14)   **Abstract noun formation in Malay**

ROOT		DERIVED FORM	
baik	'good'	kebaikan	'goodness, kindness'
bébas	'free'	kebébasan	'freedom'
cantik	'pretty'	kecantikan	'beauty'
bersih	'clean'	kebersihan	'cleanliness'
miskin	'poor'	kemiskinan	'poverty'
mati	'dead; to die'	kematian	'death'
hidup	'(to be) alive'	kehidupan	'life'
lahir	'be born'	kelahiran	'birth'
boléh	'can, may'	keboléhan	'ability'
menang	'to win'	kemenangan	'victory'
tiba	'to arrive'	ketibaan	'arrival'
naik	'to ascend'	kenaikan	'ascent'

Another example of a derivational affix that (often) changes only the syntactic category of its base is the English suffix *–ly*, which can be used to derive adverbs from adjectives with little or no change in meaning:

(15)   **English adverbialization**

ADJECTIVE ROOT	DERIVED ADVERB
happy	happily
sad	sadly
cautious	cautiously
careless	carelessly
quick	quickly
slow	slowly
rash	rashly
brave	bravely
timid	timidly

13.3.2 Change in meaning with no change in category

Many languages have DIMINUTIVE affixes which attach to noun stems to indicate smallness. German has several diminutive suffixes, e.g. *–lein* as in *Buch* 'book,' *Büchlein* 'booklet'; *fisch* 'fish,' *fischlein* 'little fish'; *Bach* 'stream,' *Bächlein* 'streamlet, brooklet.' The most productive diminutive is *-chen*, as in *Haus* 'house,' *Häuschen* 'cottage, outhouse'; *Teil* 'part,' *Teilchen* 'particle'; *Horn* 'horn,' *Hörnchen* 'little horn, croissant.' With some roots either suffix is possible, e.g. *Nagel* 'nail,' *Nägelchen* or *Näglein* 'tack'; *Vogel* 'bird,' *Vögelchen* or *Vöglein* 'little bird.' Diminutives are often used to indicate affection, rather than small size, as in *Frau* 'woman, wife,' *Frauchen* 'dear wife'; *Hut* 'hat,' *Hütchen* 'pretty hat'; *Hund* 'dog,' *Hündchen* 'nice dog' (cf. *Hündlein* 'little dog').[7]

Portuguese has both diminutive and AUGMENTATIVE suffixes. The most common diminutive suffix is *–inho* (feminine form *–inha*), as in *flor* 'flower,' *florzinha* 'little flower'; *bandeira* 'flag,' *bandeirinha* 'pennant'; *café* 'coffee,' *cafèzinho* 'small cup of strong, sweet coffee'; and the two famous members of Brazil's 2002 World Cup champion team, *Ronaldo* 'Ronald' and *Ronaldinho* 'little Ronnie.' The most common augmentative suffix is *–ão* (feminine form *–ona*), as in *sapato* 'shoe,' *sapatão* 'big shoe'; *mulher* 'woman,' *mulherona* 'big woman'; *caixa* 'box,' *caixão* 'big box, coffin'; *casa* 'house,' *casarão* 'big house.' The diminutive suffix can be added to both nouns and adjectives to express affection, tenderness, or admiration (e.g. *bonita* 'pretty,' *bonitinha* 'very pretty'), while the augmentative suffix may be used with comic or contemptuous intent.[8] In all of these uses, the category of the base form remains unchanged.

In Muna (Malayo-Polynesian; Sulawesi, Indonesia) the diminutive meaning is expressed by adding a prefix *ka-* plus reduplication: *kontu* 'stone,' *ka-kontu-kontu* 'small stone'; *wale* 'hut,' *ka-wale-wale* 'small hut'; *tomba* 'basket,' *ka-tomba-tomba* 'small basket'; *kabhawo* 'mountain,' *ka-kabha-kabhawo* 'hill.'[9]

Another example of an affix which changes meaning without changing the category of the base form is the English prefix *re-*. This prefix attaches to a verb meaning 'to do X' and produces a new verb meaning 'to do X again.' Examples include: *re-state, re-position, re-consider, re-align, re-calibrate, re-negotiate, re-open, re-appear, re-apply* (for a job), *re-hire, re-capture, re-tune* (e.g. a guitar), etc.[10] A similar example in English is the prefix *mis-*, meaning 'to do wrongly.' Examples include: *mis-represent, mis-state, mis-calculate, mis-interpret, mis-use, mis-handle*, etc.

The prefix *un-* has two different uses in English, both involving a kind of negation. It can attach to adjectives meaning 'X' to produce new adjectives meaning 'not X,' or more precisely 'the opposite of X' (*un-happy, un-lucky, un-clear, un-welcome, un-well, un-likely, un-tidy, un-certain, un-sympathetic*, etc.). It can also attach to verbs meaning 'Y' to produce new verbs meaning 'reverse the process or undo the effect of Y-ing' (*un-zip, un-tie, un-wrap, un-seat, un-leash, un-dress, un-ravel, un-load*, etc.).

Notice that the prefixes *re-* and *mis-* preserve the argument structure and subcategorization of the base form. The derived verb *re-appear* is intransitive because the base form *appear* is intransitive. The derived verb *mis-interpret* is transitive because the base form *interpret* is transitive.[11] In the next chapter we will discuss a very important class of verbal affixes, found in a wide range of languages, which do change argument structure and/or subcategorization. Some of these "valence-changing operations" are clearly derivational, e.g. CAUSATIVES (in most languages). But others are difficult to classify as either inflectional or derivational, having some properties of each type.

13.3.3 Change in category with change in meaning

As noted above, most derivational morphology involves changes in both category and meaning. A few representative examples are discussed in this section.

13.3.3.1 Nominalization

A noun derived from a verb is called a DEVERBAL NOUN. In addition to abstract deverbal nouns like those in (14), which refer to the event itself, many languages have nominalizers which name specific participants or aspects of the event: agent, patient, instrument, location, manner, cause, etc. Some of these are illustrated in the following examples.

Note that the Malay examples in (16) and (17) use the same prefix, *peN-*, but with different meanings. (The *N-* here represents a nasal sound which changes according to its environment, and may also trigger changes in the following consonant. See chapter 15 for a discussion of these issues.) It is not at all uncommon for languages to use the same nominalizer for agentive and instrumental nouns; this pattern is found in Dutch, English, French, Italian, and a number of Malayo-Polynesian languages, to name a few.[12]

(16) **Malay actor nominalizations**

ROOT		DERIVED FORM	
tulis	'write'	penulis	'writer'
bantu	'help'	pembantu	'helper'
nyanyi	'sing'	penyanyi	'singer'
pimpin	'lead'	pemimpin	'leader'
dengar	'hear'	pendengar	'listener'
pohon	'request, apply'	pemohon	'applicant'

(17) **Malay instrumental nominalizations**

ROOT		DERIVED FORM	
gali	'to dig'	penggali	'spade, shovel'
sapu	'to sweep'	penyapu	'broom'
tapis	'to filter'	penapis	'a filter'
cukur	'to shave'	pencukur	'razor'
tuai	'to harvest (rice)'	penuai	'harvesting knife'

The prefix *peN-* has another use as well. It can be added to a verbal or adjectival root to derive a noun naming a person or thing that is characterized by the property named by the root, as illustrated in (18).

(18)   **Malay characteristic nominalizations**

ROOT		DERIVED FORM	
malas	'lazy'	pemalas	'lazy person'
takut	'afraid'	penakut	'coward'
jahat	'bad, wicked'	penjahat	'bad person'
besar	'big'	pembesar	'big-shot, dignitary'
diam	'quiet'	pendiam	'quiet person'
malu	'shy'	pemalu	'shy person'
mabuk	'drunk'	pemabuk	'drunkard'
lupa	'forget'	pelupa	'forgetful person'

Karo Batak (Malayo-Polynesian, northern Sumatra) has two different ways of deriving "object nominals" from verbs; that is, nominalizations that express the patient or product of the action named by the verb. The most productive of these is formed by adding a suffix *-(e)n*, as illustrated in (19a). With certain roots, however, an infix *–in–* is used (19b).[13]

(19)   **Karo Batak object (patient or product) nominalizations**

a suffix *–(e)n*

ROOT		DERIVED FORM	
baba	'to carry'	baban	'load, burden'
inem	'to drink'	inemen	'a drink, beverage'
tangko	'to steal'	tangkon	'stolen goods'
bagi	'to divide'	bagin	'portion, share'
turi-turi	'to tell, relate'	turi-turin	'story'
kundul(-i)	'sit (on)'	kundulen	'something to sit on'
tawa(-i)	'laugh (at)'	tawan	'laughing stock'

b infix *–in–*

ROOT		DERIVED FORM	
suan	'to plant'	sinuan	'crops'
tepa	'to create'	tinepa	'creation, thing created'
tangger	'to cook'	tinangger	'something cooked'
salsal(-i)	'to shine (on)'	sinalsal	'rays, beams, glow'
gemgem	'to rule'	ginemgem	'subjects; those ruled'
jujung	'carry on head'	jinujung	'personal spirit'[14]

As a final example of deverbal nominalization, example (20) shows how nouns which name the place of an event are derived in Karo Batak. Notice that two different "circumfixes" (see chapter 16) are used: *peN-X-(e)n* (mostly with transitive roots) vs. *per-X-(e)n* (with intransitive roots).

(20)   **Karo Batak locative nominalizations**

ROOT		DERIVED FORM	
tutu	'to pound (e.g. rice)'	penutun	'pounding place'
suan	'to plant'	penuanen	'place to plant'
kirah(-ken)	'to dry (clothes)'	pengkirahen	'place for drying clothes'
cinep	'to perch'	percinepen	'a perch'
ridi	'to bathe'	peridin	'bathing place'
(er-)cidur	'to spit'	perciduren	'spitoon'
(er-)burih	'wash fingers before eating'	perburihen	'fingerbowl'

.

13.3.3.2 Verbalizers

VERBALIZATION is a process which derives verbs from roots or stems of other categories. Example (21) shows the derivation of INCHOA-TIVE forms (intransitive verbs of becoming), mostly from adjective roots, in Malay.

(21)   **Malay inchoatives**

ROOT		DERIVED FORM	
besar	'big'	membesar	'to grow'
kuning	'yellow'	menguning	'turn yellow'
pucat	'pale'	memucat	'turn pale'
tinggi	'high'	meninggi	'rise high'
batu	'stone'	membatu	'petrify (become stone)'

Example (22) illustrates the derivation of verbs from noun roots. The verb *ber-X* (where X is a noun) can have many different meanings, including *to use X, to possess X,* or *to produce X.*

(22)   **Malay verbs of using, having, producing, etc**.

ROOT		DERIVED FORM	
buah	'fruit'	berbuah	'to bear fruit'
telur	'egg'	bertelur	'lay an egg'
topi	'hat'	bertopi	'wear a hat'
sekolah	'school'	bersekolah	'go to school'
nama	'name'	bernama	'to be named'
kuda	'horse'	berkuda	'ride a horse'

13.3.3.3 Adjectivizers

Both German and Portuguese have several suffixes which derive adjectives, either from verbal stems or from nouns. Some examples are listed in (23). Notice that many of the English glosses for the derived forms involve English suffixes which have a similar function, and in some cases are actually historically related (i.e. COGNATE) to the German or Portuguese suffix.

(23)   **Adjectives derived from verbs and nouns**
       a **German** (Curme 1922/1952:417ff.).

VERB ROOT		DERIVED ADJECTIVE	
danken	'to thank'	dankbar	'thankful'
lesen	'to read'	lesbar	'legible
beissen	'to bite'	bissig	'inclined to bite'
gefallen	'to please'	gefällig	'pleasing, agreeable'
glauben	'to believe'	glaublich	'believable'
		gläubig	'faithful, devout'
verstehen	'to understand'	verständlich	'understandable'
		verständig	'sensible, intelligent'

       b **Portuguese**

VERB ROOT		DERIVED ADJECTIVE	
amár	'to love'	amável	'lovable, amiable'
notár	'to notice'	notável	'remarkable'
crer	'to believe'	crível	'credible'

       c **Portuguese**

NOUN ROOT		DERIVED ADJECTIVE	
orgulho	'pride'	orgulhoso	'proud'
perigo	'danger'	perigoso	'dangerous'
mentira	'falsehood, lie'	mentiroso	'untruthful'
maravilha	'a marvel'	maravilhoso	'wonderful'

13.4 Word structure revisited

13.4.1 Limitations of the position class chart

In chapter 2 we introduced the position class chart as a way of representing the morphological structure of a word. These charts are especially well suited to inflectional affixation where the affixes are arranged in paradigm sets occurring in a fixed order. Position class charts are often less successful as a way of displaying derivational morphology, for a variety of reasons.

First, we have noted that derivational morphology does not typically form paradigm sets such that only one affix in each set may occur in any given word. This means that each derivational affix in the language could potentially occupy its own position in the chart, which would require a large number of positions in many languages. Of course, there are often semantic reasons why two derivational affixes cannot occur together. For example, Manipuri (a Tibeto-Burman language spoken in northeast India) has a pair of derivational modality markers which indicate the appropriateness of the time at which an action was performed: *-həw* 'just in time' and *–khi* 'still (not done).'[15] Since these two concepts are mutually contradictory, they cannot occur in the same verb form.

There are also categorial requirements which limit the co-occurrence of derivational affixes. For example, English has a number of nominalizing suffixes: *-ment, -tion, -ity*, etc. No two of these can occur next to each other, since they each attach to a base form which is not a noun and produce a stem which is a noun: e.g. *creation, containment*, but **creationment, *creationity*. However, these affixes can co-occur if they are separated by some other affix which derives a stem of a different category: *compart-ment-al-iz-ation; constitu(te)-tion-al-ity; argu-ment-ativ-ity*, etc. The possibility of co-occurrence shows that these nominalizing suffixes do not form a paradigm set.

Second, derivational affixes can sometimes occur more than once within the same word. This is at least marginally possible in English, as in *re-reinstate, re-reinvent*, etc. (School principal to teacher: *If you expel my nephew again, I will simply re-reinstate him.*) Clearer examples are found in other languages. Manipuri has another modality marker, *-lə ~ -rə*, which indicates likelihood or probability. This suffix can be doubled or even tripled to indicate certainty: *saw-rə-ni* 'is probably going to be angry'; *saw-rə-rə-rə-ni* 'is definitely going to be angry.' Double causatives are reported in a number of languages, including Turkish (24c) and Quechua (25c).

(24)   **Turkish** (Aissen 1974:348; Comrie 1981a:169)

    a Müdür   mektub-u   imzala-dï.
      director letter-ACC sign-PAST
      'The director signed the letter.'

    b Dişçi   mektub-u   müdür-e   imzala-t-tï.
      dentist letter-ACC director-DAT sign-CAUS-PAST
      'The dentist got the director to sign the letter.'

    c Mektub-u   müdür-e   imzala-t-tïr-dïm.
      letter-ACC director-DAT sign-CAUS-CAUS-PAST.1sg
      'I got someone to get the director to sign the letter.'

(25)   **Imbabura Quechua** (Cole 1982:183)

    a Juzi   wañu-rka.
      José die-PAST.3SUBJ
      'José died.'

    b Juzi   Marya-ta   wañu-chi-rka.
      José Maria-ACC die-CAUS-PAST.3SUBJ
      'José caused Maria to die; José killed Maria.'

    c Juzi   Juan-ta=mi   Marya-ta   wañu-chi-chi-rka.
      José Juan-ACC=EVID[16] Maria-ACC die-CAUS-CAUS-PAST.3SUBJ
      'José caused Juan to kill Maria.'

Third, the ordering of derivational affixes may be variable, with different semantic interpretations indicated by the differences in affix order. The causative and desiderative suffixes in Cuzco Quechua can appear in either order, as illustrated in (26).

(26)   **Cuzco Quechua** (Muysken 1988:278)

a mikhu-*naya-chi*-wa-n
eat-DESID-CAUS-1OBJ-3SUBJ
'it causes me to feel like eating'

b mikhu-*chi-naya*-wa-n[17]
eat-CAUS-DESID-1OBJ-3SUBJ
'I feel like making someone eat'

In Chichewa (Bantu, East Africa), the causative and reciprocal suffixes may appear in either order, as in (27). If the causative suffix appears next to the benefactive suffix, the causative must come first as in (28a). However, the benefactive suffix may precede the causative provided that some other affix intervenes, as in (28c). (Note that these examples involve only stems; all inflectional affixation, including subject agreement and tense, are omitted.)

(27)   **Chichewa** (Hyman and Mchombo 1992:350)

a mang-an-its-
tie-RECIP-CAUS-
'cause to tie each other'

b mang-its-an-
tie-CAUS-RECIP-
'cause each other to tie (something)'[18]

(28)   **Chichewa** (Hyman and Mchombo 1992:352)

a mang-its-ir-
tie-CAUS-BEN-
'cause to tie for (someone)'

b *mang-ir-its-
tie-BEN-CAUS-

c mang-ir-an-its-
tie-BEN-RECIP-CAUS-
'cause to tie for each other'

Examples like these are not uncommon, but they are difficult to deal with in any satisfying way in a position class chart. Multiple occurrences of the same affix, or variable ordering with respect to other affixes, would force us to assign a single affix to more than one position class. For these reasons, it is often more helpful to show only the inflectional categories in our position class chart. A possible chart for Chichewa verbs is presented in (29), without listing the inflectional affixes in each position.[19] Note that the stem of the verb may consist of a single root, or of a root with one or more derivational affixes. The internal structure of the stem is, in general, "invisible" to the rest of the grammatical system.

(29)

	−2	−1	0	+1
	SUBJ-AGR	TENSE	V-STEM	MOOD/ASPECT

13.4.2 Word Formation Rules

At the beginning of this chapter, we introduced derivational morphology by saying that it changes one lexeme into another. A common way of representing this kind of process is by writing a WORD FORMATION RULE (WFR). While we begin with the intuition that a WFR changes one lexeme into another, we will argue that it is more helpful to think of the WFR as expressing a pattern of regular correspondence between pairs of lexemes.

Word Formation Rules must contain at least three kinds of information: (a) the phonological effects on the base form (e.g. the shape of the derivational affix and where it is attached); (b) the semantic changes associated with this process; and (c) the syntactic category of the base (input) and of the resulting stem (output). To take a specific example, let us begin with the Portuguese diminutive suffix *-inho*. The WFR for this suffix might look something like (30).

(30) **Portuguese diminutive (preliminary)**:

$[X]_{NOUN} \quad \rightarrow \quad [X\text{-}inho]_{NOUN}$

meaning: 'x'   meaning: 'little x'

The "X" in this rule stands for the phonological shape of the base. The rule says that the suffix *–inho* can be added to a noun stem meaning 'x' to create another noun which means 'little x.' To take another example, let us consider the Malay prefix illustrated in (16–17), which derives nouns from verbs:

(31) **Malay agentive/instrumental nominalization (preliminary)**:

$[X]_{VERB} \quad \rightarrow \quad [peN\text{-}X]_{NOUN}$

meaning: 'to x'   meaning: (a) 'person who x-es'

or: (b) 'instrument used for x-ing'

One way of interpreting a rule like (30) or (31) is to assume that only the base form is listed in the lexicon, while the derived form is produced by a rule of the grammar (specifically, a WFR). This would be similar in some ways to the distinction between words, which are listed in the lexicon, vs. phrases and sentences, which must be produced by Grammatical Rules.

However, many authors have pointed out that this view of word formation leads to a number of difficulties. It is more useful to assume that both forms are listed in the lexicon. We refer to the morphologically simpler form as the base, and the morphologically more complex form as the derived form, but both lexical entries are listed. Under this view, a WFR is an expression of regular correspondences between pairs of lexical entries.

It may seem surprising to think of every derived form (or lexeme) in the language as having a separate lexical entry, but adopting this hypothesis will help us to account for a number of characteristic properties of derivational morphology. Let us consider some of these properties. First, derivational morphology is lexically specific; specific affixes may apply to certain base forms and not to others within the same category. For example, a particular nominalizing suffix in English will apply to certain adjective stems but not to others: *superior-ity* vs. **superior-ness*; *truth* vs. **true-ness*; *strange-ness* vs. **strange-ity*; *firm-ness* vs. **firm-th*; etc. Similarly, the English prefix *en-* attaches to nouns and adjectives to create transitive verbs; but the set of base forms that take this prefix is fairly limited: *encourage, enthrone, entitle, entangle, enliven, enlarge* (cf. **em-big*), *embolden* (**em-brave(n)*), *enrich* (**en-wealth(y)*), etc.

Clearly the lexicon must specify in some way which base forms can take which affixes. One approach might be to include a set of features in the lexical entry of each root to indicate which derivational affixes or combinations of affixes could be added to that root; but in any language with even a modest number of derivational affixes, this would add an enormous amount of complexity to the lexicon. By assuming that each lexeme is already listed in the lexicon, we avoid this problem. A WFR "applies" to a particular root or stem just in case the lexicon contains both the "input" form (the base) and the corresponding "output" (derived) form.

There are also cases where what looks like a derived form does not correspond to any actual base form. For example, words like *ostracize* and *levity* seem to end in derivational suffixes, but there are no corresponding basic forms in English (**ostrac, *lev*). Similarly, *disambiguate* clearly contains the prefix *dis-*, but **ambiguate* is not a real verb. *Ambigu-ous* and *ambigu-ity* are related to *dis-ambigu-ate* in meaning, but their common root (**ambigu-*) does not exist. If each real word is listed in the lexicon, these examples are not a problem. There may be lexical gaps (i.e. non-existent forms) corresponding to either the base or the derived form for a particular WFR, but the rule can still help us to understand the meaning and structure of the forms that do exist.

As we noted in section 13.2, derivational morphology tends to be semantically irregular or unpredictable. German diminutive nouns sometimes have special meanings which could not be predicted from the base form alone: *Frau* 'woman, wife,' *Fräulein* 'unmarried woman.' The English word *transmission* can refer to the act of transmitting something (the predictable meaning), or to a specific part of a car (unpredictable meaning). Clearly the WFR itself cannot tell us everything we need to know about each specific derived form. But if each derived form is already listed in the lexicon, then any semantic, phonological, or other irregularities will be listed in the lexical entry for that particular form.

Our hypothesis also helps us to understand another aspect of word formation, namely, that speakers react to unknown or novel words as being "unreal" in some sense. Derivational affixes are occasionally used to create brand new words. The suffix *-ize*, for example, has been used to coin the word *mesmerize* (from the surname of an early pioneer in the practice of hypnotism, F. A. Mesmer) in the early 1800s; the word *bowdlerize* (from the name of Dr. T. Bowdler) a few decades later; and the term *Balkanize*, probably around 1915.

However, most of the time these affixes occur in words which are already known, that is, already part of the lexicon. If an English speaker produces a new word, e.g.?*methodicalize*, hearers will probably guess that it means 'to make something methodical' (cf. *radicalize*). But they are also likely to protest: "There is no such word." This sense that certain possible derivations are not real words, the ability to distinguish between newly coined words and actual existing forms, gives additional support to our assumption that both input and output forms are already listed in the lexicon.

Under these assumptions, then, the Portuguese lexicon contains entries for both *bandeira* 'flag' and *bandeirinha* 'pennant.' The rule in (30) does not actually "create" a new stem; rather, it expresses a regular correspondence that exists between these two particular stems, and between many similar pairs. For this reason, it is somewhat misleading to show the rule as a one-way process. It would be more accurate to use a double arrow, as illustrated below, to indicate that the WFR expresses a two-way relationship.

(30′)   **Portuguese diminutive (revised):**
$$[X]_{NOUN} \quad \leftrightarrow \quad [X\text{-}inho]_{NOUN}$$
meaning: 'x'   meaning: 'little x'

One could say that word formation rules are redundant, in the sense that they do not add new entries to the lexicon. But this does not mean they are useless or unimportant. The fact that speakers can use WFRs creatively to coin completely new words, and that other speakers can understand these new words, shows that speakers in some sense (subconsciously) "know" these rules. Knowing the rules may also help speakers to recall and understand complex words more efficiently.

WFRs allow us to determine the morphological structure of stems, which is often important for both semantic and phonological interpretation. Consider the word *unreliability*. This stem clearly contains the root *rely* although there is no single WFR which could express the relationship between the root and the derived form. It would take a sequence of several WFRs, applying in the correct order, to connect the two, as illustrated in (32).[20] The use of labeled brackets, as in (32d), is a common way to represent the internal structure of a stem.

(32) a [*rely*]$_V$ BASE FORM
      b [*rely*]$_V$ *-able*]$_{ADJ}$ *-able* RULE
      c [*un-* [*rely*]$_V$ *-able*]$_{ADJ}$] ADJ   *un-*ADJ RULE
      d [[*un-* [*rely*]$_V$ *-able*]$_{ADJ}$] ADJ *-ity*]$_N$ *-ity* RULE

13.5 Conclusion

In section 13.2 we presented a number of criteria for distinguishing inflectional vs. derivational morphology. We should emphasize again that this distinction is not always clear cut. We sometimes find affixes that have properties of both types, e.g. inflectional affixes that can change meaning, or derivational affixes that form a paradigm set. However, the basic prototypes are still useful and important.

If two words are the same except for their inflectional morphology, we consider them forms of the same lexeme. Word Formation Rules express derivational relationships between different lexemes: each rule describes a minimal unit of derivational morphology which can make two lexemes different from each other.

WFRs like those in (30) and (31) express the regular and predictable parts of a derivational process; but the rule itself cannot list all the base forms which that process could apply to, nor the irregular or specialized meanings associated with specific derived forms. This information must be contained in some way in the lexicon, the speaker's mental dictionary. For this and other reasons, we adopt the assumption that each lexeme has its own lexical entry. Thus WFRs not only determine the morphological structure of each individual stem, but also express regular patterns of morphological relationship between lexical entries. Under this view, WFRs describe patterns of regularity within the lexicon itself. Accounting for such regularities is an important goal of linguistic analysis.

Practice exercise

Luiseño (N. America; Langacker 1972:76)
Write WFRs to represent the derivational affixes in the following examples. Could these affixes be displayed in a position class chart?

1.	nóo ŋéeq	'I am leaving'
2.	nóo ŋéeviĉuq	'I want to leave'
3.	nóo póy ŋéeniq	'I am making him leave'
4.	nóo póy ŋéeviĉuniq	'I am making him want to leave'
5.	nóo póy ŋéeniviĉuq	'I want to make him leave'
6.	nóo póy ŋéeviĉuniviĉuq	'I want to make him want to leave'

Exercises

13A Tawala derivation (Papua New Guinea; Ezard 1992; and p.c.)
Describe the verbal prefixes in the following examples. Include WFRs for any derivational prefixes, and a "residue" section discussing any questions that cannot be resolved on the basis of the data provided. Do not attempt to explain the suffixes (only some of these are glossed), but list them in the residue section.

1. bulumakau kayakayana.
    cattle   red-3s
    'It (is) a brown cow.'

2. mayau amaka   ilata.
    tree   already 3s.grow
    'The tree has already grown.'

3. atogo   po ayeuyeu.
    1s.wash and 1s.clean
    'I washed and I am clean.'

4. iyana taulona.
    fish   1p.INCL.cook
    'Let's cook fish.'

5. houga idao.
    time   3s.long
    'The time is long (i.e. it is a long time).'

6. naka nae pilipilina.
    that   go   rolled.up-3s
    'That (is) a difficult way.'

7. wihiya iwopilipilihi.
    flower 3s.rolled.up-3p
    'She crumpled flowers.'

8. towoiyana   pahi-yai.
    1p.EXCL.fish totally-1p.EXCL
    'We (excl.) are loaded with fish (to take to a feast).'

9. dobu iwiitala duma.
    area 3s.rat   really
    'The village is really infested with rats.'

10. pusi iluitala po i'mam.
    cat 3s.rat and 3s.eat(PROG)
    'The cat caught a rat and was eating it.'

11. tonae   tolumayau.
    1p.EXCL.go 1p.EXCL.tree
    'We (excl.) are going to collect firewood.'

12. hewali iwogaima.
    youth 3s.stone
    'The youth held a stone (ready to throw).'

13. bada iligaimaya.
    man 3s.stone-3s
    'The man became a stone.'

14. dobu iwigaigaima.
    area 3s.stone(PROG)
    'The village is very stony.'

15. Dawida amaka iwihewali.
    David   already 3s.youth
    'David has already become a young man.'

16. dobu iwilawa.
    area 3s.person
    'The village become more populated.'

17. naka dobu iwiginahi   duma.
    that area 3s.sago.palm really
    'There are many sago palms in that village.'

18. neula   iliginahi.
    coconut 3s.sago.palm
    'The coconut palm became a sago palm.'

19. mayau awokayakaya.
    wood 1s.red
    'I shook the fire-brand (making sparks).'

20. tu   manini a baha=gei   polo ililawaya.
    person power 3s word=from pig 3s.person-3s
    'At the magicians's word, the pig became a person.'

21. numa iwibubu.
    house 3s.sand
    'The floor is covered with sand.'

22. tanae   talububu.
    1p.INCL.go 1p.INCL.sand
    'Let's go and get sand.'

23. bada ibaha po kedawa ilipoloya.
    man 3s.talk and dog   3s.pig-3s
    'When the man spoke the dog became a pig.'

24.   ega   nou-we   ma   awinouna.
       NEG sister-1s but 1s.sister-3s
       'She is not my sister, but I call her sister.'

25.   a   baha   iwidaoya.
       3s talk   3s.long-3s
       'He spoke for a long time.'

26.   a   numa   ilidaoya.
       3s house 3s.long-3s
       'He extended his house.'

27.   Gibson meyagai   iliyeuyeuya.
       G.   village.area 3s.clean-3s
       'Gibson kept the grounds tidy.'

Additional exercises

Merrifield et al. (1987a) prob. 240, 242, 243, 244, 245, 246, 251;
Healey (1990b), ex. G.1, 3

Notes

1. The term "base" is used in this chapter in a non-technical sense meaning simply the form to which an affix is added. A base may be either a root or a stem.
2. Some scholars prefer to treat compounding and derivational morphology as two different types of WORD FORMATION. In this book, we will not distinguish between word formation and derivation.
3. There are a few exceptional cases in English, such as *brothers-in-law, passers-by, hangers-on, attorneys general,* etc.
4. This discussion is based on Bickford (1998:114–116, 138–140); Stump (1998:14ff.); and Aronoff (1976:2).
5. This principle is challenged by Haspelmath (1996), who identifies constructions such as gerunds and participles as examples of "category-changing inflection." He also points out that this kind of morphology creates "mixed categories." Gerunds, for example, select the same kinds of dependents as the verbs they are based on, but the phrases which they head have the external distribution of NPs rather than VPs. See also Bresnan (1997); Bybee (1985:85).
6. Anderson (1982), Bickford (1998), and some other authors take this characteristic to be the principle defining feature of inflectional morphology.
7. Curme (1922/1952:411).
8. Sá Pereira (1948:195).
9. See ch. 16 for a discussion of reduplication. Muna data is taken from van den Berg (1989).
10. Notice that this prefix gets a secondary stress, which helps to distinguish between the words *rè-cóver* (e.g. put a new cover on a book or chair) and *recóver* 'to get something back.'

11. The same basic pattern holds for verbal *un-* as well, except that derived forms like *untie* and *unwrap* do not normally take an instrument even though the base forms *tie* and *wrap* do.
12. Booij (1986).
13. The Karo Batak data is taken from Wollams (1996:81–83, 89–90).
14. A personal spirit, worshipped by animists, is believed to be carried on one's head.
15. All Manipuri examples in this chapter are taken from Chelliah (1992).
16. *=mi* is an evidential clitic indicating first-hand information.
17. The experiencer triggers object agreement, rather than subject agreement, on stems formed with the desiderative suffix like (26b). Cole (1982:182) refers to such verbs as "impersonal verbs."
18. Hyman and Mchombo (1992:360) point out that (27b) is actually ambiguous; it can also have the interpretation given for (27a). Example (27a), however, allows only one interpretation.
19. The chart in (29) does not include the "object agreement" position. Bresnan and Mchombo (1987) present evidence that the object marker in Chichewa is actually an incorporated pronoun. See ch. 17 for a discussion of a similar pattern in Muna.
20. Since *un-* is the only prefix in this form, it may not be obvious that it needs to be attached at any particular stage of the derivation. However, we know that it cannot attach to nouns, so it cannot be added after *-ity*; there is no such verb as *unrely*; therefore the only possible base in this example is the adjective *reliable*, as indicated in (32c). The change from *–able* to *–abil* when *–ity* is added is an example of ALLOMORPHY, which will be discussed in ch. 15.

14 Valence-changing morphology

In chapter 5 we defined the (syntactic) VALENCE of a verb to be the number of terms (i.e. non-oblique arguments) it subcategorizes for. Intransitive verbs have only one term, namely the subject; so their valence is one. Transitive verbs take an object as well as a subject; so their valence is two. Ditransitive verbs have a valence of three (SUBJ, OBJ, OBJ$_2$).

In many languages there are morphological processes which apply to verbs and change their valence, either increasing or reducing the number of term arguments. For example, some intransitive verbs in English become transitive when the prefix *out-* is added. This prefix triggers an increase in valence from one to two.[1]

(1) a Jack *ran* faster than the giant.
     b Jack *outran* the giant.

(2) a This watchband will *last* longer than the watch.
     b This watchband will *outlast* the watch.

We can classify these processes in two different ways: syntactic and semantic. In terms of the syntactic effect, we distinguish processes that increase the valence of the verb from those that decrease the valence. The examples in (1–2) illustrate a VALENCE-INCREASING process; VALENCE-DECREASING examples will be provided below. In terms of the semantic effect, we distinguish processes that involve a change in meaning from those that do not. The alternation in (1–2) is one which changes meaning, since the meaning of the derived transitive form contains elements which are not present in the meaning of the intransitive base form; e.g. *outrun* means 'run *faster than* (someone).'

In section 14.1 we will consider several examples of MEANING-PRESERVING alternations. We will note in particular that these operations do not affect the argument structure of the verb, but only the assignment of Grammatical Relations. In section 14.2 we will look at examples of MEANING-CHANGING alternations, specifically operations that add a new argument to the argument structure. In section 14.3 we will look at a very interesting process known as NOUN INCORPORATION.

14.1   Meaning-preserving alternations

14.1.1   Passive

Consider the following pair of Japanese sentences (from Tsujimura 1996):

(3)   a   Sensei=ga   Taroo=o   sikat-ta.
          teacher=NOM   Taroo=ACC   scold-PAST
          'The teacher scolded Taroo.'

       b   Taroo=ga   sensei=ni[2]   sikar-are-ta.
          Taroo=NOM   teacher=OBL   scold-PASSIVE-PAST
          'Taroo was scolded by the teacher.'

Clearly the two sentences are quite similar. Their meaning is essentially the same, in the sense that they describe the same kind of event, and it would be impossible for one to be true while the other is false. The word order is essentially the same: in both cases the subject (marked with nominative case) comes first, and the verb comes last. In fact, there seem to be only two significant differences. First, the verb in (3b) contains an additional morpheme, the suffix *-(r)are*, which does not occur in (3a). Second, while the same participants bear the same semantic roles in both sentences, there is a shift in the assignment of Grammatical Relations. The patient *Taroo* is the direct object in (3a), but the subject in (3b); the agent *sensei* is the subject in (3a), but an oblique argument in (3b).

The pair of Malayalam sentences in (4) illustrates the same kind of alternation. We have already seen (chapter 7) that word order in Malayalam is quite free, provided the verb comes last. In both of these sentences the patient occurs before the agent, but once again the change in case marking indicates a change in the Grammatical Relations: the patient is the OBJ in (4a) and the SUBJ in (4b).

(4)   **Malayalam** (Mohanan 1982:583–584)
       a   kuṭṭiye   pooliissukaar   ikkiḷiyaakki.
          child-ACC   policemen-NOM   tickle-PAST
          'The policemen tickled the child.'

       b   kuṭṭi   pooliissukaaṛaal   ikkiḷiyaakkappeṭṭu.
          child-NOM   policemen-INSTR   tickle-PASS-PAST
          'The child was tickled by the policemen.'

Examples (3a) and (4a) are referred to as ACTIVE clauses, in contrast to (3b) and (4b), which are called PASSIVE. Notice that in both cases the active verb is morphologically simpler than the passive.[3] The terms "active" and "passive" are used primarily for clauses which contain a transitive (or ditransitive) verb stem, and refer to specific patterns of Grammatical-Relation assignment. In an active clause, like (3a) and (4a), the agent is the subject and the patient is the direct object. In a passive clause, like (3b) and (4b), the patient is "promoted" to become the subject. At the same time, the agent is "demoted" to become an optional oblique argument. In Japanese and Malayalam this is indicated by the use of an oblique case marker; in English, the passive agent is marked with the preposition *by*. The two configurations are represented in (5), using the English verb *bite* (active) ~ *be bitten* (passive):

(5)   a *bite*   < agent, patient >   **Active**
                    | |
                  SUBJ   OBJ

       b *bitten*   < agent, patient >   **Passive**
                    | |
                  (OBL)   SUBJ

As the diagrams in (5) indicate, the active verb has two terms, SUBJ and OBJ, while the passive verb has only one (its SUBJ). Thus passivization is a valence-decreasing process. It is also sometimes referred to as a DETRAN-SITIVIZING process, because it changes transitive verbs into intransitives. Notice that the passive agent is optional in English: *This rope was deliberately cut (by a vandal)*. The same is true in most other languages that have a passive construction. In fact, in a number of languages the passive agent is rarely if ever expressed.

One way to represent the relationship between an active verb and its passive counterpart is through the use of Word Formation Rules similar to those introduced in chapter 13. In this book we will not be able to develop a detailed account of the passive, or of the other constructions we will discuss in this chapter. However, a rough approximation to the kind of passive rule we might propose is suggested in (6).

(6)   **Japanese passive rule**:
           $[X]_{VERB}$ ↔ $[X–(r)are]_{VERB}$
       < agent, patient >   < agent, patient >
           | | | |
         SUBJ   OBJ   (OBL)   SUBJ

The active–passive contrast is the most common example of a VOICE alternation. "Voice" is a traditional term for alternations that affect the identity (i.e. the semantic role) of the subject. As we have seen, passivization causes the patient, rather than the agent, to be expressed as subject.

An important warning is needed here. In chapter 4 we pointed out that Grammatical Relations like SUBJ and OBJ must be identified on the basis of syntactic properties. In our discussion of the passive, we have been assuming that case marking is a reliable indicator of Grammatical Relations. While the normal expectation in languages like Japanese and Malayalam is that subjects will take nominative case and objects will take accusative case, there are certain contexts in a number of languages where this expected pattern does not hold. These issues are too complex to address in the present book.[4] For the purposes of this chapter we will continue to choose examples where case and word order have been shown to be reliable indicators of Grammatical Relations. But the reader should bear in mind that claims of this kind need to be confirmed by syntactic evidence which we cannot present here.

14.1.2 Applicatives

An APPLICATIVE affix is one which increases the syntactic valence of a verb by introducing a new primary object. Typically the applicative "promotes" an oblique argument to primary object, and so does not affect the argument structure of the verb. If the verb was transitive to begin with, the derived verb will be ditransitive (taking two objects). Pangutaran Sama has a suffix *-an* which functions in this way, as illustrated in (7). The basic transitive verb *(N)bəlli* 'buy' can take an optional oblique beneficiary marked with *ma* 'dative.' When the applicative suffix is added to form *N-bəlli-an*, the dative case marker is lost. There is also a change in word order, with the NP that expresses the beneficiary appearing before the patient NP.

(7)   **Pangutaran Sama** (Malayo-Polynesian, southern Philippines; Walton 1986)
      a N-bəlli   aku   taumpa' ma   si   Andi.
        ACT-buy 1sg.NOM shoe   DAT PERS Andy
        'I bought some shoes for Andy.'

      b N-bəlli-*an*   aku   si   Andi taumpa'.
        ACT-buy-*APPLIC* 1sg.NOM PERS Andy shoe
        'I bought Andy some shoes.'

Many African languages have applicative affixes, including the Bantu language Chichewa. As the examples in (8–9) illustrate, the promoted oblique argument may be a recipient or instrument; benefactive and locative uses are also possible, but are not illustrated here. In Chichewa the oblique arguments are marked with prepositions (*kwa* for recipients; *ndi* for instruments). When the applicative suffix (*-ir* ~ *-er*) is added to the verb, this argument becomes the primary object and is expressed as a bare NP.

(8)   **Chichewa** (Malawi; Baker 1988:229–230, 260; tone not marked)
      a Ndi-na-tumiz-a   chipanda cha mowa kwa mfumu.
        1sg.S-PAST-send-ASP calabash of beer   to   chief
        'I sent a calabash of beer to the chief.'

b Ndi-na-tumiz-*ir*-a   mfumu chipanda cha mowa.
1sg.s-PAST-send-*APPL*-ASP chief   calabash of   beer
'I sent the chief a calabash of beer.'

(9)   a Msangalatsi a-ku-yend-a   ndi   ndodo.
entertainer   S.AGR-PRES-walk-ASP with stick
'The entertainer is walking with a stick.'

b Msangalatsi a-ku-yend-*er*-a   ndodo.
entertainer   S.AGR-PRES-walk-*APPL*-ASP stick
'The entertainer is walking with a stick.'

As with the passive alternation, the applicative affixes in these examples
do not seem to change the basic meaning of the verb. The same participants are involved in the same type of event in both the (a) and (b)
forms, suggesting that the argument structure of the verb remains the same.
The effect of the applicative affix is to change the association (or linking)
between semantic roles and Grammatical Relations, increasing the number
of terms (i.e. the syntactic valence) by one. This change is illustrated in (10),
which shows the argument structures corresponding to the sentences in (8).
Again, we could express the relationship between the two verb forms with a
WFR.

(10)   a *tumiz* < agent, theme, recipient > **Base form (8a)**
| | |
SUBJ   OBJ   OBL$_{rec}$

b *tumiz-ir* < agent, theme, recipient > **Applicative (8b)**
| | |
SUBJ   OBJ$_2$ OBJ

Notice that the beneficiary in (7a) and the instrument in (9a) are optional;
so in addition to the changes in Grammatical Relations noted above, the
applicative suffixes in (7b) and (9b) change an optional argument into an
obligatory argument. In some languages, applicative affixes may promote
certain kinds of adjuncts to arguments, or introduce a new argument into
the argument structure. However, the defining function of an applicative is
to create a new primary object, and in most cases this does not involve a
change in argument structure.

14.1.3 Reflexives and reciprocals

In chapter 8 we noted that English, like many other languages,
has a set of REFLEXIVE pronouns that are used in certain restricted
contexts. Grammatically, reflexive pronouns are special in that they can
(and frequently must) take an argument of their immediate clause as their

antecedent. This pattern is illustrated in the following sentences, repeated from chapter 8:

(11)   a John has bought *himself* a new Mercedes.
         b I surprised *myself* by winning the dancing competition.
         c Mary tried to control *herself*, but could not resist tickling the Governor.

Reflexives are also special in terms of their semantic function. Reflexives are used when a single individual plays more than one role within a given situation. A reflexive pronoun is used to indicate that *John* is both agent and beneficiary in (11a); that the speaker is both agent and experiencer in (11b); and that Mary is both agent and patient in (11c).

Another type of pronominal element that can take an antecedent within its immediate clause is the RECIPROCAL. This is illustrated in (12):

(12)   a John and Mary bought *each other* new bicycles for Christmas.
         b My wife and I blame *each other* for the collapse of our business.
         c Fred and Martha seem to love *each other*, in a strange sort of way.

There are two important differences between reflexives and reciprocals. First, the antecedent of a reciprocal must name a group which contains two or more individuals, whereas the antecedent of a reflexive may be a single individual. Second, a reflexive is used to describe a relationship between an individual and himself (e.g. X does something to X). A reciprocal is used to describe a relationship between two or more people which is viewed as being mutual and symmetric (e.g. X does something to Y and Y does that same thing to X).

In some languages, these types of relationships are expressed using verbal affixation rather than special types of pronouns. For example, in Kimaragang Dusun (Malayo-Polynesian, northeast Borneo) the prefix *pising-* is used to form reflexive verbs. Typically the prefix is added to transitive verb roots, as in example (13). (The reflexive verbs are shown in the normal Active Voice form, which changes the initial *p-* to *m-*.) The derived reflexive is intransitive, taking only a single argument, because the same participant fills both the agent and patient roles. Thus morphological reflexivization is a detransitivizing, or valence-decreasing, process.

(13)
Root		**Reflexive form**	
garas	'slaughter'	misinggaras	'slit one's own throat'
patay	'die, kill'	misingpatay	'kill oneself'
timbak	'shoot'	misingtimbak	'shoot oneself'
tobok	'stab'	misingtobok	'stab oneself'
wanit	'poison'	misingwanit	'poison oneself'
lapis	'slap'	misinglapis	'slap oneself'
rayow	'praise'	misingrayow	'to praise oneself'

We might represent the effect of this prefix as in (14). The right side of the rule in (14) indicates that the reflexive verb assigns two semantic roles to the same participant. That participant bears only one Grammatical Relation (SUBJ), and so must be expressed by a single NP. This rule expresses the fact that reflexivization changes transitive verbs into intransitives.

(14)   **Kimaragang reflexive WFR**:

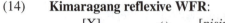
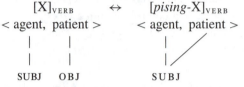

Kimaragang also has a reciprocal prefix, *pi-*. This is illustrated in (15), again using the active voice form.

(15)

Root		**Reciprocal form**	
sambat	'meet'	m-(p)i-sambat	'meet each other'
patay	'die, kill'	m-(p)i-pa-patay[5]	'fight, kill each other'
bobog	'beat'	m-(p)i-bobog	'beat each other'
balas	'repay'	m-(p)i-ba-balas	'repay each other'
talib	'pass by'	m-(p)i-talib	'pass each other'
boros	'speak, say'	m-(p)i-bo-boros	'speak to each other'
tabang	'help'	m-(p)i-ta-tabang	'help each other (e.g. with farm work)'
obpinee	'sibling'	m-(p)i-obpinee	'related to each other as siblings'

Chichewa is another language which has a reciprocal affix. As (16) illustrates, the suffix *–an* changes a transitive verb stem into an intransitive reciprocal verb. So reciprocal formation, like reflexivization, is a valence-decreasing process.[6]

(16)   **Chichewa** (Bantu; Mchombo 1993:191)

a Mbidzi   zi-ku-meny-a   nkhandwe.
   10-zebras 10.SUBJ-PRES-hit-ASP 10-foxes
   'The zebras are hitting the foxes.'

b Mbidzi   zi-ku-meny-*an*-a.
   10-zebras 10.SUBJ-PRES-hit-*RECIP*-ASP
   'The zebras are hitting each other.'

The argument structure configuration for a reciprocal verb like that in (16b) would look essentially the same as the reflexive structure shown on the right side of (14). The difference in meaning between reflexives and reciprocals would need to be spelled out as part of the semantic representation, which we will not discuss here.

14.2   Meaning-changing alternations

14.2.1   Causatives

In chapter 13 we presented some Turkish examples involving
CAUSATIVE verbs. One of these is repeated in (17b).

(17)   **Turkish** (Comrie 1981:169)
   a Müdür   mektub-u   imzala-dï.
      director letter-ACC sign-PAST
      'The director signed the letter.'

   b Dişçi   mektub-u   müdür-e   imzala-*t*-tï.
      dentist letter-ACC director-DAT sign-*CAUS*-PAST
      'The dentist got the director to sign the letter.'

The base verb in (17a) means 'to sign.' The verb in (17b) carries the
causative suffix, -*t*, and means 'cause to sign.' Notice that sentence (17b)
also contains an extra participant. The letter and its signer (in this case the
director) are participants in both clauses, but in (17b) there is a new participant who is responsible for bringing about the signing event. This new
participant is referred to as the CAUSER. The participant who is caused
to do something, corresponding to the subject of the base verb, is called
the CAUSEE. So in (17b) the dentist is the causer and the director is the
causee.

Causatives always introduce a new participant, the causer, which is normally the subject of the derived verb.[7] If the base verb is intransitive, as in
the Chichewa example (18), then the derived causative will be transitive.
So causative formation is a valence-increasing process.

(18)   **Chichewa** (adapted from Baker 1988:216)
   a Atsikana a-na-vin-a.
      girls   S.AGR-PAST-dance-ASP
      'The girls danced.'

   b Asilikari a-na-vin-*its*-a   atsikana.
      soldiers S.AGR-PAST-dance-*CAUS*-ASP girls
      'The soldiers made the girls dance.'

When the base verb is transitive, the derived causative will follow one of
three basic subcategorization patterns. In some languages, the causee will
be expressed as primary object while the patient is demoted to secondary
object, as in (19b). In other languages, the causee will be expressed as a
secondary object, as in (17b). The third possibility is for the causee to be
expressed as an oblique argument, as in (20b).

(19)   **Chimwi:ni** (Bantu; Baker 1988:183; Kisseberth and Abasheikh 1977:189)

  a Wa:na   wa-(y-)andish-iłe   xati.
    children s.AGR-O.AGR-write-ASP letter
    'The children wrote a letter.'

  b Mwa:limu Ø-wa-andik-*ish*-iłe   wa:na   xati.
    teacher   s.AGR-O.AGR-write-*CAUS*-ASP children letter
    'The teacher made the children write a letter.'

(20)   **Chichewa** (adapted from Baker, 1988:163)

  a Buluzi a-na-meny-a   ana.
    lizard s.AGR-PAST-hit-ASP children
    'The lizard hit the children.'

  b Anyani   a-na-meny-*ets*-a   ana   kwa buluzi.
    baboons s.AGR-PAST-hit-*CAUS*-ASP children to   lizard
    'The baboons made the lizard hit the children.'

The argument structure of a causative verb derived from an intransitive base verb, like the verb in (18b), is illustrated in (21a). The corresponding diagram for a causative derived from a transitive base is shown in (21b). These diagrams indicate that the causative affix introduces an abstract CAUSE predicate which takes two arguments: the causer (role = agent) and the caused event. The argument structure of the caused event corresponds to the argument structure of the base verb. So the causative verb is semantically complex: it expresses two predicates, each of which takes its own arguments. But there is only one set of Grammatical Relations assigned by the verb as a whole.[8]

(21)   a CAUSE < agent, Event >   (= 18b)
                       | |
                       | *dance* < agent >
                       | |
                    SUBJ   OBJ

        b CAUSE < agent, Event >   (= 20b)
                       | |
                       | *hit* < agent, patient >
                       | | |
                    SUBJ   OBL   OBJ

  c **Chichewa causative**:

    $[X]_{VERB}$ ↔ $[X\text{-}its]_{VERB}$
    meaning: 'x'   meaning: 'cause to x'

A simple WFR expressing the function of the Chichewa causative suffix is presented in (21c). The changes in argument structure and Grammatical Relations can be fairly complex, so in this book we will simply write out the change of meaning in words.

14.2.2 Adversatives

Another type of derivational process which changes the argument structure of the verb is the ADVERSATIVE. In Malay, the *ke-X-an* circumfix which we saw functioning as a nominalizer in chapter 13 can also be used to form adversatives, as shown in (22) and (23). As these examples illustrate, the adversative construction changes an intransitive root into a transitive verb by adding a new argument, namely the person who suffers as a result of the event being described.

(22)　a Kelapa itu jatuh.
　　　　 coconut that fall
　　　　 'The coconut fell.'

　　　b Tomo *ke*-jatuh-*an*　kelapa.
　　　　 Tomo -fall-ADVRS coconut
　　　　 'Tomo was fallen on by a coconut.'

(23)　a Anak Tomo telah mati.
　　　　 child Tomo PAST die
　　　　 'Tomo's child has died.'

　　　b Tomo *ke*-mati-*an*　anak.
　　　　 Tomo -die-ADVRS child
　　　　 'Tomo suffered the death of a child.'

Adversatives are sometimes described as being special type of passive construction.[9] Some languages, including Japanese, use the same affix for both the passive and the adversative. Compare the adversatives in (24b) and (25b) with the normal passive in (3b) above.[10]

(24)　a Kodomo=ga sinda.
　　　　 child=NOM died
　　　　 'A child died.'

　　　b Taroo=ga　　 kodomo=ni sin-are-ta.
　　　　 Taroo=NOM child=OBL die-PASSIVE-PAST
　　　　 'Taroo was adversely affected by the death of his child.'

(25)　a Sensei=ga　　 kodomo=o sikat-ta.
　　　　 teacher=NOM child=ACC scold-PAST
　　　　 'The teacher scolded the child.'

　　　b Taroo=ga　　 sensei=ni　　 kodomo=o sikar-are-ta.
　　　　 Taroo=NOM teacher=OBL child=ACC scold-PASSIVE-PAST
　　　　 'Taroo was adversely affected by the teacher scolding his child.'

Notice that the same passive suffix (*-[r]are*) is used in both constructions. In discussing example (3) we noted that passivization does not affect the argument structure of the clause: the same participants fill the same semantic roles in both active and passive. But in (24) and (25) we see that the adversative sentence contains an extra argument which is not found in the corresponding active sentence. This new participant is the person who is adversely affected by the action.

14.3   Incorporation

In chapters 2 and 7 we presented a few examples like (26), in which the noun that expresses the object ('dog') is morphologically included as part of the verb. This pattern is called NOUN INCORPORATION (NI), and we say that the object noun has been "incorporated" into the verb. NI is a special type of compounding: a verb root and a noun root combine to form a complex stem whose category is V.

(26)   **Southern Tiwa** (North America; Allen and Frantz 1983)
       (repeated from chapter 7)
       ben-*khwien*-wia-ban
       2sg:1sg:3sg-*dog*-give-PAST
       You (sg) gave me the dog.

The most common kind if NI is that in which the incorporated noun functions as the object of the verb. Sometimes this results in a decrease in syntactic valence. For example, (27a) contains a transitive verb 'sharpen' which agrees with both SUBJ and OBJ. The subject NP gets ergative case and the object gets absolutive case. In (27b) the object 'knife' has been incorporated into the verb, so the verb is no longer marked for object-agreement. Moreover, the SUBJ of (27b) is now marked with absolutive case, indicating that it is the subject of an intransitive clause. We will refer to this pattern as valence-decreasing incorporation.[11] Further examples of this pattern are given in (28b) and (29b).

(27)   **Chukchee** (Siberia; Spencer 1991:255)
       a Morgənan mət-re-mne-ŋənet   walat.
         we.ERG   1pl.S-FUT-sharpen-3pl.O knives(ABS)
         'We will sharpen our knives.'

       b Muri   mət-ra-*wala*-mna-gʔa.
         we.ABS   1pl.S-FUT-*knife*-sharpen-1pl.S
         'We will sharpen knives.'

(28)   **Huahtla Nahuatl** (Mexico; Merlan 1976:185; Mithun 1984:860–861)
       a aške:man ti-ʔ-kʷa   nakatl.
         never   2sg.S-3sg.O-eat meat
         'You never eat meat.'

       b naʔ ipanima ni-*naka*-kʷa.
         1sg always   1sg.S-*meat*-eat
         'I eat meat all the time.'

(29)　**Huahtla Nahuatl** (Merlan 1976:187–189)

　　a ti-ki-išmati　　　　Katarina? ke:na ni-ki-išmati . . .
　　　 2sg.S-3sg.O-know Katarina yes　1sg.S-3sg.O-know
　　　 'Do you know Katarina? Yes, I know her . . .'

　　b tla?ke šočitl? aš　　ni-*šoči*-išmati.
　　　 what　flower　NEG　1sg.S-*flower*-know
　　　 'What (kind of) flower is it? I don't know flowers.'

In other languages, however, NI does not reduce the valence of the verb. In (30b), for example, we see that the Mohawk verb continues to agree with its OBJ even when the OBJ is incorporated. If the verb is inflected as an intransitive, agreeing only with its SUBJ as in (30c), the sentence is ungrammatical. Similarly, a transitive verb in Southern Tiwa shows the same agreement pattern whether the object is an independent NP (31a) or an incorporated noun (31b). We will refer to this pattern as valence-preserving incorporation.

(30)　**Mohawk** (North America; Postal 1962:123, 285; Baker 1988:125)

　　a i?i　khe-nuhwe?-s　　　　ne　yao-wir-a?a.
　　　 1sg　1sgS:3femO-like-ASP the　PRE-baby-SUFF
　　　 'I like the baby.'

　　b i?i　khe-*wir*-nuhwe?-s.
　　　 1sg　1sgS:3femO-*baby*-like-ASP
　　　 'I like the baby.'

　　c *i?i　k-*wir*-nuhwe?-s.
　　　 1sg　1sgS-*baby*-like-ASP

(31)　**Southern Tiwa** (Allen, Gardiner, and Frantz 1984:294–295)

　　a yede seuan-ide　a-mũ-ban.
　　　 that　man-SUFF　2sg.SUBJ:3sg.OBJ-see-PAST [12]
　　　 'You (sg) saw that man.'

　　b a-*seuan*-mũ-ban.
　　　 2sg.SUBJ:3sg.OBJ-*man*-see-PAST
　　　 'You (sg) saw a/the man.'

　　c yede a-*seuan*-mũ-ban.
　　　 that　2sg.SUBJ:3sg.OBJ-*man*-see-PAST
　　　 'You (sg) saw that man.'

In many languages with valence-preserving incorporation, the incorporated noun can be modified by words or phrases that appear outside the verb: determiners (31c), numerals (32), and even relative clauses (33). These examples provide additional evidence that the verbs in these constructions are still transitive.[13]

(32)   **Southern Tiwa** (Allen, Gardiner, and Frantz 1984:295)
    a wisi seuan-in   bi-mū-ban.
      two man-SUFF 1sg.SUBJ:3pl.OBJ-see-PAST
      'I saw two men.'

    b wisi bi-*seuan*-mū-ban.
      two 1sg.SUBJ:3pl.OBJ-*man*-see-PAST
      'I saw two men.'

(33)   **Southern Tiwa** (Allen, Gardiner, and Frantz 1984:297)
    te-*pan*-tuwi-ban   ku-kha-ba-'i.
    1sg.SUBJ:3inan.OBJ-*bread*-buy-PAST 2sg.SUBJ:3inan.OBJ-bake-PAST-SUBORD
    'I bought the bread that you baked.'

A simple WFR which represents incorporation as a process of N+V compounding is suggested in (34). However, we will not attempt to write specific rules to express the differences between valence-decreasing and valence-preserving incorporation here.

(34)   **Noun Incorporation**:
    $[X]_{NOUN}$ + $[Y]_{VERB}$ ↔ $[X\text{–}Y]_{VERB}$
    'x'   'y'   'do y to x'

14.4   Conclusion

There are two basic ways of changing the syntactic valence of the verb. Some of the processes we have considered in this chapter, notably the causative and adversative, introduce a new semantic argument into the verb's argument structure. Others (e.g. the passive) do not affect the argument structure but only change the Grammatical Relations that are assigned to one or more arguments.

Morphological processes of both types can, and often do, produce a change in the valence of the verb. However, it is not the case that every occurrence of one of these affixes must involve a change in syntactic valence. For example, the causative example in (20b) is mono-transitive, and so is the basic clause from which it is derived (20a). So changes to argument structure do not always produce a change in syntactic transitivity.[14] Syntactic valence changes only if the derived verb has a different number of term relations (subject plus objects) from the base form. For this reason, some authors refer to the kinds of alternations we have discussed in this chapter as RELATION-CHANGING PROCESSES. Whichever term is used, it is important to investigate both the semantic effects, including but not limited to changes in argument structure; and syntactic effects, in particular, changes in Grammatical Relations.

Practice exercises

A Kinyarwanda (Rwanda; Kimenyi 1980; Givón 1984)
Describe the italicized suffixes in prose, and write a WFR for each one.

1. **Reason/"Goal"**
   a Karooli y-a-fash-ije   abaantu *ku*=busa.
      Charles he-PAST-help-ASP people *for*=nothing
      'Charles helped the people for nothing.'

   b Karooli y-a-fash-*ir*-ije   ubusa   abaantu.
      Charles he-PAST-help-*GOAL*-ASP nothing people
      'Charles for nothing helped the people.'

2. **Instrument**
   a Umualimu a-ra-andika   ibaruwa *n*=ikaramu.
      teacher   he-ASP-write letter   *with*=pen
      'The teacher is writing the letter with a pen.'

   b Umualimu a-ra-andik-*iish*-a   ikaramu ibaruwa.
      teacher   he-ASP-write-*INSTR* pen   letter
      'The teacher is using the pen to write the letter.'

3. **Associative/Manner**
   a Mariya y-a-tets-e   inkoko *n*=agahiinda.
      Mary   she-PAST-cook-ASP chicken *with*=sorrow
      'Mary cooked the chicken with regret.'

   b Mariya y-a-tek-*an*-ye   agahiinda inkoko.
      Mary   she-PAST-cook-*ASSOC*-ASP sorrow   chicken
      'Mary regretfully cooked the chicken.'

4. **Accompaniment**
   a Mariya y-a-tets-e   inkoko *ni*=Yohani.
      Mary   she-PAST-cook-ASP chicken *with*=John
      'Mary cooked the chicken with John.'

   b Mariya y-a-tek-*an*-ye   Yohani inkoko.
      Mary   she-PAST-cook-*ACCOMP*-ASP John   chicken
      'Mary together with John cooked the chicken.'

5. **Benefactive** (Note: there is no corresponding prepositional form)
   umkoobwa a-ra-som-*er*-a   umuhuungu igitabo.
   girl   she-PRES-read-*BEN*-ASP boy   book
   'The girl is reading a book for the boy.'

B Hopi (USA; Gronemeyer 1996)
Describe the derivational process(es) illustrated in the following examples.
Note: subjects take NOM case (unmarked), while objects, possessors, and
most other NPs get ACC case. Modifiers agree with the case marking of the

head noun. Gronemeyer states: "Hopi verbs always agree with the number of both the subject and the object; thus the verb 'to kill' has the four-way agreement paradigm shown in (1)."

1.   'to kill'   **sg/du** OBJ   **pl** OBJ
     sg/du SUBJ   *niina*   *qöya*
     pl SUBJ   *nina-ya*   *qö-qya*

2.   Pas   nu' pu' wuko-taqa-t   kaneelo-t   niina
     PRT   1sg now big-male -ACC   sheep-ACC   kill(sg/du.OBJ-sg/du.SUBJ)
     'I killed a big male sheep this time.'

3.   Itam taavok   kanel-nina-ya
     we   yesterday   sheep-kill-(sg/du.OBJ-pl.SUBJ)
     'We killed a sheep yesterday.'

4.   Höq-na'ya-t   engem lööq-mu-y   kanel-nina-ya.
     harvest-work. party-ACC for   two-PL-ACC   sheep-kill(sg/du.OBJ-pl.SUBJ)
     'They butchered two sheep for the harvesting party.'

5.   Mö'wi-t   engem na'ya-t   ep a'ni   kanèl-qö-qya.
     bride-ACC for   work.party-ACC at many sheep-kill(pl.SUBJ-pl.OBJ)
     'At the bride's wedding work party they butchered a lot of sheep.'

6.   Nu' pu' totokmi   naalöq kanèl-qöya.
     1sg this dance.day four   sheep-kill(sg/du.SUBJ-pl.OBJ)
     'This year I butchered four sheep for the dance day.'

7.   Nu' lööq-mu-y   ho'ap-ta.
     1sg two-PL-ACC basket-make
     'I made two baskets.'

8.   Pas   wuu-wupa-t   angap-soma.
     really PL-long-ACC cornhusk-tie
     'She tied really long husks in bundles.'

9.   Nu' ung   ma-qwhi-k-na-ni.
     1sg you.ACC   hand/arm-break-SINGLE-CAUS-FUT
     'I'll break your arm.'

10. Piikuyi-t   paa-mòy-ta.
     milk-ACC   water-take.in.mouth-CAUS
     'He took a mouthful of milk'.

Exercises

14A Southern Azerbaijani (Iran; Lee 1996)
Describe the verbal affixes that are found in the following examples, and write WFRs to express the function of any derivational or valence-changing affixes. As noted in exercise 7B, suffix vowels are affected by "vowel

harmony." You do not need to account for changes of vowel quality in suffixes. Aside from this factor, are there any other cases of a verbal affix appearing in more than one form? (This topic will be addressed in chapter 15.)

1.   a Eldar bu məqaləni yazdɨ.
        Eldar this article-ACC write-PAST
        'Eldar wrote this article.'

      b Bu məqalə Eldar tərəfindən yazɨldɨ.
        this article Eldar by
        'This article was written by Eldar.'

2.   a Məhbub kitabɨ   aldɨ.
        Mahbub book-ACC buy-PAST
        'Mahbub bought the book.'

      b Kitab Məhbub tərəfindən alɨndɨ.
        book Mahbub by
        'The book was bought by Mahbub.'

      c Nəsib Məhbuba   kitabɨ   aldɨrdɨ.
        Nasib Mahbub-DAT book-ACC
        'Nasib made Mahbub buy the book.'

3.   a Ata   maşɨna mindi.
        father car-DAT ride-PAST
        'Father got in the car.'

      b Ata   məni   maşɨna   mindirdi.
        father 1sg-ACC car-DAT
        'Father made me get in the car.'

4.   a qɨz Məmədi   gördi
        girl Memed-ACC see-PAST
        'The girl saw Memed.'

      b Məməd qɨz tərəfindən göründi
        Memed girl by
        'Memed was seen by the girl.'

5.   a inək öldi.
        cow die
        'The cow died.'

      b Məməd inəyi   öldürdi.
        Memed cow-ACC
        'Memed killed the cow (lit.: caused the cow to die).'

      c inək Məməd tərəfindən öldürüldi.
        cow Memed by
        'The cow was killed by Memed.'

14B Sayula Popoluca (Mexico; compiled by W. Merrifield, based on Merrifield et al. 1987, prob. 31 and 217)

Describe the word order and affixation patterns revealed in the following examples. Use a position class chart for inflectional affixes and WFRs for any derivational or valence-changing operations. Hint: it may be helpful to begin by analyzing transitive and intransitive clauses separately. You may need to assume that a morphophonemic process of METATHESIS (i.e. XY → YX) applies in certain contexts; see chapters 15 and 16 for further discussion.

1.	tʌkoyw	'I arrived.'
2.	mikoyp	'You are arriving.'
3.	koyp wan	'John is arriving.'
4.	tʌʔiikp ʔʌʌ	'I am playing.'
5.	miʔiikw mii	'You played.'
6.	ʔiikw	'He played.'
7.	tʌnhuyw šʌhk	'I bought beans.'
8.	mii ʔinhuyp šiš	'You are buying meat.'
9.	ʔihuyw	'He bought it.'
10.	ʔʌʌ tʌntoʔkw šʌhk	'I sold beans.'
11.	ʔintoʔkp ʔakš	'You are selling fish.'
12.	wan ʔitoʔkp šiš	'John is selling meat.'
13.	ʔʌʌ tʌtsakp mii	'I am pushing you.'
14.	ʔištsakp mii	'You are pushing me.'
15.	tʌštsakw ʔʌʌ	'He pushed me.'
16.	tʌʔeʔp	'I am looking at you.'
17.	tʌnʔeʔp	'I am looking at him/it.'
18.	ʔinʔeʔp	'You are looking at him/it.'
19.	tʌšʔeʔp heʔ	'He is looking at me.'
20.	ʔišʔeʔp heʔ	'He is looking at you.'
21.	tʌnhuhyaw šiš	'I bought meat from him.'
22.	mii ʔišhuhyap šʌhk	'You are buying beans from me.'
23.	tʌtoʔhkaw ʔʌʌ	'I sold it to you.'
24.	heʔ ʔištoʔhkap šiš mii	'He is selling meat to you.'
25.	ʔišmoyw mii	'You gave it to me.'
26.	tʌšmoyp	'He is giving it to me.'
27.	ʔinmoyw šiš wan	'You gave John the meat.'
28.	pek ʔimoyp šiš	'Peter is giving him meat.'
29.	mišišhuyw mii	'You bought meat.'
30.	šišhuyp	'He is buying meat.'
31.	tʌšištoʔkp	'I am selling meat.'
32.	ʔakštoʔkw pek	'Peter sold fish.'

Additional exercises

Merrifield et al. (1987) prob. 247, 248.

Notes

1. This prefix can also appear on transitive verbs; but if the base verb is ambiguous between a transitive and an intransitive sense, it is generally the intransitive sense that is selected when the prefix is present.
2. The clitic =*ni* can also be used to mark Dative case. This gloss follows the analysis adopted by Tsujimura.
3. It is harder to see the morpheme boundaries in the Malayalam verb in (4b) than in its Japanese counterpart (3b), because of morphophonemic changes (see ch. 15). But in both examples it is clear that the active verb is morphologically simpler than the passive. In some languages, there is no passive affix. Rather, the passive is marked by the use of a special auxiliary element or some other function word.
4. See Kroeger (2004, ch. 10) for a discussion of the relationship between case marking and Grammatical Relations; and ch. 3 for evidence that the applied object (promoted oblique) in examples like (7–9) is the primary object.
5. With some roots it is more natural to REDUPLICATE the reciprocal form; see ch. 16.
6. Mchombo (1993, 1998) shows that the reciprocal suffix is part of the verb stem and functions as a derivational affix, reducing the syntactic valence of the verb. The Chichewa reflexive prefix, in contrast, is not part of the verb stem and functions as an incorporated pronoun, like the other object-agreement prefixes. It does not reduce syntactic valence.
7. That is, the causer will be the SUBJ when the causative verb appears in the active voice.
8. See Kroeger (2004), ch. 8 for a discussion of the evidence supporting this claim.
9. A number of Southeast Asian languages have passive constructions which are only used to express something unpleasant or undesirable. These so-called "adversative passives" are normal passives in terms of their syntactic effect. Unlike the adversative construction discussed in sec. 14.2.2, they do not change argument structure but only affect the assignment of Grammatical Relations, as indicated by the passive rule in (6).
10. (24–25) are from Tsujimura (1996).
11. Rosen (1989) and Gerdts (1998) refer to this type as "compounding incorporation," and to our valence-preserving incorporation as "classifying incorporation."
12. Allen, Gardiner, and Frantz's glosses for OBJ-agreement actually refer to noun classes, which they label A, B, and C. These classes in turn are largely, but not entirely, determined by person, number, and animacy.
13. Under the analyses proposed by Mithun (1984) and Rosen (1989), the incorporated noun in the valence-preserving examples (30–33) is not the OBJ but only a kind of classifier, which restricts the semantic class of possible objects. Stranded modifiers like those in (31c, 32b, 33) involve a null N as head of the OBJ NP.
14. It is also possible to change the assignment of Grammatical Relations without affecting syntactic valence. A well-known example of this type is the "locative alternation," *John sprayed paint on the wall* vs. *John sprayed the wall with paint.* The Indonesian suffix –*kan* often marks a similar kind of change.

15 Allomorphy

In most languages there are certain morphemes which appear in different forms depending on their environment. A familiar example of this is the indefinite article in English:

(1)   a dog   an apple
        a man   an orchid
        a bus   an elephant
        a ticket an umbrella

In this case it is easy to predict which form of the article will occur in any given context: we always find *an* before vowels and *a* before consonants. In other words, the form of the article depends entirely on the phonological shape of the word which follows it. A similar example is the Korean nominative case marker:

(2)   **Korean**
        BASE FORM   **NOMINATIVE FORM**   **GLOSS**
        cekkun   cekkun-i   'enemy'
        haksæng   haksæng-i   'student'
        salam   salam-i   'person'
        tal   tal-i   'moon'
        pap   pap-i   'cooked rice'
        ttok   ttok-i   'cake'
        oppa   oppa-ka   'brother'
        holangi   holangi-ka   'tiger'
        tongmu   tongmu-ka   'comrade'
        hæ   hæ-ka   'sun'
        kho   kho-ka   'nose'

Once again, it is easy to predict which form of the case marker will be used simply by observing the phonological shape of the noun. The form *-ka* is found whenever the noun ends in a vowel, while *-i* is found whenever the noun ends in a consonant.

In other cases, however, it is not so easy to predict which form will occur. Consider the past participle suffixes of the following English verbs. Some verbs take *-ed* while others take *–en*; but as the list in (3) demonstrates, there is no phonological basis for predicting which suffix any particular verb will take:

(3)   **Base form**   **Past participle**
         give   given
         take   taken
         hide   hidden
         bite   bitten
         know   known

         live   lived
         bake   baked
         guide   guided
         sight   sighted
         owe   owed

A similar pattern can be seen in the Huichol possessive markers in (4). Once again there appears to be no way to predict, based on either phono-logical patterns or semantic features, which form of the possessive marker will occur with which stem. Some nouns take the suffix *-ya* while others take the prefix *yu-*, but the choice seems to be quite arbitrary. A language learner would simply have to memorize which nouns take which form on a case-by-case basis.

(4)   **Huichol** (Mexico; Merrifield et al. 1987, prob. 53; length and tone not indicated)
         qaicʌ   'fish hook'   qaicʌ-ya   'his fish hook'
         kuka   'bead'   kuka-ya   'his bead'
         kʌye   'tree'   kʌye-ya   'his tree'
         haca   'axe'   haca-ya   'his axe'
         maku   'pumpkin'   maku-ya   'his pumpkin'
         muza   'sheep'   muza-ya   'his sheep'

         hauri   'candle'   yu-hauri   'his candle'
         huye   'road'   yu-huye   'his road'
         micu   'cat'   yu-micu   'his cat'
         zʌnai   'nit'   yu-zʌnai   'his nit'

All these examples have two important features in common. In every case, the variant forms (a) have the same meaning, and (b) are in complementary distribution, i.e. never occur in the same environments. It is these two factors which allow us to identify them as variant forms of the same morpheme, rather than two different morphemes.

Variant forms of the same morpheme are called ALLOMORPHS. If the choice of which allomorph occurs in which environment is predictable on the basis of phonological patterns, as in (1–2), the alternation is said to be PHONOLOGICALLY CONDITIONED. If the choice of allomorph is essentially arbitrary and must be learned on a word-by-word basis, as in examples (3–4), the alternation is said to be LEXICALLY CONDITIONED.

Phonologically conditioned allomorphy may be of two basic types. If the change in form is the result of a phonological process, that process is said to be MORPHOPHONEMIC.[1] A process in which one allomorph simply replaces another – that is, a change in form that cannot be described as a phonological process – is referred to as SUPPLETION. We will consider each of these possibilities in turn, beginning with suppletion.

15.1   Suppletion

Consider the paradigm of inflection for degree in English adjectives, which is illustrated in (5). The irregular comparative and superlative forms for *good* and *bad* seem totally unrelated to the basic (positive) form. *Better* and *best* do not contain any trace of the root form *good*, unlike such irregular plural forms as *ox/oxen*, *child/children*, *criterion/criteria*, etc. in which the original root can still be seen in the plural form.

(5)	POSITIVE	COMPARATIVE	SUPERLATIVE
	big	bigger	biggest
	fast	faster	fastest
	funny	funnier	funniest
	great	greater	greatest
	good	better (*gooder)	best (*goodest)
	bad	worse (*badder)	worst (*baddest)

An alternation like *good/better/best*, in which the inflectional paradigm for a certain word involves more than one root form, has traditionally been referred to as SUPPLETION. Other examples in English include the irregular verb forms *go–went* and *am–is–are–was–were*. These suppletive forms of the root cannot be derived or predicted by any regular phonological rule, but must be listed in the lexical entry of the word.

Total suppletion (the existence of two unrelated roots or stems for the same word, as in *go–went*) occurs primarily as a marker of inflectional categories, and rarely (if ever) in derivational processes. Since derivational morphology is often semantically irregular and does not form paradigms, it would actually be very difficult to identify suppletive stems as belonging to the same morpheme. For example, on semantic grounds we might be tempted to say that *kill* is the causative form of *die*, or that *drop* is the causative form of *fall*. But there is no evidence that these pairs of forms are related morphologically; the best analysis seems to be that they are distinct (i.e. unrelated) lexical items which share certain components of meaning.

Modern linguists extend the term SUPPLETION to apply to affixes as well as roots.[2] For example, the two allomorphs of the Huichol possessive marker in (4) stand in a suppletive relationship because neither form can be derived from the other by a phonological process (one is a prefix, the other a suffix). Since there is no way to predict which allomorph occurs with which noun, the choice must be indicated in some way in the lexical entry of each noun. This is an example of LEXICALLY CONDITIONED SUPPLETION.

The two forms of the Korean nominative case marker in (2) also stand in a suppletive relationship. However, in this case it is possible to predict which form will occur with which noun: *-ka* occurs after a vowel, while *-i* occurs after a consonant. This is an example of PHONOLOGICALLY CON-DITIONED SUPPLETION, meaning that the choice of allomorph depends only on the phonological environment.

A third possibility is that affix suppletion may be MORPHOLOGICALLY CONDITIONED. This means that the choice of allomorph for a particular affix depends on what other specific affixes are present in the word. For example, Muysken (1981) reports that in Quechua verbs, the normal third person agreement suffix *–n* is replaced by a zero allomorph *–Ø* when the verb also bears the past tense suffix *–rqa*.

Morphologically conditioned suppletion appears to be less common than the lexical or phonological conditioning discussed above; at least it is harder to find cases where this is clearly the correct analysis. As another example, the future tense prefix in Lalana Chinantec has two allomorphs: /ri^2-/ when the verb is marked for first or second person vs. /ri^{23}-/ when the verb is marked for third person. (The number 3 represents low tone, 1 is high tone.) This change in tone is not phonologically conditioned. The subject agreement suffixes appear in several different allomorphs, which are lexically conditioned. However, the tone pattern associated with the suffix does not affect the tone of the prefix; this seems to be determined strictly on the basis of person, as illustrated in (6).[3]

(6) **Lalana Chinantec** (Mexico; Merrifield et al. 1987, prob. 49)
     V-class 1:

     ri^2-kwẽ-n^{31} 'I will sneeze'
     FUT-sneeze-1sg
     ri^2-kwẽ-hn^2 'you will sneeze'
     FUT-sneeze-2sg
     ri^{23}-kwẽ-h^2 'he will sneeze'
     FUT-sneeze-3sg

     V-class 2:

     ri^2-lø-n^{232} 'I will speak'
     FUT-speak-1sg
     ri^2-lø-hn^2 'you will speak'
     FUT-speak-2sg
     ri^{23}-lø-h^{23} 'he will speak'
     FUT-speak-3sg

V-class 3:

rɨ[2]-nø̃-hn[1]   'I will knead'
FUT-knead-1sg
rɨ[2]-nø̃-n[31]   'you will knead'
FUT-knead-2sg
rɨ[23]-nø̃-h[2]   'he will knead'
FUT-knead-3sg

Haspelmath (2002) cites Welsh pluralization as another example of morphologically conditioned suppletion. Welsh has about a dozen different ways of marking plural number on nouns. In derived nouns, the form of the plural marker depends on which nominalizing suffix is used, as illustrated in (7).

(7)   **Welsh** (Haspelmath 2002:119)

BASE		NOMINALIZATION		PLURAL	
swydd	'job'	swyddog	'official'	swyddog-ion	'officials'
march	'horse'	marchog	'horseman'	marchog-ion	'horsemen'
pechu	'sin'	pechadur	'sinner'	pechadur-iaid	'sinners'
cachu	'feces'	cachadur	'coward'	cachadur-iaid	'cowards'
tywysog	'prince'	tywysoges	'princess'	tywysoges-au	'princesses'
Sais	'Englishman'	Saesnes	'Englishwoman'	Saesnes-au	'Englishwomen'

In section 15.3 we will discuss the kinds of rules we could use to represent each of these kinds of suppletion. But before proceeding further with our study of suppletion, it will be helpful to discuss the other major type of allomorphy, namely MORPHOPHONEMIC change.

15.2   Morphophonemic changes

We can think of suppletion as a process which replaces one allomorph with another, as the name suggests. Morphophonemic change involves not replacing but changing the phonological shape of a morpheme. A morphophonemic process can be described as a change in one or more phonemes triggered by the phonological properties of a neighboring morpheme. A very familiar example occurs in the suffix that marks regular plurals in English.

(8)   **Plural nouns**:

cat-s   dog-z   kiss-ɨz
book-s   bed-z   wish-ɨz
map-s   star-z   rose-ɨz
tusk-s   hall-z   judge-ɨz
         cow-z   church-ɨz
         boy-z

English plural nouns are marked in several different ways, some of which are illustrated in (8). As in (1) and (2), the choice between the variant forms of the plural suffix is phonologically determined. It depends only on the final phoneme of the stem: the form /-ɨz/ occurs after sibilants (grooved fricatives); the voiceless fricative /-s/ occurs after other voiceless consonants; and the voiced fricative /-z/ occurs elsewhere.

But there is an important difference between the pattern in (8) and those in (1) and (2). In (2) there is no phonological similarity at all between the two allomorphs (/-i/ vs. /-ka/). In (1), there is a partial phonological similarity between the two allomorphs (*a* vs. *an*); but it seems unlikely that the two can be related by any regular process. The alternation between *a* and *an* is unique: there are no other morphemes in modern English in which a final /n/ is always deleted before consonants, or inserted before vowels.[4] The alternation in (8), however, is part of a more general pattern. Essentially the same changes are observed in the third person singular agreement suffix (9a) and the possessive clitic (9b).

(9)   a **Present 3rd singular verbs**:

eat-s	hug-z	kiss-ɨz
look-s	bid-z	wish-ɨz
nap-s	stir-z	rise-ɨz
risk-s	call-z	judge-ɨz
think-s	bow-z	teach-ɨz
	enjoy-z	
	swim-z	

   b **Possessive nouns (N-'*s*)**:

Pat-s	Meg-z	Joyce-ɨz
Mark-s	Ted-z	Trish-ɨz
Skip-s	Bob-z	Roz-ɨz
Ernest-s	Bill-z	George-ɨz
Ruth-s	Sam-z	Butch-ɨz
	Mary-z	
	Lou-z	

In cases like this, where two (or more) variant forms of a single morpheme are similar in phonological shape and the difference between them follows a regular phonological pattern observed elsewhere in the language, the relationship between the two forms is best analyzed as being morphophonemic. The alternation between two forms is accounted for by a special type of phonological rule, called a MORPHOPHONEMIC RULE. For example, to account for the different forms of the plural morpheme in (8) we could assume that /-z/ is the basic form and formulate morphophonemic rules to derive the other two forms. We will not discuss the details of how to write such rules in this book; for readers who have no previous training in phonology, it may be helpful to consult an introductory phonology textbook.[5] But the essence of the rules needed to account for example (8) would be the following:

(10)   a plural /-z/ → /-ɨz/   following sibilants
        b plural /-z/ → /-s/   following other voiceless consonants

We have identified the alternations in the regular English plural marker, illustrated in (8), as a morphophonemic process. The alternation in the Korean nominative case marker (2), on the other hand, is clearly not morphophonemic in nature. As we have noted several times, even though the choice between the two allomorphs is phonologically conditioned, there is no phonological similarity between the variant forms (/-i/ vs. /-ka/). There is no plausible phonological process which would change one form into the other. Thus, the Korean alternation seems to be a clear case of suppletive allomorphy, as stated in the preceding section.

The contrast between these two cases raises an obvious question: for any given example of phonologically conditioned allomorphy, how can we determine whether the alternation is morphophonemic or suppletive?[6] The basic intuition here, to oversimplify somewhat, is that a morphophonemic process replaces one *phoneme* with another, while a suppletive process replaces one *allomorph* with another. These two kinds of rules are conceptually very different, and they would play different roles in the overall organization of the grammar. But how can we decide which type of analysis is best in any particular case? Unfortunately there is no hard and fast answer to this question, but the following criteria will help to guide our decisions.

a   NATURALNESS: If the process is phonologically natural, i.e. a process which is found in the phonological systems of many different languages, it is more likely to be morphophonemic. A morphophonemic rule should be phonologically plausible. This criterion alone rules out a morphophonemic analysis of the Korean nominative allomorphy in (2).

b   PRODUCTIVITY: If the same process applies to several different morphemes, it is more likely to be morphophonemic. Patterns observed only in a single morpheme are more likely to be suppletive. Returning to the English definite article (1), it would not be implausible to find word-final /-n/ deleted by a phonological rule whenever the following word begins with a consonant. This may well be the historical source of the alternation. However, we argued above that this process is not productive in modern English; the alternation *a* vs. *an* is unique. We took this fact as evidence against a morphophonemic analysis, treating it rather as a case of phonologically conditioned suppletion.

c	SIMPLICITY: In any area of linguistic analysis, we generally look for the simplest possible grammar which will account for the data. However, it is important to look at the simplicity of the entire rule system, not just of one area (e.g. the phonology). We can always simplify one part of the grammar by adding complex rules to some other part. In the present context, we are interested in comparing two very different kinds of rules. This is not an easy thing to do; but in general, phonological rules are of a simpler type than rules of suppletive allomorphy. Thus if a plausible morphophonemic analysis is available, the criterion of simplicity would tend to favor that approach over a suppletive analysis.

To illustrate how these criteria can be applied, let us consider the Wantoat data in (11a). The allomorphs of the possessive suffixes are summarized in (11b).

(11)	**Wantoat** (Papua New Guinea; Merrifield et al. 1987, prob. 78)

a GLOSS

		'my _'	'your _'	'his _'	'our _'
'hand'		katakŋa	katakga	kataknʌ	katakŋin
'house'		yotna	yotda	yotnʌ	yotnin
'foot'		kepina	kepika	kepinʌ	kepinin

b ENVIRONMENT

	1sg	2sg	3sg	1pl
after -k	-ŋa	-ga	-ŋʌ	-ŋin
after -t	-na	-da	-nʌ	-nin
after -V	-na	-ka	-nʌ	-nin

Three of these morphemes show exactly the same pattern of allomorphy: initial /ŋ-/ following a velar alternating with initial /n-/ in other environments. If we were to treat this as a case of phonologically conditioned suppletion, we would have to write three separate allomorphic rules, one for each suffix. But it is possible to write just one simple morphophonemic rule which will account for all three alternations:

(12)	/n/ → /ŋ/	following a velar consonant

Thus the morphophonemic analysis is clearly simpler (one rule vs. three rules). The rule in (12) is a case of nasal assimilation, an extremely natural and familiar phonological process. And it is productive in this language, applying to at least three distinct suffixes. Thus all three of the criteria listed above support the morphophonemic analysis for these morphemes.

The second person possessive suffix, however, is more complicated. Here we have three distinct allomorphs in the three attested environments. Taking the form which occurs following a vowel as the basic form, the phonological changes involved are: (i) /k/ becomes /g/ following a /k/ (voicing dissimilation); and (ii) /k/ becomes /d/ following a /t/ (assimilation in place of articulation plus voicing dissimilation).

Which type of analysis is preferable in this case? Rules of dissimilation, and voicing dissimilation in particular, are found in many languages; but they are much less common than rules of assimilation. Thus the criterion of naturalness neither rules out nor strongly supports a morphophonemic analysis. The data set is extremely limited, and so offers no evidence regarding productivity (do the same changes occur in other morphemes?). And based on the very limited data available, there is no clear advantage of simplicity for one analysis over the other; either way, we will need two rules to account for the three possible forms. In the absence of additional data, either approach seems possible in this case. But since, as noted above, phonological rules are inherently simpler than rules of allomorphy, a morphophonemic analysis would probably be preferred as a preliminary hypothesis.

15.3   Rules for suppletive allomorphy

Linguists have expended a great deal of effort trying to develop precise formal notations for writing phonological rules, and a certain amount of consensus has emerged; but there is less agreement as to how rules of suppletive allomorphy should be written. For our purposes the exact form of the rule is not so important, but it must be stated clearly and precisely. It is always good practice to state any rule twice, once in prose and once in some more precise type of notation. A possible format for writing suppletive rules is illustrated below.

We have identified the alternation in the form of the Korean nominative marker as a case of phonologically conditioned suppletion: one allomorph replaced by another in a specific phonological environment. In addition to describing the alternation in prose, we need some kind of formal rule to make our description more precise. One possibility is shown in (13).

(13)
$$\{-ka\} \rightarrow \begin{cases} \text{-ka / V} + \_ \\ \text{-i / C} + \_ \end{cases}$$

In this rule, one allomorph is chosen as the basic form or label for the morpheme. This form is shown in braces {xx} on the left side of the rule, with the phonemic form of each specific allomorph listed on the right side. The "+" in the environment on the right side indicates a morpheme boundary. The rule in (13) can be interpreted as follows: "the suffix {-ka} is realized as /-i/ when it attaches to a stem ending in a consonant, but as /-ka/ when it attaches to a stem ending in a vowel."

A possible variation of this format would be to use a grammatical category, e.g. NOMINATIVE, as the label for the morpheme, rather than a phonological form. This is illustrated in (14).

(14)

$$\{\text{-NOM}\} \rightarrow \begin{Bmatrix} -\text{ka} / \text{V}+\_ \\ -\text{i} / \text{C}+\_ \end{Bmatrix}$$

As an example of lexically conditioned affix suppletion, let us return to the English past participle suffixes illustrated in (3). We will refer to the set of verbs that take the *–en* allomorph as "class 1" and the set of verbs that take the *–ed* allomorph as "class 2." (For simplicity, let us assume that these two classes are all that we need to deal with.) The lexical entry for each verb in English will have to contain a feature showing which class it belongs to. The rule of allomorphy specifies which allomorph will be chosen based on which of these features is found in the lexical entry. A simple way of writing such a rule is shown in (15b).

(15)   a **CLASS 1   CLASS 2**
        give   live
        take   bake
        hide   guide
        bite   sight
        know   owe

b $\{\text{-}en\} \rightarrow \begin{Bmatrix} -\text{en in V-class 1} \\ -\text{ed in V-class 2} \end{Bmatrix}$

15.4 Inflectional classes

Our analysis of the English past participle forms in (15) illustrates how a lexical category, e.g. Verb, can be divided into subclasses on the basis of suppletive allomorphy. When an affix has a limited number of allomorphs (in this case *–en* vs. *–ed*), and the choice of allomorph is lexically conditioned, we can classify words according to the allomorph they select. The lexical entry for each word in that category must include a feature that shows which subclass the word belongs to. A similar example was presented in (4), where we discovered that there are (at least) two distinct classes of nouns in Huichol: those that take *-ya* vs. those that take *yu-*.

Now consider the data in (16). It is clear that the markers for singular and plural number in Wali have several different allomorphs, and there seems to be no phonological pattern that would allow us to predict which allomorph will occur with which stem. The lexical entry for each common noun must include a feature that shows which form of the number markers that noun requires. These features will divide the set of common nouns into several different sub-classes: [N-class 1], [N-class 2], etc. Since sub-classes of this kind are based on shared patterns of allomorphy involving inflectional affixes, they are often referred to as INFLECTIONAL CLASSES.

(16)   **Wali** (Ghana; Merrifield et al. 1987, prob. 54)

SINGULAR		PLURAL	
nuɔ	'fowl'	nuɔ-hi	'fowls'
daa	'market'	daa-hi	'markets'
biɛ	'child'	biɛ-hi	'children'
wadze	'cloth'	wadze-hi	'cloths'
wɔɔ	'yam'	wɔɔ-hi	'yams'
dzel-a	'egg'	dzel-ii	'eggs'
n-a	'cow'	n-ii	'cows'
dau	'man'	dau-ba	'men'
poɣa	'woman'	poɣa-ba	'women'
nɔgba-ni	'lip'	nɔgba-ma	'lips'
kpakpa-ni	'arm'	kpakpa-ma	'arms'
gbɛbi-ri	'toe'	gbɛbi-ɛ	'toes'
libi-ri	'coin'	libi-ɛ	'coins'
lumbi-ri	'orange'	lumbi-ɛ	'oranges'
nubi-ri	'finger'	nubi-ɛ	'fingers'
nimbi-ri	'eye'	nimbi-ɛ	'eyes'

In traditional grammar, inflectional sub-classes of nouns are often referred to as DECLENSIONS; for verbs, inflectional sub-classes are called CONJUGATIONS. These labels are used especially when the subclassification determines not just the choice of allomorph for a single morpheme, but the allomorphs for an entire paradigm set.

Latin nouns are inflected for case and number, with both of these categories being marked by a single portmanteau suffix. The suffix which marks a particular combination of case and number, e.g. dative plural, can appear in several different forms (or allomorphs), and the distribution of these allomorphs is lexically conditioned. Each Latin noun can be assigned to one of five distinct sub-classes, or declensions, depending on the set of inflectional allomorphs which attach to that particular stem. Three of these declensions are illustrated in (17); for simplicity, only the singular paradigms are listed.

(17)   a **Latin 1st declension nouns (singular only)**

	woman	*star*	*sailor*
NOM	femin-a	stell-a	naut-a
GEN	femin-ae	stell-ae	naut-ae
DAT	femin-ae	stell-ae	naut-ae
ACC	femin-am	stell-am	naut-am
ABL	femin-ā	stell-ā	naut-ā

b **Latin 2nd declension nouns (singular only)**

	god	*slave*	*man*
NOM	de-us	serv-us	vir
GEN	de-i	serv-i	vir-i
DAT	de-ō	serv-ō	vir-ō
ACC	de-um	serv-um	vir-um
ABL	de-ō	serv-ō	vir-ō

c **Latin 3rd declension nouns (singular only)**

	city	*lion*	*father*	*body*
NOM	urbs[7]	leō	pater	corpus
GEN	urb-is	leōn-is	patr-is	corpor-is
DAT	urb-ī	leōn-ī	patr-ī	corpor-ī
ACC	urb-em	leōn-em	patr-em	corpus[8]
ABL	urb-e	leōn-e	patr-e	corpor-e

Each of the suffixes in this paradigm (i.e. each case-number marker) would have its own rule of allomorphy, conditioned by the declension class of the noun. Two sample rules are presented in (18).

(18) a $\{-\text{GEN.SG}\} \rightarrow$ $\left\{\begin{array}{ll} \textit{-ae} & \text{in N-class 1} \\ \textit{-i} & \text{in N-class 2} \\ \textit{-is} & \text{in N-class 3} \end{array}\right\}$

b $\{-\text{ABL.SG}\} \rightarrow$ $\left\{\begin{array}{ll} \textit{-ā} & \text{in N-class 1} \\ \textit{-ō} & \text{in N-class 2} \\ \textit{-e} & \text{in N-class 3} \end{array}\right\}$

It is important to distinguish inflectional classes like those illustrated in (15–17) from the gender classes discussed in chapter 8. Inflectional classes are determined by patterns of allomorphy appearing on the noun itself. Gender classes are determined by patterns of agreement observed in words which co-occur with the noun: modifiers, determiners, verbs, etc. So we may find two nouns of the same gender appearing in different inflectional classes, and nouns belonging to the same inflectional class which have different genders. The Latin 3rd declension, for example, includes nouns of all three genders. In (17c), *leō* 'lion' and *pater* 'father' are masculine; *urbs* 'city' is feminine; and *corpus* 'body' is neuter. The gender of these nouns is reflected in the form of their modifiers, as seen in *leō magnus* 'large lion,' *urbs magna* 'large city,' *corpus magnum* 'large body' (all in the nominative singular).

15.5   Conclusion

We have identified two basic types of allomorphy: morphophonemic change, in which the shape of a morpheme is altered by some phonological process; and suppletion, in which there is no regular phono-logical relationship between the two allomorphs. Suppletion may occur in roots or affixes, and is generally used to mark inflectional categories (tense, person, number, etc.), rather than derivational processes.

In the case of root suppletion, all of the suppletive forms must simply be listed in the lexical entry of the root. Affix suppletion, in contrast, can be described by rules like those illustrated in (13–15) and (18). These rules may be conditioned by the phonological shape, morphological structure, or lexical sub-class of the stem. When the suppletion is lexically conditioned, the lexical entry for each stem of the relevant category must include a class feature (e.g. [N-class 1], [N-class 2], etc.). These class features divide the words within that category into sub-classes, based on the allomorphs which appear on each word. In the case of nouns, it is important to remember that these inflectional classes may be different from the gender classes in the same language, which are determined on the basis of agreement patterns.

These different types of allomorphy are summarized in (19), which is adapted from Bickford (1998:163). This tree shows a logical way of clas-sifying the various patterns of allomorphy that we have discussed in this chapter, but it does not necessarily match the procedural order we would follow in analyzing a particular pattern.

(19)

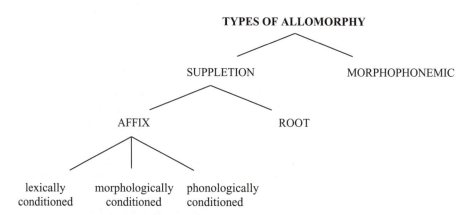

When we set out to analyze the patterns of allomorphy in a body of data, the first step is normally to observe which morphemes appear in more than one form. This will include noticing whether alternations occur in roots or affixes. The second step is (typically) to look for a phonological conditioning environment. If the choice of allomorph is predictable on phonological grounds, we need to decide whether it is best analyzed as a morphophon-emic process, or as a case of phonologically conditioned suppletion. If the choice of allomorph is not phonologically predictable, there are two basic options. Suppletive forms of the same root will be listed in the lexical entry of that root; suppletive forms of an affix will be related by a rule which refers to lexical sub-classes of the words which bear that affix, as discussed above.

Practice exercises

A Spanish verbs (Merrifield et al. 1987, prob. 48; contrastive stress not indicated)

The table below contains a small part of the verb paradigm for Spanish. Based on the data presented here:

(i)   state what kind of allomorphy is observed;

(ii)   write rules of the appropriate type to account for all of the allomorphs;

(iii)   does your analysis require assigning Spanish verbs to distinct sub-classes (conjugations)? if so, list the verbs in each conjugation.

	INFINITIVE	1st SG	3rd SG	1st PL	PARTICIPLE
'create'	kre-ar	kre-o	kre-a	kre-amos	kre-ado
'stop'	par-ar	par-o	par-a	par-amos	par-ado
'throw out'	bot-ar	bot-o	bot-a	bot-amos	bot-ado
'burn'	kem-ar	kem-o	kem-a	kem-amos	kem-ado
'believe'	kre-er	kre-o	kre-e	kre-emos	kre-ido
'insert'	met-er	met-o	met-e	met-emos	met-ido
'eat'	kom-er	kom-o	kom-e	kom-emos	kom-ido
'drink'	beb-er	beb-o	beb-e	beb-emos	beb-ido
'depart'	part-ir	part-o	part-e	part-imos	part-ido
'stir'	bat-ir	bat-o	bat-e	bat-imos	bat-ido
'live'	bib-ir	bib-o	bib-e	bib-imos	bib-ido

B Latin nouns (continued)

Based on the table below:

(i)   identify the noun class (declension) and gender of each noun;

(ii)   state the specific criteria that you use to identify declensions and genders;

(iii)   list the affixes which occur on modifiers (including both adjectives and quantifiers) in a position class chart.

GLOSS	NOMINATIVE	ACCUSATIVE
'one good letter'	una epistula bona	unam epistulam bonam
'one good girl'	una puella bona	unam puellam bonam
'many good letters'	multae epistulae bonae	multās epistulās bonās
'many good girls'	multae puellae bonae	multās puellās bonās

'one good farmer'	unus agricola bonus	unum agricolam bonum
'one good poet'	unus poēta bonus	unum poētam bonum
'many good farmers'	multī agricolae bonī	multōs agricolās bonōs
'many good poets'	multī poētae bonī	multōs poētās bonōs
'one good mother'	una māter bona	unam mātrem bonam
'one good method/reason'	una ratiō bona	unam ratiōnem bonam
'many good mothers'	multae mātrēs bonae	multās mātrēs bonās
'many good methods'	multae ratiōnēs bonae	multās ratiōnēs bonās
'one good soldier'	unus mīles bonus	unum mīlitem bonum
'one good king'	unus rēx bonus	unum rēgem bonum
'many good soldiers'	multī mīlitēs bonī	multōs mīlitēs bonōs
'many good kings'	multī rēgēs bonī	multōs rēgēs bonōs

Exercises

15A Southern Azerbaijani (Iran; Lee 1996)

List the affixes you find in the following verb forms, grouped according to their semantic function (e.g. tense, aspect, modality, etc.). Write the appropriate rules to account for any cases of allomorphy. Based on the available evidence, construct a tentative position class chart for these verbs, and discuss remaining areas of uncertainty (or "residue") in your analysis.

gəldim	'I came'	gəldik	'we came'
gəldin	'you (sg) came'	gəldiz	'you (pl) came'
gəldi	'he came'	gəldilər	'they came'
gəlirəm	'I am coming'	gəlirik	'we are coming'
gəlirsən	'you (sg) are coming'	gəlirsiz	'you (pl) are coming'
gəlir	'he is coming'	gəlirlər	'they are coming'
gələcəyəm	'I will come'	gələcəyik	'we will come'
gələcəksən	'you (sg) will come'	gələcəksiz	'you (pl) will come'
gələcək	'he will come'	gələcəxlər	'they will come'
gəlmişəm	'I have come'	gəlmişik	'we have come'
gəlibsən	'you (sg) have come'	gəlibsiz	'you (pl) have come'
gəlib	'he has come'	gəliblər	'they have come'
getdim	'I went'	getdin	'you (sg) went'
getdi	'he went'	getdilər	'they went'
gedəcəksən	'you (sg) will go'	gedəcək	'he will go'
gedirəm	'I am going'	gedirsən	'you (sg) are going'
gedirdi	'he was going'	getməlisən	'you (sg) must go'
getməli	'he must go'	getməlilər	'they must go'
getmişdi	'he had gone'	gedib	'he has gone'
getmiş	'reportedly he went'	getmisən	'reportedly you (sg) went'

gedirmişlər	'reportedly they were going'	getmişlər	'reportedly they went'
*getmişdi	(for: 'reportedly he went')	*getdimiş	(for: 'reportedly he went')
almɨşɨx	'we have taken'	alacağɨx	'we will take'
alɨbsɨz	'you (pl) have taken'	alacaxsiz	'you (pl) will take'
alɨblar	'they have taken'	alacaxlar	'they will take'
alsam	'if I take'	alsax	'if we take'
alsan	'if you (sg) take'	alsaz	'if you (pl) take'
alsa	'if he takes'	alsalar	'if they take'
gəlsə	'if he comes'	verdi	'he gave'
gəlirdi	'he was coming'	versəm	'if I give'
gəlibmiş	'reportedly he has come'	verirmiş	'reportedly he was giving'
gedərdi	'he used to go'	verərmiş	'reportedly he used to give'

zefer qazanmişmişam 'reportedly I have won' (*zefer* 'victory'; *qazan-* 'win')

Additional exercises

Merrifield et al. (1987) prob. 44, 45, 46, 47, 56, 61, 62, 63, 65, 70, 78, 110, 115, 117, 246
Healey (1990b), ex. H.4, 16, 17, 22, 23, 26

Notes

1. We are ignoring simple allophonic variation for the purposes of this chapter.
2. The term is sometimes also applied to cases where some similarity of form remains between the allomorphs but the relationship is phonologically irregular, as in the plural forms *man/men*, *goose/geese*, *mouse/mice*, etc. So, in this extended usage of the term, any allomorphy which cannot be analyzed as morphophonemic can be considered to be a case of suppletion.
3. This analysis is based on Bill Merrifield's unpublished teacher's guide for Merrifield et al. (1987). Thanks to Cal Rensch for additional clarification.
4. In earlier forms of English, this kind of alternation did occur in other forms such as *my ~ mine*, *thy ~ thine*. Evidence of this alternation is preserved in poetic forms, e.g. *Mine eyes have seen the glory . . .*
5. In particular, the issue of which form to take as the "basic" or underlying form is extremely important; but we cannot address it in the present volume.
6. We can assume, at least for the purposes of this book, that lexically conditioned allomorphy is always suppletive.
7. René van den Berg has pointed out to me that the *-s* in *urbs* preserves the old nominative case marker.
8. Neuter 3rd declension nouns do not take the *–em* suffix.

16 Non-linear morphology

Up to this point we have discussed only two kinds of morphological markers: prefixes and suffixes. For that reason, most of the word structures we have examined thus far have been quite "linear": a simple sequence of morphemes (root plus affixes) strung together one after another, like beads on a string. However, we have already seen a few examples of more complex word structure.

In chapter 9, section 9.4, we discussed the Tagalog aspect markers. We saw that realis non-active verbs are marked by an affix *-in-* that occurs, not before or after the root, but *inside* it, as illustrated in the "past" forms in (1). This marker is neither a prefix nor a suffix; we referred to it as an INFIX. We also saw that non-completive aspect is marked by copying the first consonant and vowel of the root, as seen in the "future" forms in (1). We referred to this process as REDUPLICATION.

(1)   **Tagalog aspect markers**
Gloss	**Infinitive**	**"Past"**	**"Future"**
'to be given'	bigy-an	b[in]igy-an	*bi*-bigy-an
'to be made, done'	gawa-in	g[in]awa	*ga*-gawa-in

In chapter 13 we referred to the Malay nominalizer *ke-. . . -an*, illustrated in (2), as a CIRCUMFIX. Again, this affix is neither a prefix nor a suffix; it seems to be both at once, or rather a combination of the two.

(2)   **Malay abstract noun formation**
ROOT		DERIVED FORM	
baik	'good'	ke-baik-an	'goodness, kindness'
bersih	'clean'	ke-bersih-an	'cleanliness'
miskin	'poor'	ke-miskin-an	'poverty'
mati	'dead; to die'	ke-mati-an	'death'
lahir	'be born'	ke-lahir-an	'birth'

Hockett (1954) discussed two different approaches that linguists have taken to the analysis of word structure. One of these, which he called the ITEM AND ARRANGEMENT (IA) model, assumes that all morphology is affixation. The rules of grammar must arrange the morphemes in the correct linear order, after which the rules of phonology will apply to produce the form that is actually pronounced.

The second approach, which Hockett called the ITEM AND PROCESS (IP) model, treats affixation as just one among many ways in which morphological rules may modify the form of the base. The IP model does not treat a morpheme as a string of phonemes which gets attached to the base, but rather as a pattern of phonological change which is associated with some consistent semantic or grammatical effect. Of course, one way in which the base form can be modified is simply to add a specific string of phonemes to it, resulting in affixation of the familiar sort. But many other kinds of modification are attested in human languages as well, as we will see in the following sections.

Circumfixes, infixes, and reduplication are examples of morphological marking which is not simple, linear, affixation. These patterns, and others to be discussed below, are difficult to represent in a position class chart, and (at least at first glance) seem to cause serious problems for the IA model. However, recent developments in phonological theory have made it possible to describe many of these processes as special types of affixation. So the debate between the IA and IP viewpoints continues to be a major topic of discussion in morphological theory.

The theoretical issues involved are far beyond the scope of the present book. Our primary goal in this chapter will be to introduce the standard terminology used for various types of non-linear morphology, and to help you recognize these patterns when you encounter them.

16.1   Non-linear sequencing of affixes

16.1.1   Infixation

As mentioned above, an INFIX is an affix that is added inside another morpheme. Two well-known examples are found in Tagalog: the realis marker *-in-*, mentioned above; and the Active Voice marker *-um-*. Cognate forms occur in Kimaragang Dusun, with slightly different functions. (3a) shows the use of the past tense marker *–in–* (see chapter 9 (2)) with transitive roots in the passive voice, while (3b) shows the use of both infixes with intransitive roots. Another example is the plural marker on Oaxaca Chontal nouns (4).

(3)   **Kimaragang Dusun**

    a past tense marker *–in–* with transitive roots (shown in passive voice)

ROOT	PAST (PASSIVE)	GLOSS
patay	p-in-atay	'was killed'
takaw	t-in-akaw	'was stolen'
babo'	b-in-abo'	'was carried (on back)'
garas	g-in-aras	'was butchered'

b active voice *–um–* plus past tense *–in–* with intransitive roots

ROOT	NON-PAST	PAST	GLOSS
talib	t-um-alib	t-in-um-alib	'to pass by'
rikot	r-um-ikot	r-in-um-ikot	'to arrive'
laguy	l-um-aguy	l-in-um-aguy	'to leap'
silaw	s-um-ilaw	s-in-um-ilaw	'to turn yellow'

(4)   **Oaxaca Chontal** (Mexico; Merrifield et al. 1987, prob. 17)

ROOT		PLURAL	
cece	'squirrel'	cełce	'squirrels'
sewiʔ	'magpie'	sełwiʔ	'magpies'
akan'oʔ	'woman'	akałn'oʔ	'women'

In analyzing and describing an infix, it is crucial to specify precisely where the infix occurs. Usually the point of insertion will be one phonological unit (e.g. one phoneme or syllable) from an edge (beginning or end) of the stem. In the Tagalog and Kimaragang examples, the infixes are inserted immediately after the initial consonant. In the Chontal example (4), the infix is inserted immediately before the final syllable.

It is also important to remember that the term "infix" cannot be applied to every affix that occurs in the middle of a word. It refers specifically to an affix which is inserted inside another morpheme. Many languages allow long strings of affixes, but as long as they occur one after another, rather than one inside another, none of them would be called infixes. For example, consider the negative marker in (5b), repeated from chapter 11. If we compare the negative verb in (5b) with the corresponding positive form in (5a), we could say that the negative affix gets inserted in the middle of the word. However, it does not occur inside another morpheme, but between the root and its suffixes; so it is not an infix, but just another suffix.

(5)   **Turkish** (Underhill 1976:48, 57)

a kitab-ï   oku-du-nuz.
  book-ACC read-PAST-2pl
  'You (pl) read the book.'

b kitab-ï   okú-*ma*-dï-nïz.
  book-ACC read-NEG-PAST-2pl
  'You (pl) did not read the book.'

Typically infixes are inserted into the root, but they may also occur inside other affixes as in the following Kimaragang examples: root *omot* 'to harvest (rice),' active transitive *mong-omot*, past tense *m[in]ong-omot* 'harvested'; root *talib* 'pass by', causative *pa-talib*, past tense *p[in]a-talib* 'allowed (someone) to pass.'

16.1.2 Circumfixes and other discontinuous morphemes

A CIRCUMFIX is a discontinuous affix, with elements added both before and after the stem, as illustrated from Malay in (2) and Basari in (6). Nouns in Basari carry markers that indicate their noun class and number (singular vs. plural). Some of these markers are circumfixes:

(6)   **Basari** (Ghana; Healey 1990b, ex. E.1)

u-ni	'person'	bi-ni-ib	'persons'
u-bɔti	'chief'	bi-bɔti-ib	'chiefs'
ku-saa-u	'farm'	ti-saa-ti	'farms'
ku-kabu-u	'basket'	ti-kabu-ti	'baskets'

A circumfix is often described as a combination of a prefix plus a suffix. But if both the prefix and suffix elements exist in the language as independent affixes, and if the meaning of the combined form is predictable from the independent meanings of the prefix and suffix, then the combination would not be regarded as a circumfix. The two parts of a circumfix must function as a single unit, both semantically and morphologically.

For example, the Malay circumfix illustrated in (2) consists of two parts, *ke-* and *-an*. The second of these elements, *-an*, does occur on its own as a suffix; it is relatively productive and has a variety of uses. The prefix *ke-*, however, is not productive and occurs only in a small number of frozen forms. Moreover, the meaning of the nominalizer *ke-* . . . *-an* cannot be derived from the meanings of its two component parts on their own. That is why the combination is considered to be a single affix, i.e. a circumfix.

Circumfixes are a fairly common type of discontinuous morpheme, but there are other types as well. A frequently cited example is the complex pattern of morphology in Semitic languages, in which the root consists only of consonants, while the vowels and syllable patterns are determined by derivational and inflectional processes.

(7)   **Hebrew** (Saad and Bolozky 1984:106; Merrifield et al. 1987, prob. 20)

ROOT		CAUSATIVE	
naħal	'inherit'	hinħil	'bequest'
qaraʔ	'read'	hiqriʔ	'make read'
tˤaraf	'devour'	hitˤrif	'feed'
raqad	'dance'	hirqid	'make dance'
šaʔal	'borrow'	hišʔil	'lend'

16.2 Modifications of phonological features

16.2.1 Mutation

MUTATION refers to a change in the quality of one or more phonemes in the base form. Vowel mutation is relatively common, and is often referred to by the more specific term ABLAUT. German provides many examples, both in nominal forms (singular vs. plural, similar to the English *goose/geese*) and in the paradigms of the "strong" verbs. A few of the many patterns of ablaut in verb stems are shown in (8). Of course, similar examples are found in English as well: *sing/sang, drink/drank, swim/swam, run/ran, eat/ate*, etc. These examples are interesting because the change in vowel quality itself is the marker for past tense; at least superficially, there appears to be no past tense affix involved.

(8)   **German strong verbs** (Stern and Bleiler 1961:100–101)

	PRESENT STEM	PAST TENSE
'offer'	biet-	bot
'fly'	flieg-	flog
'flow'	fliess-	floss
'read'	les-	las
'give'	geb-	gab
'help'	helf-	half
'roast'	brat-	briet
'fall'	fall-	fiel
'catch'	fang-	fing

One of the most famous examples of consonant mutation is found in Welsh:

(9)   **Welsh** (Robins 1964:201)

ta:d	'father'	garð	'garden'
və nha:d	'my father'	və ŋarð	'my garden'
i da:d	'his father'	i arð	'his garden'
i θa:d	'her father'	i garð	'her garden'
i ta:d	'their father'	i garð	'their garden'

16.2.2 "Suprafixes"

The term SUPRAFIX is sometimes used to refer to a morphological marker which consists only of a change to some SUPRASEGMENTAL feature: tone, stress, length, nasalization, etc. A famous example is found in Terena, in which nasalization is used to indicate a first person singular possessor:

(10)   **Terena** (Brazil; Bendor-Samuel 1960)

emoʔu	'his word'	ẽmõʔũ	'my word'
ayo	'his brother'	ãyõ	'my brother'
owoku	'his house'	õwõkũ	'my house'

Tone changes are used morphologically in a number of tone languages. High tone is used as a derivational affix in Birom, marking deverbal nominalization:

(11)   **Birom** (Nigeria; Bouquiaux 1970:193–194; Matthews 1991:141)
         Note: mid tone is unmarked.

	VERB	**NOMINALIZATION**
'surpass'	dàl	dál
'break'	mɔ̀pɔ̀s	mɔ́pɔ́s
'follow'	ra:	rá:
'roast'	halaŋ	háláŋ
'see'	dí	dí
'run'	télé	télé

16.3   Copying, deleting, re-ordering, etc.

16.3.1   Reduplication

REDUPLICATION involves the repetition of all or part of the base form. Reduplication is extremely widespread, and occurs in many different forms. A few representative examples are given in (12). Some of the critical issues which must be clarified in the analysis of reduplication include the following.

a   How much material is copied: the whole word, just one syllable, just a CV sequence?

b   If less than the whole word is copied, which specific portions are copied: which syllable, or which CV sequence?

c   Where does the copy attach? Reduplication most often occurs as a prefix or suffix (i.e. at an edge of the stem to which it applies); but reduplicative infixes are also found.

d   Is the reduplicated element an exact copy, or are there changes in vowel quality, initial consonant, etc.?

(12)   a **Full reduplication in Malay**

BASE FORM		**REDUPLICATED**	
kanak	'child'	kanak-kanak	'children'
negara	'country'	negara-negara	'countries'
pemimpin	'leader'	pemimpin-pemimpin	'leaders'
pelajar	'student'	pelajar-pelajar	'students'

b **Partial reduplication in Tagalog**

ROOT		ACTIVE PRESENT
bigay	'give'	nag-bi-bigay
ʔusap	'converse'	nag-ʔu-ʔusap
trabaho	'work'	nag-ta-trabaho

c **Modified reduplication in Malay**

ROOT		COLLECTIVE
sayur	'vegetable'	sayur-mayur
kuih	'cake'	kuih-muih
lauk	'gravy, viand'	lauk-pauk
saudara	'cousin, relation'	saudara-mara
gunung	'mountain'	gunung-ganang
rumput	'grass'	rumput-rampai
kayu	'wood'	kayu-kayan
batu	'stone'	batu-batan
asal	'origin'	asal-usul

16.3.2 Subtractive morphology

Subtractive morphology (or just SUBTRACTION) is a relatively rare phenomenon. The term refers to a morphological process which, instead of adding material, actually deletes one or more phonemes from the base. Consider the Papago forms in (13).

(13)   **Papago** (N. America; Hale 1965:301; stress not shown)

	BASE	PERFECTIVE
'haul'	huhag	huha
'laugh'	huhuɯm	huhuɯ
'cook'	hidoḍ	hido
'swing'	wiḍut	wiḍu
'shoot'	gatwid	gatwi
'wake'	wuhan	wuha
'give'	maak	maa
'split'	taapan	taap
'descend'	huḍuɲ	huḍ
'shell corn'	kɯliw	kɯl

If we consider any single pair in isolation, we might suppose that the base form is created by adding a suffix to the perfective form. But this analysis could require us to recognize as many allomorphs of the suffix as there are consonants in the language (in fact more, under Hale's analysis), and no way to predict which suffix occurs with which root. By far the simpler analysis is to assume that the perfective is formed by deleting the final consonant of the base form.[1]

16.3.3 Metathesis

The term METATHESIS refers to the reversal of two elements: $xy \rightarrow yx$. PHONOLOGICAL METATHESIS, i.e. a morphophonemic process that reverses the order of two phonemes in a particular phonological context, is not too unusual. For example, some roots in Tagalog lose the vowel of their final syllable when a suffix is added, as illustrated in (14a). If this vowel deletion creates a consonant cluster in which a labial follows a dental/alveolar, as in (14b), the order of the consonants in the cluster is reversed. This kind of metathesis can be viewed as a "repair strategy" which a language may use to deal with impermissible clusters or other syllable patterns which are not allowed in that language.

(14) **Suffixation in Tagalog** (Kenstowicz and Kisseberth 1979:72; Aspillera 1969; English 1986)

	ROOT		SUFFIXED FORM
a	bukas	'open'	buks-an
	putol	'cut'	putl-an
	bilih[2]	'buy'	bilh-in
	sunod	'follow, obey'	sund-in
b	tanim	'plant'	tamn-an
	talab	'pierce, affect'	tabl-an
	dilim	'dark'	ma-diml-an

Cases of MORPHOLOGICAL METATHESIS, i.e. cases in which the metathesis itself is used as the marker for a particular grammatical feature, are much harder to find. One of the most famous examples is the Malayo-Polynesian language Rotuman, spoken east of Fiji. The basic syllable pattern in Rotuman is (C)V, so most words end with a vowel in their basic or "citation" form. This is also the form that would be used in a noun phrase that refers to a definite, specific entity. When a noun phrase is used with indefinite or non-specific reference, the last word in the NP is marked by reversing the order of the final vowel and consonant. The resulting CVVC sequence is then "squeezed" down into a single C(C)VC syllable by various phonological processes such as glide formation, vowel coalescence, etc. Some of these processes are illustrated in (15). (Notice that many of the words in this list are not nouns. This is because indefiniteness is marked only on the last word of the NP, which is not necessarily the head noun. In relative clauses, for example, the modifying clause follows the head noun, so the last word of the phrase could belong to virtually any category.) The key point here is that the metathesis is triggered by a syntactic (or perhaps pragmatic) feature, [-definite], rather than a specific phonological context. Such examples are quite rare.

(15)   **Rotuman indefinite marking** (Besnier 1987:208–209)

DEFINITE	INDEFINITE (underlying)	INDEFINITE (surface)	GLOSS
pija	piaj	pyɔj	'rat'
tife	tief	tyɔf	'pearl shell'
hepa	heap	hyap	'broad'
puka	puak	pwɔk	'creeper species'
loŋa	loaŋ	lwaŋ	'towards interior of island'
rito	riot	ryot	'to glitter'
ulo	uol	wol	'seabird species'
toŋi	toiŋ	tøŋ	'to buy'
fuli	fuil	fül	'deaf'
pɔti	pɔit	pɛt	'scar'

16.4   Inflectional rules

The phenomena discussed in this chapter seem to raise problems for the Item and Arrangement (IA) model of morphology. It is not easy to see (at first glance) how infixes, circumfixes, suprafixes, mutation, reduplication, metathesis, and subtraction can be adequately represented using only linear sequences of morphemes. As we stated in the introduction to this chapter, recent developments in phonological theory do, in fact, provide ways of handling many of these processes as kinds of affixation, though whether this is the best analysis remains a hotly debated issue. In any case, such analyses require a more sophisticated knowledge of phonology than we can assume in this book, so we will not attempt to discuss them here.

Our immediate goal is to provide a way of describing non-linear morphological processes as part of a basic grammatical description. For this purpose, we will adopt an approach closer to the Item and Process (IP) model. In a sense, such an approach is already built into our format for writing Word Formation Rules. The phonological change involved in the derivation need not be simple affixation. Using the format developed in chapter 13, for example, we could write a rule for the Malay circumfix in (2) as follows:

(16)   **Malay deverbal nominalization**:

$[X]_{VERB}$ $\leftrightarrow$ $[ke\text{-}X\text{-}an]_{NOUN}$
meaning: 'to x'   meaning: 'the act of x-ing'

But WFRs are designed to represent only derivational processes. As we have seen, non-linear morphological processes may be used to mark either inflection or derivation, so we need a different kind of rule to handle the

inflectional cases. Until now we have been assuming that inflectional morphology can be represented in a position class chart, but the processes we
have discussed in this chapter are precisely those for which such a chart is
likely to be inadequate.

Inflectional morphology is used to mark grammatical features such as
tense, person, case, etc. Some linguists assume that these features are added
to the stem by a special type of syntactic rule, based on the word's syntactic
environment. Under this approach, the presence of the feature would trigger
an inflectional rule to produce the correct word form, whether by adding an
affix or by some other process.

We will adopt a slightly different approach here. Let us assume that
the inflectional rules themselves introduce the grammatical features and at
the same time modify the phonological shape of the base in some way.
The inflected forms produced by these rules are then available for lexical insertion whenever their grammatical features are compatible with the
syntactic context.

Let us consider some concrete examples, without trying to provide a completely rigorous system for writing such rules. The first person possessive
morpheme in Terena (10) could be represented roughly as in (17). This rule
is intended to describe a process which: (i) nasalizes all the vowels in the
word; and (ii) adds the grammatical feature [1st pers. poss].

(17)   **Terena possessive marking**
       $[\ldots V \ldots]_{\text{NOUN}} \rightarrow [\ldots \tilde{V} \ldots]_{\text{NOUN}}$
       [1st pers. poss]

Similarly, the function of the Kimaragang past tense marker *-in-* (3) could
be represented as in (18a). The perfective morpheme in Papago (13) could
be represented as a process which deletes the final consonant in the word, as
shown in (18b). And, of course, this same notation could be used to describe
ordinary prefixes and suffixes, if desired. Remember to supplement each rule
with a prose description of the pattern that it expresses.

(18)   a **Kimaragang past tense**
         $[CVX]_{\text{VERB}} \rightarrow [CinVX]_{\text{VERB}}$
         [past tense]

       b **Papago perfective**
         $[\ldots VC]_{\text{VERB}} \rightarrow [\ldots V]_{\text{VERB}}$
         [perfective]

16.5   Conclusion

The IP approach makes it much easier to describe the kinds of non-
linear morphology discussed in this chapter. It achieves this by setting up

a special kind of rule for morphological processes. These rules are potentially powerful enough to describe any sort of modification at all, but this descriptive power is both good and bad. It has the virtue of accounting for all attested morphological patterns in a fairly uniform manner. The problem is that it would be just as easy to write the same kind of rule for patterns which are not attested in any human language. Thus, a major focus of research for this approach is the question of how to define a possible morphological rule.

The IA approach avoids the need to recognize a special class of morphological processes. Given the power and complexity of current phonological frameworks, it turns out to be possible to analyze most of the phenomena discussed above in terms of affixation (of a somewhat abstract kind) plus phonological rules. This approach makes it possible to maintain a simpler model of how the different parts of the grammatical system relate to each other. On the other hand, it is not always clear that the "phonological" processes needed to account for these phenomena are, in fact, purely phonological. A few problem areas remain for which no really adequate IA analysis has been found; and in other cases there is disagreement as to whether the IA approach can provide a truly adequate account of the data. The attempt to overcome these problems has been one of the driving forces in the development of recent phonological theories.

Exercises

16A Bekwarra (Nigeria; Roberts 1999, ex. M-13.2)
Describe the verbal morphology illustrated in the following data, using both prose and charts or rules of the appropriate type.

1.   abe éfàà   'they grind'
2.   abe éfaà   'they learn'
3.   abe éfaa   'they roast'
4.   abe efàà   'they ground'
5.   abe èfàà   'they should grind'
6.   abe éhàrà   'they answer'
7.   abe ehàrà   'they answered'
8.   abe èhàrà   'they should answer'

16B Palantla Chinantec (Mexico; based on Merrifield et al. 1987, prob. 157, adapted by W. Merrifield; phonemic tone is not indicated)
Describe the grammatical structure of the following examples, including any examples of affixation and allomorphy. Use PS rules, position class charts, or other types of rules as appropriate, and give a complete list of roots for each lexical category.

1.	laʔʔniw	'You will buy it.'
2.	kabǎhni	'I struck (the animal).'
3.	kalãhni zɯy	'I bought the dog(s).'
4.	bǎza ŋyé	'He will strike the pig(s).'
5.	kalahni ʔma	'I bought the wood.'
6.	báza ŋyí	'He will strike the metal object(s).'
7.	kalãʔʔniw ŋyé pã	'You bought the fat pig(s).'
8.	bǎʔʔniw ow ŋyé	'You will strike two pigs.'
9.	kabáza kũw ʔma	'He struck one piece of wood.'
10.	bǎʔʔniw úw zɯy	'You will strike three dogs.'
11.	bǎhni zɯy cǎʔ	'I will strike the dirty dog(s).'
12.	kalaʔʔniw ŋyí pa	'You bought the big metal objects.'
13.	kabáʔʔniw tõ ŋyí	'You struck two metal objects.'
14.	lahni ʔma cǎʔ	'I will buy the dirty wood.'
15.	báhni ʔnɯa ŋyí cǎʔ	'I will strike three dirty metal objects.'
16.	lãhni ow zɯy cǎʔ	'I will buy two dirty dogs.'
17.	kalaʔʔniw ʔnɯa ʔma pa	'You bought three big pieces of wood.'
18.	lahni kũw ŋyí cǎʔ	'I will buy one dirty metal object.'
19.	kalãhni hã ŋyé cǎʔ	'I bought one dirty pig.'
20.	kabǎza hã zɯy pã	'He struck one fat dog.'
21.	lãza	'He will buy (the animal).'

Additional exercises

Merrifield et al. (1987) prob. 16, 17, 19, 20, 21, 51, 58, 77, 86, 87, 88, 89, 96, 97, 118

Healey (1990b), ex. H.24

Notes

1. The forms given in (13) are based on Hale's phonetic representations. The vowel preceding the final consonant is also deleted in the last three forms by a regular but somewhat complex morphophonemic process. In terms of Hale's Underlying Representations for these verbs, the rule of perfective formation always deletes the final-CV of the stem.

2. The final –h in *bilih* is not written in the standard orthography, but is assumed to be present in the underlying form.

17 Clitics

In chapter 2 we identified two basic classes of morphemes, free vs. bound. We said that free morphemes are those which can occur as independent words, while bound morphemes are those which cannot occur by themselves as complete words. An important difference between affixes and roots is that affixes are always bound, while roots may be (and in English usually are) free.

In this chapter we will discuss forms which are difficult to classify as either free or bound, forms that in some ways seem like independent words but in other ways seem more like affixes. Ambiguous elements of this type are called CLITICS.

To begin with a specific example, let us look at verbal inflection in Amele, a Papuan language of New Guinea. Verbs in Amele are marked for subject agreement, object agreement (optional), tense, mood, and certain other categories. In most sentences, these markers appear as suffixes on the verb, as in (1).

(1)   **Amele** (PNG; Roberts 1988:59)
        Waga   q-it-igi-an . . .
        crocodile hit-1sg.OBJ-3sg.SUBJ-FUT
        'The crocodile will get me . . .'

However, in certain contexts these "suffixes" may be separated from the verb and occur as free forms; that is, they can be pronounced as independent words. Some examples are given in (2–4).

(2)   **Amele** (PNG; Roberts 1996:26–27, 37, 58)
    a Mel aid   uqa ahul   eu himéc gel-*ad-éi-a*.[1]
      boy female 3sg coconut that only   scrape-3pl.OBJ-3sg.SUBJ-REC.PAST
      'The girl scraped only those coconuts.'
    b Mel aid   uqa ahul   eu gél   himéc *ad-éi-a*.
      boy female 3sg coconut that scrape only   3pl.OBJ-3sg.SUBJ-REC.PAST
      'The girl only scraped those coconuts.'

(3)   a Ege cain   cucui-*uq-aun*.
      1pl do.not! fear-1pl.SUBJ-NEG.FUT
      'We must not be afraid.'

b Ege cucui cain   *uq-aun.*
1pl fear   do.not! 1pl.SUBJ-NEG.FUT
'We MUST NOT be afraid.'

(4)   a Uqa ho-*na.*
3sg come-3sg.SUBJ-PRES
'He is coming.'

b Uqa l-i   l-i   h-u   h-u   *ena.*
3sg go-PRED go-PRED come-PRED come-PRED 3sg.SUBJ-PRES
'He comes and goes.'

Roberts (1996) demonstrates that the tense and agreement markers are not affixes (in the usual sense) but auxiliaries which occur in clause-final position.[2] When these auxiliaries occur next to the verb stem, as in (1), (2a), (3a), and (4a), they are "phonologically bound" to the verb, i.e. pronounced as part of the same PHONOLOGICAL WORD. This is the most common pattern. However, in a number of contexts they may also stand alone as separate phonological words, as illustrated in (2b), (3b), and (4b).

Notice that the syntactic position of the Amele auxiliaries is the same in both cases. The attachment of the auxiliaries to the verb stem in the (a) examples appears to be purely phonological. The rules of syntax which determine the order of elements in the clause must treat these auxiliaries as independent words, whether they are finally pronounced that way or not. Thus, the bound forms of the auxiliaries in (1), (2a), (3a), and (4a) match very well a standard definition of a CLITIC: an element which is "syntactically free but phonologically bound."

The phrase "syntactically free" means that the rules of syntax treat the clitic as an independent word. The phrase "phonologically bound" means that the clitic is pronounced as if it were affixed to an adjacent word. (This word is called the clitic's HOST.) So we need to be able to make a distinction between phonological words and syntactic words; a clitic and its host constitute a single phonological word but two separate syntactic words. In the following section we will discuss this issue in greater detail.

17.1   What is a "word?"

We have said that, in the prototypical case, clitics have the syntactic status of independent words but the phonological status of affixes. This means that a clitic does not constitute an independent phonological word. It may seem surprising to speak of a difference between phonological words and syntactic words; but consider the traditional description of the "contracted" forms of English auxiliaries in sentences like the following:

(5)   a I'm going home now.
b She'll be coming around the mountain.

In traditional terms we say that forms like *I'm* and *she'll* are CONTRAC-TIONS, meaning that two separate syntactic words, a pronoun and an auxiliary verb, are pronounced as a single phonological word. The second elements in these contracted forms (the reduced auxiliary verbs, *'m* and *'ll*) are shortened to the point that they can no longer be pronounced meaningfully in isolation, since they contain no vowels. Thus they are no longer independent phonological words, and are often analyzed as clitics.

How are we to tell the difference between phonological words and syntactic words? How can we identify the word boundaries of each type? Let us begin by focusing on the phonological word.

First, a phonological word is the smallest possible utterance in the language; speakers do not normally say anything which is smaller than a complete phonological word. As noted above, the reduced auxiliary forms *'m* and *'ll* cannot be pronounced meaningfully in isolation, because they are too "short" to be independent phonological words. Furthermore, deliberate pauses and intonation breaks occur only at phonological word boundaries, and never in the middle of a phonological word.[3]

Second, each phonological word is composed of one or more well-formed syllables (i.e. syllables which satisfy the constraints on syllable structure in the language). The contracted forms *I'm* and *she'll* each contain only a single syllable, so they cannot contain more than one phonological word.

Third, stress placement is frequently determined by phonological word boundaries, and each phonological word normally contains only a single primary stress. Notice, for example, the contrast in stress placement indicated in the last few words of (2a) vs. (2b); the acute accent in those examples marks primary stress. In particular, note that the root *gel-* in (2a) does not receive a primary stress because it is part of a larger phonological word.

Many other phonological rules are also sensitive to phonological word boundaries in various languages. Harmony systems frequently apply only within a phonological word, and fail to apply across phonological word boundaries. Many allophonic rules apply only at phonological word boundaries, e.g. the devoicing of word-final obstruents in various languages. Such rules provide additional tests for identifying phonological words. These rules typically do not treat the boundary between the clitic and its host as a word boundary; they are likely to treat the two together as a single phonological word.

Let us turn now to the identification of syntactic words. In the approach we have adopted in this book, the terminal nodes of a PS tree are always words. Thus the syntactic word is the smallest possible constituent in the language: the smallest unit which can be moved, replaced, or deleted by syntactic operations, assigned a position by Phrase Structure rules, etc.

In trying to identify clitics, the main problem will be to distinguish phonologically bound forms which are syntactically free (clitics) from those which are syntactically bound (affixes). There are two general principles which can help in this regard. First, the arrangement of affixes in a word is normally quite rigid, while the order of words in a clause or phrase is often more flexible; and second, lexically specific irregularities are more typical of affixation than of syntactic word combinations. Zwicky and Pullum (1983) offer the following specific criteria for distinguishing between clitics and affixes.

a   Affixes "select" their stems; that is, they usually appear only on stems of a certain category (nouns, verbs, etc.). Clitics, on the other hand, may attach to a wide variety of word classes.

b   Restrictions on co-occurrence, or gaps in the set of possible combinations, are more common with affixes than with clitics.

c   Irregular morphophonemic changes and suppletive forms are more common with affixes than with clitics.

d   Irregular semantic composition is more common with affixes than with clitics. The meaning of the word + clitic combination is usually predictable from the meaning of each separately, whereas a particular stem + affix combination may take on an unpredictable meaning.

e   Clitics can attach outside other clitics (e.g. *you'd've*), but affixes usually cannot attach outside clitics.

f   Syntactic rules will re-order affixed words (affix plus stem) as a unit, but generally treat a clitic and its host as separate elements. The following examples strongly suggest that the contracted form *should've* contains two distinct syntactic words, since it cannot be fronted as a unit in question formation. This means that the reduced form *'ve* (from *have*) is a clitic, rather than an affix.

(6)   a You should've seen it.
          b *Should've you seen it?
          c Should you have seen it?

Notice that all of these criteria are stated as tendencies, rather than as absolute principles. Specific clitics in particular languages may exhibit these properties in various combinations and to varying degrees. Our job as linguists is to find the analysis that best accounts for the whole range of properties of a given form.

17.2   Types of clitics

The definition quoted in the introduction to this chapter may be thought of as the prototypical case. In reality, the term "clitic" has been applied to such a bewildering array of particles that it is very difficult to find a definition that will cover them all. As languages change over time, it is common for function words to undergo phonological reduction and become clitics. It is also common for clitics to become "morphologized," that is, incorporated into their host word and re-analyzed as affixes. These changes are often gradual and may involve changes in one specific feature or property at a time, rather than sudden shifts from one category (e.g. clitic) to another (e.g. affix). So we sometimes encounter forms that seem to be at an intermediate stage of development, with some properties that are characteristic of clitics and others that are characteristic of affixes. Nevertheless, we can identify a few basic types of clitics which are relatively common across languages.

One way of classifying clitics is by position: those which attach to the right edge of their host are called ENCLITICS, while those which attach to the left edge of their host are called PROCLITICS.[4] However, a more significant basis for classification relates to their position in the sentence. Our examples thus far have involved the Amele and English auxiliaries, clitics whose position was predictable based on normal rules of syntax. The only reason for identifying these elements as clitics was their phonological attachment to an adjacent word. Zwicky (1977) refers to clitics of this type as SIMPLE CLITICS.

There are other words, however, which are identified as clitics primarily because of a special syntactic position. These forms are often unstressed, and may or may not be phonologically bound to another word. The crucial fact is that their position in the sentence cannot be predicted from the normal rules of syntax; some special rule or process is needed to account for their distribution. Zwicky refers to clitics of this type as SPECIAL CLITICS.

17.2.1 Simple clitics

17.2.1.1 Bound words

Bound words are the most obvious kind of simple clitic: words which are phonologically bound (attached to a host), but otherwise behave like normal words. Bound words belong to one of the established lexical categories of the language, and generally have the same distribution and other syntactic properties as free words belonging to the same category. The Indonesian clitic pronouns provide a typical example.

Indonesian has two different kinds of personal pronouns, bound (i.e. clitic) and free. For simplicity, we will focus on the third person singular forms: the free pronoun *dia* and the enclitic *=nya*. The fact that *=nya* is phonologically bound to its host can be demonstrated by stress placement. Cohn (1989) states that primary stress in Standard Indonesian always occurs on the next-to-last syllable of the phonological word. This makes it easy to identify phonological word boundaries, since wherever we find a syllable that bears primary stress, we know that the next syllable must occur at the end of a phonological word. As Cohen demonstrates, primary stress must shift one syllable to the right when either a suffix (7d) or an enclitic (7c) is added.

(7)   a Siapa náma orang itu?
          who name person that
          'What is that person's name?'

        b Siapa náma dia?
          who name 3sg
          'What is his name?'

        c Siapa namá=nya?
          who name=3sg
          'What is his name?'

        d Dia me-namá-kan   anak=nya Elvis.
          3sg ACT-name-APPLIC child=3sg Elvis
          'He named his child Elvis.'

Pronouns belong to the category NP, and can occur wherever NPs occur. The clitic pronouns occur in the same position as the free forms; in most contexts the two are freely interchangeable, as illustrated in (8–9), except that clitic pronouns cannot occur in subject position. Notice that the clitic pronoun =*nya* attaches to a variety of different hosts: nouns (7c), verbs (8b), prepositions (9b), etc. This pattern of "promiscuous attachment" is a strong indication that =*nya* is a clitic and not a suffix.

(8)   a Narti menúnggu dia/Pak Sastro.
          Narti wait.for   him/Mr. Sastro
          'Narti is waiting for him/Mr. Sastro.'

        b Narti menunggú=nya.
          Narti wait.for=3sg
          'Narti is waiting for him.'

(9)   a Tolong berikan buku ini kepáda dia.
          please give   book this to   3sg
          'Please give this book to him.'

        b Tolong berikan buku ini kepadá=nya.
          please give   book this to=3sg
          'Please give this book to him.'

The English reduced auxiliary forms illustrated in (5) and (6) are frequently cited as examples of bound words. Again, these forms are largely interchangeable with equivalent free forms. The existence of a corresponding free form is not, however, a necessary property of bound words. For example, Roberts (1996) states that all the post-positions in Amele are clitics (bound words); there are no alternate free forms.

17.2.1.2 Phrasal affixes

The English possessive marker -'s is somewhat difficult to analyze, and has been the topic of much debate. It is obviously not a phonological word in its own right, since it contains no vowels.[5] Some people have analyzed it as a clitic postposition, partly based on the similarity of meaning and function between the possessive -'s and the preposition *of*. But this analysis is thrown into doubt by the fact that there are no other postpositions in English. Prepositions in English always precede their object, whereas the possessive -'s always follows the NP which it is associated with. On the other hand, there is no other lexical category to which we could reasonably assign -'s if we need to recognize it as a syntactically independent word.

Another possible analysis might be to treat it as a suffix marking genitive case. This seems plausible, since many languages do use affixes to mark case. The problem is that, as noted in section 17.1, affixes are usually restricted to appearing only on stems of a certain category. The possessive -'s marks NPs, but it does not always attach to the head noun, or to any noun. Rather, it attaches to the last word in the NP, whether that word is a noun, verb, preposition, etc.

(10)   the Queen of England's crown
        a man I know's oldest son
        the woman you were talking with's daughter

So the possessive -'s looks very much like an affix which takes an entire noun phrase as its host, rather than any individual word in that phrase. Elements of this kind are sometimes referred to as PHRASAL AFFIXES (Nevis 1988).

Let us summarize the differences between these two types of simple clitic. Bound words have most of the properties of "normal" words: they belong to one of the regular lexical categories of the language; often occur in the same positions as free words of the same category; and can carry the same range of meanings as any other word in that category. However, unlike normal words, they are phonologically dependent.

Phrasal affixes have most of the properties of "normal" affixes: they are always attached to another word; do not fit into any of the established lexical categories (parts of speech) for the language; and tend to express grammatical (specifically inflectional) rather than lexical meanings. However, unlike normal affixes, they are "promiscuous" in their attachments, meaning that they may attach to words of almost any category. Rather than being bound to a particular class of stems, their position is defined relative to the boundaries of a particular kind of phrase.

17.2.2 Special clitics

We have defined SPECIAL CLITICS as being particles that occupy a special syntactic position, one which is not determined by the normal rules of syntax. Halpern (1998) states that the two most common types of special clitics are: (i) second position (2P) clitics; and (ii) verbal clitics.

17.2.2.1 Second position clitics

Tagalog has a number of particles which must occur as the second element of their immediate clause. These particles include nominative and genitive pronouns, question markers, aspectual particles, various markers of speaker's attitude, evidentials, etc. Normal word order in Tagalog is verb-initial, so these clitics normally occur immediately after the verb, as in (11). When a negative or other adverbial element appears in pre-verbal position, as in (12), the clitics also precede the verb. And in sentences which contain two clauses, the clitic elements of each clause occur in second position within that clause (12–13).

(11) Ibinigay *ko* *na* ang=pera kay=Charlie.
IV-PFV-give 1sg.GEN already NOM=money DAT=Charlie
'I already gave the money to Charlie.'

(12) Hindi *mo* *pa* *ako* mahahagkan sa=noo,
not 2sg.GEN IMPERF 1sg.NOM ABIL.FUT-kiss-DV DAT=forehead
[sariwa *pa* ang=sugat].
fresh IMPERF NOM=wound
'You cannot kiss me on the forehead yet, the wound is still fresh.'
(Wolfenden 1967, DL-118)

(13) Sinabihan *ako* ni=Luz na
PFV-say-DV 1sg.NOM GEN=Luz COMP
[ibinigay *mo* *na* ang=pera kay=Charlie].
IV-PFV-give 2sg.GEN already NOM=money DAT=Charlie
'I was told by Luz that you already gave the money to Charlie.'

The reason these elements are classified as special clitics is that their position is not determined by normal syntactic rules. For example, regular (non-pronominal) NPs do not occur before the verb even when a pre-verbal negative marker or adverb is present. Compare the position of the nominative NP *si Linda* in (14a) with the corresponding pronoun *siya* in (14b).

(14) a Hindi sinisisi ni=Charlie *si=Linda*.
not OV-PRES-blame GEN=Charlie NOM=Linda
'Linda is not blamed by Charlie.'

　 b Hindi *siya* sinisisi ni=Charlie.
not 3sg.NOM OV-PRES-blame GEN=Charlie.
'She is not blamed by Charlie.'

"Second position" in Tagalog means immediately after the first constituent of the clause. That constituent may be a single word, as in (11–14), or it may be an entire phrase, as in (15a,b). In other languages, however, second-position elements may occur after the first word of the phrase, clause, or sentence that contains them.

(15)   **Tagalog** (Schachter and Otanes 1972:496–498, 512)

a [Para=kay Pedro] *ko*   binili   ang   laruan.
  for=DAT Pedro 1sg.GEN PFV-buy-OV NOM toy
  'For Pedro I bought the toy.'

b [Bukas   ng   gabi nang alas.otso]   *siya*   aalis.
  tomorrow GEN night ADV eight.o'clock 3sg.NOM FUT.AV-leave
  'It's tomorrow night at eight that he's leaving.'

As we saw in chapter 11, Yes–No questions in Russian may be formed by the use of the enclitic particle =*li*, which attaches to the first word of the sentence as illustrated in (16). In a sense, the interrogative marker in Russian is a second-position clitic. However, the position of the clitic depends on phonological constituent boundaries as well as syntactic structure.

(16)   **Russian** (King 1995:137, 140, 143)

a Pročitala=li Anna knigu?
  read=QUES Anna book
  'Did Anna read a book?'

b Knigu=li   Anna pročitala?
  book=QUES Anna read
  'Was it a book that Anna read?'

King (1995) states that the interrogative particle attaches as an enclitic to the first PHONOLOGICAL WORD of the focused constituent. Verbs always constitute a single phonological word, but a phrasal constituent (such as an NP) may contain more than one phonological word. When a phrasal constituent containing more than one phonological word is focused, the clitic will occur inside the boundaries of the constituent which it marks, as in (17a,b). In (17b), the preposition *na* is not a phonological word; so the clitic attaches to the string *na etom* 'at this,' which is a single phonological word even though it is not a syntactic constituent.

(17)   a [Interesnuju=li   knigu Ivana]   on čitaet?
           interesting-ACC=QUES book Ivan-GEN he reads
           'Is it an interesting book of Ivan's that he is reading?'

        b [Na ètom=li   zavode] on rabotaet?
           at this=QUES factory he works
           'Is it at this factory that he works?'

        c *[Na ètom zavode]=li   on rabotaet?
            at this factory =QUES he works

17.2.2.2 Verbal clitics

Verbal clitics are clitic particles (normally pronouns) which always take a verb as their host. In Spanish, for example, non-emphatic object pronouns appear as clitics attached to the verb. They occur as proclitics with finite verbs, but enclitics with non-finite verbs (infinitives or gerunds), as illustrated in (18–19). (The alternation in the position of the pronoun observed in (19b,c) will be discussed briefly in section 17.3.) Again, the position of these clitics is "special" in the sense that it is different from the normal position of NPs or independent pronouns which bear the same Grammatical Relations.

(18)   **Spanish** (Aissen and Perlmutter 1983:362)

    a Eduardo *la*=vio.
        Eduardo 3sg.FEM=saw
        'Eduardo saw her.'

    b Quiere ver=*la*.
        wants   see.INF=3sg.FEM
        'He wants to see her.'

(19)   a Luis quiere comer   las   manzanas amarillas.
        Luis wants eat.INF the(FEM.PL) apples   yellow
        'Luis wants to eat the yellow apples.'

    b Luis quiere comer=*las*.
        Luis wants eat.INF=3pl.FEM
        'Luis wants to eat them.'

    c Luis *las*=quiere   comer.
        Luis 3pl.FEM=wants eat.INF
        'Luis wants to eat them.'

17.3   Clitic pronouns or agreement?

Many languages have clitic pronouns, whether as the only available form (like the nominative and genitive pronouns in Tagalog) or as allomorphs of corresponding free pronouns, as in Indonesian. In Tagalog, it is clear that the nominative and genitive pronouns are clitics and not affixes; they always occur in second position regardless of where the verb is. But in many other languages, clitic pronouns are always attached to the verb or auxiliary. In this case, it can be very difficult to tell whether the bound forms are actually clitics (syntactically independent pronouns) or affixes (agreement markers).

As Givón (1976) and others have pointed out, clitic pronouns often develop into agreement markers as languages change over time. As a result, we sometimes encounter intermediate forms with mixed properties, which can be very difficult to classify. But it is important to try to distinguish between clitic pronouns and agreement affixes wherever possible. Here are a few criteria which can help:

(i)   if the bound forms sometimes attach to words other than the verb which selects them, they are almost certainly clitic pronouns; if they are always attached to the verb, they could be either clitic pronouns or agreement markers.

For example, object pronouns in Italian (as in Spanish) generally appear as clitics attached to the verb which assigns their semantic role. In certain constructions, a clitic pronoun which functions as the object of a subordinate verb can optionally appear before the main verb of the sentence (20b, 21b). Spanish is similar, as illustrated in (19). This pattern is often referred to as "clitic climbing," since the clitic appears to "climb" up to a higher verb. This pattern constitutes strong evidence that the clitic forms are true pronouns, rather than agreement affixes.

(20)   **Italian** (Rizzi 1978; Spencer 1991:385)
    a Mario vuole risolver=*lo*   da.solo.
       Mario wants to.solve=it(ACC) alone
       'Mario wants to solve it on his own.'

    b Mario *lo*=vuole   risolver(e) da.solo.
       Mario it(ACC)=wants to.solve   alone
       'Mario wants to solve it on his own.'

(21)   a Gianni ha   dovuto parlar=*gli*   personalmente.
           Gianni has had   to.speak=them(DAT) personally
           'Gianni has had to speak to them personally.'

    b Gianni *gli*=ha   dovuto parlare   personalmente.
       Gianni them(DAT)=has had   to.speak personally
       'Gianni has had to speak to them personally.'

(ii)   if the bound forms are in complementary distribution with free pronouns (or full NP arguments), they are more likely to be clitic pronouns; if they can co-occur with free pronouns (or full NP arguments), they are more likely to be agreement markers.

(iii)   if the bound forms occur inside (i.e. closer to the verb root than) one or more inflectional affixes, they are almost certainly agreement markers.[6] Clitics do not normally invade the word boundary of their host.

(iv)   if the bound forms are obligatory, they are more likely to be agreement markers.

To take a concrete example, let us consider the Muna language of southern Sulawesi, Indonesia. A transitive verb in Muna can carry both a subject-marking prefix and an object-marking suffix. The subject marker is obligatory, occurring whether or not there is an overt subject NP in the sentence.[7] This suggests that the subject markers are agreement affixes, rather than clitic pronouns.

(22)   **Muna** (van den Berg 1989)
a inodi *a*-leni   'I am swimming.'
  I   *1sg*-swim

b ihintu *o*-leni   'You are swimming.'
  you   *2sg*-swim

c ama-ku   *no*-leni   'My father is swimming.'
  father-my *3sg*-swim

d *a*-leni   'I am swimming.'
  1sg-swim

e *o*-leni   'You are swimming.'
  2sg-swim

f *no*-leni   'He is swimming.'
  3sg-swim

The behavior of the object suffixes is different in several ways. First of all, the object-marking suffixes are in complementary distribution with free object pronouns. That is, a transitive clause may contain either an object suffix or an object pronoun, but not both:

(23)   a a-ghondohi-*ko*   'I am looking for you.'
         1sg-look.for-*2sg*

       b a-ghondohi ihintu   'I am looking for you.'
         1sg-look.for you

       c *a-ghondohi-*ko* ihintu
         1sg-look.for-*2sg* you

(24)   a madaho fumaa-*kanau*   'In a while you can eat me.'
         later   (IMP-)eat-*1sg*

       b madaho fumaa   inodi 'In a while you can eat me.'
         later   (IMP-)eat me

       c *madaho fumaa-*kanau*   inodi
         later   (IMP-)eat-*1sg* me

The object markers may co-occur with a full NP object phrase, as in (25a,b), but when they do the construction seems to involve a kind of apposition.[8] Van den Berg (1989:164) states: "In most of the[se] cases . . . the direct object [NP] is a known entity that is supplied for the sake of clarification, almost as an afterthought." This strongly suggests that the verb's object "suffix" is actually a pronoun, and it is this pronoun which bears the OBJ relation. The "object" NP is actually a kind of appositional or adjunct phrase. This hypothesis is supported by the fact that, when the object NP is topicalized (moved to a pre-verbal position), as in (25c), the verb normally carries an object "suffix" as well.

(25)   a na-h[um]ela-*e*   kae-kabua-ha-no.
           3sg.IRR-pull-*3sg* NOM-fish-INSTR-his
           'He will pull it in, his fishing line.'

        b no-wora-*e* foo   amaitu.
           3sg-see-*3sg* mango that
           'He saw it, the mango.'

        c sabhara   kawaaghoo no-kiido-*e*.
           all.kinds gift   3sg-refuse-*3sg*
           'All the different gifts, he refused them.'

So, while the subject-marking prefixes in Muna have the properties we expect of agreement affixes, the object markers seem more like clitic pronouns. A very similar pattern is reported in the Bantu language Chichewa (Bresnan and Mchombo 1987).

As we have mentioned on several occasions, our analysis needs to be based on a cluster of criteria like those listed at the beginning of this section. No one type of evidence taken by itself will be a reliable indicator. For example, the complementary distribution mentioned in point (ii) is an important characteristic of clitic pronouns, but there are certain well-known cases where this test breaks down. In Spanish (and a number of other languages) clitic pronouns may be co-referential with independent NPs, provided those NPs are marked by a preposition. This will normally be the case for recipients (OBJ$_2$) or definite animate objects.

The co-occurrence of a clitic pronoun with a co-referential NP argument is called CLITIC DOUBLING. Halpern (1998) states that clitic doubling in Spanish is impossible when the object is a bare NP (26a), optional when the object is a dative NP (26b), and obligatory when the object is a free pronoun (26c).

(26)   a Eduardo (*lo=)vio   el   edificio nuevo.
           Eduardo 3sg.MASC=see-3sg-PAST the(MASC.SG) building new(MASC.SG)
           'Eduardo saw the new building.'

        b Eduardo (la=)vio   a   Maria.
           Eduardo 3sg.FEM=see-3sg-PAST DAT Maria
           'Eduardo saw Maria.'

        c Eduardo *(la=)vio   a   ella.
           Eduardo 3sg.FEM=see-3sg-PAST DAT 3sg.FEM
           'Eduardo saw her.'

So we need to consider a variety of evidence and adopt the analysis which best accounts for the whole range of data. The general principle here is that agreement markers will tend to have properties we expect to find in inflectional categories, while clitic pronouns tend to have properties we expect to find in arguments.

17.4   Conclusion

Clitics are interesting for the same reasons that they are difficult to analyze. They behave in some ways like affixes, and in other ways like independent words. Their "affix-like" properties are normally phonological: they form a single phonological word with their host for purposes of stress placement and other phonological processes. The rules of syntax, however, do not generally treat the clitic and its host as a unit. Clitics, unlike normal affixes, may attach to hosts from many different categories, and clitics are less likely than true affixes to exhibit semantic or morphophonemic irregularities.

SIMPLE CLITICS are clitics only because they are phonologically bound to some other word. The majority of these are BOUND WORDS which share the normal syntactic and semantic properties of an established lexical category. Bound words are more likely to be function words (e.g. pronouns, determiners, auxiliaries, or prepositions) than content words (nouns, verbs, adjectives, etc.).

SPECIAL CLITICS are elements whose position in the sentence is not predicted by the rules of syntax needed to account for the ordering of other elements. The most common types are verbal clitics, which attach to the verb, and second position clitics. Special clitics are normally unstressed and often phonologically bound, though they may also stand alone as unstressed particles. Their special position is the defining feature.

Practice exercise

Inga evidentials (Colombia; Bendor-Samuel and Levinsohn 1986, ex. E.9; and Healey 1990b, ex. D.9)
Discuss the form and function(s) of the evidential markers as illustrated in the following examples. (The Inga data have been simplified. Italics are used to indicate focal stress in the free translation.)

1. caina   runa iscay huagra chipi huañuchi-mi.
   yesterday man two cow   there killed-DIRECT
   'Yesterday the man killed two cows there.' (action witnessed by speaker)
2. caina   huagra chipi huañuchi-si.
   yesterday cow   there killed-INDIRECT
   'Yesterday he killed a cow there.' (action not witnessed by speaker)

3.   chipi runa-mi   huañuchi.
      there man-DIRECT killed
      '*The man* killed it there.' (witnessed by speaker)

4.   huamra chipi sug cuchi-si   huañuchi.
      boy   there one pig-INDIRECT killed
      'The boy killed one *pig* there.' (not witnessed by speaker)

5.   huamra cuchi caina-si   huañuchi.
      boy   pig   yesterday-INDIRECT killed
      'The boy killed a pig *yesterday*.' (not witnessed by speaker)

6.   caina   iscay cuchi chipi-mi   huañuchi.
      yesterday two   pig   there-DIRECT killed
      'Yesterday he killed two pigs *there*.' (witnessed by speaker)

7.   huañuchi-si.
      killed-INDIRECT
      'He killed it.' (not witnessed by speaker)

Exercises

17A Sama Pangutaran (Philippines; data from C. Walton)
Identify the bound morphemes in the following examples. State whether
they are affixes or clitics, and, if clitics, which type. State the reasons for
your decision. (Note: the particle *si*, glossed PERS, is a personal name
marker.)

1.   Bonoʔna iya.
      fight-3sg 3sg
      'He fights him.'

2.   Bonoʔna aku.
      fight-3sg 1sg
      'He fights me.'

3.   Bonoʔna pagkahina.
      fight-3sg neighbor-3sg
      'He fights his neighbor.'

4.   Bonoʔna bantaʔna.
      fight-3sg enemy-3sg
      'He fights his enemy.'

5.   Bonoʔ si   Abdul bantaʔ əmmaʔna
      fight   PERS Abdul enemy   father-3sg
      'Abdul fights his father's enemy.'

6.   Kəlloʔ inaʔku   boheʔ.
      fetch   mother-1sg water
      'My mother fetches water.'

7.   Kəllo?ku pagkahi si   Abdul.
       fetch-1sg neighbor PERS Abdul
       'I fetch Abdul's neighbor.'

8.   Kəllo? əmma?ku pagkahina.
       fetch   father-1sg neighbor-3sg
       'My father fetches his neighbor.'

9.   Bono? banta? əmma?ku si   Abdul.
       fight enemy father-1sg PERS Abdul
       'My father's enemy fights Abdul.'

10.   Kəllo? əmma? si   Abdul pagkahiku.
       fetch father PERS Abdul neighbor-1sg
       'Abdul's father fetches my neighbor.'

17B Tlingit Obliques (Alaska; adapted from Bendor-Samuel and Levinsohn 1986, ex. K.4)[9]
Ignoring verb morphology, identify all other bound morphemes in the following examples. State whether they are affixes or clitics, and, if clitics, which type. State the reasons for your decision.

1.   aχ hídeet   uwagút.
       my house-POSS-to he.went
       'He went to (and arrived at) my house.'

2.   aχ hídee   tlént uwagút.
       my house-POSS big-to he.went
       'He went to (and arrived at) my big house.'

3.   aχ hídeedéi   woogòot.
       my house-POSS-to he.went
       'He went to (towards) my house.'

4.   aχ hídee   tléndèi woogòot.
       my house-POSS big-to he.went
       'He went to (towards) my big house.'

5.   du àatGáa   woogòot.
       his aunt-for he.went
       'He went for (to fetch) his aunt.'

6.   du àat   hásGàa woogòot.
       his aunt PL-for he.went
       'He went for (to fetch) his aunts.'

7.   aχ àat náq   aχ hídeedéi   woogòot.
       my aunt without my house-POSS-to he.went
       'He went to (towards) my house without my aunt.'

8.   du àat hás náq   woogòot.
       his aunt PL without he.went
       'He went without his aunts.'

9.   tléil du àat tèen woogòot.
     NEG his aunt with he.went
     'He did not go with his aunt.'

10.   du àat hás tèen woo?àat.
      his aunt PL with they.went
      'He went with his aunts.'

17C Tagalog case

Based on the following examples, state whether you would analyze the case markers *ang-*, *nəng-*, and *sa-* as affixes or clitics, and, if clitics, which type. State the reasons for your decision. Note: the "linking particle" *na* ~ *=ng*, glossed LNK in the following data, appears between the head noun and its modifiers and determiners. The relative order of these elements is extremely free. Possessive pronouns have two forms, one occurring before the noun and the other after the noun. Indefinite, non-human direct objects are marked with genitive case.[10]

1.   a bumili   siya   nəng-maliit na   bahay.
        buy(PFV) 3sg.NOM GEN-small   LNK   house
        'He bought a small house.'

     b bumili   siya   nəng-bahay na   maliit.
        buy(PFV) 3sg.NOM GEN-house   LNK   small
        'He bought a small house.'

2.   a i-hulug   mo   sa-koreyo ang-akin=ng   sulat.
        PASS-throw you(SG.GEN) DAT-mail   NOM-my=LNK   letter
        'Please mail my letter.' (lit.: 'My letter will be mailed by you.')

     b i-hulug   mo   sa-koreyo ang-sulat   ko.
        PASS-throw you(SG.GEN) DAT-mail   NOM-letter my
        'Please mail my letter.' (lit.: 'My letter will be mailed by you.')

3.   a nagbigay   siya   nəng-pera   sa-matanda ko=ng   kapatid.
        give(PFV) 3sg.NOM GEN-money DAT-old   my=LNK   sibling
        'He gave money to my older brother.'

     b nagbigay   siya   nəng-pera   sa-kapatid ko na   matanda.
        give(PFV) 3sg.NOM GEN-money DAT-sibling my LNK   old
        'He gave money to my older brother.'

4.   a maglalakad siya   buhat sa-Maynila.
        walk(FUT)   3sg.NOM from   DAT-Manila
        'He will walk from Manila.'

     b litson-in   mo   ito=ng   baboy para sa-pista.
        PASS-roast 2sg.GEN this=LNK   pig   for   DAT-party
        'Roast this pig for the party.' (lit.: 'This pig will be roasted by you . . .')

Additional exercises

Merrifield et al. (1987) prob. 187, 273, 275
Healey (1990b), ex. H.16.

Notes

1. As noted below, the acute accents in (2) represent primary stress.
2. These auxiliary elements are followed only by sentence-final elements such as question particles, sentence-level conjunctions, complementizers, etc.
3. Of course, hesitations, self-correction, and false starts can and frequently do produce pauses in the middle of words.
4. Bill Merrifield (p.c.) points out that the terms ENCLITIC and PROCLITIC are actually much older than the word CLITIC. Both of these specific terms are borrowed from late Latin, and ultimately derive from the Greek word *klít(os)* 'slope'; they refer to forms which must "lean on" another word. The first use of the more general term CLITIC in print was by K. L. Pike (1947:165).
5. More precisely, no syllabic segments.
6. Apparent counter-examples to this generalization are found in Portuguese, Polish, and a number of languages in Sulawesi, including Tabulahan and perhaps Muna.
7. The use of independent pronouns as subjects in Muna seems to give special emphasis to the subject NP.
8. Two NPs are in apposition when they refer to the same participant in the same function or role within the clause (as opposed to, for example, reflexives); see ch. 8.
9. The data for this exercise were originally provided by Gillian Story and Constance Naish. My thanks to Gillian Story for her comments and suggestions.
10. The case markers *ang*, *nəng* (spelled *ng*), and *sa* are written as separate words in the standard Filipino orthography, but they are never stressed and never occur in isolation. At least for the purposes of this exercise, we assume that they are phonologically bound to the following word.

Appendix: Swahili data for grammar sketch

Write a "grammar sketch," i.e. a short description of Swahili grammar, based on the data provided here. Write your description in prose, including charts and/or tree diagrams where helpful. You may follow the suggested outline below, or you may create your own. Data sources: Ashton (1944); Barrett-Keach (1985); Comrie (1976b); Healey (1990b); Vitale (1981).

Possible outline for grammar sketch

0. INTRODUCTION: language name, where spoken, number of speakers, basic typological information. (Swahili is spoken primarily in Tanzania and Kenya, and is recognized as a national language in both countries. Many different dialects exist; this exercise is based on "Standard Swahili," as reflected in various published grammars.)

I. MORPHOLOGY.

A.   inflectional morphology of the verb
B.   other inflectional morphology
C.   derivational morphology, including any valence-changing processes

II. BASIC CLAUSE STRUCTURE

A.   Verbal clauses (including how subjects, objects, etc. are distinguished: case, agreement, word order, etc.). Include PS rules and trees for a few sample sentences.
B.   NP structure (including PS rules and trees, agreement patterns)
C.   Non-verbal predicates (stative, equative, and locative/possessive clauses)

III. SENTENCE PATTERNS

A.   Questions, commands, etc.
B.   Complement clauses
C.   Adverbial clauses
D.   Relative clauses

IV. RESIDUE (a list of issues which are unclear and need further data and research).

Data: Part A

1.	ninasema	'I speak'
2.	unasema	'you (sg) speak'
3.	anasema	'he speaks'
4.	tunasema	'we speak'
5.	mnasema	'you (pl) speak'
6.	wanasema	'they speak'
7.	ninaona	'I see'
8.	niliona	'I saw'
9.	nitaona	'I will see'
10.	nimeona	'I have seen'
11.	ninawaona	'I see them'
12.	nilikuona	'I saw you (sg)'
13.	ananiona	'he sees me'
14.	utaniona	'you (sg) will see me'
15.	alituona	'he saw us'
16.	nilimwona	'I saw him'
17.	aliwaona	'he saw them'
18.	nilipika	'I cooked'
19.	anapika	'he is cooking'
20.	nipike	'I should cook/let me cook'
21.	wapike	'let them cook!'
22.	tupike	'let's cook!'
23.	pika!	'(you sg) cook!'
24.	pikeni!	'(you pl) cook!' (by vowel harmony; underlying form: *pikani*)

Part B

1.   a mpishi amepika nini? 'What has the cook cooked?'
        cook   cook   what

    b amepika mikate. 'He has cooked bread.'
       cook   bread

2.   waimbaji wanaimba vizuri. 'The singers are singing well.'
    singers   sing   well

3.   a watoto   wapike nini? 'What should the children cook?'
       children cook   what

    b wapike viazi.   'They are to cook potatoes.'
      cook   potatoes

4.   a watoto   wanalala wapi? 'Where are the children sleeping?'
        children sleep   where

     b wanalala nyumba-ni. 'They are sleeping in the house.'
        sleep   in.house

5.   a nani amevunja kikombe hiki?
        who break   cup   this
        'Who has broken this cup?'

     b alifika lini   mgeni   huyu?
        arrive when stranger this
        'When did this stranger arrive?'

6.   a umemwona mpishi wetu?
        see   cook   our
        'Have you seen our cook?'

     b umeona kisu   changu?
        see   knife my
        'Have you seen my knife?'

     c kisu   changu umekiona?
        knife my   see
        'Have you seen my knife?'

     d wamesoma kitabu chako? wamekisoma.
        read   book your   read
        'Have they read your book? (Yes) they have read it.'

7.   a mtoto ali(ki)vunja kikombe.
        child break   cup
        'The child broke the cup.'

     b kikombe kilivunjwa (na   mtoto).
        cup   break   by child
        'The cup was broken (by the child).'

8.   a mzee   ali(vi)vunja vikombe.
        old.man break   cup
        'The old man broke the cups.'

     b vikombe vilivunjwa (na   mzee).
        cup   break   by old.man
        'The cups were broken (by the old man).'

9.   a mvulana ali(ki)pika chakula.
        boy   cook   food
        'The boy cooked food.'

     b chakula kilipikwa na mvulana.
        food   cook   by boy
        'Food was cooked by the boy.'

c mvulana ambaye alipika chakula
  boy   cook food
  'the boy who cooked the food'

d chakula ambacho mvulana alikipika
  food   boy   cook
  'the food which the boy cooked'

e chakula ambacho kilipikwa na mvulana
  food   cook   by boy
  'the food which was cooked by the boy'

f mvulana ambaye chakula kilipikwa na *(yeye)
  boy   food   cook   by him
  'the boy by whom the food was cooked'
  [recall that *(X) means X is obligatory]

10.   a kitabu ambacho ninakisoma
        book   read
        'the book that I am reading'

      b vitabu ambavyo vilisomwa na mvulana
        books   read   by boy
        'the books which were read by the boy'

      c baarua ambazo zitafika
        letters   arrive
        'the letters which will arrive'

      d baarua ambazo wataziandika
        letters   write
        'the letters which they will write'

      e mtu   ambaye nilimwona
        person   saw
        'the person whom I saw'

      f mtu   ambaye alimwona simba
        person   saw   lion
        'the person who saw the lion'

      g mtu   ambaye aliwaponya watoto
        person   cure   children
        'the man who cured the children'

      h nyumba ambazo zilijengwa na wavulana
        houses   build   by boys
        'houses which were built by the boys'

      i wavulana ambao nyumba zilijengwa na *(wao)
        boys   houses build   by them
        'the boys by whom the houses were built'

11.   a Halima anapika ugali.
          Halima cook   porridge
          'Halima is cooking porridge.'

        b Juma alimpikia Ahmed ugali.
          Juma cook   Ahmed porridge
          'Juma cooked Ahmed some porridge.'

        c nikupikie chakula?
          cook   food
          'Shall I cook you some food?'

        d wagonjwa wasagiwe mahindi.
          sick.folk grind   maize
          'Let maize be ground for the sick folk.'

12.   a mwalimu anawaimbisha watoto.
          teacher   sing   children
          'The teacher is making the children sing (i.e. giving them a singing lesson).'

        b Sudi alimpikisha mke wake uji.
          Sudi cook   wife his   gruel
          'Sudi made his wife cook some gruel.'

        c mke wake alipikishwa uji   na Sudi.
          wife his   cook   gruel by Sudi
          'His wife was made to cook gruel by Sudi.'

        d *uji   ulipikishwa mke wake na Sudi.
          gruel cook   wife his by Sudi
          (for: 'The gruel was caused to be cooked by his wife by Sudi.')

13.   a msichana ali(u)fungua mlango.
          girl   open   door
          'The girl opened the door.'

        b mwalimu alimfunguzisha msichana mlango.
          teacher   open   girl   door
          'The teacher made the girl open the door.'

14.   a Juma anampenda Halima.
          Juma love   Halima
          'Juma loves Halima.'

        b Juma na   Halima wanapendana.
          Juma with Halima love
          'Juma and Halima love each other.'

        c Juma anajipenda.
          Juma love
          'Juma loves himself.'

15.   a Sudi alijitupa kwa simba.
      Sudi throw   to   lion
      'Sudi threw himself to the lions.'

    b Juma na   Ahmed walipigana.
      Juma with Ahmed hit
      'Juma and Ahmed hit (i.e. fought with) each other.'

16.   a Juma yu daktari. 'Juma is a doctor.'
      Juma   doctor

    b Juma alikuwa daktari. 'Juma was a doctor.'
      Juma   doctor

    c Fatuma na   Halima watakuwa wanafunzi.
      Fatuma with Halima   students
      'Fatuma and Halima will be students.'

17.   a Ahmed ni mbaya. 'Ahmed is bad.'
      Ahmed   bad

    b kitabu hiki ni kizuri. 'This book is good.'
      book this   good

    c kitabu hiki kilikuwa kizuri. 'This book was good.'
      book this   good

    d watu   ambao walimpiga Ahmed ni washenzi.
      people   hit   Ahmed   savages
      'The people who hit Ahmed are savages.'

18.   a nina kisu. 'I have a knife.'
      with knife

    b Ahmed ana   mpenzi. 'Ahmed has a lover.'
      Ahmed with lover

    c Juma alikuwa na   pesa   nyingi.
      Juma   with money much
      'Juma had a lot of money'

19.   a Juma alimwambia Ahmed kwamba Fatuma alikuwa na   chunjua upaja-ni.
      Juma tell   Ahmed   Fatuma   with wart   thigh-on
      'Juma told Ahmed that Fatuma had a wart on her thigh.'

    b Juma aliniambia kwamba Ahmed atakulipa wiki   ijayo.
      Juma tell   Ahmed pay   week coming
      'Juma told me that Ahmed will pay you next week.'

20.   a Juma alimwuliza Ahmed aje   nyumba-ni kwake.
      Juma ask   Ahmed come to.house   his
      'Juma asked Ahmed to come to his (Juma's) house.'

    b Ahmed alimshurutisha Fatuma anywe chang'aa.
      Ahmed persuade   Fatuma drink   moonshine
      'Ahmed persuaded Fatuma to drink moonshine.'

21.   a Ahmed na   Fatuma walienda mji-ni (ili)   waone senema.
       Ahmed with Fatuma go   to.town so.that see   movie
       'Ahmed and Fatuma went to town to see a movie.'

    b Halima alimpa Juma pesa   (ili)   anunue ndizi.
      Halima give   Juma money so.that buy   banana
      'Halima gave Juma some money so he could buy bananas.'

Glossary

Ablative semantic case that marks a location from which motion originates (ch. 15)

Ablaut (see MUTATION)

Absolutive case or agreement marker used for transitive objects and intransitive subjects in an ergative system (ch. 7)

Accompaniment (or comitative) semantic role of an entity which accompanies or is associated with the performance of an action (ch. 4)

Accusative case marker used for primary objects (ch. 7)

Active (see PASSIVE)

Adjuncts non-arguments; clausal dependents which are not selected by the verb, but which are added to the sentence to provide various kinds of information (ch. 4)

Adversative either: a passive construction used only for misfortunes; or, a distinct construction which adds a new argument to the argument structure of the predicate, namely a participant who suffers as a result of the event being described (ch. 14)

Affix a bound morpheme which is not a root; subtypes include PREFIX, SUFFIX, etc. (ch. 2)

Agent semantic role of the causer or initiator of an event (ch. 4)

Agreement a syntactic relationship in which the grammatical or semantic features of a noun or noun phrase determine the form of some other word (ch. 7)

Allative semantic case that marks a location toward which motion occurs (ch. 8, ex. 8A)

Allomorphs variant forms of the same morpheme (ch. 15)

Anaphora relationship between a pronoun or other pro-form (the ANAPHOR) and the phrase that it is co-referential with (its ANTECEDENT) (ch. 8)

Applicative affix that increases the syntactic valence of a verb by creating a new primary object (ch. 14)

Apposition two phrases stand in apposition to each other when they refer to the same thing and bear the same semantic role within a single clause (ch. 8)

Argument participant selected by the predicate of a clause (ch. 4)

Argument structure a representation of how many arguments a predicate takes, and what semantic roles it assigns to each of them (ch. 4)

Article words like *a* and *the*; see also DETERMINER (ch. 6)

Aspect the distribution of an event or situation over time; see PERFECTIVE, IMPERFECTIVE, HABITUAL, TELIC, PROGRESSIVE, INCEPTIVE, COMPLETIVE, INCHOATIVE, ITERATIVE (ch. 9)

Attributive clause a clause whose semantic predicate is an adjective phrase; typically used to describe a quality or attribute of the subject (ch. 10)

Auxiliary a "helping verb" or particle which expresses verbal inflectional categories such as tense, aspect, modality, and/or agreement, but does not have lexical semantic content like a normal verb

Beneficiary semantic role of the participant for whose benefit an action is performed (ch. 4)

Biased question question with an expectation on the part of the speaker for a particular answer to be given (ch. 11)

Bound morpheme a morpheme that cannot occur as an independent word by itself, but must occur as part of a larger word (ch. 2)

Case a system in which the Grammatical Relation or semantic role of an NP is indicated by a marker on the NP itself (ch. 7)

Category (see SYNTACTIC CATEGORIES)

Causative valence-increasing derivation in which the added argument (the CAUSER) causes or brings about the event named by the basic predicate (ch. 14)

Causee participant who is caused to do something, corresponding to the subject of the basic predicate (ch. 14)

Circumfix a discontinuous affix, with elements added both before and after the base form (ch. 16)

Classifier a separate word that occurs inside the NP in certain contexts and indicates the sub-class of the head noun; cf. GENDER (ch. 8)

Clause a simple sentence; the smallest grammatical unit which expresses a complete proposition (chs. 3, 4)

Clause-mates two elements are clause-mates if the smallest clause that contains either one of them contains the other as well (ch. 5)

Clitic a form which is syntactically free but phonologically bound (SIMPLE CLITIC); or whose distribution is not determined by the normal syntactic patterns of the language (SPECIAL CLITIC) (ch. 17)

Closed question a question which allows only a small, fixed range of answers; e.g. YES–NO QUESTIONS (*Do you like durian?*) and ALTERNATIVE QUESTIONS (*Would you like coffee or tea?*) (ch. 11)

Coherence (see INCOHERENT)

Collocational clash a violation of a SELECTIONAL RESTRICTION; combination of words that is semantically unacceptable (chs. 4, 5)

Comparative inflectional category for adjectives indicating "more than" (ch. 3)

Complement dependent (non-head) constituent that is selected by the head of its phrase (chs. 3, 5)

Complementary distribution two elements are in complementary distribution when they never occur in the same environments, or for other reasons never co-occur (ch. 15)

Complementizer special word that introduces a complement clause (ch. 12)

Completeness (see INCOMPLETE)

Completive aspect that describes the completion or termination of an event (ch. 9)

Compound a stem consisting of more than one root (chs. 2, 13)

Conjugations traditional grammatical term for inflectional sub-classes of verbs (ch. 15)

Constituent a group of words which functions as a unit, especially with respect to word order; in a tree, a string of words which is exhaustively dominated by a single node (see PHRASE STRUCTURE) (ch. 3)

Content question (see OPEN QUESTION)

Continuous aspect (see PROGRESSIVE)

Coordinate structure two constituents belonging to the same category conjoined to form another constituent of that category (ch. 12)

Copula a linking verb, e.g. English *to be* (ch. 10)

Count nouns nouns that can be pluralized (ch. 5)

Dative case marker used for secondary objects, especially for goal or recipient objects (ch. 7)

Declarative major mood normally used to express statements (chs. 9, 11)

Declensions traditional grammatical term for inflectional sub-classes of nouns (ch. 15)

Deictic words that refer to something in the immediate speech situation, e.g. *here, now, this, you, me* (ch. 8)

Demonstrative *this, that*, etc.; see also DETERMINER (ch. 6)

Deontic agent-oriented modality that expresses obligation or permission (ch. 9)

Dependents the non-head elements of a phrase (ch. 3)

Derivation a morphological process that changes one word (or LEXEME) into another (ch. 13)

Desiderative modality which expresses a desire rather than an actual event (ch. 9)

Determiner a word that occurs in a noun phrase to indicate features such as definiteness, distance from speaker, number or quantity, etc.; subtypes include ARTICLES, DEMONSTRATIVES, and in many languages QUANTIFIERS (chs. 3, 6)

Detransitivizing (see VALENCE-DECREASING)

Deverbal noun noun derived from a verb (ch. 13)

Diminutive affixes, primarily attached to nouns, which indicate smallness (ch. 13)

Direct arguments (see TERMS)

Direct quote speaker reports the exact words spoken by another person (ch. 12)

Direct speech act sentence in which the major mood category matches the intended function (e.g. interrogative for questions) (ch. 11)

Ditransitive a verb that takes two objects (ch. 4)

Dual a number category referring to a group that contains exactly two individuals; contrasts with singular and plural (chs. 7, 8)

Dubitative modality which indicates that the speaker is in doubt about the truth of the proposition expressed (ch. 9)

Dummy subject pro-form (e.g. English *it* or *there*) that occupies the subject position but has no semantic content (ch. 10)

Ellipsis omission of an element which is understood from the context, often because it has been previously mentioned (ch. 3)

Enclitic clitics which attach to the right edge of their host (ch. 17)

Epistemic speaker-oriented modality that expresses possibility or certainty (ch. 7)

Equative clause a clause whose semantic predicate is a noun phrase; typically used to identify one NP with another (ch. 10)

Ergative a form (usually case or agreement) used for transitive subjects but not for intransitive subjects (ch. 7)

Ergative system a system in which objects of transitive clauses are marked in the same way as subjects of intransitive clauses, while transitive subjects are marked differently (ch. 7)

Exclusive a first person plural or dual that excludes the hearer (chs. 7, 8)

Existential a verb or clause-type used to indicate that something exists or doesn't exist (ch. 10)

Experiencer semantic role of a participant who thinks, feels, or perceives something (ch. 4)

Externally headed a relative clause in which the modifying clause occurs either before or after the head noun (ch. 12)

Extraposition a way of avoiding sentential subjects by using a dummy subject and moving the embedded clause to the end, e.g. *It is strange that John doesn't eat durian.* (ch. 12)

Finite verb or auxiliary which is specified for tense (ch. 12)

Focus the crucial piece of new information in a sentence (ch. 11)

Free morpheme a morpheme that can occur as an independent word (opposite of BOUND MORPHEME) (ch. 2)

Free relative a Wh- question used as a noun phrase, e.g. [*What you see*] *is* [*what you get*] (ch. 12)

Gap strategy within a relative clause, the role of the head noun (i.e. the RELATIVIZED FUNCTION) is indicated only by a gap or missing argument in the modifying clause (ch. 12)

Gender a system of noun classes determined by patterns of agreement (ch. 8)

Genitive case marker used for possessors (ch. 7)

Gloss a translation equivalent

Grammatical case case marking which indicates the Grammatical Relation of the NP (ch. 7)

Habitual sub-type of imperfective aspect, indicating that a situation is, or was, characteristic of a certain period of time (e.g. *I used to listen to the BBC news every evening*) (ch. 9)

Head the most important word in a phrase; the word that determines the category and many other grammatical features of the whole phrase (ch. 3)

Headless relative clause a relative clause that lacks a head noun; often translatable into English as 'the one that . . .' (ch. 12)

Hortative mood category used for softened commands or exhortation (ch. 9)

Host the word that a clitic attaches to (ch. 17)

Imperative major mood normally used to express commands (chs. 9, 11)

Imperfective opposite of PERFECTIVE; any type of aspect that describes the internal time structure of a situation (ch. 9)

Impersonal constructions sentences that contain no subject (ch. 10)

Inalienable possession possessive construction which indicates a necessary and/or permanent relationship between possessor and possessed, in contrast to other possessive relationships (ALIENABLE POSSESSION) which can be terminated by selling, losing, giving away, etc. (ch. 6)

Inceptive aspect which refers to the beginning of a situation (ch. 9)

Inchoative aspect which refers to a change of state or entering a state (e.g. *get rich*) (ch. 9)

Inclusive a first person plural or dual that includes the hearer (chs. 7, 8)

Incoherent an incoherent clause is one that contains a complement which is not permitted by the verb's SUBCATEGORIZATION (ch. 5)

Incomplete an incomplete clause is one that lacks a complement which is required by the verb's SUBCATEGORIZATION (ch. 5)

Incorporation (see NOUN INCORPORATION)

Indirect arguments (see OBLIQUE ARGUMENTS)

Indirect object traditional term used to refer to semantic role of recipient or beneficiary (ch. 4)

Indirect quote speaker reports the content of what was said by another person, but not the exact words that were used (ch. 12)

Indirect speech act sentence in which the major MOOD category does not matches the intended function (e.g. interrogative for commands); see also RHETORICAL QUESTION (ch. 11)

Infix an affix that occurs inside another morpheme (ch. 16)

Infinitive a non-finite verb form (i.e. unmarked for tense) often used as the citation form, e.g. *to swim, to conquer*, etc.

Inflection a morphological process that determines the grammatical features of a particular word (or LEXEME), but does not change one lexeme into another; cf. DERIVATION (ch. 13)

Instrument semantic role of an inanimate entity used by an agent to perform some action (ch. 4)

Instrumental case marker used for instruments (ch. 7)

Intensifiers adverbs of degree (e.g. *very*) (chs. 3, 6)

Internally headed a relative clause in which the head noun occurs inside the modifying clause; cf. EXTERNALLY HEADED (ch. 12)

Interrogative major mood normally used to express questions (chs. 9, 11)

Intransitive does not take an object (chs. 4, 5)

Irrealis verb form used for future tense in contrast to present and past, and for unrealized, possible, or potential events; cf. REALIS (ch. 9)

Iterative aspect marking for events that occur repeatedly; also called REPETITIVE (ch. 9)

Lexeme a word, or lexical item, including all of its inflected forms (ch. 13)

Lexical ambiguity ambiguity of a phrase or sentence due to the presence of a word that has two or more distinct meanings (ch. 3)

Lexical category part of speech for individual words; see SYNTACTIC CATEGORIES (ch. 3)

Lexical entry an entry (or record) in the lexicon which lists the unique phonological, semantic, and grammatical properties of a particular word (ch. 5)

Lexical insertion phrase structural principle that allows a lexical category (N, V, etc.) to have a single daughter which is a word of the same category (ch. 3)

Lexicon a speaker's "mental dictionary"; the collection of all the words in the language (ch. 5)

Location semantic role of the place where a situation occurs; SOURCE, GOAL, and PATH can be treated as sub-types of location (ch. 4)

Locative case marking for NPs that express location (ch. 7)

Locative clause a clause whose semantic predicate is a prepositional phrase; typically used to express location or possession (ch. 10)

Major categories lexical categories that can function as the head of a phrase, e.g. N, V, A, and P (ch. 3)

Marked (see UNMARKED)

Mass nouns nouns that cannot be pluralized (cf. COUNT NOUNS) (ch. 5)

Matrix clause clause within which a subordinate clause is embedded (ch. 12)

Measure words words which allow the quantification of mass nouns, as in *a cup of salt* (ch. 8)

Meteorological verbs words that describe weather events or conditions, e.g. *raining* (ch. 10)

Minor categories lexical categories that do not normally function as the head of a phrase, e.g. conjunctions (ch. 3)

Modality an indicator of either the speaker's attitude toward the proposition being expressed (SPEAKER-ORIENTED MODALITY) or the actor's relationship to the described situation (AGENT-ORIENTED MODALITY) (ch. 9)

Modifier adjunct, e.g. within a noun phrase (ch. 6)

Mood grammatical reflection of the speaker's purpose in speaking; indicates what the speaker is doing with a proposition in a particular discourse situation; the three MAJOR MOODS (DECLARATIVE, INTERROGATIVE, and IMPERATIVE) indicate the speech act (chs. 9, 11)

Morpheme a minimal individually meaningful element; every word consists of one or more morphemes (ch. 2)

Morphology the study of word structure (ch. 10)

Morphophonemic alternation allomorphy due to a phonological process; a phonological change affecting one morpheme in the presence of a neighboring morpheme (ch. 15)

Mutation a change in some feature(s) of a particular phoneme, e.g. the voicing contrast in *grief* ~ *grieve*. ABLAUT is a change in vowel quality, e.g. *foot* ~ *feet*. (ch. 16)

N′ or N̄ (pronounced "N-bar") constituent headed by a noun but smaller than a noun phrase (ch. 6)

Node a labeled point or junction in a tree diagram (ch. 3)

Nominalization derivational process that derives nouns from roots or stems of some other category (ch. 13)

Nominative case marking used for grammatical subjects (ch. 7)

Nonfinite a verb form which is not inflected for tense; cf. FINITE (ch. 12)

Non-restrictive (see RELATIVE CLAUSE)

Noun incorporation special type of compounding in which a verb root and a noun root combine to form a complex stem whose category is V (ch. 14)

Null invisible, unpronounced

Oblique arguments non-terms; arguments which are not subjects or objects (ch. 4)

Open question a question that contains a question word and so allows an unlimited range of answers; also called a WH-QUESTION or CONTENT QUESTION (ch. 11)

Optative mood category marking a proposition that the speaker hopes or wishes would be true (ch. 9)

Paradigm set of inflected forms of a single word (LEXEME) encoding all of the possible values for some grammatical feature(s) (ch. 13)

Part of speech (see SYNTACTIC CATEGORIES)

Participle a non-finite verb form that can also be used as an adjective, e.g. *John arrived smiling but left discouraged.*

Passive clause pattern in which the patient is expressed as grammatical subject while the agent is expressed as an optional oblique argument. An ACTIVE clause is one in which the agent is expressed as subject and the patient as object. (ch. 14)

Patient semantic role of the entity which is acted upon, affected, or created; or of which a state or change of state is predicated (ch. 4)

Paucal number category that refers to a group consisting of a few individuals, in contrast to dual and plural (ch. 8)

Perfect tense/aspect category marking a completed event whose result is relevant to the present moment (PRESENT PERFECT) or to some other designated reference point (PAST PERFECT or FUTURE PERFECT), e.g. *I have just eaten* (ch. 9)

Perfective aspect that describes an event as a whole, without reference to its internal time structure (ch. 9)

Phonology the study of the linguistic aspects of sound patterns (ch. 1)

Phrasal affix a clitic that expresses an inflectional feature and takes an entire phrase as its host, rather than a single word (ch. 17)

Phrase a group of words that can function as a constituent within a simple clause (ch. 3)

Phrase structure a representation of word order, constituent boundaries, and syntactic categories (ch. 3)

Polarity whether a sentence is stated positively (*I won*) or negatively (*I did not win*) (ch. 11)

Portmanteau morpheme a single affix that expresses several grammatical categories at once (ch. 2)

Possessor agreement the marking of a possessed noun to indicate the person and number of the possessor (chs. 6, 7)

Post-position like a preposition except that it follows its object

Pragmatics the study of how context affects the meaning of an utterance (ch. 1)

Predicate the element of meaning which identifies the property or relationship being described (ch. 4)

Predicate complement a complement, i.e. a phrase selected by the verb, which functions as a predicate rather than an argument (ch. 10)

Proclitic CLITICS which attach to the left edge of their host (ch. 17)

Pro-drop zero anaphora; the omission of a pronoun whose reference is understood or preserved by verb agreement (ch. 5)

Progressive aspect aspect that describes an event in progress or a continuing situation (ch. 9)

Pronoun retention strategy within a relative clause, the relativized function is indicated by a pronominal "copy" of the head noun; this pronoun is called a RESUMPTIVE PRONOUN (ch. 12)

Quantifiers words like *some, all, no, many, few*, etc.; see also DETER-MINER (ch. 6)

Quote formula simple clause such as "John said" which introduces or frames a direct quotation (ch. 12)

Realis verb form used for actual events occurring in the past or present; cf. IRREALIS (ch. 9)

Recipient semantic role of a participant that receives or acquires ownership of something (ch. 4)

Reciprocal a pronoun or a verb form which is used to express a mutual activity or relationship, e.g. English *each other* (chs. 8, 14)

Recursive rule a Phrase Structure rule which allows a mother node of some phrasal category to have a daughter of the same category (ch. 6)

Recursive structure one constituent embedded within another constituent of the same category (chs. 6, 12)

Reduplication an affix formed by copying part or all of the base form (ch. 16)

Reflexive a pronoun that must (or may) take an antecedent which is an argument of its immediate clause, e.g. English *myself, himself*; or a verb form which indicates that the agent and patient are the same participant, e.g. Kimaragang *misingrayou* 'to praise oneself' (chs. 8, 14)

Relative clause a clause that functions as a modifier within a noun phrase; in a RESTRICTIVE relative clause the modifying clause determines the reference of the head noun, whereas in a NON-RESTRICTIVE relative clause the reference of the head noun is assumed to be already known (ch. 12)

Relative tense (see TENSE)

Relativized function the Grammatical Relation that is assigned to the head noun of a relative clause construction within the modifying clause (ch. 12)

Relativizer special type of complementizer that introduces the modifying clause in a relative clause construction (ch. 12)

Restrictive (see RELATIVE CLAUSE)

Resumptive pronoun (see PRONOUN RETENTION)

Rhetorical question type of INDIRECT SPEECH ACT in which the interrogative form is used for some purpose other than asking questions (ch. 11)

Root the morpheme that forms the core of a word, providing the lexical semantic content (ch. 2)

Root node the top-most node in a tree diagram (ch. 3)

S′ or S̄ (pronounced "S-bar") constituent containing a complementizer (COMP) plus a subordinate clause (ch. 12)

Secondary object NP object of a verb which is distinguished from the PRIMARY OBJECT by grammatical criteria such as position, case marking, passivization, and/or verb agreement (ch. 4)

Selectional restrictions semantic constraints imposed by a predicate on its arguments (chs. 4, 5)

Semantics the study of linguistic meaning (ch. 1)

Semantic case case marking which indicates the semantic role of the NP (ch. 7)

Sentential complement complement clause which contains its own subject NP (ch. 12)

Speech situation the time and place where a conversation or speech act takes place (ch. 8)

Split ergativity a situation in which both ergative and non-ergative case or agreement patterns are found in a single language (ch. 7)

Stative a clause or predicate which expresses a state rather than an event (ch. 9)

Stem the portion of a word that all forms of a given LEXEME have in common; includes the root plus any derivational morphology, but no inflectional morphology (ch. 13)

Stimulus semantic role of an object of perception, cognition, or emotion; an entity which is seen, heard, known, remembered, loved, hated, etc. (ch. 4)

Structural ambiguity ambiguity that arises when a single sentence can have more than one structural analysis (chs. 3, 4)

Subcategorization the set of Grammatical Relations which the verb assigns (ch. 5)

Subjunctive mood category used to mark propositions which the speaker does not assert to be true (ch. 9)

Subordinate clause a clause embedded within another clause (ch. 12)

Subtraction morphological process which, instead of adding material, actually deletes one or more phonemes from the base (ch. 16)

Superlative the form of an adjective marking the highest degree, e.g. *biggest, best* (chs. 3, 15)

Suppletion the replacement of one root form by another for the same word, to express some inflectional feature (e.g. *go* ∼ *went*); or, by extension, any allomorphy which cannot be analyzed as morphophonemic change (ch. 15)

Suprafix morphological marker which consists only of a change in some suprasegmental feature such as tone, stress, length, nasalization, etc. (ch. 16)

Suprasegmental a phonological feature like tone, ATR, or nasalization, which is (in a particular language) associated with a syllable or word rather than a single phoneme (ch. 16)

Syntactic categories parts of speech (Noun, Verb, etc.); word classes defined by shared grammatical properties (ch. 3)

Syntax study of the structure of phrases and sentences (ch. 1)

Tag question a short question added on to a statement to seek confirmation, e.g. *You have eaten, haven't you?* (chs. 4, 11)

Telic aspect TELIC events are bounded in time, i.e. they have a natural end point; ATELIC events have no natural end point (ch. 9)

Tense "location in time" (cf. ASPECT); an affix or auxiliary that indicates the time of an event or situation, relative to some reference point. In an ABSOLUTE TENSE system, that reference point is the time of the speech event. In a RELATIVE TENSE system, the reference point is the time specified by some other verb, e.g. the verb of the matrix clause. (ch. 9)

Terminal node nodes in a tree structure which do not dominate any other node; the lowest node on a particular branch (ch. 3)

Terminal string the sequence of elements in the terminal nodes (ch. 3)

Terms subjects or objects; sometimes referred to as DIRECT ARGUMENTS (ch. 4)

Theme semantic role of an entity which undergoes a change of location or possession, or whose location is being specified (ch. 4)

Topic what the sentence is about (ch. 11)

Transitive taking an object (chs. 4, 5)

Trial a number category used for a group that contains exactly three individuals, in contrast to dual and plural (ch. 8)

Uniqueness well-formedness condition which states that no Grammatical Relation may be assigned more than once by a single verb (ch. 5)

Unmarked the most basic, neutral, or default form; the form having the widest distribution (ch. 11)

Valence the number of terms (subjects and objects) listed in a verb's subcategorization. The phrase "semantic valence" is sometimes used to refer to the number of semantic arguments in the verb's argument structure (ch. 5)

Valence increasing/decreasing derivational process that increases/ decreases the number of terms in a verb's subcategorization (ch. 5)

Verbalization morphological process that derives verbs from roots or stems of other categories (ch. 13)

Voice alternations which alter the semantic role of the subject (ch. 14)

Well-formedness conditions set of constraints on possible clause structures which ensure that each clause contains the right number and type of complements (ch. 5)

Word Formation Rule (WFR) rule that expresses the function of a derivational affix (ch. 13)

Yes–no question (see CLOSED QUESTION)

Zero-anaphora omitting a pronoun where the reference can be understood in context (ch. 5)

References

Aaltio, M. H. 1964. *Finnish for foreigners*. Helsinki: Kustannusosakeyhtiö Otava. (5th edn., 1971).

Aikhenvald, A. Y. 2000. *Classifiers: a typology of noun categorization devices*. Oxford and New York: Oxford University Press.

Aissen, J. L. 1974. Verb raising. *Linguistic Inquiry* 5:325–366.

Aissen, J. L. and D. M. Perlmutter. 1983. Clause Reduction in Spanish. In Perlmutter (ed.), pp. 360–403.

Allen, B. and D. Frantz. 1983. Advancements and verb agreement in Southern Tiwa. In Perlmutter (ed.), pp. 303–314.

Allen, B., D. Gardiner, and D. Frantz, 1984. Noun incorporation in Southern Tiwa. *International Journal of American Linguistics* 50:292–311.

Allen, J. H. and J. B. Greenough. 1931. *New Latin grammar*. Aristide D. Caratzas, New Rochelle, NY (1992).

Anderson, S. 1982. Where's morphology? *Linguistic Inquiry* 13:571–612.

Aronoff, M. 1976. *Word formation in generative grammar*. Cambridge, MA: MIT Press.

Asher, R. E. 1985. *Tamil*. London, Sydney and Dover: Croom Helm.

Ashton, E. O. 1944. *Swahili grammar (including intonation)*. (2nd edn. 1947). London: Longman.

Asmah Hj. O. and R. Subbiah. 1985 (1968). *An introduction to Malay grammar*. Dewan Bahasa dan Pustaka, Kuala Lumpur.

Aspillera, P. S. 1969. *Basic Tagalog for foreigners and non-Tagalogs*. Rutland, VT: Charles E. Tuttle.

Baker, C. L. 1978. *Introduction to Transformational-Generative syntax*. Englewood Cliffs, N.J.: Prentice-Hall.

Baker, M. 1988. *Incorporation: a theory of grammatical function changing*. University of Chicago Press.

Barrett-Keach, C. 1985. *The syntax and interpretation of the relative clause construction in Swahili*. New York: Garland.

Beller, R. and P. Beller. 1979. Huasteca Nahuatl. In Ronald Langacker (ed.), *Studies in Uto-Aztecan grammar, Vol. 2: Modern Aztec grammatical sketches*. Dallas: Summer Institute of Linguistics and the University of Texas at Arlington, pp. 199–306.

Bendor-Samuel, J. T. 1960. Some problems of segmentation in the phonological analysis of Tereno. *Word* 16:348–355.

Bendor-Samuel, J. and S. H. Levinsohn. 1986. *Exercises for use in conjunction with the text Introduction to Grammatical Analysis*. 3rd edn. Mimeo, SIL British School, Horsleys Green, Bucks.

Besnier, N. 1987. An autosegmental approach to metathesis in Rotuman. *Lingua* 73:205–233.

Bickford, J. A. 1998. *Tools for analyzing the world's languages: morphology and syntax*. Dallas: Summer Institute of Linguistics.

Blake, B. 1987. *Australian aboriginal grammar*. London and Sydney: Croom Helm.

Bloomfield, L. 1917. *Tagalog texts with grammatical analysis*. University of Illinois Studies in Language and Literature, Vol. 3.

Booij, G. 1986. Form and meaning in morphology: the case of Dutch 'agent nouns'. *Linguistics* 24:503–517.

Bouquiaux, L. 1970. *La langue birom (Nigéria septentrional): phonologie, morphologie, syntaxe*. Bibliothèque de la Faculté de philosophie et lettres de l'Université de Liège; fasc. 185. Paris: Les Belles Lettres.

Bresnan, J. (ed.). 1982. *The mental representation of grammatical relations*. Cambridge, MA: MIT Press.

    1997. Mixed categories as head sharing constructions. Proceedings of the LFG97 Conference, University of California, San Diego, ed. by M. Butt and T. Holloway King. On-line, Stanford University: http://www-csli.stanford.edu/publications/LFG2/lfg97.html

    2001. *Lexical-Functional syntax*. Oxford: Blackwell.

Bresnan, J. and J. Grimshaw. 1978. The syntax of free relatives in English. *Linguistic Inquiry* 9:331–391.

Bresnan, J. and S. A. Mchombo. 1987. Topic, pronoun and agreement in Chichewa. *Language* 63/4:741–782.

Bybee, J. 1985. *Morphology: a study of the relation between meaning and form*. Amsterdam: John Benjamins.

Cárdenas, D. 1961. *Applied linguistics: Spanish: a guide for teachers*. Boston: D. C. Heath & Co.

Chelliah, S. L. 1992. Pretty derivational morphemes all in a row. *Berkeley Linguistics Society* 18, *Parasession on the place of morphology in a grammar*, pp. 287–297.

Chomsky, N. 1957. *Syntactic structures*. The Hague: Mouton.

Chung, S. and A. Timberlake. 1985. Tense, aspect, and mood. In Shopen (ed.), Vol. 3, pp. 202–258.

Clark, E. V. 1970. Locationals: a study of the relations between 'existential', 'locative', and 'possessive' constructions. In *Working Papers on Language Universals 3*, Stanford University, pp. 1–36.

    1978. Locationals: existential, locative and possessive constructions. In Greenberg et al. (eds.), *Universals of human language, Vol. 4: syntax*. Stanford, CA: Stanford University Press, pp. 85–126.

Clayre, B. and L. Cubit. 1974. An outline of Kayan grammar. *Sarawak Museum Journal* 43:43–91.

Cohn, A. C. 1989. Stress in Indonesian and bracketing paradoxes. *Natural Language and Linguistic Theory* 7/2:167–216.

Cole, P. 1982. *Imbabura Quechua*. Lingua Descriptive Studies, 5. Amsterdam: North-Holland.

Comrie, B. 1976a. *Aspect*. Cambridge and New York: Cambridge University Press.

    1976b. The syntax of causative constructions: cross-language similarities and divergences. In Shibatani (ed.), *The grammar of causative constructions. Syntax and semantics*, Vol. 6. New York: Academic Press, pp. 261–312.

    1978. Ergativity. In W. Lehmann (ed.), *Syntactic typology: studies in the phenomenology of language*. Austin: University of Texas Press, pp. 329–394.

    1981a. *Language universals and linguistic typology*. University of Chicago Press.

    1981b. Ergativity and grammatical relations in Kalaw Lagaw Ya (Saibai dialect). *Australian Journal of Linguistics* 1/1:1–42.

    1985. *Tense*. Cambridge and New York: Cambridge University Press.

Coope, A. E. 1976. *Malay–English English–Malay dictionary*. Kuala Lumpur: Macmillan.

Craig, C. 1977. *The structure of Jacaltec*. Austin: University of Texas Press.
  1986a. Jacaltec noun classifiers. *Lingua* 70:241–284.
  (ed.). 1986b. *Noun classes and categorization: proceedings of a symposium on categorization and noun classification, Eugene, Oregon, October 1983*. Amsterdam and Philadelphia: John Benjamins.
Culy, C. 1990. Grammatical relations and verb forms in internally headed relative clauses. In Dziwirek, Farrell and Bikandi (eds.), *Grammatical relations: a cross-theoretical perspective*. Stanford, CA: CSLI Publications.
Curme, G. O. 1952 (1922). *A grammar of the German language*. New York: F. Ungar.
Day, C. 1973. *The Jacaltec language*. Language Science Monographs 12. Bloomington, IN: Indiana University.
De Guzman, V. P. 1978. *Syntactic derivation of Tagalog verbs*. Oceanic Linguistics Special Publication 16. Honolulu: University of Hawaii Press.
Dixon, R. M. W. 1972. *The Dyirbal language of north Queensland*. London and New York: Cambridge University Press.
  1977. *A grammar of Yidiɲ*. Cambridge and New York: Cambridge University Press.
  1979. Ergativity. *Language* 55.1:59–138.
  1980. *The languages of Australia*. Cambridge and New York: Cambridge University Press.
  1986. Noun classes and noun classification in typological perspective. In C. Craig (ed.), pp. 105–112.
Donaldson, T. 1980. *Ngiyambaa, the language of the Wangaaybuwan*. Cambridge and New York: Cambridge University Press.
Doron, E. 1986. The pronominal 'copula' as an agreement clitic. In H. Borer (ed.), *The syntax of pronominal clitics. Syntax and semantics* 19. New York: Academic Press, pp. 313–332.
Downing, P. 1986. The anaphoric use of classifiers in Japanese. In C. Craig (ed.), pp. 345–375.
Dowty, D. R. 1979. *Word meaning and Montague grammar: the semantics of verbs and times in generative semantics and in Montague's PTQ*. Dordrecht and Boston: Reidel.
Dutton, T. 1973. *Conversational New Guinea pidgin. Pacific Linguistics*, D12. Canberra: Research School of Pacific Studies, Australian National University.
Ellison, F., F. Gomes de Matos, et al. 1971. *Modern Portuguese: a project of the Modern Language Association*. New York: Knopf.
Elson, B. and V. Pickett. 1988. *Beginning morphology and syntax*. 2nd edn. Dallas: SIL.
Emonds, J. E. 1976. *A transformational approach to English syntax: root, structure-preserving, and local transformations*. New York: Academic Press.
English, L. J. 1986. *Tagalog–English Dictionary*. Manila: National Book Store.
Ezard, B. 1992. Tawala derivational prefixes: a semantic perspective. In M. D. Ross (ed.), *Papers in Austronesian Linguistics, 2. Pacific Linguistics* A82. Canberra: Australian National University, pp. 147–250.
Foley, W. A. 1986. *The Papuan languages of New Guinea*. Cambridge and New York: Cambridge University Press.
  1991. *The Yimas language of New Guinea*. Stanford, CA: Stanford University Press.
Gerdts, D. 1998. Incorporation. In Spencer and Zwicky (eds.), pp. 84–100.
Givón, T. 1972. Studies in ChiBemba and Bantu grammar. *Studies in African Linguistics*, Supplement 3:1–247.
  1976. Topic, pronoun, and grammatical agreement. In Li (ed.), pp. 149–188.
  1984. *Syntax: a typological functional introduction*, Vol. 1. Amsterdam: John Benjamins.

Glover, W. 1974. *Semantic and grammatical structures in Gurung (Nepal)*. Norman, OK: SIL.

Greenberg, J. H. 1963. Some universals of grammar with particular reference to the order of meaningful elements. In Greenberg (ed.), *Universals of language*. (2nd edn. 1966) Cambridge, MA: MIT Press, pp. 73–113.

Gronemeyer, C. 1996. Noun incorporation in Hopi. *Working Papers* 45:25–44. Lund University, Department of Linguistics.

Haiman, J. 1992. Iconicity. In Bright (ed.), *International Encyclopedia of Linguistics*, Vol. 2. New York: Oxford University Press, pp. 191–195.

Hale, K. 1965. Some preliminary observations on Papago morphophonemics. *International Journal of American Linguistics* 31/4:295–305.

1981. *On the position of Walbiri in a typology of the base*. Indiana University Linguistics Club.

Halpern, A. 1998. Clitics. In Spencer and Zwicky (eds.), pp. 101–122.

Haspelmath, M. 1996. Word-class-changing inflection and morpological theory. In G. Booij and J. van Marle (eds.), *Yearbook of Morphology 1995*. Dordrecht: Kluwer Academic Publishers, pp. 43–66.

2002. *Understanding morphology*. London: Arnold; and New York: Oxford University Press.

Healey, J. 1990a. *Doing grammar*. Kangaroo Ground, Vic.: SPSIL.

1990b. *Grammar exercises*. Kangaroo Ground, Vic.: SPSIL.

Hinnebusch, T. 1992. Swahili. In Bright (ed.), *International encyclopedia of linguistics*, Vol. 4. Oxford: Oxford University Press, pp. 99–106.

Hockett, C. F. 1954. Two models of grammatical description. *Word* 10:210–231.

1958. *A course in modern linguistics*. New York: Macmillan.

Huddleston, R. 1984. *Introduction to the grammar of English*. Cambridge and New York: Cambridge University Press.

Hudson, J. 1978. *The core of Walmatjari grammar*. Canberra: Australian Institute for Aboriginal Studies.

Hutchisson, D. 1986. Sursurunga pronouns and the special uses of quadral number. In Wiesemann (ed.), pp. 1–20.

Hyman, L. and S. Mchombo. 1992. Morphotactic constraints in the Chichewa verb stem. *Berkeley Linguistics Society*, 18, *Parasession on the place of morphology in a grammar*, pp. 350–364.

Ingram, D. 1978. Typology and universals of personal pronouns. In Greenberg et al. (eds.), *Universals of human language, Vol. 3: Word structure*. Stanford, CA: Stanford University Press, pp. 213–247.

Jackendoff, R. S. 1983. *Semantics and Cognition*. Cambridge, MA: MIT Press.

Jespersen, O. 1924. *The philosophy of grammar*. London: Allen & Unwin; New York: H. Holt & Co.

Kaplan, R. and J. Bresnan. 1982. Lexical–Functional Grammar: a formal system for grammatical representation. In Bresnan (ed.), pp. 173–281.

Keenan, E. L. 1985. Relative clauses. In Shopen (ed.), Vol. 2, pp. 141–170.

King, T. H. 1995. *Configuring topic and focus in Russian*. Stanford, CA: CSLI.

Kennedy, R. 1985a. Clauses in Kalaw Lagaw Ya. In S. Ray (ed.), *Aboriginal and islander grammars: collected papers*. Work papers of SIL-AAB, Series A, Vol. 9. Darwin: Summer Institute of Linguistics, pp. 59–79.

1985b. Kalaw Kawaw verbs. In S. Ray (ed.), *Aboriginal and islander grammars: collected papers*. Work papers of SIL-AAB, Series A, Vol. 9. Darwin: Summer Institute of Linguistics, pp. 81–103.

Kenstowicz, M. and C. Kisseberth. 1979. *Generative phonology: description and theory*. New York: Academic Press.

Kimenyi, A. 1980. *A relational grammar of Kinyarwanda*. Berkeley, CA: University of California Press.

Kisseberth, C. and M. Abasheikh. 1977. The object relationship in Chi-Mwi:ni, a Bantu language. In Cole and Sadock (eds.), *Grammatical relations. Syntax and semantics, 8*. New York: Academic Press, pp. 179–218.

Klima, E. S. 1964. Negation in English. In J. Fodor and J. Katz (eds.), *The structure of language*. Englewood Cliffs, N.J.: Prentice-Hall, pp. 246–323.

Kroeger, P. R. 1993. *Phrase Structure and grammatical relations in Tagalog*. Stanford, CA: CSLI.

    1998. Clitics and clause structure in Tagalog. In Lourdes Bautista (ed.), *Pagtanaw: essays on language in honor of Teodoro A. Llamzon*. Manila: Linguistic Society of the Philippines, pp. 53–72.

    2004. *Analyzing syntax: a lexical-functional approach*. Cambridge: Cambridge University Press.

Langacker, R. W. 1972. *Fundamentals of linguistic analysis*. New York: Harcourt Brace Jovanovich.

Larsen, T. W. 1987. The syntactic status of ergativity in Quiché. *Lingua* 71/1:33–59.

Lee, S. N. 1996. *A grammar of Iranian Azerbaijani*. Ph.D. thesis, University of Sussex.

Lehmann, C. 1988. On the function of agreement. In M. Barlow and C. A. Ferguson (eds.), *Agreement in natural language: approaches, theories, descriptions*. Stanford, CA: CSLI, pp. 55–65.

Li, C. N. (ed.). 1976. *Subject and topic*. New York: Academic Press.

Li, C. N. and S. Thompson. 1981. *Mandarin Chinese: a functional reference grammar*. University of California Press, Berkeley.

Lyons, J. 1966. Towards a 'notional' theory of the 'parts of speech.' *Journal of Linguistics* 2:209–236.

Maling, J. 1983. Transitive adjectives: a case of categorial reanalysis. In Heny and Richards (eds.), *Linguistic categories: auxiliaries and related puzzles*, Vol. 1. Boston: Reidel, pp. 253–289.

Matsumoto, Y. 1993. Japanese numeral classifiers: a study of semantic categories and lexical organization. *Linguistics* 31:667–713.

Matthews, P. H. 1991. *Morphology* (2nd edn.). Cambridge and New York: Cambridge University Press.

McCawley, J. D. 1988. *The syntactic phenomena of English*. University of Chicago Press.

Mchombo, S. A. 1993. On the binding of the reflexive and reciprocal in Chichewa. In Mchombo (ed.), *Theoretical aspects of Bantu grammar*. Standford, CA: CSLI Publications, pp. 181–207.

    1998. Chichewa (Bantu). In Spencer and Zwicky (eds.), pp. 500–520.

Merlan, F. 1976. Noun incorporation and discourse reference in modern Nahuatl. *International Journal of American Linguistics* 42:177–191.

Merrifield, W., C. Naish, C. Rensch, and G. Story (eds.). 1987. *Laboratory manual for morphology and syntax*. 6th edn. Dallas: SIL. (7th edn. 2003).

Mithun, M. 1984. The evolution of noun incorporation. *Language* 60:847–894.

Mohanan, K. P. 1982. Grammatical relations and clause structure in Malayalam. In Bresnan (ed.), pp. 427–503.

    1983. Move NP or lexical rules? Evidence from Malayalam causativization. In L. Levin, M. Rappaport, and A. Zaenen (eds.), *Papers in Lexical-Functional grammar*. Bloomington, IN: Indiana University Linguistics Club, pp. 47–111.

Mosel, L. U. and A. So'o, 1997. *Say it in Samoan*. Pacific Linguistics D88. Canberra: Research School of Pacific and Asian Studies, Australian National University.

Muysken, P. 1981. Quechua word structure. In Heny (ed.), *Binding and filtering*. Cambridge, MA: MIT Press, pp. 279–327.

1988. Affix order and interpretation: Quechua. In M. Everaaert, A. Evers, R. Huybregts, and M. Trommelen (eds.), *Morphology and modularity*. Dordrecht: Foris, pp. 259–279.

Nevis, J. 1988 (1985). *Finnish particle clitics and general clitic theory*. Outstanding Dissertations in Linguistics. New York: Garland.

Nichols, J. 1986. Head-marking and dependent-marking. *Language* 62:56–117.

Nik Safiah K., Farid Onn, Hashim Hj. Musa, and A. Hamid Mahmood. 1986. *Tatabahasa Dewan, Jilid 1: Ayat*. Kuala Lumpur: Dewan Bahasa dan Pustaka.

Palmer, F. R. 1986. *Mood and modality*. Cambridge and New York: Cambridge University Press.

Parkinson, S. 1992. Portuguese. In Bright (ed.), *International Encyclopedia of Linguistics*, Vol. 3. Oxford University Press, pp. 252–256.

Payne, J. R. 1985. Negation. In Shopen (ed.), Vol. 1, pp. 197–242.

Payne, T. 1997. *Describing morphosyntax: a guide for field linguists*. Cambridge and New York: Cambridge University Press.

2002. *Analytical methods in morphology and syntax*. Unpublished MS., ORSIL, Eugene OR.

Perlmutter, D. (ed.). 1983. *Studies in Relational Grammar I*. University of Chicago Press.

Pike, K. L. 1947. *Phonemics: a technique for reducing languages to writing*. University of Michigan Publications: Linguistics, 3. Ann Arbor: University of Michigan Press.

Pike, K. L. and E. G. Pike. 1982. *Grammatical analysis*. (2nd edn.). Dallas: SIL and The University of Texas at Arlington.

Postal, P. 1962. *Some syntactic rules of Mohawk*. Ph.D. dissertation, Yale University. (1979, New York: Garland Press).

Radford, A. 1988. *Transformational Grammar: a first course*. Cambridge and New York: Cambridge University Press.

Ramos, T. V. 1971. *Tagalog structures*. PALI Language Texts: Philippines. Honolulu: University of Hawaii Press.

Reed, J. and D. Payne. 1986. Asheninca (Campa) pronominals. In Wiesemann (ed.), pp. 323–331.

Reesink, G. P. 1999. *A grammar of Hatam: Bird's Head Peninsula, Irian Jaya*. Pacific Linguistics C-146. Canberra: Australian National University.

Rizzi, L. 1978. A restructuring rule in Italian syntax. In Keyser (ed.), *Recent transformational studies in European languages*. Linguistic Inquiry Monograph, 3. Cambridge, MA: MIT Press, pp. 113–158.

Roberts, J. R. 1988. Amele switch reference and the theory of grammar. *Linguistic Inquiry* 19:45–63.

1996. A Government and Binding analysis of the verb in Amele. *Language and Linguistics in Melanesia* 27:1–66.

1999. *Grammar exercises for Tools for analyzing the world's languages (Bickford 1998)*. Mimeo, SIL UK Training and Research Dept., Horsleys Green, Bucks.

Robins, R. H. 1964. *General linguistics: an introductory survey*. Bloomington, IN: Indiana University Press; and London: Longmans.

Rosen, C. 1990. Rethinking Southern Tiwa: the geometry of a triple-agreement language. *Language* 66:669–713.

Rosen, S. T. 1989. Two types of noun incorporation: a lexical analysis. *Language* 65:294–317.

Saad, G. N. and S. Bolozky. 1984. Causativization and transitivization in Arabic and Modern Hebrew. *Afroasiatic Linguistics* 9:101–110.

Sadock, J. and A. Zwicky. 1985. Speech act distinctions in syntax. In Shopen (ed.), Vol. 1, pp. 159–196.

Sá Pereira, M. de Lourdes. 1948. *Brazilian Portuguese grammar*. Boston: D. C. Heath and Co.

Schachter, P. 1977. Reference-related and role-related properties of subjects. In P. Cole and J. Sadock (eds.), *Grammatical Relations*, Syntax and Semantics 8. New York: Academic Press, pp. 279–306.

1985. Parts-of-speech systems. In Shopen (ed.), Vol. 1, pp. 3–61.

Schachter, P. and F. T. Otanes. 1972. *Tagalog Reference Grammar*. Berkeley, CA: University of California Press.

Schmitt, C. J. 1972. *Schaum's outline of Spanish grammar*. New York: McGraw-Hill.

Shopen, T. (ed.). *Language typology and syntactic description*, Vols. 1–3. Cambridge, New York, and Melbourne: Cambridge University Press.

Silverstein, M. 1976. Hierarchy of features and ergativity. In R. M. W. Dixon (ed.), *Grammatical categories in Australian languages*. Canberra: Australian Institute of Aboriginal Studies, pp. 112–171.

Sityar, E. M. 1989. Pronominal clitics in Tagalog. M.A. thesis, University of California, Los Angeles.

Sneddon, J. 1996. *Indonesian reference grammar*. London and New York: Routledge; and St. Leonards, NSW: Allen & Unwin.

Spatar, N. M. 1997. Imperative constructions in Cambodian. *Mon-Khmer Studies* 27:119–127.

Spencer, A. 1991. *Morphological theory: an introduction to word structure in generative grammar*. Cambridge, MA and Oxford: Basil Blackwell.

Spencer, A. and A. Zwicky (eds.). 1998. *The handbook of morphology*. Oxford: Blackwell.

Stern, G. and E. Bleiler. 1961. *Essential German grammar*. New York: Dover; and London: Hodder & Stoughton.

Stump, G. 1998. Inflection. In Spencer and Zwicky (eds.), pp. 13–43.

Sussex, R. 1992. Russian. In Bright (ed.), *International encyclopedia of linguistics*, Vol. 3. Oxford University Press, pp. 350–358.

Thomas, E., J. T. Bendor-Samuel, and S. H. Levinsohn. 1988. *Introduction to grammatical analysis: self-instruction and correspondence course second (revised) edition*. Horsleys Green, Bucks: SIL.

Trechsel, F. R. 1993. Quiché focus constructions. *Lingua* 91/1:33–78.

Tsujimura, N. 1996. *An introduction to Japanese linguistics*. Cambridge, MA; and Oxford: Basil Blackwell.

Underhill, R. 1976. *Turkish grammar*. Cambridge, MA: MIT Press.

van den Berg, R. 1989. *A grammar of the Muna language*. Dordrecht: Foris.

Verhaar, J. 1995. *Toward a reference grammar of Tok Pisin: an experiment in corpus linguistics*. Oceanic Linguistics Special Publication, 26. Honolulu: University of Hawaii Press.

Vitale, A. J. 1981. *Swahili syntax*. Publications in Language Sciences, 5. Dordrecht and Cinnaminson, N.J.: Foris Publications.

Walton, C. 1986. *Sama verbal semantics: classification, derivation and inflection*. Linguistic Society of the Philippines, Special Monograph Issue, 25. Manila: Linguistic Society of the Philippines.

Weber, D. J. 1989. *A grammar of Huallaga (Huanuco) Quechua*. Berkeley: University of California Press.

Wierzbicka, A. 1981. Case marking and human nature. *Australian Journal of Linguistics* 1/1:43–80.

Wiesemann, U. (ed.). 1986. *Pronominal systems*. Tübingen: Narr.

Wolfenden, E. P. 1961. *A restatement of Tagalog grammar*. Manila: Summer Institute of Linguistics and the Institute of National Language.

1967. Tagalog concordance. Unpublished MS., University of Oklahoma Computer Laboratory.

Wollams, G. 1996. *A grammar of Karo Batak, Sumatra. Pacific Linguistics* C-130. Canberra: Research School of Pacific Studies, Australian National University.

Woodbury, H. 1975. Noun incorporation in Onandaga. Ph.D. dissertation, Yale University.

Woolford, E. B. 1979. *Aspects of Tok Pisin grammar. Pacific linguistics* B66. Canberra: Research School of Pacific Studies, Australian National University.

Zwicky, A. 1977. *On clitics*. Bloomington, IN: IULC.

1985. Clitics and particles. *Language* 61/2:283–305.

Zwicky, A. and G. Pullum. 1983. Cliticization vs. inflection: English n't. *Language* 59/3:502–513.

Language index

Agatu 98
Amele 100, 116, 191, 220, 316–317, 321
Amharic 185
Arabic 143, 151, 185
Asheninca 146n.5
Azerbaijani, Southern 120, 229, 284, 302

Bariba 99
Basari 307
Bekwarra 314
Bengali 195n.15
Biatah 140, 185
Birom 309
Buru 117

Cambodian (Khmer) 133, 201
Cashinahua 109
ChiBemba 151, 161
Chichewa 261–262, 273, 276, 277–278, 328
Chimwiini 278
Chinantec, Lalana 291
Chinantec, Palantla 314
Chinese 80, 131–132, 141, 160, 175, 185,
    206–208, 234, 246n.21
Chinook 150
Chontal, Oaxaca 305
Chukchee 280

Dogon 233
Dusun 150, 185
Dutch 256
Dyirbal 109, 129, 130

Ekpeye 169
English 17, 34–35, 37, 56, 63, 90–92, 103,
    105, 112, 200, 204–205, 223, 234–235,
    241, 244n.1, 248–249, 288, 292–294,
    317
  adverbial clause as PP 227–229
  auxiliary verbs 82, 165
  derivational morphology 12, 252, 254, 255,
    260, 263–264, 270
  imperfective aspect 157
  noun phrases 87–89, 90–92, 97
  possessor phrase 92, 95, 322

"strong" verbs 308
subject–aux inversion 225
subjecthood properties 56–57
suppletive morphology 23, 290
VP constituent 81–82
Eskimo 185
Eskimo, Greenlandic 204, 206
Estonian 195n.15

Finnish 24, 195n.15, 213, 215, 252
French 80, 140, 172n.4, 185, 256

Gee 18–21
German 80, 128, 129, 137, 139, 140, 160, 186,
    233, 235, 254, 259, 263, 308
Greek 185
Gurung 163

Hatam 93
Hausa 181
Hebrew 182, 185, 213, 238, 307
Hindi 110, 195n.15, 234
Hokkien 185
Hopi 217n.7, 283
Huichol 289
Hungarian 195n.15, 217n.9

Indonesian (see Malay)
Inga 329
Irish 185
Italian 80, 172n.4, 256, 326

Jacaltec 144, 204
Japanese 80, 84, 134, 271, 279

Kalaw Lagaw Ya 124
Kalkatungu 118
Karo Batak 257–258
Kashmiri 195n.15
Kayan 141
Khmer (see Cambodian)
Kimaragang Dusun 141, 149, 166, 185,
    226–227, 275–276, 305, 306
Kinyarwanda 283
Korean 288

Subject index